Herman Wadsworth Hayley

The Alcestis of Euripides

Edited with an introduction and Critical and Exegetical Notes

Herman Wadsworth Hayley

The Alcestis of Euripides
Edited with an Introduction and Critical and Exegetical Notes

ISBN/EAN: 9783337682408

Printed in Europe, USA, Canada, Australia, Japan

Cover: Foto ©Thomas Meinert / pixelio.de

More available books at **www.hansebooks.com**

THE
ALCESTIS OF EURIPIDES

EDITED, WITH AN INTRODUCTION AND CRITICAL AND
EXEGETICAL NOTES

BY

HERMAN WADSWORTH HAYLEY, Ph.D. (Harvard)
INSTRUCTOR IN LATIN AT WESLEYAN UNIVERSITY

"*Nobilissima fabula, Euripidis Alcestis*"
— MACROBIUS

BOSTON, U.S.A.
GINN & COMPANY, PUBLISHERS
The Athenæum Press
1898

MEMORIAE
GEORGI·MARTINI·LANE
ET
FRIDERICI·DEFOREST·ALLEN
PRAECEPTORVM·CARISSIMORVM

PREFACE.

THE object with which this little book has been prepared is twofold, — to provide a convenient text-book for the use of students who are just beginning the critical study of the Greek drama, and to contribute something toward the constitution of a sound text of the *Alcestis*.

The play in question is often said to be an "easy" one; yet it abounds in critical difficulties and presents many interesting problems. These are thrown into stronger relief by the very simplicity and clearness of many portions of the play, and so can more easily be noted and discussed by the beginner in the critical art, who would be completely baffled by the manifold and complex difficulties of such a drama as the *Agamemnon* or the *Trachiniae*. Hence the *Alcestis* seems peculiarly adapted for the use of our classical "seminaries" and "pro-seminaries," and is often selected as a subject for their labors. In writing the present work, and especially in preparing the introduction and *apparatus criticus*, I have had in view the needs of students in these seminaries.

This, however, is not the sole object of the book. Some five years since, when looking over a large collection of works relating to the Greek drama, I was impressed by the fact that since the edition of Professor Monk no edition of the *Alcestis* which had for its chief purpose the critical constitution of the text had appeared in English. This seemed all the more strange because the play is one of the best known and most popular of all the Euripidean dramas. There appeared, therefore, to be need of a new edition which should gather up the scattered critical material which has appeared during this century — which should, in other words, "bring Monk up to date." To do this adequately would require a much larger and more elaborate work than the present one; but I have tried to make at least a beginning in this direction.

In the treatment and constitution of the text I have been, on the whole, conservative. I have no sympathy with what some one has called "the yelping chorus of those who carp at conjectural criticism"; but the need of caution in the exercise of the art can scarcely be too strongly emphasized. Nothing is easier than to make conjectures; nothing is harder than to make a *certain* one. Still, I have received not a few conjectures into the text, especially from those suggested by Wecklein, F. W. Schmidt, Herwerden, Wilamowitz, Earle, and the early editors and critics. Variations in the text from the reading of the MSS. have been indicated by using bold-face type in the words where the change occurs.

The *apparatus criticus* is necessarily based upon that of Prinz; but I have made many changes and additions, and have omitted those *testimonia* which show no variant from the reading of the Euripidean MSS. Through the kindness of Professor U. von Wilamowitz-Moellendorff, a few readings from *d* (Cod. Laurent. 31, 15) have been added. Under the heading "Select Conjectures" have been collected a number of emendations which for one reason or another seemed worthy of mention, but which I did not venture to receive into the text. These have been very carefully sifted from the great mass of conjectures upon the *Alcestis*, which could not have been reprinted as a whole without preserving a great deal of rubbish. In the critical notes, which form the larger part of the book, I have tried to discuss, or at least to point out, most of the difficulties which confront the student of the play. Many of the problems are still unsolved; some, perhaps, are incapable of solution, but I have honestly striven to blink none of them. At the end a brief "Metrical Appendix" has been added to help the student in dealing with the lyric metres of the play.

Though I have been under constant obligation to the labors of my predecessors, this edition is not "based" on that of any previous commentator, German or otherwise, and I have tried in all cases to exercise an independent judgment. I have aimed to make due acknowledgment for whatever is not the common property of scholars, though in so small a book it is not always possible "*suum cuique reddere.*" I wish to express my special obligation to the following: to former editions of the play (particularly that of Monk), especially for "parallel passages"; to Professor von Wilamowitz-Moellendorff, of Göttingen, for valuable information and advice; to Professor M. L. Earle, of Bryn Mawr, who very kindly communicated to me a number of unpublished readings and conjectures, with permission to make use of them; to Professors C. L. Smith, M. H. Morgan and A. A. Howard, of Harvard, for advice and encouragement, and above all to the late Professor F. D. Allen, of the same university, without whose kindly counsel this book would probably never have been written. I am much indebted, also, to my colleague, Dr. J. M. Paton, of Wesleyan University, for the valuable chapter (on the works of art in which scenes from the *Alcestis* are represented) which he has contributed to the introduction.

It may appear to some that I have been too cautious in many of my statements, and that "probably," "perhaps," "it would seem," etc., recur too often in these pages; but I have thought it best to run the risk of erring in this direction rather than in that of over-confidence and "cocksureness." It behooves the classical scholar to be very cautious in his assertions in these days, when the very next discovery in Egypt may prove him to be in the wrong. I may perhaps be permitted to add that this is (if I mistake not) the first mainly critical edition of a Greek play that has been published by an American scholar. *Sit venia tironi!*

H. W. HAYLEY.

MIDDLETOWN, CONN., September 1, 1897.

LIST OF CONTENTS.

	PAGE
INTRODUCTION	xi
TEXT AND APPARATUS CRITICUS	3
SELECT CONJECTURES	53
CRITICAL AND EXEGETICAL NOTES	61
METRICAL APPENDIX	169

INTRODUCTION.

A. The Myth of Alcestis.

Its History and Literary Treatment.

Few Greek myths have become more celebrated or have furnished a greater stimulus to literary effort than that of Admetus and Alcestis. It would be both interesting and profitable to trace the evolution of the story from its origin down to the time of Euripides; but, unfortunately, so many links in the chain are wanting that much must be left to conjecture. With the various "solar-myth" theories that have been suggested to account for the legend I will not weary the reader; they have long since been "gathered to their fathers." They may be found stated at length in the dissertation by Karl Dissel, "*Der Mythus von Admetos und Alkestis*" (Brandenburg, 1882) pp. 6 ff. The Euhemeristic explanation of the myth which was proposed by Gottfried Hermann (see the dissertation prefixed to his *Alcestis* pp. xiii. ff.) may also be dismissed as quite untenable.

That keen-sighted scholar, K. O. Mueller, in his *Prolegomena zu einer wiss. Mythologie* pp. 300–306 (cf. his *Dorier*, Eng. trans. I. p. 340 f.), advanced a different and much more probable theory. Noting that Ἄδμητος, "the unconquered," is a common title of Pluto, and that Ἀδμήτου κόρη (see Hesychius *s. v.*) was a name of Hecate, he made the suggestion that Admetus was originally not the hero of later legend, but the king of the under-world himself. After slaying the Python, Apollo was obliged to atone for the blood-guilt thus incurred by descending into Hades and serving Ἄδμητος (i.e. Pluto) for a time. That form of the legend which connects Apollo's servitude with the killing of the Cyclopes is, as we shall see, of later origin (see also Pauly, *Real-Encyclop.*² *s. v.*

Apollon III. 12 and IV. 2). This view of Mueller's is extremely plausible, and is probably correct,* though it cannot, with our present *data*, be absolutely proved. As he points out (*Dorier l.s.c.*), it is confirmed by the obscure traditions which represent Apollo as actually dying and descending into the lower world (Euhemerus in Minucius Felix c. 21. 2, etc.). If Mueller is right, it becomes probable that Ἄλκηστις (cf. ἀλκή, Ἄλκιμος, Ἀλκέτας, Ἀλκμήνη, etc.) was originally a name of Persephone, Pherrhephatta, or Core, the queen of Hades. In what manner the story became localized and Pluto was transformed to a Thessalian monarch we can only guess. Possibly the fact that the name Admetus was not uncommon among the chieftains of northern Greece may have had something to do with the change. The Molossian king with whom Themistocles took refuge was an Admetus, and there were several distinguished Macedonians of that name.

In the Homeric poems we find but little about Admetus or Alcestis, but enough to show that the myth had already obtained a "local habitation." Admetus, the son of Pheres (Φηρητιάδαο *Il.* II. 763, XXIII. 376) and grandson of Cretheus and Tyro (*Od.* XI. 257-8), rules over four Thessalian cities, Pherae, Boebe, Glaphyra and Iolcus (*Il.* II. 711 f.). His wife Alcestis is mentioned (*Il. l.s.c.*) as "the fairest of the daughters of Pelias," who (as we learn from *Od.* XI. 253 f.) was the son of Poseidon and Tyro and dwelt in Iolcus. Eumelus, son of Admetus and Alcestis (*Il.* II. 713), commands twelve ships at Troy, and possesses mares famed for their speed, τὰς ἐν Πιερίῃ θρέψ' ἀργυρότοξος Ἀπόλλων (*Il.* II. 766). Eumelus appears among the contestants in the chariot race (*Il.* XXIII. 287 ff.); but he does not play a conspicuous part in the *Iliad*. His wife is Iphthime, daughter of Icarius (*Od.* IV. 797-8). It is clear, I think, that, though the *Iliad* and *Odyssey* contain no detailed statement of the myth, the story was known to the authors of the parts of the Homeric poems above cited, and had already passed through a long process of development. It will be noted, also, that Admetus, Alcestis, and Eumelus are mentioned only in portions

* See, however, Schreiber, *Apollon Pythoktonos* pp. 11, 12, who opposes Mueller's theory.

of the *Iliad* which are now generally believed to be of comparatively *late* origin (viz. the *Catalogue of Ships* and Book XXIII.).

The poet who did most to give the myth form and coloring seems, however, to have been Hesiod, or, rather, the unknown author of that curious work, the *Eoeae*. In one of the divisions of this poem the story of Admetus and Alcestis was told with considerable fullness; and, though the work itself is lost, Wilamowitz with extraordinary acuteness has succeeded in making out the plot of this particular *Eoee* (see his *Isyllos* pp. 57 ff.). This he has accomplished by piecing together bits of information from various ancient writers (the fragments of the poem, Pindar *Pyth.* III. and the schol., Apollod. *Bibl.* III. 10, 3 and I. 9, 15, Hyginus *Fab.* 49 and 51, etc.). Not all the details of his combinations are certain; but, taken as a whole, his conclusions seem well assured. According to him (*l. s. c.* p. 70 f.), the tale as told by the Hesiodic poet ran about as follows (omitting the earlier portion, in which were narrated the loves of Apollo and Coronis and the fate of the latter): Asclepius, son of Apollo and Coronis, grew up to manhood under the care of the centaur Chiron, and learned to know the medicinal powers of the herbs and the spells that stay disease. He became a physician without peer, and healed many of their ills; but when he presumed so far as to bring back the dead to life Zeus smote him with the thunderbolt and slew him at Delphi, where was his father's sanctuary. Then Apollo, in anger at his son's death and not being able to take vengeance upon Zeus, slew the Cyclopes who had forged the bolt which caused the death of Asclepius. At Leto's intercession Apollo was spared expulsion into Tartarus, but was condemned by Zeus to spend a "great year" in servitude to a mortal. So he entered the service of Admetus, king of Pherae, and pastured his master's flocks near Lake Boebeis. Being kindly treated by Admetus, he caused the latter's herds to thrive and multiply (cf. *Alc.* 588 f.). He also aided the king to yoke together to his chariot a lion and a boar, in order to win Alcestis, whose father, Pelias, would grant her hand only to the suitor who should accomplish this feat. Admetus won his bride and brought her home amid rejoicing, but he forgot to sacrifice to Apollo's sister, the cruel Artemis Βριμώ of Pherae; and, as a token of her wrath, he found a coil of snakes in his bridal chamber. Apollo interpreted to the king the will of the goddess; she demanded the life of the bridegroom, and would spare it only on condition that the life of another be voluntarily offered as a substitute. Friends and kindred all refused to make the sacrifice; only the young wife would consent to give her life for that of her husband. But when the sacrifice had been consummated, Persephone (who is Artemis Βριμώ under another aspect) had mercy on her and sent her back to the upper world. Thus, or nearly thus, the author of the *Eoeae* (see esp. Apollodorus and Hyginus *ll. s. c.*). Though both Apollodorus and Hyginus mention the interference of Heracles, the former speaks of it only as another form of the legend (ὡς δὲ ἔνιοι λέγουσιν, Ἡρακλῆς μαχεσάμενος Ἅιδῃ cf. the third schol. on Aristoph. *Vesp.* 1239). The date of the *Eoeae* is not exactly known, but probably is not far from the latter part of the seventh century B.C.; hence we may assume that as the time when the legend takes on a definite literary form. As we have seen, the poet assigns as the cause of Apollo's θητεία not the slaying of the Python but the killing of the Cyclopes; but whether he was the first who introduced this change into the story we cannot say.

Another step in the development of the myth was taken by the tragic poet Phrynichus. Among his tragedies Suidas (*s. v.* Φρύνιχος) mentions an Ἄλκηστις, and one line of this play (fr. 2 Nauck) has been preserved to us by Hesychius (*s. v.* ἀθαμβές): σῶμα δ' ἀθαμβὲς γυιοδόνητον (so Hermann; γυιοδόνιστον MS.) | τείρει. If, as seems highly probable, this refers to the struggle between Heracles and Thanatos,* it is clear that Phrynichus, or the source from which he drew, introduced Heracles into the story and ascribed the restoration of Alcestis to his intervention. Robert (*Thanatos* p. 30) holds that this form of the myth is the older one, on the ground that "die Lösung eines Konflikts durch physische Kraft ist in aller Sagenentwickelung älter und ursprünglicher als die Versöhnung durch das Eingreifen ethischer Motive." But, though this is undoubtedly true as a general principle, it is hardly a safe criterion in individual cases.

* Cf. Fahlenberg, *De Hercule Tragico* p. 37 and note 4.

We learn further from Servius (on *Aen.* IV. 694) that Phrynichus brought Thanatos ("Orcus"; some hold that Hades is meant) upon the stage, bearing a sword with which to cut off a lock of hair from the head of Alcestis; a feature which was borrowed by Euripides. Aeschylus (*Eum.* 713 ff.) says (the Erinnyes are addressing Apollo) τοιαῦτ' ἔδρασας καὶ Φέρητος ἐν δόμοις· | Μοίρας ἔπεισας ἀφθίτους θεῖναι βροτούς. . . . σύ τοι παλαιὰς διανομὰς καταφθίσας | οἴνῳ παρηπάτησας ἀρχαίας θεάς: cf. *Eum.* 171 f. παρὰ νόμον θεῶν βρότεα μὲν τίων, | παλαιγενεῖς δὲ Μοίρας φθίσας. As the schol. on *Alc.* 12 points out, this obviously refers to the same incident as *Alc.* 11 ff. παιδὸς Φέρητος, ὃν θανεῖν ἐρρυσάμην, | Μοίρας δολώσας κ.τ.λ. That form of the legend according to which Apollo made the Moerae intoxicated and then obtained from them permission for Admetus to offer a substitute is therefore older than the Euripidean *Alcestis*, and probably goes back to the play of Phrynichus, if not farther (cf. Apollod. *Bibl.* I. 9, 15, 2).

In the Aristophanic hypothesis to the *Alcestis* is the statement: παρ' οὐδετέρῳ (i.e. neither Aeschylus nor Sophocles) κεῖται ἡ μυθοποιία. This is not quite correct: for, though Aeschylus seems not to have written on this subject, Plutarch (*De defect. orac.* c. 15 p. 417 F) has preserved a line of Sophocles in which Admetus says, οὑμὸς δ' ἀλέκτωρ αὐτὸν ἦγε πρὸς μύλην. As G. Hermann long ago pointed out, this looks like a passage from a satyric drama, and Aristophanes may have neglected to mention the play because it was of that character. What form of the legend Sophocles adopted we have no means of knowing.

Pherecydes (doubtless the Lerian, who flourished about B.C. 450) seems to have related the myth, or a part of it, in his Ἱστορίαι. He asserted that not the Cyclopes themselves, but their sons, were slain by Apollo (schol. on *Alc.* 1 = Mueller *F. H. G.* fr. 76), doubtless because the Cyclopes were commonly believed to be immortal. What other innovations he may have tried to introduce into the legend we do not know, but he seems to have followed Hesiod pretty closely (cf. the schol. on Pindar *Pyth.* III. 59 = *F. H. G.* fr. 8; Wilamowitz *l. s. c.* p. 62).

The story of Admetus seems to have been very popular about this time: the famous skolion

> Ἀδμήτου λόγον ὦ 'ταῖρε μαθὼν τοὺς ἀγαθοὺς φίλει,
> τῶν δειλῶν δ' ἀπέχου, γνοὺς ὅτι δειλοῖς ὀλίγη χάρις

was probably written by Praxilla of Sicyon, a contemporary of Pherecydes, though some attributed it to Alcaeus, others to Sappho (schol. on Aristoph. *Vesp.* 1240; Pausanias in Eustath. on *Il.* II. 711, p. 326, 36). This song is mentioned by Cratinus (fr. 236 Kock) and twice by Aristophanes (*Vesp.* 1239, fr. 430 K.), and was so much in vogue that Ἀδμήτου μέλος passed into a proverb (Hesych. and Suidas *s. v.*; see also Hesych. *s. v.* Ἀδμήτου λόγον, Athenaeus XV. p. 695 C). Even in antiquity its precise application seems to have been disputed (see Eustath. *l. s. c.* and the schol. on the *Vespae* 1239). Aristophanes puts it into the mouth of the flatterer and parasite Theorus, and it probably reflects on the courage of Admetus; though some (schol. on the *Vespae l. s. c.*) took it as referring merely to the refuge which the Thessalian king, when driven into exile, was said to have taken with Theseus.

This brings us to the time of Euripides. He seems to have followed the Hesiodic form of the myth, with those modifications which were shown in the Phrynichean play. It is not clear that he introduced any important change, except, possibly, that he makes Admetus king of *all* Thessaly (*Alc.* 590 ff.). Euripides seems, also, to have laid greater stress upon the hospitality of Admetus, as shown to Heracles in the midst of the mourning for Alcestis, than did the earlier poets; though whether he *invented* that part of the story which represents Heracles as entertained at that time in the house of the Thessalian monarch, we cannot say. Probably, however, he borrowed this, too, from Phrynichus.

Two poets of the Old (or early Middle) Comedy, Aristomenes and Theopompus, each wrote an Ἄδμητος (see the fourth hypoth. to Aristoph. *Plutus*, and Athenaeus XV. 690 A), but of the contents of these plays we know little or nothing.

Better known is the Ἄλκηστις of the comic poet Antiphanes, from which two (perhaps three) fragments have been preserved. The first of these (Athenaeus III. 122 D = fr. 29 K.),

ἐπὶ τὸ καινουργεῖν φέρου
οὕτως, ἐκείνως, τοῦτο γιγνώσκων ὅτι
ἓν καινὸν ἐγχείρημα, κἂν τολμηρὸν ᾖ,
πολλῶν παλαιῶν ἐστι χρησιμώτερον,

looks like a piece of advice given by Admetus to Heracles (or by some one to Admetus) as to the way to recover Alcestis. Athenaeus says (XII. 553 C = fr. 30 K.): Ἀντιφάνης ἐν Ἀλκήστιδι ἐλαίῳ τινὰ ποιεῖ χριόμενον τοὺς πόδας. Apparently Heracles had his feet anointed with oil to relieve them after the long journey down to Hades.* A third fragment (Ath. II. 47 B = fr. 276 Koek) *may* belong to the same play: ἓν νόσημα τοῦτ' ἔχει· | ἀεὶ γὰρ ὀξύπεινός ἐστι. B. Θετταλὸν λέγεις | κομιδῇ τὸν ἄνδρα.

In accordance with the erotic taste of the time, the poet Rhianus (second half of the third century B.C.) ascribed (in his Θεσσαλικά?) the servitude of Apollo to his love for Admetus, whose servant he voluntarily became (schol. on *Alc.* 1). This form of the story was, as might be expected, popular with later writers. The Delphian periegete Anaxandrides, on the other hand, retained the older, Delphian version which represented Apollo as undergoing the θητεία to atone for his slaying the Python (schol. on *Alc. l. s. c.*).

The Atthidographer Phanodemus (schol. on the *Vespae l. s. c.* = *F. H. G.* fr. 9) related that Admetus, being driven out of Pherae, came with his wife Alcestis and his youngest son Hippasus to Theseus at Athens, and settled there. This addition to the legend may have been suggested by *Alc.* 954 f., which clearly implies that some of Admetus' subjects were disaffected toward him. (For other minor features and variations of the legend, see Wentzel's admirable article "Admetos" in Pauly's *Real-Encyclopaedie* ².)

Fulgentius (*Expos. Serm. Ant. s. v. friguttire*) gives what purports to be a quotation from an *Alcestis* of the Roman poet Ennius; but as no such play of Ennius is mentioned elsewhere, and Fulgentius is known to have forged many quotations, his statement is now generally disbelieved.

---

* That a form of the legend existed in which Heracles brought Alcestis up from Hades is shown by the works of art. See p. 13 ff.

The tragic poet L. Accius, however, wrote an *Alcestis*, of which one line — *cum striderat retracta rursus inferis* — has been preserved to us by Priscian (IX. p. 867 P., X. p. 893 P.). What version of the myth he followed is quite unknown (see Ribbeck, *Römische Tragödie* p. 551; *Frag. Scaen. Rom. Po.* I. p. 143).

We have also a fragment (*Gellius* XIX. 7, 3; Nonius *s. v. obesum*: Baehrens *Po. Lat. Min.* VI. p. 288) from an *Alcestis* of the poet Laevius, which, however, was probably not a play,* but a part of his *Erotopaegnia* (see Weichert, *De Laevio poeta* pp. 55 ff. in his *Poet. Lat. Reliq.*). The fragment runs (the text is somewhat uncertain): *corpore pectoreque undique obeso ac | mente exsensa tardigenuclo | senio obpressum.* It may be a description of Pheres.

It would appear from Lucian *De Saltu* 52 (cf. Juvenal *Sat.* VI. 652) that under the empire the myth of Alcestis was often made the subject of mimetic performances.

It is clear, both from this brief sketch and from the number and character of the allusions to the legend in classical writers, that it never occupied a commanding position in Greek mythology or literature, such a position, for instance, as was held by the story of the Atridae or of the house of Laius. The reason for this is twofold: the scene of the legend is in northern Greece, removed from the great centres of life and civilization, and the family involved is not one which played a very conspicuous part in the mythical history of the heroic age; and secondly, the conception of conjugal love and fidelity which the story reveals is so elevated that it could scarcely be appreciated by the great mass of the Greeks of classical times. But later, when the romantic element in the relation between the sexes began to appear more prominently, the myth came at once into vogue. The influence of Christianity was favorable rather than unfavorable to its popularity; it was often referred to by the fathers of the church, to whom the servitude of Apollo and the self-sacrifice of Alcestis offered convenient illustrations; and, in one way or another, it has exercised no slight influence upon modern literature.†

---

* Menozzi (*Rivista di filol. class.* 185 pp. 191 ff.) holds that it was a tragedy.

† See Ellinger, *Alceste in der modernen Litteratur*, Halle, 1885; Patin, *Tragiques Grecs*,³ *Euripide* vol. 1. pp. 221 ff.

B. The Euripidean Play.

The *Alcestis* is the earliest of the plays which are known* to have been written by Euripides that has come down to us. Its date was long uncertain, for that part of the Aristophanic hypothesis which contained information as to this point had been lost. It was known, however, from internal evidence, such as the severity of the metrical treatment, the friendly mention of Sparta (l. 448 f.), and the fact that vv. 367-8 are parodied in the *Acharnians* (which appeared B.C. 425), that the play was an early one. In 1834 W. Dindorf published in his edition of the *Alcestis* a new fragment of the hypothesis, which he had found in the Vatican MS. (*B*). This fragment contained (in addition to other matter previously known) the following words: τὸ δρᾶμα ἐποιήθη ιζ. ἐδιδάχθη ἐπὶ Γλαυκίνου ἄρχοντος τὸ λ. πρῶτος (πρῶτον MS.) ἦν Σοφοκλῆς, δεύτερος (δεύτερον MS.) Εὐριπίδης Κρήσσαις Ἀλκμέωνι (ἀλκμαίονι MS.) τῷ διὰ Ψωφῖδος (διαψωφίλῳ MS.) Τηλέφῳ Ἀλκήστιδι. τὸ δὲ δρᾶμα κωμικωτέραν ἔχει τὴν καταστροφήν. As we know from other sources (see Diodor. XII. 30, who gives the name as Glaucides; schol. on Aristoph. *Achar.* 67; Clinton, *Fasti Hellen.* II. p. 62-3), Glaucinus or Glaucines was archon in the second year of the 85th Olympiad; hence Dindorf substituted for the meaningless τὸ λ of the MS. (which is certainly corrupt) ὀλυμπιάδος πέ ἔτει δευτέρῳ (or β'). The fragment gives us the following facts: the play was the seventeenth in order of composition. As Earle has pointed out (p. 4 f. of his edition),† this probably means that it belonged to the seventeenth group of plays brought out by the poet. We know from the *Vita* that Euripides presented his first drama in 455; hence either ιζ is a mistake for ιη, or (more probably) the poet let one year pass without exhibiting. The *Alcestis* was presented in the year of Glaucinus, i.e. 439-8, and hence must have been performed (if, as is probable, it appeared at the Greater Dionysia) in the

---

* The *Rhesus* is, of course, disputed.
† Cf., however, Teuffel in the *Rheinisches Museum* 1866, p. 471.

spring of 438. It was the fourth member of a tetralogy (the other plays being the *Cretan Women*, the *Alcmeon in Psophis* and the *Telephus*), thus occupying the place usually held by a satyric drama. Euripides gained only the second prize, Sophocles being first.

The *Alcestis*, then, is the work of no prentice hand. It appeared when Euripides was in at least the forty-second year of his life (probably several years older; the statement of the Parian Marble that he was born in Ol. 72, 4 is much more likely to be right than the other version, which makes his birth occur in the year, and even on the day, of the battle of Salamis) and the eighteenth of his career as a dramatist. It belonged to the same tetralogy as two of his most famous plays,—the *Alcmeon in Psophis* and the *Telephus*. Whatever imperfections the play may contain cannot, therefore, be ascribed to the poet's youth or inexperience. The period at which the drama was presented was that when the greatness of Athens was at its height, seven years before the outbreak of the Peloponnesian War and while the Parthenon was still in process of building.

The *Alcestis*, like the first play of Euripides (the *Peliades*) and the *Medea*, has to do with the fortunes of the royal family of Iolcus. As Wilamowitz has pointed out, during the earlier part of his dramatic career Euripides tried to please the Athenians by treating new subjects with which they were not already familiar. It may be suspected, also, that there was some strong tie which bound Euripides himself to northern Greece. We know that later in life he went to Macedonia to the court of Archelaus; and doubtless some other attraction beside the liberality and literary taste of the king drew him thither. It is possible that he had kinsfolk in Thessaly or Macedonia.

The question arises, in what relation did the *Alcestis* stand to the other three dramas of the tetralogy? Were the four plays connected in plot or by some other internal bond, or was the connection between them merely external? That they were not linked together in plot seems clear; their subjects are too different and the myths of which they treat cover too wide a range for this to be possible. It has been suggested, however, by Bernhardy (art.

"Euripides" in Ersch and Gruber's *Encycl.*) and G. A. Schoell (*Tetral. d. Att. Theaters* pp. 52-9) that the poet's object in selecting the subjects of these plays was to show different types of woman, the lascivious adulteress Aerope being opposed to the trustful and faithful Alphesiboea (or Arsinoe), and the masculine Clytaemestra to the womanly Alcestis. Schoell notes, also, that in all four dramas the sanctity of the household hearth and the duties of hospitality are important elements. But, ingenious as this theory is, at best the verdict must be "not proven." We do not know enough of the three lost tragedies to enable us to establish such a connection.

The contents of the Euripidean play are, in brief, as follows: vv. 1-76. Prologue. Apollo makes the introductory speech, informing the spectators of the situation. The day appointed for the death of Alcestis has arrived, and hence he must leave the palace of Admetus to avoid pollution (1-27). Thanatos enters: seeing Apollo before the door, he reproaches him in a short anapaestic system. A dialogue between the two follows: Apollo entreats Thanatos to spare the queen's life, but in vain, and leaves in anger. Thanatos enters the palace (28-76). 77-135. Parodos. The chorus enters, full of anxiety to find out whether Alcestis is still alive or not. Their opinions differ; but they know that her end is near; no one can save her now that Asclepius is dead. 136-434. First Episode. An attendant comes out of the palace and is questioned by the coryphaeus. She relates the preparations made by Alcestis against her death, her prayers in behalf of her children, and her farewell to her marriage-bed and her domestics. The servant tells also of the grief of Admetus, and the dying queen's desire to see once more the light of the sun (141-212). A lyric dialogue between the two semi-choruses follows. They doubt whether there is still hope, but pray Zeus and Apollo for aid; express their sympathy for Admetus, and praise Alcestis as she is brought out of the palace (213-243). Alcestis says farewell to the sun and to her home. She believes that she sees Charon, who is impatient for her departure, and that a spectre from the under-world is trying to drag her away. Admetus entreats her to stay with him (244-279). Alcestis then makes a long and affecting speech, setting forth his obligations to her and begging him to love and care for her children and not to marry again. In a long speech he promises to comply with her wishes, and she solemnly commits the children to his care. She then says farewell and expires (280–392). The child Eumelus sings a monody lamenting his mother's death (393–415). The chorus comforts Admetus, who gives orders as to the mourning for his wife (416–434). 435–475. First Stasimon. The chorus lauds Alcestis for her devotion and prophesies that her name will live in song, expresses the wish that it could bring her back to life, and contrasts her conduct with that of the king's parents. 476–567. Second Episode. Heracles, on his way to Thrace to bring the horses of Diomedes, comes to Pherae. He explains the object of his journey and receives information from the coryphaeus as to the dangerous nature of the undertaking (476–506). Admetus, clad in the garb of mourning, comes out of the palace. Heracles questions him as to the reason for his attire, but he evades the question, presses the visitor to remain and gives orders for his entertainment. The chorus remonstrate, but Admetus persists (507–567). 568–605. Second Stasimon. The chorus recall the time when Apollo served the king, and the manner in which the god charmed the wild beasts with his music. They then extol the wealth and power of the king, and express their confidence that his hospitality will be rewarded. 606–961. Third Episode. Pheres enters and tries to condole with Admetus, but is indignantly rejected. An angry dialogue between father and son follows, and Pheres departs in wrath. Admetus renounces him. The king and chorus pass out to the burial (606–746). A servant comes out of the palace and complains of the greediness of Heracles and his lack of regard for the proprieties of the occasion. Heracles follows him and gives him a serio-comic lecture on the duties of a servant to his master's guests and the true philosophy of life; but soon discovers the truth and goes off to the tomb to rescue Alcestis (747–860). Admetus and the chorus return (ἐπιπάροδος), and Admetus laments his loss while the chorus sympathize with him and try to comfort him (861-934). Admetus then paints the wretchedness of his situation in a short speech in trimeters (935-961). 962-1005. Third Stasimon. The chorus sing the power of Necessity, and predicts the honours which await Alcestis as heroine. 1006-end. Exodus. Heracles enters, leading a veiled woman, whom, he says, he has won as a prize in certain games in which he has contested. He asks Admetus to take charge of her until his return from Thrace. The king at first refuses; but at last yields, though very reluctantly and after a long dialogue. Heracles then unveils her, and Admetus recognizes his wife. He inquires how she was rescued, and Heracles tells him. Admetus thanks his benefactor, and presses him to remain; but Heracles is in haste and cannot stay. The king then orders a general thanksgiving. The chorus march out to the closing anapaests.

Such, in brief, is the action of the play. This brings us to that most perplexed and difficult question: is the *Alcestis* a *tragedy*, and if not, what is it? On this subject volumes (I had almost said libraries) have been written, and the question is still far from being settled. It seems to have been disputed even in ancient times. We read in the last paragraph of the hypothesis: τὸ δὲ δρᾶμά ἐστι σατυρικώτερον ὅτι εἰς χαρὰν καὶ ἡδονὴν καταστρέφει ⟨καὶ⟩ ἐκβάλλεται ὡς ἀνοίκεια τῆς τραγικῆς ποιήσεως ὅ τε Ὀρέστης καὶ ἡ Ἄλκηστις, ὡς ἐκ συμφορᾶς μὲν ἀρχόμενα, εἰς εὐδαιμονίαν ⟨δὲ⟩ καὶ χαρὰν λήξαντα, ⟨ἃ⟩ ἐστι μᾶλλον κωμῳδίας ἐχόμενα· and on the other hand in the treatise περὶ κωμῳδίας published by Duebner (see his ed. of the scholia to Aristophanes p. xix.) from the Codex Parisinus 2677 we read: σατυρικῆς δὲ οὐ τὸ ἀπὸ πένθους εἰς χαρὰς ἀπαντᾶν, ὡς ὁ Εὐριπίδου Ὀρέστης καὶ Ἄλκηστις καὶ ἡ Σοφοκλέους Ἠλέκτρα, ἐκ μέρους, ὥσπερ τινὲς φασίν, ἀλλ' ἀμιγῆ καὶ χαρίεντα καὶ θυμελικὸν ἔχει γέλωτα κ.τ.λ. Aristophanes of Byzantium seems to have contented himself with the cautious remark: τὸ δὲ δρᾶμα κωμικωτέραν ἔχει τὴν καταστροφήν (the last clause of the Vatican fragment), which was amplified by later grammarians (see Trendelenburg, *Gramm. Graec. d. art. trag. jud. reliq.* p. 36 f.). He makes a similar observation in the hypothesis to the *Orestes*.

The modern literature of the subject is, as I have said, very large. The best survey of it is to be found in the very sane and careful essay by G. Bissinger, "*Ueber die Dichtungsgattung u. d. Grundgedanken d. Alcestis d. Euripides*" (Erlangen 1869–71), to which I am indebted for many points.

The theories which have been advanced respecting the nature of the *Alcestis* may be divided into seven classes: —

I. Many authorities regard the play as a *tragedy* in the strict sense. So Sponheim, Buhl, Wieland, Firnhaber, Preller, G. Hermann, Goethe, Kolanowski, Wilken, Sittl, Cucuel, etc. (For references see list at the end of this section.) Steinberger regards the drama as a "distorted tragedy" (verzerrtes Trauerspiel), the poet having at first intended to write a comic play, but having found the subject unsuitable for that purpose.

II. Few writers, if any, have openly expressed the view that the *Alcestis* is a *comedy*. The Frenchman Brumoy, however, seems to have held nearly this opinion, and (as Bissinger points out) Köchly's view (see below) involves nearly this conception of the play. Schöne believes that the *Alcestis* is a parody on the play of Phrynichus.

III. Others have held that the *Alcestis* is a satyr-drama. So Hedelin, d'Aubignac, Danina, Lessing, Glum, Hartung, Klein.

IV. Others, still, have seen in the play a tragi-comedy (or *hilarotragoedia*) with an intentional admixture of tragic and comic elements. So O. Mueller, Buchholz, Duentzer.

V. Others believe the *Alcestis* to be neither a tragedy nor a comedy nor a mere combination of the two, but rather what the Germans call a "Schauspiel," a "play" in the modern sense, with varying moods and situations, not falling wholly within the limits either of comedy or tragedy. So Eichstädt, Wagner, Rauchenstein, Ritter.

VI. Others still, while holding that Euripides was endeavoring, by producing the *Alcestis*, to strike out a new path in the drama, do not attempt to classify the play under any one of these heads. So Köchly, whose view is so peculiar that I quote him more at length: "An die Stelle der Satyrn und Silene setzte er aus dem eigenen Kreise des gewöhnlichen Alltagslebens die fadesten Personen, mit denen er einen tragischen Charakter umgab, in Berührung und Wechselwirkung brachte. Das Wesentliche dieser neuen Gattung nun wurde der Conflict eines tragischen Charakters mit der Philisterwelt der Gegenwart, der Gegensatz einer idealen Weltanschauung zu der kahlen, nüchternen Prosa des wirklichen Lebens." The humor of the piece lies in the fact that in this conflict the idealist is saved by the materialist, the tragic heroine by the "Philistine." Bernhardy expresses a similar view, and so Jöhring.

VII. Lastly, Mr. Verrall holds that the play is what the Germans would call a "Tendenz-Schrift," a covert attack on the popular religion, bearing one meaning to the multitude and another to the "advanced thinkers" of the day.

The theory that the *Alcestis* is a comedy does not, I think, require any extended refutation. Neither the subject of the play, nor its arrangement, nor the position which it occupied in a tetralogy is consistent with the Greek conception of a comedy. Whatever we may pronounce the play to be, the tragic element in it clearly preponderates over the comic.

Nor is it easy to believe that the *Alcestis* was a satyric drama. True, it occupied the place of one; but the characteristic features of the satyric drama, the chorus of satyrs, the rude jests and unrestrained merriment, are conspicuously absent. The *Alcestis* differs less widely from the *Agamemnon* than from the *Cyclops*.

It is clear, however, that the drama is not an *ordinary* tragedy. The fact that it held the place usually occupied by a satyr-play is proof positive of this; and the comic tinge of certain portions of it, though slight, is unmistakable. In what, then, does the difference consist? Not in the fortunate ending; for this criterion, if strictly applied, would exclude many plays the tragic nature of which has never been questioned. True, Aristotle *preferred* that in a tragedy the change of fortune should be from prosperity to adversity (*Poet.* 1453 b 12); but he also knew and *recognized as tragedies* plays in which the change was in the opposite direction (1453 a 25, 1455 b 29). Nor yet does it lie in the nature of the characters who appear in the play. True, the *Alcestis* is a drama of domestic life, and the personages who take part in it are very much like ordinary men and women; but who could be more ordinary (I had almost said vulgar) than the characters who rail and wrangle through so many lines of the *Andromache* or the *Orestes*? Nor does the difference consist wholly in the more subdued nature of the action. It is true that the characters move in a calmer atmosphere than in many of the Euripidean plays; but surely the spectacle of a young and lovely woman snatched away in her prime by a merciless and irresistible power is sufficient to excite both terror and pity.

It has seemed, and still seems, to the present writer that, after all, the main difference between the *Alcestis* and an ordinary tragedy is in the comic element which appears in the play; and even this difference is one of degree rather than of kind. It has often been noted that occasional comic touches are found even in Aeschylean and Sophoclean tragedies, (e.g. the nurse's speech in *Choeph.* 715 ff., esp. l. 735 f.); and they are much more frequent in Euripides. What is more natural, then, than for the poet, having to provide a substitute for a satyric drama, to offer a tragedy in which these occasional comic features have been slightly intensified? I say slightly; for the comic element in the *Alcestis* is in reality much less prominent than some have claimed.

Wherein does this comic element appear? Some have thought that it may be traced in the scene between Apollo and Thanatos (vv. 28–76). That there may be a slight touch of humor here I will not deny; but, taken as a whole, the scene is merely an angry dialogue of the kind so common in Greek tragedies. Almost the same may be said of the scene between Pheres and Admetus, which is simply an ἀγών of the kind so dear to Athenian audiences. Neither contains anything which is inconsistent with the idea of a tragedy; and the Apollo-Thanatos scene cannot weigh very heavily in any case, as it lies under grave suspicion (see below). Nor is the comic element prominent in the closing scene (1006 ff.). Some have thought that the long hesitation and timid consent of Admetus to receive the woman were intended to *amuse* the audience. They have, I think, missed to a large extent the real purport of this scene. Why does Heracles tantalize Admetus with a feigned tale and press him to receive a (supposed) stranger woman into his house, instead of restoring Alcestis to him at once? Partly, no doubt, to test his faithfulness to his wife's memory; partly, too, because Euripides wished by the suspense to heighten the interest of the spectators; but there is a stronger reason. The poet's attitude toward the conduct of Admetus (and this it is the great merit of Mr. Verrall to have pointed out) is by no means one of *unmixed* praise. The first words which Heracles speaks on his return are words of *censure* (1008 f.). Admetus has deceived him, though with kindly intent; has evaded his questions and dealt in language of double meaning. The king is now requited in full measure for this deception. Every evasion, every *double-entendre* is repaid to him with interest. Not until he has atoned for his deceit is Alcestis restored to him. In this scene, then, there is nothing inconsistent with the conception of a tragedy. There remains the scene between Heracles and the servant. This is undeniably tinged with comic humor. The poet lets us see for an instant the gluttonous, riotous Heracles of the popular conception; though even here, when we consider in what light the hero was represented in the comedy of the day, we see that Euripides has confined himself within relatively narrow bounds. In this scene, then, the difference between the *Alcestis* and an ordinary tragedy mainly lies.

Did this comic element belong to the original plan of the play? At the close of "Balaustion's Adventure" Robert Browning has sketched a plot which in his judgment (and surely he was no mean judge) would have been preferable to that of the Euripidean *Alcestis*. Curiously enough this plot follows very nearly the story as (according to Wilamowitz) it was told in the Hesiodic *Eoeae*. Why should Euripides, when he had this form of the myth ready to his hand, have preferred the Phrynichean version?

The late Prof. F. D. Allen long entertained doubts as to the authenticity of the Apollo-Thanatos scene in the prologue. He kindly permitted me to use the following brief abstract of his arguments: —

"1. If Thanatos goes into the house (at 76), how and when does he leave it? He is next heard of at the tomb (845, 1140 ff.). Does he depart by a postern gate, or does he become all at once invisible to the spectators?

2. After the announcement of Thanatos at 74 ff. (cf. 47, 48), it is strange that Alcestis dies quietly on the stage, *in the absence of Thanatos*, then is carried into the house, and presently carried out again and actually buried. (In 253 ff. she does indeed see 'Αΐδας and Charon, but this is, of course, only in her *mind's eye*.)

3. Alcestis is in the death-throe (20) *before* the arrival of Thanatos.

4. Altogether there is confusion between two notions. (α) In the Thanatos scene the notion is that Thanatos comes to despatch Alcestis in person, goes into the house for the purpose, and is to carry her off bodily to Hades (47, 49, 73, etc.). (β) In the rest of the play, the notion is that Alcestis dies quietly in the ordinary way, is buried, and that *then* Thanatos comes to *the tomb* to fetch her, and is overcome by Heracles, who is awaiting him in ambush (1142).

5. If Apollo knows that Alcestis is to be released by Heracles (64–69), why his distress in the earlier part of the prologue, and his effort to dissuade Thanatos from his purpose?

6. A notion runs through the Thanatos scene (32, 34 [αὖ], 43, 45) that Admetus' death-day is already past, a separate death-day being set for Alcestis (the present day). But the conception of the play itself (12 ff., 523 f., especially 694–700) is that Alcestis dies on Admetus' appointed day."

These are certainly weighty reasons, and show, I think, conclusively that the Thanatos scene is an insertion. Whether it was put into the text long after the time of Euripides or not is hard to say. The *cruces* and ineptitudes which occur in it favor this view. Another possibility that has presented itself to me is: that Euripides may have originally intended to make of the *Alcestis* a pure tragedy of the ordinary type, *perhaps* taking as its groundwork that form of the myth found in the *Eoeae*. Then, finding that he had no satyric play on hand to complete a tetralogy, he may have taken the unfinished drama and worked it over, using the other form of the legend, which was better adapted to a comic treatment. If this view be correct, vv. 24–76, 476–605, 747–860, 1006-end will be later additions by the poet, which did not belong to the original plan of the play. Except in these portions there is no allusion whatever to Heracles. When we remember that Euripides is believed to have written over ninety plays and that he seems to have exhibited in at least seventeen of the first eighteen years of his dramatic career, we cannot wonder if he was forced to resort to such an expedient. The defects and incongruities which have so often been noted in the play could be easily explained on this hypothesis; and Professor Allen's arguments against the authenticity of the prologue would not lose their force, but simply point in a new direction. I make this merely as a suggestion; a demonstration of the theory from our present data would be difficult, perhaps impossible.

Be this as it may, I believe the *Alcestis* to be a *tragedy*, with only so much of the comic element as was absolutely necessary in a play which was to replace a satyric drama. The ancient writers, though they speak of it as σατυρικώτερον or as having a κωμικωτέραν καταστροφήν, regularly call it a δρᾶμα or a tragedy, not a comedy, a satyr-play or a *hilaro-tragoedia*. By their judgment we must abide.

This subject must not be dismissed without a few words as to the theory lately propounded by Dr. Verrall. Ingenious and instructive as his essay is, the present writer, for one, must wholly dissent from his main position; and this for the following reasons.

(1) Euripides (especially during the earlier part of his career) was a *poet* first and foremost, and only secondarily a moral teacher. It is not probable that he would have sacrificed a fine play in order to covertly disseminate his opinions.

(2) No ancient writer, so far as I know, gives us even a hint of the secret meaning which Dr. Verrall has discovered in the *Alcestis*. Not even that most keen-eyed and merciless of critics, Aristophanes, betrays a suspicion of it. If Euripides really was concealing a rationalistic doctrine under the garb of a drama, he hid it "not wisely but too well," so that for more than two thousand years no one was able to penetrate the disguise.

(3) It appears to me that, *from the Greek point of view*, Dr. Verrall has unduly depreciated the characters both of Admetus and

Heracles. That the former cuts a contemptible figure it would be vain to deny; but we must not forget that (in spite of some brilliant exceptions) the Greek sense of personal honor and personal responsibility was less keen than that of modern people. What person ever reads the story of the typical Greek hero, Odysseus, without partly despising the "man of many wiles"? Macaulay has pointed out that an Italian audience of Machiavelli's day would have felt more sympathy for Iago than for Othello. I will not say that an Athenian audience of the time of Euripides would have been in full sympathy with Admetus; but it would certainly have felt much less repugnance for him than modern readers of the play necessarily feel. There is force, also, in the hackneyed argument that in the eyes of the Greeks a king was of more importance than any woman, even though she were a queen. — Heracles, too, has suffered at Dr. Verrall's hands. The rescuer of Alcestis is no mere "athlete-adventurer"*: the true idea of him is as far from Dr. Verrall's materialized notion on the one hand as it is from Browning's idealized conception on the other. The complaints of the domestic (v. 747 f.), like the grumblings of discontented servants in every age of the world, should not be taken too literally. Heracles is slightly flushed with wine,† it is true; but the clearness and coherence of his speech show that he is not by any means intoxicated. The philosophy which it expresses is not a very lofty one; but such as it is, it is set forth consistently enough. The reason why Heracles pretends to bring a stranger woman and quarter her upon Admetus (a piece of seeming discourtesy of which Dr. Verrall makes a great deal) has been already stated. Deceit must be repaid with deceit; the punishment, though a kindly one, is none the less a punishment. In short, I believe that instead of *lowering* the popular conception of Admetus and Heracles, Euripides has distinctly *raised* it.

---

* Note the extreme brevity and modesty of his replies in ll. 1140 ff., without a particle of self-praise or braggadocio.

† "Non ebrius est, sed paulum incaluit vino," as Hermann rightly observes; but Dr. Verrall repeatedly (pp. 8, 26) says or implies that Heracles "*got very drunk*."

(4) The strongest point of Dr. Verrall's argument, and one to which he was the first to call attention, is "the haste and precipitancy, irregular and indecent in any case, and in this particular case nothing less than outrageous, with which the corpse of the noble heroine is conveyed to the grave" (p. 44). This is a real and serious difficulty. Dr. Verrall has, I think, somewhat overstated the amount of repugnance which a Greek would feel toward the hasty burial of a corpse.* Still, it must be admitted that such a proceeding was contrary both to Attic law and Attic custom. In our play something had, no doubt, to be conceded to dramatic convenience, in order to bring the action within a comparatively short space of time. But this is clearly not a sufficient reason for so marked a violation of Greek usage. As Dr. Verrall says (p. 45), "it would have been perfectly easy to present a story like that of Alcestis, a story of death and revival, without introducing any funeral at all,† and so that a day or a few hours should naturally cover events from first to last." Moreover, the poet has emphasized the haste of the burial in the most striking way. The chorus actually speak of the funeral before they know that Alcestis is dead (v. 96). "Scarce a minute (says Dr. Verrall, p. 48) has passed since her last 'Farewell!' was spoken, the wail of her frightened child has scarcely sunk into sobbing, and the friend who stands by has barely proffered his first word of condolence, when Admetus . . . runs on, as it were in one sentence, to invite the immediate assistance of his visitors in conveying 'this corpse' to the cemetery."

But is there no reason for all this? The circumstances are most exceptional; the Moerae have been cheated of their destined victim by a disgraceful trick, and there is every reason to believe that the payment of the debt will be enforced with the utmost rigour. The

* Cf. Eustathius on *Il.* VIII. 410 (p. 688, 7): νεκροῦ μείλιγμα μὲν ἡ οἰκεῖα ταφὴ . . . μήνιμα δὲ τὸ μὴ ταχὺ θάπτεσθαι. The sooner the burial took place, the sooner the soul would pass through the "gates of Hades."

† But if, as I believe, the *Alcestis* was worked over by the author and the plot changed, the funeral certainly belonged to the *original plan* of the drama (according to which Alcestis probably died, was buried, went down to Hades and was sent back by Persephone, as in the *Eoeae*), and hence could not be cut out without destroying too much of the whole framework of the play.

appointed day has come, and the substitute is ready; the offering must be promptly made, and the chthonian powers receive their γέρας. If there is one moment's delay beyond the time which has been set, all will be lost. But *the payment is not complete, and Admetus is not safe, until the funeral with its attendant offerings has taken place;* hence Alcestis must be buried on *the very day* of her death. The preparations made by the queen before her decease (158 f.), the promptness with which the chorus appear at the palace on the appointed day, the arrangements which are made for the funeral immediately after Alcestis dies, all point in this direction; and surely the proclamation of Admetus to all the Thessalians (425 ff.) does not look as though the proceedings were "clandestine" (Dr. Verrall, p. 56)!

I append a partial list of the essays and articles dealing with the nature of the *Alcestis*. For the older literature, see the essays of Buchholz and Bissinger, mentioned below. I include only works that have appeared in this century. Much additional matter may be found in the different editions of the play, the histories of Greek literature (esp. Bernhardy,[3] vol. III. pp. 458 ff.), and special works on Euripides (see esp. Hartung, *Euripides restitutus* I. pp. 229 ff.).

Glum, *De Euripidis Alcestide commentatio.* Berlin, 1836.

Firnhaber, review of Glum in *Zeitschr. f. Alterthumswiss.* 1837. pp. 411–421 (esp. 414 ff.).

Duentzer, *De Euripidis Alcestide, N. Jahrb. f. Philol.* Suppl.-Bd. V. (1839) pp. 192 ff.

Koechly, *Die Alcestis des Euripides, Literarhistor. Taschenbuch von Prutz.* 1847. pp. 359–390.

Rauchenstein, *Die Alcestis des Euripides als besondere Gattung des griechischen Dramas.* Aarau, 1847.

Bendixen, *De Alcestide Euripidis commentatio.* Altona, 1851.

Buchholz, *Commentatio de Alcestide Euripidea.* Osnabrück, 1864.

Kolanowski, *De natura atque indole fabulae Eurip. quae Alcestis inscribitur.* Ostrowo, 1868.

Bissinger, *Ueber die Dichtungsgattung u. d. Grundgedanken d. Alcestis.* Erlangen. Th. I. 1869, Th. II. 1871. (This is by far the best treatise on this subject.)

Ritter, *De Euripidis Alcestide.* Jena, 1875.
Wilken, *De Alcestide Euripidea.* Berlin, 1876.
Humphreys, *The fourth Play in the Tetralogy,* Am. Jour. Philol. I. (1880) pp. 191 ff.
Cucuel, *Phérès, Admète et Hercule dans l'Alceste,* Revue de Philol. 1887. pp. 17 ff.
Steinberger, *Goethe u. d. Alkestisfrage,* Blätter f. d. Bayer. Gymn.-Wesen XXV. (1889) pp. 24 ff.
Jöhring, *Ist die Alkestis des Euripides eine Tragoedie?* Feldkirch, 1894.
Schoene, *Ueber die Alkestis des Euripides.* Kiel, 1895.
Verrall, *Euripides the Rationalist.* Cambridge, 1895. (The *Alcestis* is treated in pp. 1–128 of the book.)

The short article by Bremi (in the *Allgemeine Schulzeitung,* 1829 no. 48, pp. 393-7), and the dissertation of Bendixen and article of Koechly mentioned above I have been unable to consult at first hand.

C. The Critical Basis for the Text.

The Manuscripts, Scholia, Editions, etc.

As every scholar knows, the MSS. of Euripides are comparatively late and poor. Fortunately, however, the *Alcestis* was a favorite drama in post-classical times, and was included in the Byzantine edition of ten* selected plays (the *Hecuba, Orestes, Phoenissae, Hippolytus, Medea, Alcestis, Andromache, Rhesus, Troades* and *Bacchae;* see Wilamowitz, *Herakles* pp. 195 ff.) as well as in the larger one of nineteen plays. Hence we have the advantage of two † recensions of the play, each of which acts as a check upon the other. *I have followed Prinz in designating the MSS.;* for his nomenclature, though not entirely satisfactory, is more widely

---

* On the question as to whether there were *nine* (so Kirchhoff) or *ten* see Wilamowitz, *Analecta* p. 51, *Herakles* I. p. 207 and note.

† I ought strictly to say *three;* for *a c d* probably represent a recension differing somewhat from *B,* though much less widely than from *L P.* But the exact relation of *a* to *c d* is not yet known.

used than any other. To introduce a new nomenclature would be almost a crime.

Unfortunately for us, the best of the Euripidean MSS., the Marcianus 471, does not contain the *Alcestis*. It formerly did include the play; but the part which contained it had been torn out of the codex even before the latter was brought to Italy (Wilamowitz, *Herakles* I. p. 206 note). The text of the *Alcestis* rests mainly upon four MSS. These are:—

(1) The *codex Vaticanus* 909 (*B* Prinz = B Kirchhoff = V Dindorf and Wilamowitz = A Schwartz = Rom. A Elmsley). This is a paper (bombycine) MS. of the twelfth (Kirchhoff) or thirteenth (Prinz) century, containing the *Hecuba, Orestes, Phoenissae, Medea, Hippolytus, Alcestis, Andromache, Troades* and *Rhesus*, with scholia and glosses. It has been corrected in many places by the first hand (marked B^1 by Prinz); and many corrections and variant readings were added by later hands (marked *b* by Prinz). Kirchhoff ranked this MS. next to the *Marcianus*. Later critics have, for the most part, held it in somewhat lower esteem (see esp. Wilamowitz, *Herakles* p. 206). The extreme carelessness with which it is written greatly diminishes its value, and it is sometimes hard to tell whether its readings are mere blunders of the copyist or really represent what stood in its source. Still, for the *Alcestis* I should be inclined to rank it higher than any other *single* MS., though when it stands *alone* it is inferior to *L* and *P* conjoined.

(2) The *codex Parisinus* 2713 (*a* Prinz = a Kirchhoff = (Par.) B Wilamowitz, Schwartz and the older edd.). This is a fine vellum MS. of the thirteenth century, written in an elegant hand and containing the *Hecuba, Orestes, Phoenissae, Hippolytus, Medea, Alcestis* and *Andromache*, with glosses and very copious scholia, mostly written by the first hand. Beside the first hand (a^1 Prinz), a second hand (a^2 Prinz) and several later ones (a^3 Prinz) have corrected the MS. In the *Alcestis* this codex has suffered much from interpolation; but, on the whole, it is not to be despised, particularly when it confirms the testimony of *B*. When it stands *alone*, however, it is to be used with extreme caution, as the scribe (or the

maker of the recension which he followed) was a man of some learning and prone to arbitrary emendation. Good examples of his conjectures are 289 (where by leaving out δῶρ' and retaining the gloss or interpolation ἐγώ he has contrived to make a tolerable trimeter), 329 ἐμοῦ γυνὴ for ἐμὴ γυνὴ (to avoid the rhyme), 426 θέλω for λέγω, 434 λίαν, 531 γυναικὸς δ' (δ' inserted to remove asyndeton), 794 (οἶμαι μέν given to the servant), 811 θυραῖος for οἰκεῖος (the most successful of his emendations, though I do not believe that Euripides wrote θυραῖος), 837 ψυχή τ' (from *Orestes* 466) for καὶ χείρ, 1038 ἀθλίους for ἀθλίου (not a bad emendation), 1048 συμφοραῖς for συμφορᾷ, 1085 σ' νῦν (an impossible elision to avoid the extra syllable), 1111 σοῖς for τήν. On the other hand, in *minutiae* this codex is often in the right against the other MSS., as the greater care or scholarship of the scribe has preserved him from many errors. In particular, L a together are very often right in small points (such as accent, the use of ν movable, etc.). In general, however, a agrees so closely with B in our play that editors are fully justified in speaking of them as belonging to one "family." a shows occasional signs of contamination with a MS. of the other class, e.g. 259 ἄγει μ' ἄγει τις ἄγει μέ τις, 1045 μή με μιμνήσῃς. It has preserved one excellent reading, 1140 κυρίῳ, which, however, was also known to the scholiast.

(Codices Florent. 31, 10 (c Prinz, c Kirchhoff) and 31, 15 (d Prinz, d Kirchhoff) agree very closely with a. They deserve, however, a new examination, especially d, which (as Professor von Wilamowitz, who has kindly communicated to me a number of readings from it, assures me) is not without importance for the *Alcestis*. I much regret that I have been unable to collate it.)

(3) The *codex Laurentianus* (or *Florentinus*) 32, 2 (L Prinz = B Kirchhoff = C Dindorf, Wilamowitz = Fl., Flor. (2) or Laurentianus older edd.). This is a paper (*chartaceus*) MS. of the fourteenth century, written by several hands. It contains (beside six plays of Sophocles, three of Aeschylus and the *Works and Days* of Hesiod) eighteen of the Euripidean plays, the *Troades* and part of the *Bacchae* being wanting. The text has been corrected by the first hand, or rather hands (L¹ Prinz), and then many corrections

and alterations have been made by a later hand (*l* Prinz). For a more minute description, see Wilamowitz, *Analecta Euripidea* pp. 4 ff.

(4) By the side of *L* stands the *codex Palatinus* 287 (*P* Prinz = *C* Kirchhoff = P Dindorf, Wilamowitz = P, Pal., Palat. or Rom. C older edd.). This codex (now in the Vatican) is a vellum MS. of the fourteenth century. It contains the *Antigone, Oedipus Col., Trachiniae* and *Philoctetes* of Sophocles, the *Andromache, Medea, Supplices, Rhesus, Ion, Iph. Taur., Iph. Aul.*, the spurious prologue to the *Danae*, the *Hippolytus, Alcestis, Troades, Bacchae, Cyclops, Heraclidae* as far as l. 1002, and the *Prometheus, Septem* and *Persae* of Aeschylus. The rest of the *Heraclidae*, the *Helena, Heracles, Electra, Hecuba, Orestes, Phoenissae*, and the *Ajax, Electra* and *Oedipus Rex* of Sophocles (with the hypothesis and list of characters of the *Antigone*) once formed part of this codex, but were torn off not long after the year 1400, and are now preserved as a separate MS., the Laurentianus 172 (*G* Prinz = Γ Wilamowitz). That *P* and Γ belong together was first pointed out by Robert (*Hermes* XIII. pp. 133 ff.). *P* has been corrected by the first hand (P^1 Prinz) and by a later hand or hands (*p* Prinz).

The exact relation in which *P* stands to *L* and their comparative value have been, and still are, matters of high dispute. In his *Analecta Euripidea* (pp. 3 ff.) Wilamowitz expressed the belief that both MSS. were copied from a lost codex which was written in minuscule letters not earlier than the twelfth century. This lost MS. he designated by Φ. From this *L* was copied near the beginning of the fourteenth century, and *P* toward the end of the same century. Prinz held substantially the same view, and indicated the lost archetype of *L* and *P* by the letter *S*. Wilamowitz, however, has now changed his opinion, and holds (*Herakles*[1] I. pp. 208 ff.) that in *P* the nine dramas which are without scholia were copied from the same MS. as was *L* (though much more carelessly); while in the other plays the scribe of *P* has constituted a text of his own, partly from the MS. which he had used for the nine dramas, partly from an unimportant manuscript akin to *Ba*. He adds: "das mischungsverhältnis ist verschieden; in den drei ersten stücken und Andromache folgt er mehr dem vulgären, in Rhesos und Alkestis stimmt er mehr zu C (i.e. *L*) : es leuchtet ein, dass P für diese dramen ganz wertlos ist; es sei denn, er hilft einmal eine überschmierte lesart von C erkennen." Prof. Vitelli, on the other hand (see the pref. to van Herwerden's *Helena* p. vii.), has long maintained that Laurent. 172 (and consequently *P*) is a copy of a copy of *L*. Though I hesitate to express an opinion contrary to such high authority, as regards the *Alcestis* at least I cannot agree either with Vitelli or with the later view of Wilamowitz. Much more probable to me seems the view of Bruhn, that in the *Alcestis L* and *P* go back to a common source, but the scribe of *L*, being a man of considerable learning, has allowed himself changes and interpolations, while the more ignorant but more faithful copyist of *P* adhered more closely to his original (*Lucubrationes Euripideae* p. 255 f.).

I do not, however, believe that *L* and *P* were derived *directly* from the same MS. The number of different readings which they contain (about 160 in the *Alcestis* alone, if I may trust a very carefully made list of mine) is much too great for this to be possible. Many of these differences, to be sure, are slight (matters of accent, etc.), but still the sum total is considerable. Space will not allow me to give a complete list, but the following are the variants for the first 300 lines : —

v. 22	κίχῃ *L*,	κιχῇ *P*.
26	συμμέτρως *L*,	σύμμετρος *P*.
27	ἦμαρ *L*,	ἦμαρ *P*.
28 ff.	θαν. pref. *L*,	χρ̄ *P* (so too 43, 45 ff., but 39, 72 θἄ).
31	is in *L*,	is not in *P*.
33	διακωλύσαι *L*,	διακωλῦσαι *P*.
40	αἰεὶ *L*,	ἀεὶ *P*.
45	κάτω *L*,	κατὰ *P*.
46	μέτα *L*,	μετὰ *P*.
47	νερτέρων *L*,	νερτέραν *P*.
57	τίθης *L*, .	τιθεὶς *P*.
58	ἢ *L*,	ἢ *P*.

58	λέληθας L,	ἐλήλυθας P.
59	ὠνοῖντ' L,	ὤνοιντ' P.
73	ἡ δ' L,	ἥδ' P.
74	κατάρξομαι L,	κατάρξωμαι P.
80	εἴποι L,	ἐννέποι P.
82	λεύσσει L,	λεύσει P.
88	γόον L,	γόων P.
91	ἡμιχ. pref. L,	ἡμιχ. omitted in P.
94	νέκυς ἤδη L,	ἤδη νέκυς P.
103	νεολαῖα L,	νεολαία P.
105	ἦμαρ L,	ἦμαρ P.
106	χορ. pref. L,	ἡμιχ. P.
107	χρή L,	χρῆν P.
108	ἡμιχ. not in L,	ἡμιχ. before the 2d ἔθιγες P.
118	ἀπό**μος L,	ἄποτμος P.
120	ἔχω 'πι L,	ἔχω ἐπὶ P.
129	πλῆκτρον L,	πλᾶκτρον P.
136	ὀπαδός L,	ὀπαδῶν P.
140	βουλοίμεθ' ἂν L,	βουλοίμεθα P.
141	βλέποι L,	βλέπ* P.
145	πάθοι L,	πάθη P.
148	οὐκοῦν L,	οὐκ οὖν P.
151	παράγραφος pref. in L,	θερ. in P.
152	" " " "	τροφ. in P.
157	θαυμάσεις L,	θαυμάσει P.
173	ἄκλαυτος L,	ἄκλαυστος P.
184	ὀφθαλμοτέκτῳ L,	ὀφθαλμοτέγκτῳ P.
188	αὑτὴν L,	αὐτὴν P.
197	δ' ἔχει L,	τ' ἔχει P.
198	οὔπoτ' οὐ L,	οὔποτε P (sic).
198	λήσεται L,	λελήσεται P.
211	πα**στάναι L,	παριστάναι P.
213–17 to χορ.		
218–25 to θερ.	} L,	213–43 to χορ. P.
226–43 to χορ.		
213	ἄν πως ** L,	ἄν πως παῖ* P.

219	εὐχώμεθα L,	εὐχόμεθα P.
227	τῆς σῆς L,	σῆς P.
228	ἀὶ ἀὶ L,	αἲ αἲ P.
234	βόασον L,	βόησον P.
239	πάροιθεν L,	πάροιθε P.
241	ὅστις (τις deleted) L,	ὅστις P.
247	θανεῖν L,	θανῇ P.
259	ἄγει *ἄγει με τις L,	ἄγει ἄγει μέ τις P.
260	εἰς L,	ἐς P.
261	ἄδης L,	ἄδας P.
263	δειλαι** L,	διλαιότατα P.
267	ποσί L,	πόσι P.
269	ὅσσοισιν L,	ὅσσοισι P.
270	τέκν' L,	τέκνα P.
271	ἔστιν L,	ἐστὶ P.
289	δῶρον L,	δῶρ' P.
295	ἔζην L,	ἔζην P.
299	δή μοι L,	δ' ἡμῖν P.

From this partial list (and still more from the complete one which I have before me) we may draw, I think, the following inferences:

(1) The two MSS. were not copied directly from the same archetype. The differences are too numerous, and in the aggregate too considerable.

(2) On the other hand, these differences are just what we should expect in two MSS. descended from a common and not very remote ancestor. Most of them are slight, and very few are what we may call *characteristic* variants.

(3) L is, on the whole, distinctly superior to P. This superiority, however, shows itself mainly in small matters. The scribe of L was evidently a man of some learning, and avoided many errors into which the more ignorant copyist of P stumbled. Probably he also corrected many small mistakes in his original, while the scribe of P seems to have merely copied what lay before him.

(4) On the other hand, P occasionally shows superiority to L,

e.g. ὀπαδῶν in 136 against ὀπαδός, λελήσεται in 198 against λήσεται, δῶρ' in 289 against δῶρον, etc. Cases like these *may* be ascribed to contamination with a MS. of the other family; but what shall be said of instances like σύμμετρος in 26, the omission of 31 (rejected by Nauck), νερτέραν in 47, κατάρξωμαι in 74, πάθη in 145, where *P* alone, or virtually alone, offers readings worthy of careful consideration and even of acceptance? Though I consider *L* the better MS., I cannot for an instant agree with Wilamowitz that *P* is almost *worthless* in the *Alcestis*.

It may be noted, also, that *L*, like *a*, occasionally indulges in daring emendations. Examples are 401 σε γὰρ (σ' ἐγὼ *P*) to avoid asyndeton, 487 μ' ἦν πόνους (πόνους *P*) to fill a lacuna, 825 μόνον for μόνη to avoid the rhyme, etc. If *P* is a copy of a copy of *L*, why do not these changes reappear in *P*? (See also the *Classical Review* X. [1896] pp. 258-9, where England has pointed out some of the difficulties which stand in the way of Vitelli's view.)

In order not to do injustice to the opinion of Wilamowitz, I intentionally selected the first 300 lines, where the differences between *L* and *P* happen to be more marked than in the rest of the play. The number of cases, however, in which *L P* agree (or substantially agree) against the whole or a part of Prinz's other MSS. is *large* (well over 220, rejecting doubtful cases), and of the readings offered by *L P* in common a very large proportion are characteristic, e.g. κλέος against γέρας in 55, the inversion of 106 and 107, the omission of ἔτι in 130, the interpolated interjections in 226, the omission of ἰδοὺ ἰδού in 233, the order in 234, the omission of μέθες με in 262 and of μὴ — ὀρφανιεῖς in 276, σοῖσι θαρσυνεῖ τέκνον against τοῖσι σοῖσι θαρσυνεῖ in 318, the omission of 376, μελαμπέπλω στολῇ in 427, πέρι against ἔτι in 520, the omission of δισσὰ — ἥδε in 760-61, and scores of others. These show conclusively that *L P* are derived from a common source.

Nor do I find any proof that in the *Alcestis P* shows the influence of the other family more strongly than *L*. Any one who will take the trouble to make a list will find that *L* agrees with *B* or *a* or *B a* about as often as *P* does. *L* and *a* in particular frequently show agreement, which I attribute not to contamination but to the fact that the scribes of these two MSS., being men of learning, often both went right in small matters where other copyists erred.

To sum up then, I believe that, in the *Alcestis* at least, *L P* spring from a common ancestor lying not very far (perhaps two or three removes) back; that, though *L* is on the whole the better MS., *P* sometimes better represents the common original, and is by no means to be despised; and that from the agreement of *L P* we can generally deduce the reading of that original, which with Prinz I have denoted by *S*.

The *codex Harleianus* 5743 (*A* Kirchhoff = H Earle = Harl. older edd.) is a late MS., containing (beside two plays of Sophocles) the *Alcestis* from v. 1029 to the end, the *Rhesus* and the *Troades*. It is said by Earle and others who have collated it to be of little value in the *Alcestis*, except in v. 1037, where it offers the reading ἀτίζων (see note ad loc.).

The *codex Havniensis* 417 (*C* Prinz = C Kirchhoff = Havn. older edd.) is a paper (*chartaceus*) MS. of the fifteenth century, containing the *Medea, Hecuba, Orestes, Phoenissae, Hippolytus, Alcestis, Andromache, Troades* and *Rhesus*. Kirchhoff ranked it comparatively high, placing it in his first class; but Prinz held it to be of less importance, and Wilamowitz believes it to be of little value. In the *Alcestis* it is certainly almost worthless. Of the readings from it given by Prinz μεγίστα in 219 (so also *a* and *d*), ἠλεκτρυόνος in 839 (which may be wrong, as Wilamowitz's conjecture is very tempting; see note ad loc.), μή 'λαβες in 1102 and κνισᾶν in 1156 are easy changes; καὶ κωκυτοῦ τε ῥεέθρων in 458 I do not believe to be right, though it has the much stronger authority of *B a* (καὶ at all events must be rejected), while μηδ' ἔτ' in 18 (see note) and θέλοις in 1079 (see Apparat. Crit.) are almost certainly wrong.

We come now to the much-vexed question as to the comparative value of the two families *B a* and *L P*. Kirchhoff, as is well known, attributed very much greater importance to the MSS. of his first class than to those of his other two classes; and hence in the *Alcestis* he has pretty consistently followed *B*, rejecting for the most part the readings of *L P*. Most recent editors of Euripides, on the other hand (including Nauck, Prinz, Wilamowitz, Barthold,

Weil, Wecklein, England, Earle and others), rate *L P* higher than did Kirchhoff. Wilamowitz in particular, as some one has remarked, "has constituted himself the champion of *L*." The general trend of critical opinion seems to be toward the verdict of Prinz (pref. to his *Medea* p. ix.): "pretium duarum classium non prorsus par est, cum numerus vitiorum et interpolationum primae classis minor sit, sed secunda classis non multo deterior ac nequaquam hercle contemnenda est." This is substantially my own view; though in the *Alcestis* I should be inclined to rate *L P* a little higher than does even Prinz. While I believe *B* to be on the whole superior to any other *single* MS. of the play, I hold the authority of *L P* combined to be *very* nearly, if not quite, equal to that of *B a*. For the grounds of this opinion I must refer the reader to the notes *passim*, as space will not permit an adequate discussion of the subject here. Useful material (which, however, must be used with caution) may be found in the essay of Krauthausen, *Der Werth der Handschrift "S" der Alcestis* (Saarlouis, 1895). I would gladly have given here a complete list of the passages in the *Alcestis* where *L P* agree against *B a*; but Kirchhoff and Prinz have not given the readings of *a* with sufficient fullness to make this possible. A list of those where *L P* agree against *B* would be of comparatively little value; for *B* is written so carelessly that it is often unsafe to trust it unless supported by *a*.

What I have said above applies only to the *Alcestis*. The general question of the value of the two families cannot be really decided until we have full and accurate collations of the principal Euripidean MSS. Scholars are eagerly awaiting from the competent hands of Wecklein the completion of the work begun by Prinz. Then, and not till then, shall we really know just what the testimony of *L P* is worth, and whether any of the less known MSS. are of value. — See also the preface to Kirchhoff's larger edition; the prefaces to Prinz's *Medea*, *Alcestis* and *Hecuba*; Wilamowitz's *Herakles*[1] I. pp. 205 ff. and *Analecta passim*; Wecklein in *N. Jahrb. f. Phil.* 1878 pp. 226–7. The article by Prinz in the *Rhein. Mus.* N. F. XXX. (1875) pp. 129 ff. (on the *cod. Harniensis*) should also be consulted.

The *Alcestis*, being one of the ten plays of the Byzantine *delectus*, possesses tolerably copious scholia, which are preserved chiefly in the MSS. *B* and *a* (A and B of Schwartz). These scholia are, of course, of a very composite character. They contain some valuable bits of Alexandrian learning, such as the Aristophanic portion of the hypothesis, the scholarly notes on vv. 1, 968, etc.; but taken as a whole they are not of great value. The best account of the origin and history of the Euripidean scholia is given by Wilamowitz, *Herakles*[1] I. pp. 144 ff.* The scholia themselves may be found to best advantage in the editions of Dindorf (Oxford, 1863; schol. to the *Alcestis* vol. IV. pp. 85 ff.) and Schwartz (Berlin, 1887–91; schol. to *Alcestis* vol. II. pp. 214 ff.). In making quotations from them I have followed the text of Schwartz.

The editions of the *Alcestis* are very numerous. I give a partial list, including especially those valuable for the history and criticism of the text. To those which are of prime importance an asterisk is prefixed.

A. Editions of Euripides which are of critical value for the *Alcestis*, but include other plays as well.

1. *Editio princeps*, Florence, 1496. Contains *Medea*, *Hippolytus*, *Alcestis*, *Andromache*. Edited by Janus Lascaris, who followed *cod. Parisinus* 2818 (a copy of *a*).

2. Aldine edition, Venice, 1503. Contains all the plays but the *Electra*. Edited by Marcus Musurus, who followed *P* (except in the *Helena*, *Hercules Fur.*, *Cyclops*, *Heraclidae* and *Ion*, where he used *Parisinus* 2817 (a copy of *L*), and in the *Hecuba*, *Phoenissae* and *Orestes*, where he used some late MS.). Musurus made numerous emendations, some of value, many worthless.

3. Hervagian editions, Basle, 1537, 1544, 1551.

4, 5. Canter's edition, Antwerp, 1571, and that of Portus, Heidelberg, 1598, are occasionally useful.

6. Barnes' edition, Cambridge, 1694, with scholia and notes. Barnes' comments may still be consulted with profit in a few

---

* See also Barthold, *De Scholiorum in Eur. vett. fontibus*, Bonn, 1864.

passages. This edition was reprinted, revised by Beck, Leipzig, 1778.

7. Musgrave's edition, Oxford, 1778. Musgrave laid a firmer foundation for the text, using *a* in addition to the MSS. employed by the earlier edd. His original edition, which is very rare, I have been unable to consult.

8. Matthiae's edition, Leipzig, 1813-29, with scholia and notes. (Notes on the *Alcestis* vol. VII. pp. 113 ff.) Matthiae used more MSS. than any of his predecessors, including *L*, *c*, *d*, *C*. He erred in the opposite direction from Kirchhoff, showing partiality toward the readings of the second family (*P L*).

9. The Glasgow edition of 1821, with scholia, notes and Beck's index. (This is the best edition to consult for the notes of Barnes, Musgrave, Markland and the older edd. and critics.* *Alcestis* vol. IV. pp. 409 ff.)

10. W. Dindorf's *Poetarum Scenicorum fabulae*, London and Leipzig, 1830, etc.; fifth ed. Leipzig, 1869. (Contains the *Alcestis* among other plays, with brief critical apparatus.)

11. W. Dindorf's edition, Oxford, 1832-9, with copious notes. (Notes on *Alcestis* vol. III. pp. 325 ff.)

12. Nauck's edition in the Teubner series, Leipzig, 1854, second ed. 1866, third ed. 1869-71. (Important for the constitution of the text.)

*13. Kirchhoff's large edition, Berlin, 1855. (This laid the foundation for the critical study of the text. The editor was too partial to the MSS. of his first class, and the collations which he used were often incomplete and inaccurate. Nevertheless the edition was an epoch-making one, and is still indispensable.)

14. Kirchhoff's smaller edition (Berlin, 1867-9, with brief critical apparatus) shows less unfairness toward *L P*.

15. Paley's edition, London, 1857 (new ed. of vol. I. 1872, of vol. II. 1875), with notes. (Not of great critical value; but the exegetical notes are sometimes useful.)

---

* (Trollope's) *Notae philol. et grammat. in Euripidis tragoedias*, London, 1828, is also a useful collection. (Notes on *Alcestis* vol. I. pp. 281 ff.)

B. Special editions of the *Alcestis* (including those which form *separate volumes* of larger editions).

1. The *Alcestis* from Barnes' edition, revised by Kaltwasser, with preface by Geissler, Gotha, 1776. (Contains the scholia to the play, Barnes' notes and Buchanan's Latin version.)

2. Kuinoel's edition, Leipzig, 1779 (also 1811). (Of little value.)

3. Wagner's edition, Leipzig, 1800. (Diffuse, and of little critical value. Introductory dissertation on the play.)

4. Gaisford's edition, Oxford, 1806, with various readings. (School edition, for the use of Westminster students.)

*5. Monk's edition, Cambridge, 1816 (second ed. 1823), with notes and Buchanan's version. (The first really *critical* edition of the play. Monk, who was Fellow of Trinity and Regius Professor of Greek at Cambridge, was a fine scholar and a worthy contemporary of Porson, Elmsley and G. Hermann. His edition is still extremely valuable.)

6. Wuestemann's edition, Gotha, 1823. (This is a reprint of the second edition of Monk, with a preface and additional notes by Wuestemann. The additions are not of great value.)

*7. G. Hermann's edition, Leipzig, 1824. (This has selections from the notes of Monk and Wuestemann, and a valuable introductory dissertation and short additional notes by G. Hermann. The editor's notes, though curt and arbitrary in tone, are often of great value.)

8. Woolsey's edition, Cambridge (Massachusetts), 1834, etc. — Hartford, 1875. (This is a school edition; but Woolsey was a sound scholar, and his exegetical notes are occasionally of service.)

*9. Pflugk's edition, Gotha, 1834. (Vol. II. sect. II. of his annotated edition of Euripides. Second ed. rev. by Klotz, Leipzig, 1858. Conservative treatment of the text; valuable for parallels and for defense of the MS. readings.)

10. Dindorf's edition, Oxford, 1834. (In this the famous Vatican fragment of the hypothesis was first published.)

xlvi INTRODUCTION.

11. Bauer's edition, Munich, 1871. Second ed. by Wecklein, 1888. (Important for Wecklein's constitution of the text, though it is a school edition.)

*12. Prinz's edition, Leipzig, 1879. (Text with critical apparatus. Full and careful collations of the leading MSS. enabled the editor to lay a firm basis for the constitution of the text. This work is indispensable for critical students of the play.)

13. Jerram's edition, Oxford, 1880, 1884, 1890, 1896. (School edition, but with some useful material.)

*14. Weil's critical edition, Paris, 1891. (Short introductory essay, critical apparatus, and explanatory notes. Valuable.)

*15. Earle's edition, London, 1894. (School edition, but with brief *apparatus criticus* and useful introduction and explanatory notes. Also short critical and metrical appendices.)

The following editions I will merely mention: Major's, London, 1838; Witschel's, Jena, 1845 (vol. III. of his edition of selected plays); the Oxford ed. of 1870, "by a First-Class man of Balliol" (the edition itself is not first-class), often reprinted; Paley's school ed., London, 1875; the London ed. of 1876 (in the "Analytical Series of Greek and Latin Classics"); the Oxford ed. of 1876 (in "Oxford Pocket Classics"); Milner's ed., London, 1879; the editions of Pessonneaux (Paris, 1880), Weil (school eds. Paris, 1881, 1883, 1887, 1891, 1896), Groussard (Paris, 1881), Huit (Paris, 1883), Desfossés (Paris, 1883), Quentier (Paris, 1883; third ed. by Ragon, 1896), Richardot (Paris, 1884), Parnajon (Paris, 1888) and Fix (Paris, 1893); the London ed. of 1886 ("with translation, notes and descriptive list of proper names"); Bayfield's ed., London, 1890; Reynolds' ed., London, 1893; Haydon's, Cambridge, 1896, and Hadley's, Cambridge, 1896. Many of these I have not seen; but I believe them to be all, or nearly all, school editions.

Of English translations I will mention the following: those of Potter (in his translation of Euripides, London, 1781; also in Morley's *Universal Library*, vol. 54); Buckley, London, 1850 (in his translation of Euripides in Bohn's series); Rice, Dublin, 1879; Coleridge (in his *Plays of Euripides*, London, 1891); Lawton (in his *Three Dramas of Euripides*, Boston, 1892) and Way, London, 1894. Browning's *Balaustion's Adventure* deserves special mention as a spirited version in a charming setting; but even in the part of it which is translated it is sometimes Browning, not Euripides, who speaks. It was published in 1871 (in London and New York). — The elegant Latin version of Buchanan (written about 1540) also deserves mention; it may be found appended to the editions of Monk and Wuestemann.

The essays, articles, etc., of a critical nature dealing with the text of the *Alcestis* are so numerous that only a small part of them can be mentioned here. Of special importance are the following: —

Nauck, *Euripideische Studien*, Th. II. pp. 49 ff. (St. Petersburg, 1862), reprinted from the Memoirs of the Imp. Acad. of Sciences, series VII. vol. 5, No. 6 (with additions* in his *Kritische Bemerkungen*, Nos. V. and VII., in vols. XII. and XXII. of the Academy's Bulletin); Kviçala, *Studien zu Euripides*, Th. II. pp. 1 ff. (Vienna, 1879); F. W. Schmidt, *Kritische Studien zu d. Griech. Dramatikern*, vol. II. pp. 1 ff. (Berlin, 1886); Von Holzinger, *Exeget. u. krit. Bemerkungen zu Euripides' Alkestis*, Sitzungsber. d. Akad. d. Wiss. zu Wien, Philol.-histor. Classe, vol. 124, X. (1891); Lenting, *Epistula critica in Eur. Alcest.* (Zutphen, 1821); the review of Monk's edition in the *Quarterly Review* for April, 1816; Wecklein's review of Prinz's edition in *N. Jahrb. f. Philol.*, 1879, pp. 657 ff.; Mekler, *Euripidea*, pp. 14, 21, 42 ff. (Vienna, 1879); Bauer in *Blätter f. Bayer. Gymn.* VII. pp. 111 ff.; Van Herwerden in *Verslagen en Mededeelingen d. Koninkl. Akad. van Wetensch.*, 2d series vol. IV. pp. 82 ff., 158 ff. Of less importance are Silber, *Lectiones Euripideae* (Oels, 1856); Kolanowski, *Quaestiones criticae in Eur. Alcest.* (Posen, 1857); Wheeler, *De Alcestidis et Hippolyti interpolationibus* (Bonn, 1879); Rassow, *De Interpolationibus Alcestidis* (Greifswald, 1888); Nindel, *Kritische Bemerkungen zu Euri-*

---

* These are to be found also in the *Mélanges Gréco-Romains* III. pp. 31, 39 and IV. p. 214.

pides (Bernburg, 1893); Holthoefer, *Animadversiones in Euripidis Herculem et Alcestin* (Bonn, 1881). — Numerous conjectures may be found collected in Schenkl's and Wecklein's reports on the Greek tragedians, *Philologus* vol. XX., *Bursian's Jahresberichte* vols. I., III., IV., IX., XIII., XVII., XXVI., XXX., XXXVIII., XLVI., LVIII., LXXI. See also Van Herwerden in *Mnemosyne* IV. (1855) p. 372 f., ib. N. S. V. (1877) p. 43 f., *Revue de Philol.*, N. S. II. (1878) p. 54, *Mnemos.* N. S. VIII. (1880) p. 110, ib. N. S. XIV. (1886) p. 62, *Mélanges Graux*, p. 202 f., *Revue de Philol.* N. S. XVII. (1893) p. 215 f., *Stud. crit. in poet. scaen. Graec.* (Amsterdam, 1872) p. 17, and his *Oedipus Rex* p. 203; Cobet, *Variae Lectiones in script. Graec.* p. 73, pp. 579 ff., *Novae Lectiones* p. 109, *Mnemosyne* V. (1856) p. 247; Wecklein, *Analecta Euripidea* in his *Ars Sophoclis emendandi* p. 179, and *Studien zu Euripides*, *Jahrb. f. Philol.* Supplementb. VII. p. 363 f.; Naber, *Mnemosyne* N. S. X. (1882) p. 6 f.; Usener, *Jahrb. f. Philol.* CXXXIX. (1889) pp. 369, 371; von Wilamowitz, *Hermes* XIV. (1879) pp. 178, 460, ib. XVII. (1882) p. 364, *Analecta* p. 246, *Herakles*[2] II. p. 214; Zacher, *Philologus* LI. p. 540; Stadtmueller, *Jahrb. f. Philol.* CXIX. (1879) p. 529; Mekler ib. p. 662; Radermacher ib. 1895, p. 235; Leutsch, *Philologus* XXIII. p. 27; Goram, *Rhein. Museum* XVIII. (1863) p. 616; Weil, *Revue de Philol.* N. S. XI. (1887) p. 10; Sarreiter, *Blätter f. Bayer. Gymn.* XIV. p. 419 f.; Dobree, *Adversaria Critica*, Berlin ed. IV. p. 70 f., etc.

D. Questions concerning the Scenic Representation of the Play.

I. *The Alcestis and the Stage-question.*

In view of the battle-royal now going on between the "old-stagers" and the "no-stagers" (as Prof. Gildersleeve has wittily called them) it behooves us to speak with extreme caution as to this point. We do not absolutely *know* how plays were represented in the fifth century B.C., but it must be admitted that the probabilities now seem to be very strongly in favor of the view advocated by Dr. Doerpfeld and his followers. Hoepken (*De theatro attico saec. a. Chr. quinti*, 1884), White (*Harv. Stud. in Class. Philol.* II. pp. 159 ff.), Capps (*Trans. of Am. Philol. Assoc.* 1891) and Pickard (*Am. Jour. Philol.* XIV. Nos. 1–3), but above all Doerpfeld and Reisch (*Das Griechische Theater*, 1896), have shown that the extant plays could never have been acted on the Vitruvian stage. The theory that there was a low, temporary stage is also liable to grave objections; and the architectural evidence against it seems conclusive.

The evidence supplied by the *Alcestis*, while not in itself decisive, strongly favors the no-stage theory. As Capps (*l.s.c.* p. 14) points out, the withdrawal of the chorus with Admetus at v. 740 f., and their return together at 860 f. would be decidedly easier if the actors and choreutae were on the same level. Moreover, the scene in 77 f. is much more effective if the chorus are on the same level as the palace than if they peer up at it from below. So, too, the words of Admetus to the chorus at 423 f. are more natural if he is standing at the same elevation as they are. — We may also infer that the front of the σκηνή, or the προσκήνιον (if one was used so early; see Doerpfeld and Reisch *l.s.c.* p. 372), had at least two doors in it, one the main door of the palace and the other the side-entrance through which Heracles retires at v. 552.

II. *The Withdrawal of the Chorus.*

As has been said above, there is a withdrawal (μετάστασις; see Pollux IV. 108) and re-entry (ἐπιπάροδος) of the chorus in this play. The reason is obvious. The chorus must withdraw at 740 f., or they will learn of Heracles' resolve to rescue Alcestis and the surprise of the last scene cannot be motived properly. If, as I believe, the play has been worked over and the plot changed, the μετάστασις may, or may not, have belonged to the original plan; but in the former case the reason for it must have been a different one. There are four other instances of μετάστασις in the extant tragedies,* viz., in the *Eumenides, Ajax, Helena* and *Rhesus* (though

* There is also a case in the *Ecclesiazusae* of Aristophanes.

some of these are disputed). See further A. Mueller, *Scenische Fragen zur Alkestis des Eur.* (Hannover, 1860) p. 10 f.; A. Mueller, *Bühnenalterthümer* p. 212 and note; Haigh, *Attic Theatre* p. 276.

III. *Distribution of the Rôles.*

As to the way in which the parts were distributed among the actors in the *Alcestis* there has been considerable dispute, and a decision is by no means easy. As Elmsley long ago pointed out, the silence of Alcestis in the last scene of the play is due in all probability to the poet's unwillingness to bring more than two speaking actors upon the scene at once. Why he was unwilling is not so clear; for three speaking actors appeared at once in the *Oresteia* of Aeschylus (458 B.C.) and probably earlier. It is noticeable, also, that (as O. Mueller pointed out in his *History of Greek Literature**) the play *can* be performed with only two actors. Putting these two facts together, it seems probable that the play was intended to be performed by two speaking actors, perhaps to save the choregus the expense of providing a third. With two actors the parts may be divided as follows (Mueller, *Scenische Fragen* p. 5 f.): protagonist Admetus, Thanatos, man-servant; deuteragonist Alcestis, Apollo, Heracles, Pheres, maid-servant. The part of the boy Eumelus (393 f.) was probably sung *ad manum* by some one behind the scenes, the actor merely going through the appropriate motions; while his sister Perimele, Alcestis from 1007 on and the servants at 546, 1110 are *mutae personae*. Another possible division is: protagonist Apollo, Alcestis, Pheres, Heracles; deuteragonist Thanatos, Admetus, maid-servant, man-servant; *mutae personae* as before. This is inferior to the first, as it gives the rôle of Admetus, which is clearly the most exacting, to the second actor. The main objection to both is that the same actor takes the parts of both Alcestis and Heracles, which are so very different. But there are other instances of this kind; e.g. in the *Prometheus* one actor took the parts of Kratos and Io. With three actors the distribution would be easy, e.g. (with Wecklein) protagonist Apollo,

---

* Vol. I. p. 603 of the fourth German edition.

Alcestis, Heracles; deuteragonist Admetus, Thanatos; tritagonist servant-maid, Eumelus, Pheres, man-servant; *mutae personae:* or, better I think (with K. F. Hermann, *De distributione personarum in trag. Graec.* [Marburg, 1840] p. 49), protagonist Admetus; deuteragonist Alcestis, Heracles, Pheres, Thanatos; tritagonist Apollo, man-servant, maid-servant; *mutae personae.** Which of these arrangements was actually adopted in ancient times we have no means of determining. — See further A. Mueller, *Lehrbuch d. Griech. Bühnenalterthümer* p. 173, note 3; A. Mueller, *Scenische Fragen zur Alkestis d. Euripides* pp. 4–8.

E. The Myth of Alcestis in Ancient Art.

By James M. Paton, Ph.D.

The works of ancient art containing scenes which may be referred to the story of Alcestis have been collected and discussed by Petersen (*Arch. Zeit.* 21, 1863, pp. 105 ff.), Dissel (*Der Mythos von Admetos und Alkestis*), Engelmann (Roscher, *Lexikon* I. 235) and Escher (Pauly-Wissowa, *Real-Encyc.* I. 1513), but none of these have aimed at completeness. In this chapter I have endeavored to bring together all known representations of this story, although, as I have been compelled to rely on published material, it is scarcely possible that none have escaped notice. The necessary limits of this introduction have prevented an exhaustive discussion of these works, but the following pages contain an outline which may serve as the basis for a more detailed study. The collection is confined to those works which are directly concerned with the story of Admetus and Alcestis, and therefore all representations of Alcestis among the daughters of Pelias, Admetus as a participant in the Calydonian Hunt, and similar scenes, have been omitted.

I., II. The statement of Pausanias (III. 18, 8), that Admetus was represented on the throne of Apollo at Amyclae yoking a lion and

---

* Hermann did not decide whether the part of Eumelus was taken by the tritagonist or was a παραχορήγημα; but see above.

a boar, has led Petersen to find the wooing of Admetus on an Etruscan ring (Abeken, *Mittelitalien* Taf. VII., 6 a). A lion and boar are driven by a man in a chariot, while in front marches a winged male* figure. The winged figure belongs to a distinctly oriental type, and only the lion and the boar suggest the story of Admetus. A similar union of these animals occurs on the bl. fig. amphora from Rhegium in a representation of the marriage of Cadmus and Harmonia (Benndorf, *Vorlegebl.* Ser. C., Taf. VII. 3). It seems better to see in this ring one of those general types which the Greek artists adapted to the representation of particular scenes. An Apollo of the type of this winged figure can scarcely be accepted, unless some other representations of the god in this form are cited.

III. If the connection of this ring with our story is more than doubtful, the reference is clear in a stucco relief, which forms part of the interior decoration of a tomb on the Via Latina. It was briefly described by Brunn (*Bull. d. Inst.* 1858, p. 81), and published by Petersen (*Ann. d. Inst.* 33, 1861, p. 227; cf. *Mon. Ined.* VI. Tav. 52, 3). On the right a bearded man is seated on a throne, and beside him stands a woman. In front of this group, and with his left foot planted on the platform on which the throne stands, is a young man, who, while looking at the king, points with his outstretched right arm to a marvellous sight. Through the open gate of the court comes a chariot drawn by a lion and a boar, beside whom walks a man crowned with laurel and probably carrying a bow. In the chariot stands a female figure in a short chiton, and with a quiver on her back. Brunn referred this scene to an otherwise unknown form of the myth in which Apollo and Artemis went to the lower world to rescue Alcestis. Petersen, however, is certainly right in interpreting it as a representation of the wooing of Admetus, who appears before King Pelias and his daughter to show how easily with divine assistance the required task has been fulfilled. The presence of Artemis in the chariot may point to a form of the story in which she also helped Admetus, whose later neglect thus appears in a stronger light, but her connection with wild beasts renders it natural that she should act as charioteer, when artistic

---

*Surely not female, as Dissel says, *l. c.* p. 10.

requirements made it necessary that Admetus should occupy another position.

This part of the legend, however, did not attract the ancient artists. As in literature, so in art, the story turned rather to the representation of Alcestis as the type of wifely devotion, and its popularity is of comparatively late development. Apparently no extant work of Greek art belonging to the fifth or fourth centuries contains any reference to this myth, with the single exception of the sculptured drum from Ephesus, of which the interpretation is by no means certain. It is found on Etruscan works of a somewhat later date, though were it not for inscriptions, which leave no doubt as to the intent of the artist, it is scarcely likely that his meaning would have been recognized.

IV. The first is an amphora from Vulci formerly in the collection of the Duc de Luynes (*Arch. Zeit.* 8, 213*). It is published by Dennis (*Cities and Cemeteries of Etruria*[2] II. front., cf. I. ci., and 437; also *Arch. Zeit.* 21, 1863, Taf. 180, 3). The centre of the picture is occupied by the husband and wife. Alcestis (*Alcsti*) has thrown her arms about the neck of Admetus (*Atmite*), but the time of their separation is at hand, for on either side there hastens forward a demon of death, behind Alcestis the Etruscan Charon with wolf's ears, huge tusks, and a great hammer in his hand, behind Admetus a winged figure with hideous face, and holding a snake in each hand. It seems needless to try to read into this picture the story of the self-sacrifice of Alcestis, who throws herself between death and her husband. The positions of the two figures are practically the same, while the snakes of the demon on the right are no more threatening to Admetus than is the hammer of Charon to Alcestis. A parting scene* specialized by the addition of legendary names, that and nothing more, in my opinion, is shown on this vase.

* A similar scene, though much ruder in conception, is published in the *Annali d. Inst.* 1866 Tav. W. An unpublished red-figured Etruscan vase of late date, now in the Boston Museum of Fine Arts, shows a man and woman parting, while a bearded and winged demon hovers over them. The addition of names could turn the scene into a representation of Admetus and Alcestis.

V. The second occurrence of this legend in Etruria is on a mirror from Civita Castellana, published by Körte (Gerhard, *Etruskische Spiegel* V. p. 217 Nachträge No. 9), and now in the Metropolitan Museum of New York. In the centre stand Admetus (*Atmite*) and Alcestis (*Alcestei*). He is clad in an himation which covers the left shoulder and the lower part of the body, while Alcestis is fully draped. They embrace one another, and a large necklace encircles both, a symbol of union found also on a mirror representing Venus and Adonis (Gerhard, *l. c.* V. Taf. XXIII.). On the right a maid seems to be smoothing the hair of Alcestis with a small rod, which has doubtless been dipped in the alabastron in her left hand. On the left is a youth in the act of leaving; in his left hand he carries a pair of shoes, and in his right an object which Professor Körte thinks may be a πεμπώβολον. As is pointed out by the editor, this scene, so far as the chief figures are concerned, is simply a transference of the type used for the Aphrodite-Adonis series. There is no reference to the death of Alcestis, and apart from the inscriptions, there is nothing to separate this group from the many similar love scenes on Etruscan mirrors.*

VI. The same lack of any sharply defined characterization renders the meaning of the artist somewhat uncertain in the class of monuments now to be discussed. Among the Etruscan urns there are a number which show a composition that has been thought to represent the death of Alcestis. This interpretation was first suggested by C. N. Grauert† in connection with an urn now in Berlin. A better example is the one published by Inghirami (*Mon. Etr.* Ser. I. Tav. 74) from Volterra. In the centre on a couch reclines a fully draped woman. She rests her left arm on the cushions and stretches her right toward a man who approaches from the left. He is closely wrapped in a large himation, which covers the back of the head and is drawn closely under the chin. His left foot rests on a footstool in front of the couch. On this stool sits a boy, who rests his chin on his right hand, while he looks

---

* Cf. Gerhard, *l. c.* V. p. 35 and the plates there cited, also plates CXLVII. 1 and CL.

† *Ann. d. Inst.* 1842, p. 40 ff. Cf. *Mon. Ined.* III. Tav. 40, B.

up at the woman on the couch. From the right there hastens to the head of the couch a young girl, whose right hand seems to rest on the pillow, while in her left she holds a ring on which hang some indeterminate objects. Back of this girl hovers a winged female figure with a torch. The ends of the relief are occupied by symmetrically grouped women, who start back from the central scene and raise a hand to the forehead in a gesture of surprise. That this is a representation of the death of a mother is very probable, and the presence of the children makes it quite possible that the artist had in mind the parting of Alcestis and Admetus. At the same time this is the only urn where the children are present, unless the grown youth at the head of the couch, and the maiden who seems to receive tablets from the dying woman on the urn in Inghirami, *l. c.* Tav. 75, are intended to take the place of the boy and girl. In the great majority of cases,* while the central group remains substantially the same, the figure at the head of the couch is a youth whose right hand seems to rest on the dying woman's shoulder, while in the left is the ring with the indistinct pendants.

These scenes were interpreted by Inghirami as Eriphyle and Amphiaraus, a view which now scarcely calls for discussion. Grauer's explanation was adopted by Dissel (*Admetos und Alkestis* p. 16) and at first by Dütschke (*l. c.* I. 8), though in a later volume (II. 381) he left the question of interpretation open. K. O. Müller (*Ancient Art* § 413, 2) saw in them a representation of the return of Protesilaus to Laodamia. In favor of this view of the meaning of some of the urns are the absence of the children, and the close veiling of the head of the figure, though the face is not covered. On the other hand, any such view seems impossible for the urn first described. Both interpretations, however, can fairly claim some consideration. The Protesilaus and Alcestis sarcophagi in spite of

---

* Cf. Inghirami, *l. c.* Tavv. 19 and 77. In Tav. 76 Admetus (?) is just entering the door. In Tav. 75 this figure has been crowded away from the couch by the interposition of the maiden. Cf. also Gori. *Mus. Etr.* I. 133; Dütschke, *Antike Bildwerke Ober- und Mittelitaliens* I. Nos. 8, 91, 99; II. 320, 381; IV. 602; V. 407; *Mus. Gregor.* II. Tav. 103, 6. This latter omits the figure at the head of the couch. Instead there seems to be a partition, behind which is a female figure, starting back from the scene on the other side.

many divergencies in detail have still a common source for the central group, and there is nothing antecedently improbable in the use by an Etruscan artist of the same general arrangement for both myths. In one relief (Inghirami, *l. c.* I. Tav. 20) a reclining figure much like "Alcestis" occupies the right half, while the left is filled by two standing figures clasping hands. Scenes of parting are too frequent on the urns to make it necessary to seek in all of them a mythological meaning. Whence the artist drew his inspiration is made clear by such a Greek relief as the stele of Plangon in the National Museum at Athens.* If a conclusion may be drawn from silence, Professor Körte may also be cited against a mythological interpretation for these urns, as they are not found in *I Rilievi delle Urne Etrusche* vol. II.

To sum up, — it seems not impossible that the death of Alcestis was in the mind of the maker of the urn (Inghir. *l.c.* I. Tav. 74), but if the same thought governed the other workmen, they gave no certain clue to its expression. In any case the *motif* is not one invented for the expression of this thought, nor even sharply and precisely differentiated for it, a sure proof in my opinion that the myth did not occupy the attention of Greek artists, at least not before the Hellenistic period.

In the Roman period scenes from the myth of Alcestis become more frequent and at the same time more clearly defined. With the exception of some Pompeian paintings these representations are on funeral monuments, either in the form of mural paintings, or as decorations of sarcophagi and other sepulchral reliefs.

VII. In Herculaneum and Pompeii seven pictures † have been found, manifestly representations of the same scene, though differing in the grouping of the persons concerned. The two types are published by Petersen in *Arch. Zeit.* 21, 1863, Taf. 180, 1 (= Helbig 1157) and 2 (= Helbig 1158). I abridge the description of Helbig.

---

* Le Bas, *Voy. Arch.*, *Mon. Fig.* Pl. 71; Καββαδίας, Γλυπτὰ τοῦ 'Εθν. Μουσ. 740; Conze, *Att. Grabreliefs* p. 70.

† Helbig, *Wandg. Campan.* Nos. 1157-1161, Sogliano, *Le pitture murale Campane*, No. 506 (this book I have not seen), *Bull. d. Inst.* 1877, p. 27.

A. At the left sits Admetus, who is represented as youthful and vigorous. He is wrapped in a mantle and rests his bowed head on his left hand. On his left and a little behind him sits Alcestis, fully draped and with a veil over the back of her head. Her right arm is passed around the shoulders of Admetus, and her left hand rests on his arm. Both are listening to a young man, who, seated on a stool in front of them, is reading from a scroll. At the right an old woman leans forward in close attention to the reader and behind her stands a bearded old man. The centre of the background is occupied by Apollo, plainly distinguished by his quiver, and in front of him stands a fully draped female figure, with a veil over her head, who raises the right hand as if in astonishment.

B. The other type contains the same groups but differs in their arrangement. Admetus and Alcestis occupy an ornamental throne at the left with the youthful reader before them. The upper part of Admetus' body is nude and he leans forward with his right arm outstretched toward the reader. Alcestis, who here wears a diadem, rests her chin on her left hand and gazes into vacancy, evidently sunk in deep thought. The old man and woman stand behind the throne, and on the extreme right, leaning on a high balustrade is Apollo. On his right a little behind him, and apparently in conversation with him is the female figure with upraised right hand. The other paintings are merely variations on these types, though one (Helbig 1159) adds to type *A* two beardless figures behind Admetus, probably attendants.

These pictures were at first explained as the recognition of Orestes and Iphigenia, and though Petersen's reference to the story of Alcestis was adopted by Helbig, it has been doubted by Dissel (*l. c.* p. 13 and Anm.), mainly because of the unexplained female figure with Apollo and the absence of any reference to an oracle in the literary versions of the myth. The interpretation seems to have been settled by Mau (*Bull. d. Inst.* 1879, p. 69) in a paper which must have escaped Dissel's notice. In a discussion of Pompeian inscriptions referable to mural paintings Mau communicated an unpublished *graffito* from the house Reg. V., Ins. 1, No. 18, consisting of two words PELIAS | ALCESTIS. On the wall to the right are found the chief groups of our first type arranged among fantastic architectural decorations, and we obviously have here the interpretation which some member of the household put upon the painting. The introduction of Pelias is well explained by Mau as due to the ignorance of the scribbler, who confused him with Pheres. We have here, therefore, the reading of the message which announces the impending death of Admetus unless he can provide a substitute, and it is easy to see that the artist has endeavored to show Alcestis as already contemplating her self-sacrifice. The old couple are of course the parents of Admetus, and the presence of Apollo requires no comment. The female figure near Apollo has hitherto baffled satisfactory explanation. Petersen calls her the Nympheutria in the first type, who has been elevated to a marriage-goddess in the second, but such a view must be supported by other examples before it can be accepted as certain.

The other paintings which contain references to this myth are concerned chiefly with the intervention of Heracles and the restoration of Alcestis.

VIII. A drawing in the Codex Pighianus of a ceiling, which was probably in a columbarium in Rome.* Two panels are connected with this story. In one, a young man, his chlamys floating over his left shoulder, hastens toward Heracles, who stands at the right with lion's skin over his left arm, and club in hand, and stretches his right hand toward his welcomer. The sarcophagi show that these two figures are taken from a scene which has usually been interpreted as the reception of Heracles, but is regarded by Robert, following Dissel, as representing Admetus entreating his rescuer to remain with him. As the interpretation must depend on the sarcophagi, it will be considered later. As to the other panel there can be no doubt.† Out of an arched door-

---

* Jahn, *Deckengem. d. Cod. Pigh.* in *Ber. d. s. k. Ges. d. Wiss.* 1869, pp. 12-14, Taf. I., ll. 2, 3. Robert, *Sark.-Rel.* III. 1, p. 27, calls this a stucco relief, which certainly seems more probable.

† Cf. Beger, *Alc. pro mar. mor.* p. 24 ; Michaelis, *Röm. Mitth.* viii. 174, B′, who wrongly cites this as the end of a sarcophagus. Cf. Robert, *Sark.-Rel.* III. 1, p. 26.

way at the left, Heracles is leading a veiled woman, certainly Alcestis. His right hand is laid encouragingly on her shoulder, while her left hand rests on his arm. This rescue of Alcestis from the lower world is also found on the sarcophagi, and it seems clear that the painter of the ceiling had the same copy-book which furnished the stone-cutters with their designs.

IX. The same scene of the rescue of Alcestis forms the subject of a painting from Antium at Dresden.* In this example the doorway is omitted, and Heracles leads Alcestis, holding her right hand with his left, toward the left.

X. In the tomb of the Nasones † is a painting which has been referred to this myth, though its interpretation is far from certain. At the left is seated on a rock (?) a bearded man with his mantle covering the lower part of the body, and thrown over the right shoulder, leaving the upper part of the body bare. His right hand rests on the rock, and his left elbow on what looks like the unornamented arm of a throne, while the left hand supports his chin. At his left stands a female figure in Doric chiton with girdle, on her left arm an arm-ring and in her left hand a spear, though the copyist has made it a sceptre. On her *right* arm is a shield. Opposite this group stand Heracles and a woman. His club is in his right hand, and on his *right* side hang his bow and quiver. His left hand is laid on the shoulder of the woman, who wears the veil over her head in such a way as to leave the face exposed. The irregularities in the position of the shield and bow and quiver show that in the process of engraving the figures have been reversed, and Bartoli's accuracy as an artist is never above suspicion. If Athena is really present the scene can scarcely be the release of Alcestis by Hades, and to assume that the copyist has transformed Persephone into Athena seems rather violent. Petersen suggests that it represents Heracles with Alcmena or Hebe before Zeus and Athena. No exactly similar representation of Hebe is

* Hettner, *Bildw. d. königl. Antikensamml. 440d.*; W. G. Becker, *Augusteum*, Taf. 92. The circumstances under which the picture was discovered are unknown.

† Bartoli, *Pict. Vet. in Sep. Nas. Tub. X.* Cf. Parker, *Arch. of Rome* ix. p. 31.

cited, and though we hear of Heracles leading his mother before Rhadamanthus (cf. Furtwängler in Roscher, *Lexikon* I. 2248), I do not know of any authority for Alcmena's reception into Olympus. Robert (*Sark.-Rel.* III. 1, p. 33) compares with this a Pompeian painting (Helbig 1149),* and considers it the restoration of Alcestis to Admetus. Athena has been created by Bartoli out of the doryphorus of Admetus. This may be correct, though as it rests on a mutilated painting and a conjectural emendation it cannot be regarded as conclusive.

XI. This painting can scarcely be called a scene from the story of Alcestis, but is interesting as showing the typical character which her self-sacrifice came to assume in later times. In the Catacomb of S. Praetextatus at Rome is the burial-vault of Vincentius, priest of Sabazius. It is decorated in part with paintings† representing the mystical reception of his wife Vibia into the future life. The only picture which need be mentioned here is in the first chamber. In the centre *Dispater* and *Aeracura* (*Abracura* Cumont) are enthroned on a high platform; on the left are the three *Fata Divina*; on the right *Mercurius* introduces *Vibia* attended by *Alcestis*. It is clear that the latter is present to vouch for the dead Vibia as a faithful and devoted wife.

XII. One more painting calls for mention, though it has commonly been referred to the sacrifice of Iphigenia. It is the Pompeian picture No. 1305 in Helbig, published by Zahn (*Die schönsten Ornamente u. s. w.* II. 61) and discussed by Jahn (*Arch. Beitr.* p. 378). In the centre, facing the right, is a female figure in a long chiton and wearing a wreath on her head, but with loosely flowing hair. Next to her stands a bearded man in a short chiton, girt up at the waist, and likewise wearing a wreath. With his left hand he draws forward a long lock of the woman's

---

* On the right a man in a chlamys and hunting boots sits on a rock; his left hand holds two spears and his right is raised to his head. Before him stands Heracles, behind whom advances a female figure in chiton and mantle. The upper part of all the figures is missing.

† First published by Garrucci and Marchi, *Tre sepolcri etc.*, Naples, 1852. This book I have not seen. Cf. Cumont, *Culte de Mithras* II. p. 412, and the literature there cited.

hair, and in his right he holds the sword with which he is about to sever this lock and thus consecrate his victim to the gods of the nether world. Behind the woman, with his back to this scene, sits a man wrapped in his mantle, and evidently sunk in deep grief.

The application to the story of Iphigenia is clear, and seems rendered certain by the close resemblance to the so-called altar of Cleomenes at Florence. Robert,* however, prefers to see in it Thanatos in the act of cutting off the lock of Alcestis' hair, as mentioned in the prologue of this play. A full discussion of this question can hardly find space here, but it may be said that Robert himself cites no similar representation of Thanatos. On the Attic lecythi he is always winged, and the sword and costume alone can scarcely be considered sufficient to differentiate him from a priest.

It remains to consider the most important group of scenes from this myth, — the Sarcophagi.†

Four complete Roman sarcophagi contain this story on the front; in two instances it furnishes scenes for the ends, once it decorated a cover, while several fragments show that it occupied a prominent place on lost works.

XIII. The complete Sarcophagi. — I give these with the numbering of Robert, which is the same in the text and on the plates.

22. [Mich. A., B.; Dissel D.] Sarcophagus at the Villa Faustina near Cannes, belonging to M. de Courcel. It was formerly in Rome and is mentioned by Zoega (*Bassiril.* I. 205) and Gerhard (*Hyperb.- röm. Stud.* I. 154). Robert seems to have proved that it is the

---

* *Arch. Zeit.* xxxviii. p. 42, in *Ber. d. arch. Gesellsch.*, 2 März, 1880. Cf. *Arch. Märchen*, pp. 175 ff.

† Cf. Robert, *Die antiken Sarkophag-Reliefs* III. 1, pp. 24-38, Taf. VI., VII.; Michaelis, *Röm. Mitth.* VIII. 174 ff. Robert's work was not accessible until this chapter was completed, though I have endeavored to incorporate all the new information which it brings. As there was no time for a careful review of his interpretations, I have thought it best to make few changes in the treatment of disputed points, and to be content in general with a simple statement of his views.

original of the drawing in the Cod. Coburg. 44, 208 and Cod. Pigh. f. 265, No. 205,* published by Beger (*Alcestis pro marito moriens*, p. 3). It belongs to the first half of the second century.

23. [Mich. C.; Dissel C.] Front of a sarcophagus in the Villa Albani-Torlonia, No. 140. Published by Winckelmann (*Mon. Ined.* Tav. 86), Zoega (*Bassiril.* I. Tav. 43), Millin (*Gall. Myth.* pl. 108, No. 428), and Guignaut (*Relig. d. Ant.* IV. pl. 228, No. 175). It belongs to the first half of the second century.

24. [Mich. D.; Dissel B.] Robert says it was found near Rome in the time of Ficoroni,† who sent a copy of the inscription to Gori in 1732. It was bought in 1734 by the Duc de St. Aignan, and is now at the Chateau St. Aignan in France. It is careful work of the early second century. It bears a Greek inscription in memory of Ulpia Cirilla. Published by Roulez (*Gaz. Arch.* 1875, p. 105, pl. 27).

26. [Mich. F.; Dissel A. and plate.] Sarcophagus of C. Iunius Euhodus and Metilia Acte, his wife, from Ostia, now in the Vatican. (*Mus. Chiaram.* III. Tav. 10; Helbig, *Guide to the Antiquities in Rome*, 74; Gerhard, *Ant. Bildw.* Taf. 28, *Prodromos*, pp. 273 ff.) Its date is between 161 and 170 A.D.

The variations in the sarcophagi have been pointed out by Michaelis, and I have used his account freely in the description, checking it with the text of Robert and the various plates. Through the kindness of Professor C. L. Smith of Harvard University and Professor Petersen of the German Archaeological Institute in Rome I have been able to use photographs of 22 and 26, which seem to me much better than the published drawings. Twenty-two and 23 are very closely connected, and 24, though by no means identical, evidently belongs in the same group. Twenty-six also follows similar models, but treats the whole material with such freedom that it requires a separate discussion. For 22 and 23 I use the lettering of Michaelis, and have kept the same notation for 24, so far as possible.

* Matz, *Monatsb. d. Berl. Ak.* 1871, p. 492; Jahn, *Sitzb. d. k. s. Ges. d. Wiss.* 1868, p. 223.

† Cf. Jahn, *Sitzb. d. k. s. Ges. d. Wiss.* 1869, p. 14 Anm. 44.

22, 23 $a\ b\ c\ d\ e\ f\ g\ \Big|\ h\ {{i}\atop{k}}\ l\ {{m}\atop{n}}\ o\ \Big|\ p\ q\ r\ s.$

24. $t\ u\ v\ w\ x\ i\ h\ l\ o\ \Big|\ p\ q\ r\ y\ s.$
          $k\ n$

In 22 *a* and *b* are female figures, who raise the left hand to the face in a gesture of grief. While *b* leans forward toward the other figures, *a* stands with bowed head, as if in thought. In 23 the gestures are different; *b* faces the left, her right hand raised to her head, while *a* seems to be trying to dry her tears, though the gesture is uncertain, as at least the right forearm of *a* has been restored. *c* is a doryphorus, who stands in full front, but looks toward the right. *d* is a male figure in profile to the right. His chlamys is gathered over the left shoulder and arm, so as to leave the greater part of the body nude. In 22 he seems unarmed, but in 23 he has a sword at his side, and the point of a spear appears over the left shoulder. He is in animated converse with the next two figures, of which *e* occupies the background, and in 22 is a woman, apparently old, fully draped and with a veil over the back of the head. In 23, owing evidently to the thoughtlessness of the artist, this figure has become a youth in a long chlamys. *f* is a bent old man who faces the left, leaning on a staff. *g* is a youthful doryphorus, who also faces the left. The meaning of this group can scarcely be doubtful. Admetus (*d*) having heard the terms on which he can survive, entreats his parents (*e* and *f*) to come to his rescue. The doryphori are probably attendants on Admetus and Pheres. At such a scene it seems as if Alcestis should be present, as in the Pompeian paintings, and Petersen has already suggested that in 23 she must be the second figure (*b*), who is momentarily overwhelmed by the evil news; in 22, on the other hand, she must be the first (*a*), who with hand to face meditates on the deed.

In 24 the place of these figures is taken by a group which for the most part is connected with the central scene, though the first two figures may perhaps be regarded separately. At the left is a young man (*t*), facing the right, naked save for the chlamys on his left shoulder, bearing a spear in his left hand, and in his right a sheathed sword. In the background in very low relief a youth (*u*) in girded chiton advances toward *t*. The third figure (*v*), which faces the right, is an older man, bearded, a lagobolon (?) in his right hand, while his left is concealed in his chlamys, which is tightly wound about the arm. In the background is another youth (*w*) in girded chiton, facing the right and plainly an attendant of *x*. This is a young man, who stands with his back to the spectator, his right hand raised to his mouth and his head turned to the right in contemplation of the central scene. He wears a sword, and carries two spears in his left hand. It is possible that the scene represents the return of Admetus (*x*) and his followers, who on their arrival at the house find that the fatal day has come. The artist does not seem to have had the skill to bring Admetus into closer connection with the central scene, and so has placed him on the edge, differing but little from a mere spectator. Robert's interpretation of this scene is entirely different. He calls attention to the unanimity of the literary sources in representing the fatal day as well known, so that a return of Admetus from the hunt is scarcely justified. At the left is Admetus, clearly marked as in the other scenes, accompanied by his servant, sorrowing at his fate. The other figures belong to the death scene. The chief difficulty is the bearded man (*v*), who shows no sign of sorrow but seems almost a *pendant* to the figure of Heracles at the other end. The object in his hand is not properly carried for a lagobolon; otherwise he might be regarded as a representative of the chorus. He is in the proper place for Thanatos, but is a figure more suited to the Roman belief, and if the object he holds can be a key, he is probably *Ianitor Orci*.

The central scene on 22 and 23 shows no important variation, and on 24 the differences are not such as to affect the meaning. At the left is a somewhat bent old man (*h*) in chiton and himation, who stands at the foot of a couch on which lies a woman (*l*). She supports her body on her left elbow, her head sinks on her shoulder, and her whole attitude is that of extreme weakness. Her right hand is extended and clasps the hand of the old man. In the background is an old woman (*i*), who bends forward to the right over the dying woman. At the head of the couch is a woman (*o*) who in her dishevelled hair and bared breast exhibits the usual signs of mourning, and in 22 the head of another woman (*m*) turned toward the right appears just above the head of the figure on the couch. In the foreground are two children. A girl (*k*), whose garment has fallen about her waist, rests her right knee on a footstool in front of the couch and stretches both hands upward toward her dying mother. At the other end of the footstool stands a boy (*n*). He faces the left, his right foot on the stool, his right elbow on his knee, leaning his bowed head on his right hand in an attitude of deep sorrow. In 24 the same figures occur, with the exception of *m*, but the grouping is somewhat different. The old woman (*i*) is at the foot of the couch, and holds in her right hand the right hand of the reclining figure, who has fallen farther back and seems already dead. The old man (*h*) is farther forward, between the couch and the little girl, and kneels beside the dead woman whose left hand he holds in his right. The mourner (*o*) is also placed somewhat farther from the couch, and is tearing her hair with both hands.

The meaning of this scene is evident. It is the death of Alcestis, surrounded by her children and attendants. The only question concerns the identity of the aged man and woman who are placed in such prominent positions. Petersen is inclined to call them the father and mother of Admetus, while Dissel sees in them the paedagogus and nurse, urging that Pheres cannot be present at this scene, and that the costume, so far as it is visible, favors this view. It must be remembered that this entire scene is in its origin simply the death of a mother, and that in their first significance these figures have nothing to do with Alcestis. Furthermore, the consideration of the person for whom the sarcophagus is intended is seldom wholly disregarded by the maker, and therefore Robert's view (*Sark.-Rel.* III. 1, p. 25) seems very probable that in the thought of the artist these figures are the parents of the dying woman; not Pelias and Anaxibia, but simply the father and mother who belong at the bedside of their daughter. While it must be admitted that on 22 and 23 the old woman (*i*) wears the headdress of the nurse, the old man (*h*) does not wear the costume of the paedagogus, and his position seems too prominent for even a trusted servant. Robert emphasizes his view by the greater prominence of the woman on 24, which is shown by the inscription to have been ordered by a mother.

In the third scene 22 and 23 agree, while 24 again shows divergencies. From the left hastens a young man (*p*), the chlamys over his left shoulder, a sheathed sword in his left hand, his arms outstretched toward Heracles (*r*) who, easily recognized by club and lion's skin, stands with the body in full front, his head turned toward the left and his right arm extended toward this youth. Behind Heracles stands a doryphorus, his right hand raised to his mouth, looking with interest at the scene to his right. In general appearance he forms an excellent *pendant* to the figure (*e*), near the left end. Evidently we have here a meeting between Heracles and Admetus; but at what point in the story does it belong? The answer to this question depends upon the fourth figure (*q*), and unfortunately just at this point the evidence is most unsatisfactory. On 23 only the body of Admetus (*p*) and traces of this figure (*q*) have been preserved, though the restorer has endeavored to supply this lack. On 22 the space between the heads of the mourning servant (*o*) and of Heracles (*r*) has been broken out, destroying the upper part of the head of Admetus and the face of the all-important figure. The drawing in the Coburgensis shows this figure complete, but, as will be seen, its testimony is not wholly clear. The figure is that of a woman in a long chiton and mantle, the body in full front, who stands in the background between Admetus and Heracles. The right foot is firmly planted and pointed directly toward the front. The left leg is slightly bent and only the toe touches the ground. This is plain both in the drawing and in the photograph, where the position of the feet indicates a pose almost identical with that of Heracles.* In the drawing the upper part of this figure is slightly twisted, so that in

---

* Schenck's drawing in Robert does not give the position of Heracles quite as in my copy of the photograph.

spite of the position of the feet, the woman stands at the side of Admetus, with head turned toward Heracles. In the photograph of 22, this distortion of the upper part of the body does not appear, while both shoulders are concealed, owing to the narrow space between Admetus and Heracles. Michaelis describes this figure as "accanto ad Admeto," and interprets the scene as the reception of Heracles by Admetus, where this woman and the doryphorus must be servants. As this is the opinion of one who has seen the Courcel sarcophagus, it is with great hesitation that I express a doubt as to its correctness. After a somewhat protracted search I have failed to find any figure with the lower limbs in the position shown by the photograph, and the upper part of the body as represented in the drawing. So far as my examination goes, a figure standing thus always has a tendency toward the direction indicated by the advanced and firmly planted foot. She may have halted, may even be looking backward, but the arrested motion was in the direction of the foot on which she rests. If this theory is correct, the figure on 22 is coming from the same direction as Heracles, and the position of the missing head is of less account.*
The scene then represents the restoration of Alcestis to Admetus by Heracles. Against this view can be urged, apart from the drawing, the attitude of Admetus, strikingly unlike his dignified pose at this moment on 26, and very like the ceiling-painting already described; and especially the corresponding scene on 24. Here Admetus (p) bends still more toward his visitor, whose hand he grasps and whose pose and general form suggest very strongly the reveller to whose presence the servant of Admetus takes such exception in the play. The position of the woman (q) is here open to no dispute. She stands at the side of Admetus, and slightly in front of him, clad in a chiton and mantle, her right hand raised to her chin, her gaze directed toward Heracles, whose great size is made more prominent by the stooping posture of Admetus, and by

* I regard the figure as much in the position of the figure e but in the opposite direction. In the Coburgensis the drawing of the hair of q is so like that of e that it seems not unlikely that q also had the mantle over the back of the head.

the decidedly short stature of the woman.* The figure behind Heracles no longer carries a spear, but rests his right hand on his breast, and in the left clasps what Roulez calls a scroll, but in the drawing of Eichler (*Sark.-Rel.* III. 1, Taf. vi. 24) is plainly a sheathed sword. In the background between Heracles and this youth is visible another figure (*y*) in profile to the left, but in very low relief, who is possibly the servant of Admetus already seen on the sarcophagus at *u* and *w*. In that case the figure with the sword may be a representative of the people (so Robert). As has been said, this scene can scarcely be the return of Alcestis. The small stature, the absence of any veil, the whole costume, and the position by Admetus combine to make any such view as that of Roulez more than doubtful. But does not this settle the meaning of the scene of 22 and 23? Possibly; but in view of what seems to me the position of the figure (*q*), I am inclined to see in 24 only another instance of the freedom which its sculptor has used in the other scenes, though the presence of a maid-servant at the reception of Heracles is certainly hard to explain.

Here again Robert offers a different explanation. He sees in this scene on all three sarcophagi an illustration of the closing lines of the play. Alcestis is restored to life and hence no longer wears the veil which enwraps her in the rescue scenes; hence, too, she stands beside her husband, and almost seems to join him in his earnest entreaty to Heracles to remain as their guest. This had also been suggested by Dissel, but in spite of its ingenuity I cannot feel convinced that it is beyond question. The chief difficulty in 24 is the small size, which is appropriate for a young girl or a servant, but scarcely seems to belong to Alcestis. Moreover, in the symmetry, which Robert shows is so marked in this work, this figure corresponds to the servant (*w*). The heavy figure of Heracles also, in spite of the poplar wreath† in which Robert sees the sign of his return from the lower world, is in marked contrast to his dignity

---

* Roulez's drawing gives the position and costume of the woman somewhat differently. It may be noted that the position is the reverse of that on the other sarcophagus, and is similar to that of the figure *e*.

† This wreath is not very clear even in Eichler's drawing.

in the other scenes. The attitude of Admetus in all cases suggests hasty movement, appropriate in welcoming his guest or his new-found wife, but not quite fitting in an endeavor to detain his friend. In 22 the position of Alcestis, as has been said, seems to connect her more closely with Heracles than Admetus.

The ends of the Courcel sarcophagus 22 and of a Florentine sarcophagus (Mich. E.) containing the rape of Persephone on its front, show further scenes from our story.* The left end of E shows Hermes conducting a veiled woman (Alcestis) to the lower world, the entrance to which is indicated by the arch at the left. The right end of 22 evidently represents a later moment in the story. At the right Hades from his throne stretches out his right hand toward the veiled Alcestis who has passed through the portal, which is shown behind her. In the background is another veiled head in low relief, probably that of Persephone. The left end of 22 presents a scene very similar to that on the ceiling already described (cf. supra, p. lviii). In addition the character of the gate is marked by the appearance behind Alcestis of the triple-headed Cerberus. The right end of E offers simply a variation of this scene. Cerberus is omitted, and Heracles seems to be drawing the veil of Alcestis across her face. Dissel regards the action as an unveiling, but surely any violence on the part of Heracles is excluded by all the terms of the myth.

It remains to consider the important sarcophagus from Ostia (26), whose maker has in most cases known how to express his meaning with great clearness, though he cannot be acquitted of a tendency to unite separate incidents into single scenes.

At the left is an arch in which stands a bearded man who seems distinctly larger and heavier than the other figures. He wears a chlamys over his left shoulder and carries a spear, point downward, in his left hand, while in his right he holds the leash of a dog, which is sitting just inside the arch with its head thrown back as if howling. Next to him is a bearded man, wrapped in his chlamys, who appears to turn away from the group to his left toward the figure at the door. His head is bowed, and his

* Drawings in Robert, Sark.-Rel. III. 1, pp. 28 and 35, under 31, 1.

right hand is raised to his face. In his left hand, which hangs at his side, he carries a sheathed sword, the hilt of which is visible, while the sheath is concealed behind the arm. Next to this man in the foreground is a tripod, around which coils a serpent, while in the background in profile to the right is another man, who holds in his right hand what Robert thinks may be a broken rod, though it is too indistinct in the photograph and drawings to warrant a positive opinion. As to the next figure there can be no doubt. Apollo, chlamys over left shoulder and bow in left hand, is hastening forward toward the left, though he looks back toward the central scene.

This is the death of Alcestis, in many particulars showing a close resemblance to the other sarcophagi. Alcestis on the couch, the children in the foreground, the attendant at the head, and the woman in the background are much the same, though the position of Alcestis is less indicative of immediate death, and the grief of the attendants is not so strongly marked. The place of the old man at the foot of the couch is taken by Admetus, who hastens forward, much in the attitude of the welcomer of Heracles * (*p*); his chlamys is thrown back over the left shoulder, his right hand is extended to meet the hand which Alcestis reaches toward him. In his left hand we see the hilt of the sheathed sword, though the rest of the weapon is invisible. The old man is visible in the background between Apollo and Admetus, leaning on a crooked staff.

The rest of this relief is occupied by a new combination of figures. At the extreme right sits Hades enthroned, much as on the right end of 22 (Mich. *l. c.* 177). Next to him in the background stands Persephone, the torch in her right hand, while her left rests on the shoulder of her husband, and her gaze is bent upon his face. Next comes Alcestis, a veil over her head, her face bowed, and her right hand raised to her mouth. She moves slowly toward the left, following Heracles, who with the club on his left shoulder, and the lion's skin hanging over his arm, extends his

---

* The chief difference is that the body above the hips is erect instead of bent forward. The position of the legs seems identical.

right hand to grasp the hand of Admetus, who stands facing the right, his chlamys covering his body, and again in the sunken left hand the hilt of the sword, which he carried in the central group. Beneath the clasped hands of Heracles and Admetus is the opening of a cavern in which sits the three-headed Cerberus. In the background, filling the vacant space between Admetus, Heracles, and Alcestis, are three female figures, evidently the Moirai. In this scene we have a combination of two distinct episodes,—the rescue of Alcestis from the lower world by Heracles, probably through the mediation of Persephone, and the restoration to Admetus. With the omission of Admetus, Cerberus is quite in place as marking the entrance to the region, whence Alcestis and her guide are to withdraw. In his present position he is meaningless, for it is scarcely possible to suppose with Roulez that Admetus has accompanied Heracles to the entrance to the world of shades. Besides, even on this theory, Admetus and Heracles are on opposite sides of the gate.

I have purposely left till the last the interpretation of the scene at the left. Three interpretations have been proposed, so far as I am aware. Roulez, followed by Dissel, sees in it Admetus returning from the hunt and met at his entrance into the palace by a sorrowing servant with the news of his wife's impending death. To this there seem to me serious objections. In both the other scenes Admetus is clearly marked, and carries the sheathed sword with the hilt projecting from the left hand. This sword is carried by the sorrowing man, and in my opinion gives strong grounds for believing that the artist meant to designate him as Admetus. Moreover, the returning hunter shows no likeness to Admetus in the other scenes, and is also much larger. Petersen interprets the scene as Admetus turning in sorrow from an inquiry of the Delphic oracle, indicated by the tripod and the presence of Apollo. The figure in the archway is a retainer. Against this view it may be urged that Apollo is manifestly interested in the central scene, not in Admetus, with whom his figure has no association whatever, and that the tripod does not necessarily indicate Delphi, but simply adds distinctness to Apollo, although it must be admitted that the bow would have been a sufficient attribute.* Moreover, the other figure seems much too large and occupies too prominent a place (his spear is across Admetus' right leg) to be a mere attendant. The third explanation has been given by Robert.† In spite of the sword the sorrowing man is not Admetus, for he has not the portrait features, doubtless those of Euhodus, by which the sculptor has elsewhere marked the husband. The figure in the door is a representative of the lower world, a Roman substitute for the Thanatos of Euripides, and may be compared with Hades and the dog on the cover of the San Lorenzo sarcophagus.‡ This certainly makes a marked parallelism between the ends of this relief. At the left the hunter enters for his prey, and at the right the rulers of the dead release their victim. It seems to me that this view gains if the husband appears helpless and weeping before the impending blow, as well as receiving his lost wife from the grave. Nor does the absence of the portrait features seem a fatal objection, though it is certainly not without weight, for, so far as I can judge from the photograph, Alcestis has the features of Metilia only in the death scene.

XIV. The Fragments of Sarcophagi.

25. The right end of the front of a sarcophagus in the Louvre (Clarac, II. pl. 194, No. 758, 214; Reinach, p. 82) shows Heracles followed by a doryphorus, with traces of another figure in the background, much as at the end of 22. Clarac calls this fragment Heracles and Iolaus, but in the opinion of Robert it may be part of the missing end of 23.

27. [Matz-Duhn, *Ant. Bildw. in Rom*, 2889.] A fragment in the Villa Pamfili shows part of the central scene in a somewhat different type. There are more figures in the background, the old man sets his left foot on the stool, and the little girl no longer kneels but is hastening toward the couch.

28. [Dütschke, *Ant. Bildw.* II. p. 161.] A Florentine fragment of the death scene, preserved in the Palazzo Antinori.

* Cf. on this point Robert, *Sark.-Rel.* III. 1, p. 32.
† *West-Deutsche Zeitschr. f. Gesch. u. Kunst*, 1885, 231. Cf. *Arch. März.* 177; *Sark.-Rel.* III. 1, p. 32. The first article I know only from the later references.
‡ Matz-Duhn, 3090; *Wien. Vorlegebl.* 1888, Taf. ix. 4a.

29. [Matz-Duhn, 2890.] This fragment shows the children from the death scene in the usual type, and traces of the couch and the figure of the old man.

30. [Matz-Duhn, 2892.] This is a fragment of a left corner, and shows three male figures, which do not agree with any of the other reliefs; though it has been proposed to see in it Admetus hastening to meet Heracles, to which view the position at the left seems fatal, or Admetus and Pheres, which seems possible. On the corner of the left end traces of a caduceus perhaps indicate a scene like that on the Uffizi sarcophagus, but the connection of this fragment with the story is more than doubtful.

30.[1] [Matz-Duhn, 2891.] A lost fragment which seems to have contained only the figure of Admetus (*d*) from the first scene of 22 or 23.

31. [Matz-Duhn, 3385.] This fragment is also lost, and its connection with the Alcestis monuments must remain very doubtful, as the description shows no marked likeness to the other reliefs. It is possible that it belonged to a variation of the scene between Admetus and his parents.

31.[1] This is a fragment in the Villa Albani, which once formed the left end of a sarcophagus. Heracles leads Alcestis into the upper world from an opening in the rock, while at the left is a figure emerging from the earth, and raising the right hand in astonishment. Robert calls him the Ianitor Orci, who appears in a similar position on the Persephone sarcophagi, and on one with scenes from the life of Heracles (*Sark.-Rel.* III. 120). He suggests to me the Hermes on the Rinuccini relief, though the mutilation is too great for any exact comparison.

XV. [*Sark.-Rel.* 32.] Another relief, which very probably formed part of the cover of a sarcophagus,* is now preserved in the Palazzo Rinuccini in Florence in a badly mutilated condition, and more completely in a drawing in the Cod. Pighianus. It was first published from the drawing by Petersen (*Arch. Zeit.* 21, 1863, Taf. 179, 1, 2), and later was discovered by Dütschke (*Ant. Bildw. in*

---

* Robert suggests it might have belonged to 23, could it be shown that this sarcophagus was known in the sixteenth century.

Oberital. II. 314), and published from the original by him (*Arch. Zeit.* 33, 1875, pp. 72 ff. Taf. 9, cf. also Baumeister, *Denkmäler* I. 46). The fragment is only 0.55 M. long and 0.21 M. high, according to Dütschke, and is broken at both ends.

At the left stands Heracles, the lion's skin over his left arm; the head and much of the right side have been restored, but even in the Pighianus the right leg and lower right arm are missing. It seems probable that the right hand rested on the club. He looks toward the right after a woman (Alcestis) in long chiton, and mantle which covers her head and is drawn around the face without covering it. She seems to be moving slowly and with bowed head toward the right. In the drawing the scene is completed by the addition on the left of Hermes,* who stands in the entrance to a cavern, and by his gesture seems to dismiss Heracles and Alcestis.

The next scene to the right is clearly separated by a column, which stands in front of the veiled Alcestis. Here we have a group of five figures. On the right a woman in long chiton and with the mantle over her head is gently urged toward the left by another woman. This group is evidently that of a bride supported by the nympheutria. The husband in this scene is a youthful figure, nude but for the chlamys over his back, who while moving toward the bride, turns away his face and grasps her right hand with his left. In the background, between the husband and wife, is a youthful figure clad in a long chlamys and holding an inverted torch, who is turning his back on the newly wedded pair, but looks over his shoulder toward the fifth figure. This is a young man, of much the same size and general appearance as the husband. He stands with his back to the spectator, his left elbow resting on the top of the pillar, and his right arm partly extended, while with the hand he seems to beckon to one of the figures at the right. His chlamys is gathered over the right arm at the elbow.

Petersen (*Arch. Zeit.* 21, 116) explained this scene as the marriage of Admetus and Alcestis, the unhappy issue of which is sug-

---

* Dütschke claims that all to the left of the figure of Heracles is due to the combination by the artist of Pighius of two distinct reliefs. In opposition to this, cf. Robert, *Arch. März.* p. 174[1], who speaks with authority on this point.

gested by Hymenaeus, who turns away and reverses his torch. To this Dilthey (*Annali d. Inst.* 1869, p. 24) added the ill-omened use of the left hand by Admetus. The fifth figure according to Petersen is the nymphagogus, who brings to Admetus the tidings of the evil omen sent by Artemis. Dütschke accepts this view in most particulars, but calls the figure to the left Hermes, and sees in his gesture a sign to Hymenaeus to return, as with the left hand the god points to the rescue of Alcestis in token of the ultimate happiness of the newly wedded pair. Against this last interpretation may be urged the uncertainty as to the exact direction and intention of the gestures of this so-called Hermes, whose relation to his fellow god is by no means distinct in the reproductions; but the most serious objection is the total absence of an attribute, which seems to me to exclude at once this identification. Robert also accepts the view that this scene is the marriage, and his interpretation of the other figures has much to commend it. The evil fate is indicated by the ill-omened use of the left hand, from which Admetus, suddenly aware of his mistake, turns his face in terror, while his nymphagogus by his gesture expresses his horror. The same emotion is shown by the turning away of the torch-bearer, who is not necessarily Hymenaeus, and this act is accompanied by a further sign of the ill-will of the gods in the inverted torch. These signs have been substituted by the artist for the traditional coil of snakes. Dissel's interpretation of this scene is entirely different. He sees in it a free imitation of the last part of Euripides' play.* The youth is Hermes, who has brought Heracles and Alcestis from the lower world. Alcestis is conducted by some maid-servant to Admetus, who unwillingly extends to her his left hand, while in the background Thanatos turns away. Apart from the difficulty in finding a Hermes Psychopompos without the customary attribute, and the exceedingly doubtful type assumed for Thanatos, this view makes Heracles belong to both scenes, or else absent at the all-important moment of the return of Alcestis to Admetus. The first alternative requires us to admit Alcestis twice in a scene, where Heracles occurs only once, and the second is surely impossible.

* This idea is due to von Duhn. Cf. Dissel, *l. c.* 18[19].

The extreme right of the relief was broken away in the time of Pighius, though his drawing shows part of a figure turned toward the right. The rest of this figure and an additional one have since been very badly restored, but we only know that there must have been still another scene, perhaps connected with the miraculous wooing, as the remains of the first figure suggest the possibility of Artemis, as on the stucco relief from the Via Latina, but behind the chariot.

The left end of the relief, in the drawing, is occupied by a scene which still waits for a satisfactory explanation. The whole style is totally unlike the rest of the sculpture; a fact which led Dütschke to his theory of contamination, though it is explained by Robert as due to the variety in the sources used by the artist. Back of the grotto in which Hermes appears, there sits on a rock a young man wearing a chlamys. He faces the left and rests his left hand on the rock and the end of a short shepherd's crook; beside the rock, looking up at the hand of his master, is a dog. Beside this man, in the background, is a young girl, her back to the spectator, and looking back at the man, while with her right hand she seems to make a gesture of dismissal. He pays no attention to her, but extends his right hand toward a boy wearing a chlamys over his back, who stands before him, holding in his left hand a bow. The boy does not look toward the man, but down over his right shoulder, toward an old woman, who stands at the extreme left and by her gestures seems to be encouraging the lad.

Petersen interpreted the scene as Admetus, who in grief at the loss of his wife has retired to his flocks, and his children, accompanied by the nurse. This does not seem very natural. The group as a whole shows no sign of sorrow, and a retirement of Admetus to the fields is a rather long step from his reluctance to enter the palace (Alc. 911 ff.). Dilthey (*Ann. d. Inst.* 1869, 25[2]), while admitting that the man is Admetus, insists that the two children are Apollo and Artemis. This view has been adopted by Robert, who interprets the scene as the entrance of Apollo into the service of Admetus. The reluctant Apollo, who, according to the Delphic version, has been condemned to servitude for slaying the

Python, and is therefore still a mere child, is urged forward by Leto, and kindly welcomed by Admetus, from whom his sister turns away in the first manifestation of that anger which was to have such a fatal termination. This explanation accounts for the representation of the divinities as children, but it must be admitted that the figure of Leto does not suggest the goddess, nor does the Delphic version seem to have enjoyed such prominence as to make its choice by an artist of a late date easily intelligible. It is probably the best interpretation yet suggested, but it certainly is by no means free from difficulties, nor can it be regarded as the final decision of a still perplexing question.

XVI. Another monument in Rome has been brought into connection with the story of Alcestis. It is an oblong basis,* which supported a column, from Porto d'Anzio, now in the Villa Albani, and published by Francke (*Annali*, 1879, pp. 53–58, Tav. E. 1). One side and the two ends contain a continuous scene. The front shows a woman on a bed, resting on her left elbow, in an attitude not unlike that of the dying Alcestis. In front of the couch, with her arms about the other, kneels an apparently aged woman. Behind the couch stand five mourning women, the upper part of the body nude, some tearing their hair, others with hands crossed on the breast. The two ends are said to show the ends of the couch, and at each a mourner of the same type as those on the front. Thus far there is nothing to show that the relief is more than a representation of the mourning of a mother (for so we might interpret the kneeling woman) for her daughter, or of a family for its mistress. Neither Admetus nor the children nor any other of the characters especially concerned in the death of Alcestis are even hinted at. The supposed connection with the myth is found on the fourth side. Here we see on the left Heracles *en face*, his right hand resting on his club, his left arm, over which hangs the lion's skin, stretched out toward a woman, on whom his gaze is directed. This woman wears a chiton and mantle, which perhaps covers the back of her head, though her entire face and neck are uncovered. With her left hand she grasps the left hand of the hero, and her

* Size 0.22 M. by 0.14 M. The height of the fragment is 0.39 M.

right seems to be touching his face. Francke thought that the original artist had here represented Admetus, but that the copyist had changed the scene for his own purpose, which was to show the love felt for the dead woman, under the types used for a well-known myth. Dissel objects to this, and sees in the last scene Alcestis resisting and rebuking Heracles for an attempt to unveil her. Considering the deference shown by Heracles toward his prize in the other representations, such an interpretation of this relief and of the end of the Florentine sarcophagus (E) seems scarcely warranted. The gestures of the woman are rather those of earnest entreaty, and the group looks as if it belonged in some other story of Heracles. While it is possible that the scenes owe their suggestion to the Alcestis monuments, I can see no reason for believing that the sculptor was endeavoring to portray that story on this occasion.

There are several representations of Heracles and a veiled woman, which seem to be taken from this legend, though the emphasis seems rather on Heracles than on Alcestis.

XVII. Near Salona in Dalmatia in a grotto is a rock-cut tomb in the form of a sarcophagus. The front is divided into three compartments in which are represented various labors of Heracles.* On the left is the capture of Cerberus, in the centre Heracles hurries to the right, the lion's skin around his shoulders, the club in his left hand, while with his right he grasps the left wrist of a veiled woman, who seems to walk slowly after him. The attitude of Heracles is very like that in the Cerberus relief. The third relief represents a combination of the shooting of the Stymphalian birds and the plucking of the apples of the Hesperides, which the artist has accomplished by putting the birds in the tree which bears the apples.

XVIII. Walled into a tower near Smederevo in Servia is a funeral relief, which seems to me very closely related to the Alcestis representations. It is published by Kanitz (*Denkschr. d. Wien.*

---

* Literature. Steinbücher, *Wiener Jahrbücher der Litteratur*, 1820, *Anz.* Taf. I. Fig. 3; *Denkschr. d. Wiener Akad.* II., Carrara, *De' scavi di Salona nel 1848*, p. 11, Tav. VI. 17; *Ib.* VII., Lanza, *Monumenti Salonitani inediti*, p. 7, Tav. II. 1.

Akad. XLI. *Röm. Stud. in Serbien* p. 11, Fig. 6), who describes it as "ein an einigen Stellen beschädigtes oblonges Relief mit zwischen zwei korinthischen Säulen trefflich angeordneter und gut ausgeführter Trauerscene." The wood-cut shows on the left a veiled woman (though the face seems uncovered) who is led toward the right by Heracles, who grasps her wrist in his right hand. He is represented nearly *en face;* in his left hand he holds the club, which rests on his shoulder, while the lion's skin, or possibly a chlamys, hangs over the left arm. The rest of the relief is somewhat badly damaged, but seems to represent a couch, at the head of which (the extreme right) is a stool, on which sits a figure with the head bowed on the right hand. The right elbow and the left hand rest on the head of the couch. On the couch seems to be another figure, and there was possibly a footstool before it.* This relief in my opinion is derived from the representations of the death and return of Alcestis, though the absence of Admetus and the children would indicate that it was not so much the myth which occupied the thought of the artist, as the idea of a death and rescue of the departed.

XIX. In the following monument the relation to Alcestis is somewhat clearer. It was discovered in Tripoli, at a place called El-Amrouni about halfway between Douîrat and Nâlout, near the border of Tunis. Here a mausoleum was unearthed by M. Lecoy de la Marche, and a short description published by M. Philippe Berger (*Rev. Arch.* 1895, 1, pp. 71–83). Two inscriptions, one Latin, the other Neo-punic, show that it was erected to Q. Apuleius Maximus Rideus (?) by his wife and three sons. It was decorated on the outside with two rows of reliefs, of which only one is of immediate interest. In the lower row, the west side represented Orpheus charming the wild beasts, the south side Orpheus and Eurydice, including a view of Sisyphus, Ixion, and Tantalus, while the north side furnished a new form of the rescue of Alcestis (Berger, *l. c.* p. 79, Fig. 3). This relief is broken longitudinally a little

---

* The relief is badly damaged near the centre, and the couch is very indistinct in the drawing. I consider it as like the relief from Servia, *Arch.-Epigr. Mitth. aus Oester.* X. 214, Fig. 6.

below the middle, but the general character of the representation is clear. On the left is Charon, pushing his boat to shore. On the end of the boat is seated a fully draped female figure (Alcestis). In front of her, on the shore, stands Heracles, the club in his left hand, and the lion's skin over his shoulder. His right hand is extended, apparently in the act of helping the woman to descend from the boat. On the right is the lower part of the gate of the lower world, and beyond this Heracles pushing Alcestis forward, up the steep incline to the world of life. The style of the reliefs is the only means of fixing the date,* and as this can scarcely be determined from the drawings published, it is not possible to give any exact statement, further than that the work evidently belongs to the late Roman time.

XX. Another relief, whose connection with this story is only known through the inscription, is now in Aquileia, where it was found in 1863. I have not seen any illustration of the relief, though a description was published by Dütschke from a sketch by Conze (*Arch. Zeit.* 33, p. 78).† On the left is a bearded man, perhaps with the chlamys over his left shoulder, and a staff in his left hand, who raises his right hand as if in conversation with a veiled woman at the right, who rests her bowed head on her right hand. The lower part of the relief is broken away. Apparently across the top of the stone is the inscription ADMETVS ET ALC (*estis*). It does not seem necessary to see in this, with Dütschke, Admetus communicating his fate to Alcestis, who is meditating her sacrifice. It rather belongs with such scenes as those on the Etruscan vases, and Admetus and Alcestis are simply typical figures to express the conjugal devotion of the pair in whose honor this funeral monument was erected.

XXI. Preller (*Ber. d. Sächs Gesellsch.* 1850, 241) mentions a terra-cotta relief in Weimar, brought from Rome, about the size of those of the Campanari collection, as representing the return of

---

* The inscription is not published in facsimile, nor does the editor assign any date.

† For the inscription, cf C. I. L. V. 2, 8265, where is cited Gregorutti, *Le antiche lapidi di Aquileja*, which I have not seen.

Alcestis to Admetus. He gives no further description, and I do not know of any other mention of it.

XXII. It is barely possible that there may be some remote connection between this story and a sardonyx of the British Museum, representing a youthful Heracles seated in weariness on a rock, while from behind him hastens away a bearded and winged man, somewhat in the type of Thanatos. (Cf. Furtwängler in Roscher, *Lexikon, s.v.* Herakles, I. 2141–42.) I do not believe this can be Thanatos flying from his conqueror, but include it for the sake of completeness.

XXIII. It now remains to consider the most difficult of the monuments which have been referred to the story of Alcestis, — the *columna caelata* from the temple of Artemis at Ephesus.* Of the figures (probably about eight in number) which originally filled this relief only four have been preserved with any approach to completeness, though there are fragments of two more. On the right is the lower part of a seated figure, probably male. In front of him is a standing female, fully draped, and holding a somewhat indefinite object, which may possibly be a necklace or taenia; the head is missing, but seems to have been turned toward the left. The third figure is the best preserved of the group, and by the *kerykeion* is easily recognizable as Hermes, who, with head thrown back and glance directed upward, is moving toward the left. Before him, apparently just starting, is a woman, fully draped, who is in the act of fastening her mantle on the left shoulder; the head is lacking, but probably was turned to the right. The next figure is also well preserved, except for a break on the right side. It represents a youth with great wings, extending even above the head, and a great sword suspended by a band over the right shoulder. He stands with the body turned very slightly toward the left, his right hand at his side, while with the left he seems to beckon to the woman behind him, toward whom he turns a somewhat sad and thoughtful face. Beyond this figure there can be distinguished

---

* Rayet, *Mon. de l'Art antique* II. Pl. 50; Curtius, *Arch. Zeit.* 1872, Taf. 65, 66; Overbeck, *Gesch. d. griech. Plast.* 11⁴. p. 131. Less complete reproductions in other publications.

traces of a naked shoulder and a left arm wrapped in a chlamys, so that it can fairly be inferred that here stood a man, who rested his left elbow on his side. It does not seem to me that the traces are sufficient to show whether he stood in the attitude of Heracles on the Rinuccini relief, as Robert thinks, or in a position more like that of Hermes on this column. If Smith is correct (see below), the position would be unlike either. Space will not permit a full account of all the attempts to interpret this scene, on which the last word, in my opinion, has not yet been spoken. Ernst Curtius (*Arch. Zeit.* 31, 1873, p. 72) in a notice of the newly discovered relief, suggested that it might be connected with a contest of the Muses before Apollo, under the leadership of Hermes, and that the youth with the sword was Agon — a view which seems to have found no adherents. Later Engelmann (*Arch. Zeit.* 37, p. 115) brought this scene into connection with the story of Phineus, interpreting the figure with the sword as a Boread. This view also labors under serious difficulties and has not met with any acceptance.

The view which has supplanted earlier theories, and has not as yet been driven from the field, was first published by C. Robert in "Thanatos. 39tes Programm zum Winckelmannsfeste," Berlin, 1879. Here was maintained very skilfully the thesis that the relief represented the return of Alcestis. Heracles having conquered Thanatos has descended to the lower world and prevailed on the deities to reward his victory. On the right are Hades and Persephone, who have consented to the return, then Hermes ready to conduct Alcestis, who stands next to him, to the upper world, while Thanatos* by his gesture indicates the release of his victim. At the extreme left must have been Heracles quietly waiting for his prize. As to the missing figures Robert refused to make any conjecture. The view was at once denied by Kekulé (*Deutsche Litteratur-Zeitung,* 1880, 382), and later by Wolters (*Gipsabgüsse ant. Bildw.* 1242), but has been accepted by many scholars, notably Rayet, Overbeck, and Collignon. Benndorf (*Bull. della Comm. Arch.* 1886, p. 54) endeavored to establish the view that the Judgment of Paris was

---

* The interpretation of this figure as Thanatos had been suggested in *Sat. Rev.* 1873, 35, p. 51.

here represented. Zeus and Hera, Eros and Aphrodite, Hermes as conductor of the goddesses, and apparently Paris waiting at the left, — such was his interpretation, which was refuted by Robert (*Arch. März.* pp. 160–175), who also endeavored to overthrow the criticism of Wolters. The last explanation with which I am acquainted is that of A. H. Smith (*Jour. Hell. Stud.* XI. pp. 278 ff.), who sees here the sending of Pandora. From the right we have Zeus, Hera, who holds a necklace or diadem, Hermes with slightly opened mouth in the act of imparting the gift of speech to Pandora, who already fastens her mantle for departure, Eros, who here in his gloomy aspect presages the unhappy result of this gift of the gods, and finally Hephaestus, his left hand on his hip, while he leans on his stick thrust under the right shoulder. The discovery of a part of the original surface showing part of a staff is very important, but the traces are evidently too faint to be entirely conclusive. Without discussing this theory in detail, it may be said that Eros with a sword still awaits an analogy in Greek art, and that all other Greek representations of this scene show Pandora as a very stiff doll-like figure, in no way like the graceful woman of the column.

Robert's theory, however, requires a brief examination. Wolters brings against it three arguments: (1) Thanatos on representations of this time ought to be a bearded man, (2) Heracles cannot wear the simple chlamys, (3) the scene here represented does not correspond with any literary version; to which Benndorf adds (4) that the necklace in the hands of Persephone is unexplained, and Furtwängler (Roscher, *Lexikon* I. 2248) (5) that the presence of Heracles is due to a conjecture. Robert (*Arch. März. l. c.*) has answered the first four objections. (1) In the fourth century the idea of Thanatos was changing from the type of the fifth century toward that conception which later led to Erotes as symbols of death; moreover, Thanatos is certainly beardless on the cylix of Pamphaios and an altar from the Esquiline (*Monum. d. Inst.* XI. Tav. X. 3). It is certainly not improbable that the beginnings of a tendency, which developed during the Hellenistic and Roman periods, should be found in the later fourth century, although the fact that Thanatos is beardless on the vases more than a century earlier can scarcely weigh very heavily, in view of the prominence of the bearded type on the Attic lecythi of the late fifth and earlier fourth centuries. That the dank and matted hair and sad expression are very appropriate to the later conception of Thanatos cannot be denied, but Robert's interpretation of this scene requires that this Thanatos be a rival of Heracles, and it seems to me very hard to imagine this youth in contest with a Heracles of the type belonging to this period. As Robert has urged in answering objection (3), the artist has combined two versions which the literature kept separate, and the sarcophagi have already made it clear that the art recognized a journey of the hero to the lower world in this connection; but the only justification for Thanatos in the Alcestis legend is that he may be conquered by Heracles, and for that purpose the type of the time of Euripides is in my opinion a necessity. As to the costume of Heracles, Robert has shown that he does appear in a chlamys on several works, but a comparison with the citations of Furtwängler (Roscher, *Lexikon* I. 2183) would indicate that this is confined to special occasions, where he is not engaged in any of his heroic labors. The object in the hand of "Persephone" is too indistinct to make argument (4) very weighty, though Robert's suggestion that it is a thank-offering of Alcestis seems to call for some analogy to justify it. The last objection (5) is of course enough to prevent certainty, and if the traces which Smith regards as proving the presence of a staff, cannot be reconciled with the theory that the hero leaned on his club, they alone would suffice to make the connection with Alcestis still more doubtful.

A modification of Robert's view has been suggested by Edward Robinson (*Catalogue of Casts in Boston Mus.* III. 526), who interprets the scene as the departure of Alcestis to the lower world with Thanatos and Hermes. Apart from the fact that this fails to explain the calm attitude of the figures at the right, whom Mr. Robinson calls the parents of Admetus, it seems difficult to account for the presence of both Thanatos and Hermes, one of whom would seem sufficient, and for the position of Hermes, who as ψυχοπομπός regularly precedes the soul on its descent to the lower world.*

* Cf. Robert, *Thanatos*, 40.

For these reasons I am unable to believe that the connection of the Ephesus column with the story of Alcestis has been proved, though it must be granted that there are perhaps fewer difficulties in this interpretation than in any other. Nor is it easy to see how certainty can be reached, unless some work of art should come to light of obvious dependence on this column, and containing some clue to the missing figures.

F. Hypotheses of the Play.

The following are the hypotheses of the *Alcestis* which have come down to us. The text is that of Schwartz in his edition of the scholia, with one slight change.

ΥΠΟΘΕΣΙΣ ΑΛΚΗΣΤΙΔΟΣ

Ἀπόλλων ᾐτήσατο παρὰ τῶν Μοιρῶν ὅπως ὁ Ἄδμητος, τελευτᾶν μέλλων, παράσχῃ τὸν ὑπὲρ ἑαυτοῦ ἑκόντα τεθνηξόμενον, ἵνα ἴσον τῷ προτέρῳ χρόνον ζήσῃ. καὶ δὴ Ἄλκηστις ἡ γυνὴ τοῦ Ἀδμήτου ἐπέδωκεν ἑαυτήν, οὐδετέρου τῶν γονέων θελήσαντος ὑπὲρ τοῦ παιδὸς ἀποθανεῖν. μετ' οὐ πολὺ δὲ ταύτης τῆς συμφορᾶς γενομένης Ἡρακλῆς παραγενόμενος καὶ μαθὼν παρά τινος θεράποντος τὰ περὶ τὴν Ἄλκηστιν ἐπορεύθη ἐπὶ τὸν τάφον καὶ τὸν Θάνατον ἀποστῆναι ποιήσας, ἐσθῆτι καλύπτει τὴν γυναῖκα· τὸν δὲ Ἄδμητον ἠξίου λαβόντα αὐτὴν τηρεῖν· εἰληφέναι γὰρ αὐτὴν πάλης ἆθλον ἔλεγε. μὴ βουλομένου δὲ ἐκείνου, ἔδειξεν ἣν ἐπένθει.

Ἄλκηστις, ἡ Πελίου θυγάτηρ, ὑπομείνασα ὑπὲρ τοῦ ἰδίου ἀνδρὸς τελευτῆσαι, Ἡρακλέους ἐπιδημήσαντος ἐν τῇ Θετταλίᾳ διασῴζεται, βιασαμένου ⟨αὐτοῦ⟩[1] τοὺς χθονίους θεοὺς καὶ ἀφελομένου τὴν γυναῖκα. παρ' οὐδετέρῳ κεῖται ἡ μυθοποιία.

τὸ δρᾶμα ἐποιήθη ιζ̄. ἐδιδάχθη ἐπὶ Γλαυκίνου ἄρχοντος ὀλ⟨υμ⟩πιάδος π̄ε ἔτει β̄. πρῶτος ἦν Σοφοκλῆς, δεύτερος Εὐριπίδης Κρήσσαις Ἀλκμέωνι τῷ διὰ Ψωφίδος Τηλέφῳ Ἀλκήστιδι. εἰσὶδ * ἐχορήγει. τὸ δὲ δρᾶμα κωμικωτέραν ἔχει τὴν καταστροφήν.

---

[1] ⟨αὐτοῦ⟩ was inserted by the ed.

ἡ μὲν σκηνὴ τοῦ δράματος ὑπόκειται ἐν Φεραῖς, μιᾷ πόλει τῆς Θετταλίας· ὁ δὲ χορὸς συνέστηκεν ἔκ τινων πρεσβυτῶν ἐντοπίων, οἳ [καὶ] παραγίνονται συμπαθήσοντες ταῖς Ἀλκήστιδος συμφοραῖς. προλογίζει δὲ Ἀπόλλων.

τὸ δὲ δρᾶμά ἐστι σατυρικώτερον ὅτι εἰς χαρὰν καὶ ἡδονὴν καταστρέφει [παρὰ τοῖς τραγικοῖς] ⟨καὶ⟩ ἐκβάλλεται ὡς ἀνοίκεια τῆς τραγικῆς ποιήσεως ὅ τε Ὀρέστης καὶ ἡ Ἄλκηστις, ὡς ἐκ συμφορᾶς μὲν ἀρχόμενα, εἰς εὐδαιμονίαν ⟨δὲ⟩ καὶ χαρὰν λήξαντα, ⟨ἅ⟩ ἐστι μᾶλλον κωμῳδίας ἐχόμενα. ⟨πολλὰ δὲ τοιαῦτα παρὰ τοῖς τραγικοῖς.⟩

Critical Signs and Abbreviations.

$B =$ Codex Vaticanus 909.
  $B^1 =$ the first hand, $b =$ the second hand.
$L =$ Codex Laurentianus 32, 2.
  $L^1 =$ the first hand, $l =$ the second and third hands.
$P =$ Codex Palatinus 287.
  $P^1 =$ the first hand, $p =$ a later hand.
$a =$ Codex Parisinus 2713.
  $a^1 =$ the first hand, $a^2 =$ the second hand, $a^3 =$ several later hands.

$C =$ Codex Havniensis 417.
$c =$ Codex Laurentianus 31, 10.
$d =$ Codex Laurentianus 31, 15.

S indicates a reading which is common to both L and P, and hence was found in their common source.
r stands for *reliqui libri*.
* denotes the erasure of a letter or an accent.

ΕΥΡΙΠΙΔΟΥ ΑΛΚΗΣΤΙΣ.

ΤΑ ΤΟΥ ΔΡΑΜΑΤΟΣ ΠΡΟΣΩΠΑ

ΑΠΟΛΛΩΝ
ΘΑΝΑΤΟΣ
ΧΟΡΟΣ
ΘΕΡΑΠΑΙΝΑ
ΑΛΚΗΣΤΙΣ
ΑΔΜΗΤΟΣ
ΕΥΜΗΛΟΣ
ΗΡΑΚΛΗΣ
ΦΕΡΗΣ
ΘΕΡΑΠΩΝ

ΑΛΚΗΣΤΙΣ.

ΑΠΟΛΛΩΝ.

Ὦ δώματ' Ἀδμήτει', ἐν οἷς ἔτλην ἐγὼ
θῆσσαν τράπεζαν αἰνέσαι θεός περ ὤν.
Ζεὺς γὰρ κατακτὰς παῖδα τὸν ἐμὸν αἴτιος
Ἀσκληπιόν, στέρνοισιν ἐμβαλὼν φλόγα·
οὗ δὴ χολωθεὶς τέκτονας Δίου πυρὸς 5
κτείνω Κύκλωπας· καί με θητεύειν πατὴρ
θνητῷ παρ' ἀνδρὶ τῶνδ' ἄποιν' ἠνάγκασεν.
ἐλθὼν δὲ γαῖαν τήνδ' ἐβουφόρβουν ξένῳ,
καὶ τόνδ' ἔσῳζον οἶκον ἐς τόδ' ἡμέρας.
ὁσίου γὰρ ἀνδρὸς ὅσιος ὢν ἐτύγχανον 10
παιδὸς Φέρητος, ὃν θανεῖν ἐρρυσάμην
Μοίρας δολώσας· ᾔνεσαν δέ μοι θεαὶ
Ἄδμητον ᾅδην τὸν παραυτίκ' ἐκφυγεῖν,
ἄλλον διαλλάξαντα τοῖς κάτω νεκρόν.
πάντας δ' ἐλέγξας καὶ διεξελθὼν φίλους, 15
[πατέρα γεραιάν θ' ἥ σφ' ἔτικτε μητέρα,]
οὐχ ηὗρε, πλὴν γυναικός, ὅστις ἤθελε
θανὼν πρὸ κείνου μηκέτ' εἰσορᾶν φάος·

3 κατ' ἀκτὰς B. 8 δὲ γαῖαν] δ' ἐς αἶαν Athenagoras Legat. pro Christ. c. 21 (p. 25 Steph.). 9 ἐς τόδ' a] ἐστὶ δ' B (with ἐς τόδ' added by b) εἰς τόδ' S. 11 ἐρρυσάμην S] ἐρυσάμην r. 12 δηλώσας B. 13 παρ' αὐτίκ' B. 15 ἔλεξας B (but with an acute accent and γ written above the λε by B¹). 16 rejected as spurious by W. Dindorf. 17 ὅστις Reiske] ἥτις MSS. 18 θανὼν Reiske] θανεῖν MSS. | μηδ' ἔτ' C.

4 ΕΥΡΙΠΙΔΟΥ

ἣ νῦν κατ' οἴκους ἐν χεροῖν βαστάζεται
ψυχορραγοῦσα· τῇδε γάρ σφ' ἐν ἡμέρᾳ   20
θανεῖν πέπρωται καὶ μεταστῆναι βίου.
ἐγὼ δέ, μὴ μίασμά μ' ἐν δόμοις κίχῃ,
λείπω μελάθρων τῶνδε φιλτάτην στέγην.
(ἤδη δὲ τόνδε Θάνατον εἰσορῶ πέλας,
ἱερέα φθινόντων, ὅς νιν εἰς Ἅιδου δόμους   25
μέλλει κατάξειν· σύμμετρος δ' ἀφίκετο,
φρουρῶν τόδ' ἦμαρ ᾧ θανεῖν αὐτὴν χρεών.

ΘΑΝΑΤΟΣ.

ἆ ἆ·
τί σὺ πρὸς μελάθροις; τί σὺ τῇδε πολεῖς,
Φοῖβ'; ἀδικεῖς αὖ τιμὰς ἐνέρων   30
[ἀφοριζόμενος καὶ καταπαύων.]
οὐκ ἤρκεσέ σοι μόρον Ἀδμήτου
διακωλῦσαι, Μοίρας δολίῳ
σφήλαντι τέχνῃ; νῦν δ' ἐπὶ τῇδ' αὖ
χέρα τοξήρη φρουρεῖς ὁπλίσας,   35
ἣ τόδ' ὑπέστη πόσιν ἐκλύσασ'
αὐτὴ προθανεῖν Πελίου παῖς.

ΛΠ. θάρσει· δίκην τοι καὶ λόγους κεδνοὺς ἔχω.
ΘΑ. τί δῆτα τόξων ἔργον, εἰ δίκην ἔχεις;

22 κιχῇ *BP*.   23 λίπω *B* | τῶνδε φιλτάτην Schol. on *Hippol.* 1437] τῶνδε φιλτάτων *B* a τήνδε φιλτάτην *S*.   25 ἱερῇ with ερέα written above the ερῇ *L* ἱερῇ r. ἱερέα Monk.   26 σύμμετρος *P* (and Nauck ex conj.)] συμμέτρως r. | φθινόντων Wecklein] θανόντων MSS.   27 ἦμαρ *L*] ἧμαρ r.   28 ΘΑΝΑΤΟΣ] *P* has χͬρ (= χάρων) here, and the same abbreviation prefixed to 43, 45, etc.; but the same MS. has θᾰ (= θάνατος) prefixed to 39 and 72. ἆ ἆ *L* ἆ ἆ ἆ ἆ *l*.   29 σὺ πρὸς] σοι πρὸς *B*.   31 is not in *P*, and was rejected by Nauck without knowledge of that fact.   33 διακωλῦσαι *P l a*] διακωλύσαι r.   37 αὐτὴ *a*] αὐτὴν r.   38 τοι] τε *S*.

ΑΛΚΗΣΤΙΣ.

ΑΠ. σύνηθες αἰεὶ ταῦτα βαστάζειν ἐμοί. 40
ΘΑ. καὶ τοῖσδέ γ' οἴκοις ἐκδίκως προσωφελεῖν.
ΑΠ. φίλου γὰρ ἀνδρὸς συμφοραῖς βαρύνομαι.
ΘΑ. καὶ νοσφιεῖς με τοῦδε δευτέρου νεκροῦ;
ΑΠ. ἀλλ' οὐδ' ἐκεῖνον πρὸς βίαν σ' ἀφειλόμην.
ΘΑ. πῶς οὖν ὑπὲρ γῆς ἐστι κοὐ κάτω χθονός; 45
ΑΠ. δάμαρτ' ἀμείψας, ἣν σὺ νῦν ἥκεις μέτα.
ΘΑ. κἀπάξομαί γε νερτέραν ὑπὸ χθόνα.
ΑΠ. λαβὼν ἴθ'· οὐ γὰρ οἶδ' ἂν εἰ πείσαιμί σε.
ΘΑ. κτείνειν γ' ὃν ἂν χρῇ; τοῦτο γὰρ τετάγμεθα.
ΑΠ. οὔκ, ἀλλὰ τοῖς μέλλουσι θάνατον ἀμβαλεῖν. 50
ΘΑ. ἔχω λόγον δὴ καὶ προθυμίαν σέθεν.
ΑΠ. ἔστ' οὖν ὅπως Ἄλκηστις ἐς γῆρας μόλοι;
ΘΑ. οὐκ ἔστι· τιμαῖς κἀμὲ τέρπεσθαι δόκει.
ΑΠ. οὔτοι πλέον γ' ἂν ἢ μίαν ψυχὴν λάβοις.
ΘΑ. νέων φθινόντων μεῖζον ἄρνυμαι γέρας. 55
ΑΠ. κἂν γραῦς ὄληται, πλουσίως ταφήσεται.
ΘΑ. πρὸς τῶν ἐχόντων, Φοῖβε, τὸν νόμον τιθεῖς.
ΑΠ. πῶς εἶπας; ἀλλ' ἦ καὶ σοφὸς λέληθας ὤν;
ΘΑ. ὠνοῖντ' ἂν οἷς πάρεστι γηραιοὶ θανεῖν.
ΑΠ. οὔκουν δοκεῖ σοι τήνδε μοι δοῦναι χάριν; 60
ΘΑ. οὐ δῆτ'· ἐπίστασαι δὲ τοὺς ἐμοὺς τρόπους.
ΑΠ. ἐχθρούς γε θνητοῖς καὶ θεοῖς στυγουμένους.

40 αἰεὶ L] ἀεὶ r. **41** ἐκδίκως S] ἐνδίκως r. **44** βίαν B a l] βία S. **45** ἔστηκ' οὐ B (corrected by b). | κατὰ χθονός P. **46** μέτα L a] μετά r. **47** νερτέραν P l] νερτέρων r. **48** πείσοιμι B. **49** γ' ὃν B] ὃν r | χρῇ Schaefer] χρὴ MSS. **50** ἄλλα B | ἀμβαλεῖν Bursian] ἐμβαλεῖν MSS. **51** δὴ] γε S. **52** ἐς S] εἰς r. **53** δοκεῖ B. **54** οὔτοι B (corrected by b). **55** γέρας] κλέος S. **57** τιθεῖς] τιθεὶς P τίθης r. **58** ἦ P l] ἢ r. | λέληθας L] λέληθας B (with πέφυκας written above by B¹) ἐλήλυθας P πέφυκας a (with λέληθας written above by a¹). **59** ὠνοῖντ' L (with ω rewritten, and ο written over the ω and αι over the οι by l)] ὤνοιντ' P a ὄνοιντ' B ὄναιντ' l. | οἷς S] οὓς B a. | γηραιοὶ W. Dindorf] γηραιοὺς MSS. **60** οὐκ οὖν a.

ΘΑ. οὐκ ἂν δύναιο πάντ' ἔχειν ἃ μή σε δεῖ.
ΑΠ. ἦ μὴν σὺ κλαύσῃ καίπερ ὠμὸς ὢν ἄγαν.
τοῖος Φέρητος εἶσι πρὸς δόμους ἀνήρ, 65
Εὐρυσθέως πέμψαντος ἵππειον μέτα
ὄχημα Θρῄκης ἐκ τόπων δυσχειμέρων,
ὃς δὴ ξενωθεὶς τοῖσδ' ἐν Ἀδμήτου δόμοις
βίᾳ γυναῖκα τήνδε σ' ἐξαιρήσεται.
[κοὔθ' ἡ παρ' ἡμῶν σοι γενήσεται χάρις 70
δράσεις θ' ὁμοίως ταῦτ', ἀπεχθήσει τ' ἐμοί.]
ΘΑ. πόλλ' ἂν σὺ λέξας οὐδὲν ἂν πλέον λάβοις·
ἡ δ' οὖν γυνὴ κάτεισιν εἰς Ἅιδου δόμους.
στείχω δ' ἐπ' αὐτήν, ὡς κατάρξωμαι ξίφει·
ἱερὸς γὰρ οὗτος τῶν κατὰ χθονὸς θεῶν 75
ὅτου τόδ' ἔγχος κρατὸς ἁγνίσῃ τρίχα.

ΧΟΡΟΣ.

τί ποθ' ἡσυχία πρόσθεν μελάθρων;
τί σεσίγηται δόμος Ἀδμήτου;
ἀλλ' οὐδὲ φίλων πέλας ⟨ἔστ'⟩ οὐδείς,
ὅστις ἂν εἴποι πότερον φθιμένην 80
χρὴ βασίλειαν πενθεῖν, ἢ ζῶσ'

64 κλαύσῃ Earle] παύσῃ MSS. 70, 71 were rejected as spurious by W. Dindorf. 73 ἡ δ' *L a*] ἥδ' *r* (with *l*). 74 κατάρξωμαι *P* (with Macrobius Sat. V. 19, 4)] κατάρξομαι *r*. 75 τῶν θεῶν] τῷ θεῷ Macrobius *l. l.* 76 ὅτου τόδ'] ὃ τοῦτο δ' *B* ὅτῳ τόδ' Macrobius *l. l.* | ἁγνίσει *S*. ΧΟΡΟΣ] χορ. was prefixed in *S*, ἡμιχ. *r*. | πρόσθεν Blomfield] πρόσθε MSS. 79 ἡμιχ. is prefixed in the MSS., but was rejected by Kirchhoff. | πέλας ⟨ἔστ'⟩ οὐδείς Monk] πέλας οὐδείς MSS. (in *L* τις has been inserted after φίλων by *l*). 80 εἴποι *B a*] εἴποι (with ἐνί written above the εἰ by *l*) *L* ἐννέποι *P*. 81 χρὴ βασίλειαν πενθεῖν Blomfield] βασίλειαν πενθεῖν χρή MSS. (in *L* a has been written above χρή and β above πενθεῖν by *l*).

ΑΛΚΗΣΤΙΣ.

ἔτι φῶς λεύσσει Πελίου τόδε παῖς
Ἄλκηστις, ἐμοὶ πᾶσί τ' ἀρίστη
δόξασα γυνὴ
πόσιν εἰς αὐτῆς γεγενῆσθαι. 85

ΗΜΙΧ. κλύει τις ἢ στεναγμὸν ἢ   στρ.
χειρῶν κτύπον κατὰ στέγας
ἢ γόον ὡς πεπραγμένων;
ΗΜΙΧ. οὐ μὰν οὐδέ τις ἀμφιπόλων
στατίζεται ἀμφὶ πύλας. 90
εἰ γὰρ μετακύμιος ἄτας,
ὦ Παιάν, φανείης.
ΗΜΙΧ. οὔ τἂν φθιμένης γ' ἐσιώπων.
⟨ΗΜΙΧ.⟩ νέκυς ἤδη.
ΗΜΙΧ. οὐ δὴ φροῦδός γ' ἐξ οἴκων.
ΗΜΙΧ. πόθεν; οὐκ αὐχῶ. τί σε θαρσύνει; 95
ΗΜΙΧ. πῶς ἂν ἔρημον . . .
τάφον Ἄδμητος
κεδνῆς ἂν ἔπραξε γυναικός;
ΗΜΙΧ. πυλῶν πάροιθε δ' οὐχ ὁρῶ   ἀντιστρ.
πηγαῖον ὡς νομίζεται
χέρνιβ' ἐπὶ φθιτῶν πυλαῖς. 100
⟨ΗΜΙΧ.⟩ χαίτα τ' οὔτις ἐπὶ προθύροις
τομαῖος, ἃ δὴ νεκύων

82 λεύσσει Πελίου τόδε Bothe] τόδε λεύσσει (λεύσει B Γ) πελίου MSS. 85 αὐτῆς Schaefer] αὐτῆς MSS. 87 χειρῶν Nauck] χερῶν MSS. 88 γόον L] γόων r. 90 στατίζεται G. Hermann] στατίζετ' MSS. 91 ἡμιχ. is prefixed in B a L, but not in P. | εἰ S] εἴ B εἴ a. 92 ὦ Matthiae] ἰώ MSS. 93 οὔ τἂν Matthiae] οὔτ' ἂν MSS. | φθιμένης Monk] φθιμένας MSS. 94 In the MSS. the words νέκυς ἤδη (ἤδη νέκυς P, ἤδη deleted in L by l) come directly after οἴκων. Kirchhoff transposed them as in the text, and prefixed to them ΗΜΙΧ. | οὐ γὰρ δὴ MSS. γὰρ was rejected from the text by Kirchhoff. 96 Earle conjectured that the lacuna is after ἔρημον. 99 πηγαῖ' l. 100 φθιτῶν S] φθιμένον r. 101 ΗΜΙΧ., which is not in the MSS., was added by Hartung. | χαίτα τ' S a] χαίτη B.

ΕΥΡΙΠΙΔΟΥ

   πένθει πίτνει· οὐ νεολαία
   δουπεῖ χεὶρ γυναικῶν.
ΗΜΙΧ. καὶ μὴν τόδε κύριον ἦμαρ,   105
ΗΜΙΧ. τί τόδ' αὐδᾷς;
ΗΜΙΧ. ᾧ χρή σφε μολεῖν κατὰ γαίας.
ΗΜΙΧ. ἔθιγες ψυχάς, ἔθιγες δὲ φρενῶν.
ΗΜΙΧ. χρὴ τῶν ἀγαθῶν διακναιομένων
   πενθεῖν ὅστις   110
   χρηστὸς ἀπ' ἀρχῆς νενόμισται.
ΧΟ. ἀλλ' οὐδὲ ναυκληρίαν   στρ.
   ἔσθ' ὅποι τις αἴας
   στείλας ἢ Λυκίαν
   εἴτ' ἐφ' ἕδρας ἀνύδρους   115
   Ἀμμωνιάδας
   δυστάνου παραλῦσαι
   ψυχάν· μόρος γὰρ ἀπότομος
   πλάθει· θεῶν δ' ἐπ' ἐσχάραν
   οὐκέτ' ἔχω τίνα μηλοθύταν πορευθῶ.   120
   μόνος δ' ἄν, εἰ φῶς τόδ' ἦν   ἀντιστρ.
   ὄμμασιν δεδορκὼς
   Φοίβου παῖς, προλιποῦσ'
   ἦλθεν ἕδρας σκοτίους   125

  103 πένθεσι S | πίτνει Elmsley] πιτνεῖ MSS. | οὐ Aldine] οὐδὲ MSS. | before οὐδέ B and a have ἡμιχ., which is not found in L and P. | νεολαία B P l] νεολαῖα r. **105** ἦμαρ L] ἦμαρ r.   **107** stands before 106 in L and P.   **106** ΗΜΙΧ.] χορ. L.   **107** ἡμιχ. B (and a³)] not in r. | χρῆν P.   **108** ΗΜΙΧ.] χορ S. P has ἡμιχ. before the second ἔθιγες.   **109** ἡμιχ. a (?)] χορ. S.   B has no sign. **112** χορ. B and a.   S has no designation of the part.   **114** Λυκίαν Monk] Λυκίας MSS.   **115** εἴτ' ἐφ' ἕδρας ἀνύδρους Ἀμμωνιάδας Nauck] εἴτ' ἐπὶ τὰς ἀνύδρους Ἀμμωνιάδας ἕδρας MSS.   **117** παραλῦσαι B (and a²)] παραλύσαι r.   **118** ψυχάν S] ψυχῆς B ψυχὰς a (but a³ has changed the grave to the circumflex and written ἦν above). | ἀπότομος Blomfield] ἀπό**mos L ἀπότμος B ἀποτμος r (with l).   **119** ff. δ' ἐπ' ἐσχάραν οὐκέτ' ἔχω τίνα Hartung] δ' ἐπ' ἐσχάραις οὐκ ἔχω ἐπὶ τίνα (ἔχω 'πὶ L) MSS. See Critical Notes.   **123** ὄμμασιν Barnes] ὄμμασι MSS.   **125** σκοτίας B.

ΑΛΚΗΣΤΙΣ.

Ἅιδα τε πύλας·
δμαθέντας γὰρ ἀνίστη,
πρὶν αὐτὸν εἷλε Διόβολον
πλῆκτρον πυρὸς κεραυνίου.
νῦν δὲ βίου τίν' ἔτ' ἐλπίδα προσδέχωμαι; 130
—— πάντα γὰρ ἤδη τετέλεσται
βασιλεῦσιν,
πάντων δὲ θεῶν ⟨εἰσ'⟩ ἐπὶ βωμοῖς
αἱμόρραντοι θυσίαι πληρεῖς,
οὐδ' ἔστι κακῶν ἄκος οὐδέν. 135
ἀλλ' ἥδ' ὀπαδῶν ἐκ δόμων τις ἔρχεται
δακρυρροοῦσα· τίνα τύχην ἀκούσομαι;
πενθεῖν μέν, εἴ τι δεσπόταισι τυγχάνει,
συγγνωστόν· εἰ δ' ἔτ' ἐστὶν ἔμψυχος γυνὴ
εἴτ' οὖν ὄλωλεν εἰδέναι βουλοίμεθ' ἄν. 140

ΘΕΡΑΠΑΙΝΑ.

    καὶ ζῶσαν εἰπεῖν καὶ θανοῦσαν ἔστι σοι.
ΧΟ. καὶ πῶς ἂν αὐτὸς κατθάνοι τε καὶ βλέποι;
ΘΕ. ἤδη προνωπής ἐστι καὶ ψυχορραγεῖ. 143
ΧΟ. ἐλπὶς μὲν οὐκέτ' ἐστὶ σῴζεσθαι βίον; 146
ΘΕ. πεπρωμένη γὰρ ἡμέρα βιάζεται.
ΧΟ. οὔκουν ἐπ' αὐτῇ πράσσεται τὰ πρόσφορα;

---

126 ἄδα S ἀΐδα r. 129 πλᾶκτρον P (with l). 130 βίου τίν' ἔτ' Hartung] τίν' ἔτι βίου B τίν' ἐπὶ βίου a τίνα βίου S. 131 προσδέχωμαι Musgrave] προσδέχομαι MSS. 132 βασιλεῦσιν L a] βασιλεῦσι B P. 133 εἰσ' was inserted by Mekler. 135 οὐδ' S] ἀλλ' οὐδ' r. 136 χορ. is prefixed in B. | ὀπαδῶν P l] ὀπαδός L ὀπαδῶν r. 140 βουλοίμεθ' ἄν L a] βουλοίμεθα r. 141 is omitted in B, but has been added by a later hand. 142 πῶς] πῶ B. | αὐτὸς Kirchhoff (?) αὐτὸς MSS. (αὐτὸς Gaisford, ωὑτὸς Aldine.) | βλέποι L a p] βλέπει B βλέπ* P. 146 σώσασθαι S. 148 οὔκουν Elmsley] οὐκοῦν B L οὐκ οὖν r. | αὐτοῖς S.

ΘΕ. κόσμος γ' ἕτοιμος, ᾧ σφε συνθάψει πόσις.
ΧΟ. ὦ τλῆμον, οἵας οἷος ὢν ἁμαρτάνεις. 144
ΘΕ. οὔπω τόδ' οἶδε δεσπότης πρὶν ἂν πάθῃ. 145
ΧΟ. ἴστω νυν εὐκλεής γε κατθανουμένη 150
γυνή τ' ἀρίστη τῶν ὑφ' ἡλίῳ μακρῷ.
ΘΕ. πῶς δ' οὐκ ἀρίστη; τίς δ' ἐναντιώσεται
τὸ μὴ οὐ γενέσθαι τήνδ' ὑπερβεβλημένην
γυναῖκα; πῶς δ' ἂν μᾶλλον ἐνδείξαιτό τις
πόσιν προτιμῶσ' ἢ θέλουσ' ὑπερθανεῖν; 155
καὶ ταῦτα μὲν δὴ πᾶσ' ἐπίσταται πόλις·
ἃ δ' ἐν δόμοις ἔδρασε θαυμάσῃ κλύων.
ἐπεὶ γὰρ ᾔσθεθ' ἡμέραν τὴν κυρίαν
ἥκουσαν, ὕδασι ποταμίοις λευκὸν χρόα
ἐλούσατ', ἐκ δ' ἑλοῦσα κεδρίνων δόμων 160
ἐσθῆτα κόσμον τ' εὐπρεπῶς ἠσκήσατο,
καὶ στᾶσα πρόσθεν ἑστίας κατηύξατο·
δέσποιν', ἐγὼ γὰρ ἔρχομαι κατὰ χθονός,
πανύστατόν σε προσπίτνουσ' αἰτήσομαι,
τέκν' ὀρφανεῦσαι τἀμά· καὶ τῷ μὲν φίλην 165
σύζευξον ἄλοχον, τῇ δὲ γενναῖον πόσιν.
μηδ' ὥσπερ αὐτῶν ἡ τεκοῦσ' ἀπόλλυμαι
θανεῖν ἀώρους παῖδας, ἀλλ' εὐδαίμονας
ἐν γῇ πατρῴᾳ τερπνὸν ἐκπλῆσαι βίον.
πάντας δὲ βωμοὺς οἳ κατ' Ἀδμήτου δόμους 170
προσῆλθε κἀξέστεψε καὶ προσηύξατο,

144 ὦ] ὣ B. 145 πάθῃ] πάθη P πάθοι r. The insertion of 144-5 after 149 was suggested by H. Mueller. 150 ἰστώ B | νυν l] νῦν r. In L the παράγραφος is prefixed to 151 and 152, so that 152 ff. are assigned to the chorus. In P θερ. (= θεράπαινα) is prefixed to 151 and τροφ. (= τροφός) to 152. | 151 μακρῶν B. 153 τὸ μὴ οὐ — τήνδ' Lenting] τί χρὴ — τὴν MSS. 157 θαυμάσῃ] θαυμάσῃ B (with ει written above η by b) θαυμάσεις L (with η written above the εις by l). 164 προσπίτνουσ' a] προσπιτνοῦσ' r (and a³). 167 ἀπόλλυται S.

ΑΛΚΗΣΤΙΣ.

πτόρθων ἀποσχίζουσα μυρσίνης φόβην,
ἄκλαυστος ἀστένακτος, οὐδὲ τοὐπιὸν
κακὸν μεθίστη χρωτὸς εὐειδῆ φύσιν.
κἄπειτα θάλαμον ἐσπεσοῦσα καὶ λέχος, 175
ἐνταῦθα δὴ 'δάκρυσε καὶ λέγει τάδε·
ὦ λέκτρον, ἔνθα παρθένει' ἔλυσ' ἐγὼ
[κορεύματ' ἐκ τοῦδ' ἀνδρός, οὗ θνῄσκω πέρι,]
χαῖρ'· οὐ γὰρ ἐχθαίρω σ'· ἀπώλεσας δέ με
μόνον: προδοῦναι γάρ σ' ὀκνοῦσα καὶ πόσιν 180
θνῄσκω. σὲ δ' ἄλλη τις γυνὴ κεκτήσεται,
σώφρων μὲν οὐκ ἂν μᾶλλον, εὐτυχὴς δ' ἴσως.
κυνεῖ δὲ προσπίτνουσα, πᾶν δὲ δέμνιον
ὀφθαλμοτέγκτῳ δεύεται πλημμυρίδι·
ἐπεὶ δὲ πολλῶν δακρύων ἔσχεν κόρον, 185
στείχει προνωπὴς ἐκπεσοῦσα δεμνίων,
καὶ πολλὰ θάλαμον ἐξιοῦσ' ἐπεστράφη
κἄρριψεν αὑτὴν αὖθις ἐς κοίτην πάλιν.
παῖδες δὲ πέπλων μητρὸς ἐξηρτημένοι
ἔκλαιον· ἡ δὲ λαμβάνουσ' ἐς ἀγκάλας 190
ἠσπάζετ' ἄλλοτ' ἄλλον, ὡς θανουμένη.
πάντες δ' ἔκλαιον οἰκέται κατὰ στέγας
δέσποιναν οἰκτίροντες. ἡ δὲ δεξιὰν
προύτειν' ἑκάστῳ, κοὔτις ἦν οὕτω κακὸς
ὃν οὐ προσεῖπε καὶ προσερρήθη πάλιν. 195

172 πόρθων B (with τ written above the π by b). | μυρσινῶν S. **173** ἄκλαυστος L. **176** 'δάκρυσε Heath] δάκρυσε MSS. **178** rejected as spurious by Nauck. **180** μόνον Blomfield] μόνην MSS. **182** οὐχὶ Suidas s. v. κλέπτης. **183** κύνει S. | προσπίτνουσα Elmsley] προσπιτνοῦσα B S (in L πιπ was written at first, but has been altered to πιτ by L¹) προσπίπτουσα a. **184** ὀφθαλμοτέγκτῳ P (and a³)] ὀφθαλμοτέκτῳ r. | δεύετο S (with an erasure in P above the o). **185** ἔσχεν Earle] εἶχεν S εἶχε r. **186** πνονωπὴς B (with προ written above πνο by b). **188** αὑτὴν L] αὐτὴν r. **190** ἐν ἀγκάλαις S. **194** πρότειν' B.

τοιαῦτ' ἐν οἴκοις ἐστὶν Ἀδμήτου κακά.
καὶ κατθανών γ' ἂν ὤλετ'· ἐκφυγὼν δ' ἔχει
τοσοῦτον ἄλγος οὔποθ' οὗ λελήσεται.
ΧΟ. ἦ που στενάζει τοισίδ' Ἄδμητος κακοῖς,
ἐσθλῆς γυναικὸς εἰ στερηθῆναί σφε χρή; 200
ΘΕ. κλαίει γ' ἄκοιτιν ἐν χεροῖν φίλην ἔχων,
καὶ μὴ προδοῦναι λίσσεται, τἀμήχανα
ζητῶν· φθίνει γὰρ καὶ μαραίνεται νόσῳ.
παρειμένη δέ, χειρὸς ἄθλιον βάρος,
ὅμως δέ, καίπερ σμικρόν, ἐμπνέουσ' ἔτι, 205
βλέψαι πρὸς αὐγὰς βούλεται τὰς ἡλίου.
[ὡς οὔποτ' αὖθις, ἀλλὰ νῦν πανύστατον
ἀκτῖνα κύκλον θ' ἡλίου προσόψεται.]
ἀλλ' εἶμι καὶ σὴν ἀγγελῶ παρουσίαν·
οὐ γάρ τι πάντες εὖ φρονοῦσι κοιράνοις, 210
ὥστ' ἐν κακοῖσιν εὐμενεῖς παρεστάναι·
σὺ δ' εἶ παλαιὸς δεσπόταις ἐμοῖς φίλος.
ΗΜΙΧ. ἰὼ Ζεῦ, τίς ἂν πῶς πᾷ πόρος κακῶν στρ.
γένοιτο καὶ λύσις τύχας ἃ πάρεστι κοιράνοις;
ΗΜΙΧ. ἔξεισί τις; ἢ τέμω τρίχα, 215
καὶ μέλανα στολμὸν πέπλων
ἀμφιβαλώμεθ' ἤδη;
ΗΜΙΧ. δῆλα μέν, φίλοι, δῆλά γ', ἀλλ' ὅμως

197 κατθανών γ' second Hervagian edition] κατθανών τ' MSS. | τ' ἔχει P. **198** οὔποθ' οὗ Nauck] οὔποτ' οὐ L a οὐ ποτ' οὐ B L οὐ ποτ' οὐ a² οὔποτε P. | λήσεται L. **199** τοισίδ'] τοῖσιδ' B a τοῖσιν S. **200** εἰ S] ἧς B (and a²) ἦι α | σφε S a] γε B. **205** The punctuation in the text was suggested by F. D. Allen. **207, 208** That these lines are an interpolation from Hecuba 411, 412 was pointed out by Valckenaer. **211** παριστάναι P πα**στάναι L παρεστάναι l. B a P assign 213-43 to the chorus; L assigns 213-17 to the chorus, 218-25 to the θεράπαινα, and 226-43 to the chorus. The assignment in the text follows Wecklein. **213** ἂν πῶς πᾷ B] ἄν πως παῖ * P ἄν πως ** L ἂν πᾶ a. **215** τέμω G. Hermann] τεμῶ MSS. **218** γ'] δ B.

ΑΛΚΗΣΤΙΣ.

θεοῖσιν εὐχώμεσθα· θεῶν γὰρ δύναμις μεγίστη.
ΧΟ. ὦναξ Παιάν, 220
ἔξευρε μηχανάν τιν' Ἀδμήτῳ κακῶν,
πόριζε δὴ πόριζε· καὶ πάρος γὰρ
τοῦτ' ἐφηῦρες, [καὶ νῦν]
λυτήριος ἐκ θανάτου γενοῦ,
φόνιον δ' ἀπόπαυσον Ἅιδαν. 225
ΗΜΙΧ. παπαῖ . . . . ἀντιστρ.
ὦ παῖ Φέρητος, οἷα πράξεις δάμαρτος σᾶς στερείς.
ΗΜΙΧ. ἆρ' ἄξια καὶ σφαγᾶς τάδε
καὶ πλέον ἢ βρόχῳ δέρην
† οὐρανίῳ πελάσσαι; 230
ΗΜΙΧ. τὰν γὰρ οὐ φίλαν ἀλλὰ φιλτάταν
γυναῖκα κατθανοῦσαν ἐν ἤματι τῷδ' ἐπόψει.
ΧΟ. ἰδοὺ ἰδού,
ἥδ' ἐκ δόμων δὴ καὶ πόσις πορεύεται.
βόασον ὦ στέναξον, ὦ Φεραία
χθών, [τὰν] ἀρίσταν 235
γυναῖκα μαραινομέναν νόσῳ
χθόνιον κατὰ γᾶς παρ' Ἅιδαν.

219 εὐχώμεσθα a d (Flor. 31, 15) l] εὐχώμεθα L εὐχόμεθα P ἐχώμεθα B | δύναμις B] ἁ δύναμις r | μεγίστη B L P] μεγιστᾶ a μεγίστα C d. 220 ὦναξ B. 221 μηχανάν τιν' S] μηχανήν τιν' a μηχανὴν ἥντιν' B. 223 τοῦτ' Monk] τοῦδ' MSS. | [καὶ νῦν] was bracketed by Monk as an interpolation. 225 δ'] τ' S. | Ἅιδαν Heath] ἄϊδαν MSS. 226 παπαῖ ὦ B a] παῖ παῖ φεῦ φεῦ ἰὼ ἰώ S. The lacuna after παπαῖ was first marked by W. Dindorf. 227 οἷα πράξεις Jacobs] οἷ' ἔπραξας MSS. | σᾶς] σῆς P τῆς σῆς L | στερεῖς Monk] στερηθεὶς MSS. 228 ἆρ' G. Hermann] αἲ αἲ P αἲ αἲ L αἲ αἲ αἲ αἲ B αἲ αἲ αἲ αἲ a. 229 καὶ is omitted in a | πλεῖον S. 230 † οὐρανίῳ] see Critical Notes. | πελάσσαι Erfurdt] πελάσαι MSS. 231 φιλτάτην S. 232 εἰν W. Dindorf] ἐν MSS. | ἤματι B L P] ἄματι d a³ ἄματι a. | τῷδε γ' ὄψει S. 233 ἰδοὺ ἰδού was not in S. 234 στέναξον ὦ βόασον (βόησον P) ὦ S. 235 [ταν] rejected as an interpolation by Erfurdt. 237 χθόνιον κατὰ γᾶς Weil] κατὰ γᾶν χθόνιον MSS. (but γᾶς B). Ἅιδαν] ἄδαν S ἀΐδαν r.

ΕΥΡΙΠΙΔΟΥ

———— οὔποτε φήσω γάμον εὐφραίνειν
πλέον ἢ λυπεῖν, τοῖς τε πάροιθεν
τεκμαιρόμενος καὶ τάσδε τύχας 240
λεύσσων βασιλέως, ὅστις ἀρίστης
ἀπλακὼν ἀλόχου τῆσδ' ἀβίωτον
τὸν ἔπειτα χρόνον βιοτεύσει.

ΑΛΚΗΣΤΙΣ.

Ἅλιε καὶ φάος ἁμέρας, στρ.
οὐράνιαί τε δῖναι νεφέλας δρομαίου. 245

ΑΔΜΗΤΟΣ.

ὁρᾷ σὲ κἀμέ, δύο κακῶς πεπραγότας,
οὐδὲν θεοὺς δράσαντας ἀνθ' ὅτου θανῇ.
ΑΛ. γαῖά τε καὶ μελάθρων στέγαι ἀντιστρ.
νυμφίδιοί τε κοῖται πατρῴας Ἰωλκοῦ.
ΑΔ. ἔπαιρε σαυτήν, ὦ τάλαινα, μὴ προδῷς· 250
λίσσου δὲ τοὺς κρατοῦντας οἰκτῖραι θεούς.
ΑΛ. ὁρῶ δίκωπον ὁρῶ σκάφος [ἐν λίμνᾳ], στρ.
νεκύων δὲ πορθμεὺς
ἔχων χέρ' ἐπὶ κοντῷ Χάρων μἤδη καλεῖ· τί μέλλεις;
ἐπείγου· σὺ κατείργεις. τάδε τοί με 255
σπερχόμενος ταχύνει.

239 πάροιθεν *L*] πάροιθε *r*. **241** λεύσσων] λεύσων καὶ *S* (but in *L* καὶ has been deleted by *l*). | ὅστις] in *L* the τις has been deleted. **242** ἀπλακὼν Wakefield] ἀμπλακών *S* ἀμπλακῶν *r* (in *B* λ is a correction by *B*¹ from some other letter). **244** ἡμέρας *S*. **247** θανεῖν *L*. **249** νυμφίδιαι *S*. | **252** ὁρῶ before σκάφος has been erased in *L*. | [ἐν λίμνᾳ] omitted in the Aldine ed., bracketed by Prinz. **254** χέρ' Aldine] χεῖρ' MSS. **256** τάδε τοί με *B a*] τάδ' ἕτοιμα *S*.

ΑΛΚΗΣΤΙΣ.

ΑΔ. οἴμοι, πικράν γε τήνδε μοι ναυκληρίαν
ἔλεξας. ὦ δύσδαιμον, οἷα πάσχομεν.
ΑΛ. ἄγει μ' ἄγει μέ τις, οὐκ ὁρᾶς; *ἀντιστρ.*
νεκύων ἐς αὐλὰν 260
ὑπ' ὄφρυσι κυαναυγέσι βλέπων, πτερωτὸς Ἄιδας.
τί ῥέξεις; ἄφες. οἵαν ὁδὸν ἁ δει-
λαιοτάτα προβαίνω.
ΑΔ. οἰκτρὰν φίλοισιν, ἐκ δὲ τῶν μάλιστ' ἐμοὶ
καὶ παισίν, οἷς δὴ πένθος ἐν κοινῷ τόδε. 265
ΑΛ. μέθετε μέθετέ μ' ἤδη,
κλίνατ', οὐ σθένω ποσίν·
πλησίον Ἄιδας.
σκοτία δ' ἐπ' ὄσσοις νὺξ ἐφέρπει.
τέκνα, τέκν' οὐκέτι δὴ 270
οὐκέτι μάτηρ σφῶν ἔστιν.
χαίροντες, ὦ τέκνα, τόδε φάος ὁρῶτον.
ΑΔ. οἴμοι· τόδ' ἔπος λυπρὸν ἀκούω
καὶ παντὸς ἐμοὶ θανάτου μεῖζον.
μὴ πρός ⟨σε⟩ θεῶν τλῇς με προδοῦναι, 275
μὴ πρὸς παιδῶν οὓς ὀρφανιεῖς,
ἀλλ' ἄνα τόλμα·
σοῦ γὰρ φθιμένης οὐκέτ' ἂν εἴην·
ἐν σοὶ δ' ἡμῖν καὶ ζῆν καὶ μή·
σὴν γὰρ φιλίαν σεβόμεσθα.

259 ἄγει μ' ἄγει με τις *l*] ἄγει * ἄγει με τις *L* ἄγει ἄγει μέ τις *P* ἄγει μ' ἄγει τίς *B* ἄγει μ' ἄγει τίς ἄγει μέ τις *a*.   260 ἐς *P*] εἰς *r* (and so corrected in *P*, whether by *P*¹ or not is uncertain).   261 ἄδας *P* ἄδης *L* αἴδας *r*.   262 τί ῥέξεις *S*] μέθες με τί ῥέξεις (πράξεις *B*) *r*.   263 δειλαι ** *L* δειλαία *l*.   266 μέθετε μέθετε μ *S*] μέθετε με μέθετε μ' *r*.   267 κλίνατ'] κλίνατέ μ' *S* | ποσίν Hermann] ποσί *L* πόσι *r*.   268 ἄδας *S* αἴδας *r*.   269 ὅσσοισι *P* ὅσσοισιν *L*.   270 τέκν' *L*] τέκνα *r*.   271 οὐκέτι δὴ *S* | σφῶν *S*] σφῶιν *r*. | ἔστιν *L* ἐστὶ *r*.   273 ὤμοι *P L*¹.   275 πρός σε θεῶν Porson] πρὸς θεῶν MSS.   276 not in *S*.   277 ἄνα τόλμα *l*] ἄνα τόλμα *B* ἀνατόλμα *r*.   278 ἡμῖν Wecklein] ἐσμὲν MSS.   279 σεβόμεθα *S* (corrected in *L* by *l*).

ΑΛ. Ἄδμηθ', ὁρᾷς γὰρ τἀμὰ πράγμαθ' ὡς ἔχει, 280
λέξαι θέλω σοι πρὶν θανεῖν ἃ βούλομαι.
ἐγώ σε πρεσβεύουσα κἀντὶ τῆς ἐμῆς
ψυχῆς καταστήσασα φῶς τόδ' εἰσορᾶν
θνήσκω, παρόν μοι μὴ θανεῖν ὑπὲρ σέθεν,
ἀλλ' ἄνδρα τε σχεῖν Θεσσαλῶν ὃν ἤθελον 285
καὶ δῶμα ναίειν ὄλβιον τυραννίδι.
οὐκ ἠθέλησα ζῆν ἀποσπασθεῖσά σου
σὺν παισὶν ὀρφανοῖσιν, οὐδ' ἐφεισάμην,
ἥβης ἔχουσα δῶρ', ἐν οἷς ἐτερπόμην.
καίτοι σ' ὁ φύσας χἠ τεκοῦσα προύδοσαν, 290
καλῶς μὲν αὐτοῖς †κατθανεῖν ἧκον βίου,
καλῶς δὲ σῶσαι παῖδα κεὐκλεῶς θανεῖν.
μόνος γὰρ αὐτοῖς ἦσθα, κοὔτις ἐλπὶς ἦν
σοῦ κατθανόντος ἄλλα φιτύσειν τέκνα.
κἀγώ τ' ἂν ἔζων καὶ σὺ τὸν λοιπὸν χρόνον, 295
κοὐκ ἂν μονωθεὶς σῆς δάμαρτος ἔστενες
καὶ παῖδας ὠρφάνευες, ἀλλὰ ταῦτα μὲν
θεῶν τις ἐξέπραξεν ὥσθ' οὕτως ἔχειν.
εἶεν· σὺ νῦν μοι τῶνδ' ἀπόμνησαι χάριν·
αἰτήσομαι γάρ σ' ἀξίαν μὲν οὔποτε· 300
ψυχῆς γὰρ οὐδέν ἐστι τιμιώτερον·
δίκαια δ', ὡς φήσεις σύ· τούσδε γὰρ φιλεῖς
οὐχ ἧσσον ἢ 'γὼ παῖδας, εἴπερ εὖ φρονεῖς·
τούτους ἀνάσχου δεσπότας τρέφων δόμων,

285 θεσσαλῶν a θεσσαλὸν r. 288 in L above οὐδ' l has written γρ. ἀλλ'. 289 ἔχουσα δῶρ' (so P, δῶρον L) ἐν οἷς ἐτερπόμην S] ἔχουσα δῶρ ἐν οἷς ἐτερπόμην ἐγώ B (but with ἐγώ deleted, by what hand is uncertain) ἔχους' ἐν οἷς ἐτερπόμην ἐγώ a. 291 see Critical Notes. 294 φιτύσειν B (and a in the margin by the first hand) φυτεύσειν r. 295 ἔζων B] ἔζην r (but in L the first hand has written ω above the η) with Etymol. Mag. p. 413, 9. 298 ἐξέπραξεν S] ἔπραξεν B (but with ἐξ written over the ἐπ by B¹) εἰσέπραξεν a. 299 νῦν μοι B] μοι νῦν a δή μοι L δ' ἡμῖν P. 304 τρέφων Wecklein] ἐμῶν MSS.

ΑΛΚΗΣΤΙΣ.

καὶ μὴ 'πιγήμῃς τοῖσδε μητρυιὰν τέκνοις,   305
ἥτις κακίων οὖσ' ἐμοῦ γυνὴ φθόνῳ
τοῖς σοῖσι κἀμοῖς παισὶ χεῖρα προσβαλεῖ.
μὴ δῆτα δράσῃς ταῦτά γ', αἰτοῦμαί σ' ἐγώ.
ἐχθρὰ γὰρ ἡ 'πιοῦσα μητρυιὰ τέκνοις
τοῖς πρόσθ', ἐχίδνης οὐδὲν ἠπιωτέρα.   310
καὶ παῖς μὲν ἄρσην πατέρ' ἔχει πύργον μέγαν,
[ὃν καὶ προσεῖπε καὶ προσερρήθη πάλιν]
σὺ δ', ὦ τέκνον μοι, πῶς κορευθήσει καλῶς,
τοίας τυχοῦσα συζύγου τῷ σῷ πατρί;
μή σοί τιν' αἰσχρὰν προσβαλοῦσα κληδόνα   315
ἥβης ἐν ἀκμῇ σοὺς διαφθείρῃ γάμους.
οὐ γάρ σε μήτηρ οὔτε νυμφεύσει ποτὲ
οὔτ' ἐν τόκοισι σοῖσι θαρσυνεῖ, τέκνον,
παροῦσ', ἵν' οὐδὲν μητρὸς εὐμενέστερον.
δεῖ γὰρ θανεῖν με, καὶ τόδ' οὐκ ἐς αὔριον   320
οὐδ' ἐς τρίτην μοι νηλὲς ἔρχεται κακόν,
ἀλλ' αὐτίκ' ἐν τοῖς μηκέτ' οὖσι λέξομαι.
χαίροντες εὐφραίνοισθε· καὶ σοὶ μέν, πόσι,
γυναῖκ' ἀρίστην ἔστι κομπάσαι λαβεῖν,
ὑμῖν δέ, παῖδες, μητρὸς ἐκπεφυκέναι.   325

ΧΟ. θάρσει· πρὸ τούτου γὰρ λέγειν οὐχ ἅζομαι·
δράσει τάδ', εἴπερ μὴ φρενῶν ἁμαρτάνει.

ΑΔ. ἔσται τάδ', ἔσται, μὴ τρέσῃς· ἐπεὶ σ' ἐγὼ
καὶ ζῶσαν εἶχον καὶ θανοῦσ' ἐμὴ γυνὴ
μόνη κεκλήσει, κοὔτις ἀντὶ σοῦ ποτε   330

---

310 B^1 has written δ' above the s of ἐχίδνης.   **312** rejected first by Pierson; cf. 195 and see Critical Notes.   **314** τοίας Reiske] ποίας MSS.   **318** σοῖσι θαρσυνεῖ τέκνον S] τοῖσι σοῖσι θαρσυνεῖ r.   **320** ἐς L] εἰς r.   **321-22** are omitted in the text of L, but have been added by L^1 in the margin.   **321** νηλὲς Hoefer] μηνὸς MSS.   **322** οὐκέτ' οὖσι S.   **326** οὐχ ἅζομαι B, and a^1] οὐ χάζομαι S (and a^2 and a^3).   **327** ἥνπερ and ἁμαρτάνῃ S.   **329** ἐμὴ] ἐμοῦ a.

ΕΥΡΙΠΙΔΟΥ

τόνδ' ἄνδρα νύμφη Θεσσαλὶς προσφθέγξεται.
οὐκ ἔστιν οὕτως οὔτε πατρὸς εὐγενοῦς
οὔτ' εἶδος ἄλλως εὐπρεπὴς οὕτω γυνή.
ἅλις δὲ παίδων· τῶνδ' ὄνησιν εὔχομαι
θεοῖς γενέσθαι· σοῦ γὰρ οὐκ ὠνήμεθα. 335
οἴσω δὲ πένθος οὐκ ἐτήσιον τὸ σόν,
ἀλλ' ἔστ' ἂν αἰὼν οὑμὸς ἀντέχῃ, γύναι,
στυγῶν μὲν ἥ μ' ἔτικτεν, ἐχθαίρων δ' ἐμὸν
πατέρα· λόγῳ γὰρ ἦσαν οὐκ ἔργῳ φίλοι.
σὺ δ' ἀντιδοῦσα τῆς ἐμῆς τὰ φίλτατα 340
ψυχῆς ἔσωσας. ἆρά μοι στένειν πάρα
τοιᾶσδ' ἁμαρτάνοντι συζύγου σέθεν;
παύσω δὲ κώμους συμποτῶν θ' ὁμιλίας
στεφάνους τε μοῦσάν θ', ἣ κατεῖχ' ἐμοὺς δόμους.
οὐ γάρ ποτ' οὔτ' ἂν βαρβίτου θίγοιμ' ἔτι 345
οὔτ' ἂν φρέν' ἐξαίροιμι πρὸς Λίβυν λακεῖν
αὐλόν· σὺ γάρ μου τέρψιν ἐξείλου βίου.
[σοφῇ δὲ χειρὶ τεκτόνων δέμας τὸ σὸν
εἰκασθὲν ἐν λέκτροισιν ἐκταθήσεται,
ᾧ προσπεσοῦμαι καὶ περιπτύσσων χέρας 350
ὄνομα καλῶν σὸν τὴν φίλην ἐν ἀγκάλαις
δόξω γυναῖκα καίπερ οὐκ ἔχων ἔχειν,
ψυχρὰν μέν, οἶμαι, τέρψιν, ἀλλ' ὅμως βάρος
ψυχῆς ἀπαντλοίην ἄν. ἐν δ' ὀνείρασι
φοιτῶσά μ' εὐφραίνοις ἄν· ἡδὺ γὰρ φίλους 355
κἂν νυκτὶ λεύσσειν χὥντιν' ἂν παρῇ τρόπον.]
εἰ δ' Ὀρφέως μοι γλῶσσα καὶ μέλος παρῆν,

333 εὐπρεπὴς οὕτω Wecklein] εὐπρεπεστάτη B a ἐκπρεπεστάτη S (in P ἐκ is written over an erasion). Perhaps ἐκπρεπὴς οὕτω is to be preferred. See Critical Notes. 337 οὑμός B. 344 κατεῖχεν ἐμοὺς B. 346 ἐξάροιμι S. 348–56 I have bracketed as an interpolation. 354 ἀπαντλείην B. 355 φίλους B] φίλοις r. 356 χὥντιν' Kvičala] ὄντιν' MSS. | τρόπον Prinz] χρόνον MSS. 357 γλῶττα S.

ΑΛΚΗΣΤΙΣ.

ὥστ᾽ ἢ κόρην Δήμητρος ἢ κείνης πόσιν
ὕμνοισι κηλήσαντά σ᾽ ἐξ Ἅιδου λαβεῖν,
κατῆλθον ἄν, καί μ᾽ οὔθ᾽ ὁ Πλούτωνος κύων 360
οὔθ᾽ οὑπὶ κώπῃ ψυχοπομπὸς ἂν Χάρων
ἔσχεν, πρὶν ἐς φῶς σὸν καταστῆσαι βίον.
ἀλλ᾽ οὖν ἐκεῖσε προσδόκα μ᾽, ὅταν θάνω,
καὶ δῶμ᾽ ἑτοίμαζ᾽, ὡς συνοικήσουσά μοι.
ἐν ταῖσιν αὐταῖς γάρ μ᾽ ἐπισκήψω κέδροις 365
σοὶ τούσδε θεῖναι πλευρά τ᾽ ἐκτεῖναι πέλας
πλευροῖσι τοῖς σοῖς· μηδὲ γὰρ θανών ποτε
σοῦ χωρὶς εἴην τῆς μόνης πιστῆς ἐμοί.

ΧΟ. καὶ μὴν ἐγώ σοι πένθος ὡς φίλος φίλῳ
λυπρὸν συνοίσω τῆσδε· καὶ γὰρ ἀξία. 370

ΑΛ. ὦ παῖδες, αὐτοὶ δὴ τάδ᾽ εἰσηκούσατε
πατρὸς λέγοντος μὴ γαμεῖν ἄλλην τινὰ
γυναῖκ᾽ ἐφ᾽ ὑμῖν μηδ᾽ ἀτιμάσειν ἐμέ.

ΑΔ. καὶ νῦν γέ φημι, καὶ τελευτήσω τάδε.

ΑΛ. ἐπὶ τοῖσδε παῖδας χειρὸς ἐξ ἐμῆς δέχου. 375

ΑΔ. δέχομαι, φίλον γε δῶρον ἐκ φίλης χερός.

ΑΛ. σὺ νῦν γενοῦ τοῖσδ᾽ ἀντ᾽ ἐμοῦ μήτηρ τέκνοις.

ΑΔ. πολλή μ᾽ ἀνάγκη, σοῦ γ᾽ ἀπεστερημένοις.

ΑΛ. ὦ τέκν᾽, ὅτε ζῆν χρῆν μ᾽, ἀπέρχομαι κάτω.

ΑΔ. οἴμοι, τί δράσω δῆτα σοῦ μονούμενος; 380

ΑΛ. χρόνος μαλάξει σ᾽· οὐδέν ἐσθ᾽ ὁ κατθανών.

ΑΔ. ἄγου με σὺν σοὶ πρὸς θεῶν ἄγου κάτω.

358 ὥστ᾽ ἢ Reiske] ὡς τὴν MSS. 362 ἔσχεν Lenting] ἔσχον MSS. 372 τινά] ποτέ S. 376 This verse is not in P, and in L is not in the text, but has been added in the margin by l. Hence in P 375 and 377 are given to Alcestis, and in L the lines which belong to Alcestis are assigned to Admetus and those of Admetus to her all the way down to 391. 378 μ᾽ Monk] γ᾽ MSS. 379 χρῆν μ᾽ c] χρή μ᾽ B a μ᾽ ἐχρῆν L (in P μ᾽ ἐχρῆν has been written by P¹ over an erasure above ἀπέρχομαι).

ΕΥΡΙΠΙΔΟΥ

ΑΛ. ἀρκοῦμεν ἡμεῖς οἱ προθνῄσκοντες σέθεν.
ΛΔ. ὦ δαῖμον, οἵας συζύγου μ' ἀποστερεῖς.
ΑΛ. καὶ μὴν σκοτεινὸν ὄμμα μου βαρύνεται.   385
ΑΔ. ἀπωλόμην ἄρ', εἴ με δὴ λείψεις, γύναι.
ΑΛ. ὡς οὐκέτ' οὖσαν οὐδὲν ἂν λέγοις ἐμέ.
ΛΔ. ὄρθου πρόσωπον, μὴ λίπῃς παῖδας σέθεν.
ΑΛ. οὐ δῆθ' ἑκοῦσά γ'. ἀλλὰ χαίρετ', ὦ τέκνα.
ΑΔ. βλέψον πρὸς αὐτοὺς βλέψον. ΑΛ. οὐδέν εἰμ' ἔτι. 390
ΑΔ. τί δρᾷς; προλείπεις; ΑΛ. χαῖρ'. ΑΔ. ἀπωλό-
         μην τάλας.
ΧΟ. βέβηκεν, οὐκέτ' ἔστιν Ἀδμήτου γυνή.

ΕΥΜΗΛΟΣ.

ἰώ μοι τύχας. μαῖα δὴ κάτω   στρ.
βέβακεν, οὐκέτ' ἔστιν, ὦ
πάτερ, ὑφ' ἁλίῳ.   395
προλιποῦσα δ' ἀμὸν βίον
ὠρφάνισεν τλάμων.
ἴδε γὰρ ἴδε βλέφαρον
καὶ παρατόνους χέρας.
ὑπάκουσον ἄκουσον, ὦ μᾶτερ, ἀντιάζω σ'·   400
ἐγώ σ', ἐγώ, μᾶτερ,
. . . καλοῦμαι ὁ
σὸς ποτὶ σοῖσι πίτνων στόμασιν νεοσσός.

386 ἄρ'] ἂν B.   389 χαιρέτω S.   391 προλείπεις L] προλείπεις με r | χαῖρ' L] χαῖρε r.   393 ἰώ μοι μοι L.   395 ἁλίῳ S] ἡλίῳ r.   397 ὠρφάνισεν Monk] ὠρφάνισε MSS.   399 χέρας a] χεράς B χεῖρας S.   400 ἀντιάζω σ' Monk] ἀντιάζω MSS.   401 ἐγώ σ' ἐγώ μᾶτηρ P l] ἐγώ σε γὰρ μᾶτηρ L, σ' ἐγώ, μᾶτερ, ἐγώ B a.   402 ὁ S] σ' ὁ r.   403 πίτνων a] πιτνῶν r | στόμασιν Barnes] στόμασι MSS.

ΑΛΚΗΣΤΙΣ.

ΑΔ. τὴν οὐ κλύουσαν οὐδ᾽ ὁρῶσαν· ὥστ᾽ ἐγὼ
καὶ σφὼ βαρείᾳ συμφορᾷ πεπλήγμεθα. 405
ΕΥ. νέος ἐγώ, πάτερ, λείπομαι φίλας   ἀντιστρ.
μονόστολός τε ματρός· ὦ
σχέτλια δὴ παθὼν
ἐγὼ ἔργα . . . σύ τε
σύγκασί μοι κούρα 410
. . . συνέτλας·
. . . ὦ πάτερ,
ἀνόνατ᾽ ἀνόνατ᾽ ἐνύμφευσας οὐδὲ γήρως
ἔβας τέλος σὺν τᾷδ᾽·
ἔφθιτο γὰρ πάρος,
οἰχομένας δὲ σοῦ, μᾶτερ, ὄλωλεν οἶκος. 415
ΧΟ. Ἄδμητ᾽, ἀνάγκη τάσδε συμφορὰς φέρειν·
οὐ γὰρ σὺ πρῶτος οὐδὲ λοίσθιος βροτῶν
γυναικὸς ἐσθλῆς ἤμπλακες· γίγνωσκε δὲ
ὡς πᾶσιν ἡμῖν κατθανεῖν ὀφείλεται.
ΑΔ. ἐπίσταμαί γε κοὐκ ἄφνω κακὸν τόδε 420
προσέπτατ᾽· εἰδὼς δ᾽ αὔτ᾽ ἐτειρόμην πάλαι.
ἀλλ᾽ ἐκφορὰν γὰρ τοῦδε θήσομαι νεκροῦ,
πάρεστε καὶ μένοντες ἀντηχήσατε
παιᾶνα τῷ κάτωθεν ἀσπόνδῳ θεῷ.
πᾶσιν δὲ Θεσσαλοῖσιν ὧν ἐγὼ κρατῶ 425
πένθος γυναικὸς τῆσδε κοινοῦσθαι λέγω
κουρᾷ ξυρήκει καὶ μελαμπέπλῳ στολῇ·

406 πάτερ λείπομαι S] λείπομαι πάτερ r.   407 τε S] not in r.   409 ff. the lacunas were indicated as in the text by G. Hermann, who also transposed σύγκασι, which in the MSS. follows μοι. S has τ᾽ ἐμοὶ σύγκασι, r τε μοι σύγκασι. 412 ἀνόνατ᾽ ἀνόνατ᾽ Matthiae] ἀνόνατα ἀνόνατα B a ἀνόνητ᾽ ἀνόνητ᾽ S.   417 σὺ F. W. Schmidt] τι MSS.   420 γε] τε r.   421 προσέπτατ᾽ B (with τ written over the πα by b).   425 πᾶσιν a l] πᾶσι r.   426 πένθους B a | λέγω θέλω a. 427 μελαμπέπλῳ στολῇ S μελαγχίμοις πέπλοις c μελαγχείμοις πέπλοις B. In a and d κουρᾷ ξυρ has been written by the first hand, but the rest of the line is wanting.

τέθριππά θ' οἳ ζεύγνυσθε καὶ μονάμπυκας
πώλους, σιδήρῳ τέμνετ' αὐχένων φόβην.
αὐλῶν δὲ μὴ κατ' ἄστυ, μὴ λύρας κτύπος 430
ἔστω σελήνας δώδεκ' ἐκπληρουμένας·
οὐ γάρ τιν' ἄλλον φίλτερον θάψω νεκρὸν
τοῦδ' οὐδ' ἀμείνον' εἰς ἔμ'· ἀξία δέ μοι
τιμᾶν, ἐπεὶ τέτληκεν ἀντ' ἐμοῦ θανεῖν.

ΧΟ. ὦ Πελίου θύγατερ, στρ. 435
χαίρουσά μοι εἰν Ἀίδα δόμοισιν
τὸν ἀνάλιον οἶκον οἰκετεύοις.
ἴστω δ' Ἀίδας ὁ μελαγχαίτας θεὸς ὅς τ' ἐπὶ κώπᾳ
πηδαλίῳ τε γέρων 440
νεκροπομπὸς ἵζει,
πολὺ δὴ πολὺ δὴ γυναῖκ' ἀρίσταν
λίμναν Ἀχεροντίαν πορεύσας ἐλάτᾳ δικώπῳ.
πολλά σε μουσοπόλοι ἀντιστρ. 445
μέλψουσι καθ' ἑπτάτονόν τ' ὀρείαν
χέλυν ἔν τ' ἀλύροις κλέοντες ὕμνοις,
Σπάρτᾳ κύκλος ἁνίκα Καρνείου περινίσσεται ὥρας
†μηνὸς ἀειρομένας 450
παννύχου σελάνας,
λιπαραῖσί τ' ἐν ὀλβίαις Ἀθάναις.
τοίαν ἔλιπες θανοῦσα μολπὰν μελέων ἀοιδοῖς.

428 θ' οἳ] τε S.   **432** τιν'] τι B.   **434** τιμῆς S | τέτληκεν Nauck] τέθνηκεν MSS. | θανεῖν Nauck] μόνη S μόνην B λίαν a.   **435** ὦ l] ἰώ r (with L).
436 εἰν] ἐν S. | Ἀίδα Lascaris] ἄϊδ* L ἄδα P ἀΐδαο r. | δόμοισιν l] δόμοις r (with L).
437 οἰκετεύοις P a] οἰκετεύεις L ἱκετεύοις B.   **438** ἄϊδας B a] ἄΐδης L ἄδης P.
439 κώπᾳ S] κώπῃ r.   **443** ἀχεροντείαν S (but in L l has written ι above the ει).   **446** ὀρείαν S] οὐρείαν r.   **447** κλέοντες Elmsley] κλείοντες MSS.   **449** κύκλο*s a | περινίσσεται BL] περινίσεται a περινείσεται (σεται written over an erasure) P περινήσεται p. | ὥρας Hesychius s.v. περι(ν)ίσσεται ὥρας] ὥρ* L ὥρα P la ὥρᾳ B.
450 I have marked μηνὸς with a dagger as suspicious.   **451** παννύχου a l] παννύχους r | σελήνας S (but σελάνας l).   **452** ἀθήναις S (but ἀθάναις l).

ΑΛΚΗΣΤΙΣ.

εἴθ᾽ ἐπ᾽ ἐμοὶ μὲν εἴη,   στρ.   455
δυναίμαν δέ σε πέμψαι
φάος ἐξ Ἀίδα τεράμνων
Κωκυτοῖό τε ῥείθρων
ποταμίᾳ νερτέρᾳ τε κώπᾳ.
σὺ γάρ, ὦ ⟨σὺ⟩ μόνα, φίλα γυναικῶν,   460
σὺ τὸν αὑτᾶς
ἔτλας πόσιν ἀντὶ σᾶς ἀμεῖψαι
ψυχᾶς ἐξ Ἀιδα. κοῦφα σοι
χθὼν ἐπάνωθε πέσοι, γύναι. εἰ δέ τι
καινὸν ἕλοιτο λέχος πόσις, ἦ μάλ᾽ ἂν ἔμοιγ᾽ ἂν εἴη
στυγηθεὶς τέκνοις τε τοῖς σοῖς.   465
ματέρος οὐ θελούσας   ἀντιστρ.
πρὸ παιδὸς χθονὶ κρύψαι
δέμας, οὐδὲ πατρὸς γεραιοῦ,

. . . .

ὃν ἔτεκον δ᾽ οὐκ ἔτλαν ῥύεσθαι,
σχετλίω, πολιὰν ἔχοντε χαίταν.   470
σὺ δ᾽ ἐν ἥβᾳ
νέᾳ προθανοῦσα φωτὸς οἴχῃ.
τοιαύτας εἴη μοι κῦρσαι
συνδυάδος φιλίας ἀλόχου· τὸ γὰρ

457 Ἀίδα] ἄδου S.   458 Κωκυτοῖό τε ῥείθρων] καὶ κωκυτοῖς ῥείθρων L (κωκυτοῖο l, who has also written above καὶ the word περισσός) καὶ κωκυτοῖς ῥείθρων P καὶ κωκυτοῦ τε ῥείθρων B a. καὶ was omitted by Matthiae as an interpolation. (Κωκυτοῖό τε ῥείθρου Earle.)   459 κωπή S (but κώπα l).   460 σὺ γάρ, ὦ ⟨σὺ⟩ μόνα, φίλα γυναικῶν Wilamowitz] σὺ γάρ, ὦ μόνα ὦ φίλα γυναικῶν MSS.   461 αὑτᾶς Erfurdt] ἑαυτᾶς L (σαυτᾶς l, who has also inserted γε before τὸν) ἑαυτῆς P σαυτᾶς r. | ἀμείψασθαι S (ἀμείψαι l).   462 Ἀιδα Lascaris] αἴδα B a ἄδαο S. | κοῦφα S] κοῦφα r.   463 ἐπάνωθε Erfurdt] ἐπάνωθεν B a P ἐπάνω L. | πέσοι] πέσειε l.   464 πόσις λέχος S | ἦ B | μάλ᾽ ἂν] μάλ᾽ S.   465 τέκνοισι P τέκνοισ* L.   469 δ᾽ οὐκ] κοὐκ P οὐκ L | ῥύσασθαι S.   470 ἔχοντες S (but ἔχοντε l).   471 νέᾳ] νέᾳ νέου S.   472 μοι L (with ε written over the οι by L¹) μοι is wanting in P. | κῦρσαι Musgrave] κυρῆσαι MSS.   473 τὸ Erfurdt] τοῦτο MSS.

ἐν βιότῳ σπάνιον μέρος· ἦ γὰρ ἂν ἔμοιγ' ἄλυπος
δι' αἰῶνος ἂν ξυνείη. 475

ΗΡΑΚΛΗΣ.

ξένοι, Φεραίας τῆσδε κωμῆται χθονός,
Ἄδμητον ἐν δόμοισιν ἆρα κιγχάνω;
ΧΟ. ἔστ' ἐν δόμοισιν παῖς Φέρητος, Ἡράκλεις.
ἀλλ' εἰπὲ χρεία τίς σε Θεσσαλῶν χθόνα
πέμπει, Φεραῖον ἄστυ προσβῆναι τόδε. 480
ΗΡ. Τιρυνθίῳ πράσσω τιν' Εὐρυσθεῖ πόνον.
ΧΟ. καὶ ποῖ πορεύῃ; τῷ συνέζευξαι πλάνῳ;
ΗΡ. Θρῃκὸς τέτρωρον ἅρμα Διομήδους μέτα.
ΧΟ. πῶς οὖν δυνήσῃ; μῶν ἄπειρος εἶ ξένου;
ΗΡ. ἄπειρος· οὔπω Βιστόνων ἦλθον χθόνα. 485
ΧΟ. οὐκ ἔστιν ἵππων δεσπόσαι σ' ἄνευ μάχης.
ΗΡ. ἀλλ' οὐδ' ἀπειπεῖν τοὺς πόνους οἷόν τ' ἐμοί.
ΧΟ. κτανὼν ἄρ' ἥξεις ἢ θανὼν αὐτοῦ μενεῖς.
ΗΡ. οὐ τόνδ' ἀγῶνα πρῶτον ἂν δράμοιμ' ἐγώ.
ΧΟ. τί δ' ἂν κρατήσας δεσπότην πλέον λάβοις; 490
ΗΡ. πώλους ἀπάξω κοιράνῳ Τιρυνθίῳ.
ΧΟ. οὐκ εὐμαρὲς χαλινὸν ἐμβαλεῖν γνάθοις.
ΗΡ. εἰ μή γε πῦρ πνέουσι μυκτήρων ἄπο.
ΧΟ. ἀλλ' ἄνδρας ἀρταμοῦσι λαιψηραῖς γνάθοις.
ΗΡ. θηρῶν ὀρείων χόρτον, οὐχ ἵππων λέγεις. 495
ΧΟ. φάτνας ἴδοις ἂν αἵμασιν πεφυρμένας.

474 βιότω B (with the οτ written over an erasure) βίω S (in L a γε has been inserted by l before βίω). | ἂν has been erased in L. | ἔμοιγ' L] ἐμοὶ γ' P ἔμοιγε r.
477 κιγχάνω L a] κιχάνω r.   479 χθόνα] πόλιν S.   480 φεραίων S (in L l has written ον over ων).   481 πόνω B.   482 συνέζευξαι S] προσέζευξαι r.
483 θρηικὸς B.   487 τοὺς πόνους Monk] πόνους P μ' ἦν πόνους L. τοῖς πόνοις B a | τ' ἐμοὶ B a] τέ μοι L τέμει P.   488 μένεις B.   492 εὐμαθὲς S (εὐμαρὲς l).
496 αἵμασιν a p] αἵμασι r.

ΗΡ. τίνος δ' ὁ θρέψας παῖς πατρὸς κομπάζεται;
ΧΟ. Ἄρεος, ζαχρύσου Θρῃκίας πέλτης ἄναξ.
ΗΡ. καὶ τόνδε τοὐμοῦ δαίμονος πόνον λέγεις·
σκληρὸς γὰρ αἰεὶ καὶ πρὸς αἶπος ἔρχεται· 500
εἰ χρή με πᾶσιν οὓς Ἄρης ἐγείνατο
μάχην συνάψαι, πρῶτα μὲν Λυκάονι,
αὖθις δὲ Κύκνῳ, τόνδε δ' ἔρχομαι τρίτον
ἀγῶνα πώλοις δεσπότῃ τε συμβαλῶν.
ἀλλ' οὔτις ἔστιν ὃς τὸν Ἀλκμήνης γόνον 505
τρέσαντα χεῖρα πολεμίαν ποτ' ὄψεται.
ΧΟ. καὶ μὴν ὅδ' αὐτὸς τῆσδε κοίρανος χθονὸς
Ἄδμητος ἔξω δωμάτων πορεύεται.
ΑΔ. χαῖρ', ὦ Διὸς παῖ Περσέως τ' ἀφ' αἵματος.
ΗΡ. Ἄδμητε, καὶ σὺ χαῖρε, Θεσσαλῶν ἄναξ. 510
ΑΔ. θέλοιμ' ἄν· εὔνουν δ' ὄντα σ' ἐξεπίσταμαι.
ΗΡ. τί χρῆμα κούρᾳ τῇδε πενθίμῳ πρέπεις;
ΑΔ. θάπτειν τιν' ἐν τῇδ' ἡμέρᾳ μέλλω νεκρόν.
ΗΡ. ἀπ' οὖν τέκνων σῶν πημονὴν εἴργοι θεός.
ΑΔ. ζῶσιν κατ' οἴκους παῖδες οὓς ἔφυσ' ἐγώ. 515
ΗΡ. πατήρ γε μὴν ὡραῖος, εἴπερ οἴχεται.
ΑΔ. κἀκεῖνος ἔστι χἠ τεκοῦσά μ', Ἡράκλεις.
ΗΡ. οὐ μὴν γυνή γ' ὄλωλεν Ἄλκηστις σέθεν;
ΑΔ. διπλοῦς ἐπ' αὐτῇ μῦθος ἔστι μοι λέγειν.
ΗΡ. πότερα θανούσης εἶπας ἢ ζώσης πέρι; 520
ΑΔ. ἔστιν τε κοὐκέτ' ἔστιν, ἀλγυνεῖ δέ με.

497 δ' ὁ L] θ' ὁ P δὲ r.   498 ἄρεος B S (and a³) ἄρεως a¹ l. | Θρῃκίας (P Θρακώας L) ζαχρύσου S | πέλλης B.   500 αἰεὶ B L] ἀεὶ r | αἶπος a (with the a corrected from an ε) ἔπος P.   501 πᾶσιν Wecklein] παισὶν MSS. | οὓς] οἷς S.   504 συμβαλῶν L (with the circumflex rewritten by l) a²] συμβαλών r.   505 γόνον] τόκον L.   506 πολεμίαν B a] πολεμί** L πολεμίων P l.   509 τ' was omitted in S.   511 δ' omitted in S.   512 τρέπεις B.   514 ἀπ' B a.   515 ζῶσι B.   519 αὐτὴν S.   520 πέρι S] ἔτι r.   521 ἔστιν τε] ἔστι τε B. | δέ με] τέ με L τ' ἐμέ P.

ΗΡ. οὐδέν τι μᾶλλον οἶδ'· ἄσημα γὰρ λέγεις.
ΑΔ. οὐκ οἶσθα μοίρας ἧς τυχεῖν αὐτὴν χρεών;
ΗΡ. οἶδ', ἀντὶ σοῦ γε κατθανεῖν ὑφειμένην.
ΑΔ. πῶς οὖν ἔτ' ἔστιν, εἴπερ ᾔνεσεν τάδε; 525
ΗΡ. ἆ, μὴ πρόκλαι' ἄκοιτιν, ἐς τόδ' ἀμβαλοῦ.
ΑΔ. τέθνηχ' ὁ μέλλων, καὶ θανὼν οὐκ ἔστ' ἔτι.
ΗΡ. χωρὶς τό τ' εἶναι καὶ τὸ μὴ νομίζεται.
ΑΔ. σὺ τῇδε κρίνεις, Ἡράκλεις, κείνῃ δ' ἐγώ.
ΗΡ. τί δῆτα κλαίεις; τίς φίλων ὁ κατθανών; 530
ΑΔ. γυνή· γυναικὸς ἀρτίως μεμνήμεθα.
ΗΡ. ὀθνεῖος ἢ σοὶ συγγενὴς γεγῶσά τις;
ΑΔ. ὀθνεῖος, ἄλλως δ' ἦν ἀναγκαία δόμοις.
ΗΡ. πῶς οὖν ἐν οἴκοις σοῖσιν ὤλεσεν βίον;
ΑΔ. πατρὸς θανόντος ἐνθάδ' ὠρφανεύετο. 535
ΗΡ. φεῦ.
εἴθ' ηὕρομέν σ', Ἄδμητε, μὴ λυπούμενον.
ΑΔ. ὡς δὴ τί δράσων τόνδ' ὑπορράπτεις λόγον;
ΗΡ. ξένων πρὸς ἄλλων ἑστίαν πορεύσομαι.
ΑΔ. οὐκ ἔστιν, ὦναξ· μὴ τοσόνδ' ἔλθοι κακόν.
ΗΡ. λυπουμένοις ὀχληρός, εἰ μόλοι, ξένος. 540
ΑΔ. τεθνᾶσιν οἱ θανόντες· ἀλλ' ἴθ' ἐς δόμους.
ΗΡ. αἰσχρὸν παρὰ κλαίουσι θοινᾶσθαι φίλοις.
ΑΔ. χωρὶς ξενῶνές εἰσιν οἷ σ' ἐσάξομεν.

524 ἂν τί *B.* **525** ᾔνεσε *B.* **526** ἆ *L*] ἀ *P* ἀ ἀ *r.* μὴ] omitted in *P.* | ἀμβαλοῦ Nauck] ἀναβαλοῦ MSS. **527** τέθνηχ' ὁ *B a*] τέθνηκε *L* (but with χ' ὁ written over the κε by *L*¹) τέθνηκεν ὁ *P* | καὶ θανὼν οὐκ ἔστ' ἔτι Schwarz] καὶ ὁ θανὼν οὐκέτ' ἔστιν *P* χὤ θανὼν οὐκ ἔστ' ἔτι *L.* κοὐκέτ' ἔσθ' (ἔστιν *B*) ὁ κατθανὼν *B a.* **530** φίλων] οὖν *P* ἦν *L* (but *L*¹ has deleted ἦν and written φίλων in the margin). **531** γυναικὸς δ' *a.* **533, 534** are wanting in the text of *L*, but have been added in the margin by *L*¹. **534** ὤλεσε *a P* ὤλεβε *B.* **536** φεῦ was omitted in *L*, but has been supplied by *l.* **537** δὴ τί *a*] δή τι *r.* **538** ξένων *a L*¹] ξένον *P l* ξεῖνων *B* | ἄλλην *S* | ἑστίαν *B.* **539** τοσόνδ' *B.* **541** ἐς *S*] εἰς *r.* **542** φίλοις] ξένοις *S.* **543** ἐσάξομεν *Pl*] εἰσάξομεν *r.*

ΑΛΚΗΣΤΙΣ.

ΗΡ. μέθες με, καί σοι μυρίαν ἔξω χάριν.
ΑΔ. οὐκ ἔστιν ἄλλου σ᾽ ἀνδρὸς ἑστίαν μολεῖν. 545
ἡγοῦ σὺ τῷδε δωμάτων ἐξωπίους
ξενῶνας οἴξας, τοῖς τ᾽ ἐφεστῶσιν φράσον
σίτων παρεῖναι πλῆθος· εὖ δὲ κλῄσατε
θύρας μεταύλους· οὐ πρέπει θοινωμένους
κλύειν στεναγμῶν οὐδὲ λυπεῖσθαι ξένους. 550
ΧΟ. τί δρᾷς; τοιαύτης συμφορᾶς προσκειμένης,
Ἄδμητε, τολμᾷς ξενοδοκεῖν; τί μῶρος εἶ;
ΑΔ. ἀλλ᾽ εἰ δόμων σφε καὶ πόλεως ἀπήλασα
ξένον μολόντα, μᾶλλον ἄν μ᾽ ἐπῄνεσας;
οὐ δῆτ᾽, ἐπεί μοι συμφορὰ μὲν οὐδὲν ἂν 555
μείων ἐγίγνετ᾽, ἀξενώτερος δ᾽ ἐγώ.
καὶ πρὸς κακοῖσιν ἄλλο τοῦτ᾽ ἂν ἦν κακόν,
δόμους καλεῖσθαι τοὺς ἐμοὺς ἐχθροξένους.
αὐτὸς δ᾽ ἀρίστου τοῦδε τυγχάνω ξένου
ὅταν ποτ᾽ Ἄργους διψίαν ἔλθω χθόνα. 560
ΧΟ. πῶς οὖν ἔκρυπτες τὸν παρόντα δαίμονα,
φίλου μολόντος ἀνδρός, ὡς αὐτὸς λέγεις;
ΑΔ. οὐκ ἄν ποτ᾽ ἠθέλησεν εἰσελθεῖν δόμους,
εἰ τῶν ἐμῶν τι πημάτων ἐγνώρισε.
καὶ τῷ μέν, οἶμαι, δρῶν τάδ᾽ οὐ δόξω φρονεῖν, 565
οὐδ᾽ αἰνέσει με· τἀμὰ δ᾽ οὐκ ἐπίσταται
μέλαθρ᾽ ἀπωθεῖν οὐδ᾽ ἀτιμάζειν ξένους.

546 τῷδε d] τῶδε a τῶνδε r. 547 ἐφεστῶσιν Gaisford] ἐφεστῶσι MSS.
548 εὖ England] ἐν MSS. (ἐνδεκλήσατε B). 549 μεταύλους Ussing] μεσαύλους
MSS. 551 τοσαύτης S | προσκειμένης Wakefield] προκειμένης MSS. 552 ξενοδοκεῖν Stephanus] ξενοδοχεῖν MSS. | μῶρος C] μωρὸς r. 558 καλεῖσθαι L (but κα
has been changed to κεκ by l) | ἐχθροξένους S] κακοξένους r. 560 ὅταν ποτ᾽]
ὅταν περ S. 563 after ἠθέλησεν the writer of B repeated by mistake the letters ὡς αὐτὸς λ from the preceding verse, but they have been cancelled with red-
lead. 564 ἐγνώρισε B] ἐγνώρισεν r. 565 οὐ δόξω φρονεῖν Herwerden] οὐ
φρονεῖν δοκῶ MSS.

ΧΟ. ὦ πολύξεινος καὶ ἐλευθέρου ἀνδρὸς ἀεί ποτ' οἶκος, στρ.
σέ τοι καὶ ὁ Πύθιος εὐλύρας Ἀπόλλων 570
ἠξίωσε ναίειν,
ἔτλα δὲ σοῖσι μηλονόμας
ἐν νόμοις γενέσθαι,
δοχμιᾶν διὰ κλιτύων 575
βοσκήμασι σοῖσι συρίζων
ποιμνίτας ὑμεναίους.
σὺν δ' ἐποιμαίνοντο χαρᾷ μελέων βαλιαί τε
λύγκες, ἀντιστρ.
ἔβα δὲ λιποῦσ' Ὄθρυος νάπαν λεόντων 580
ἁ δαφοινὸς ἴλα·
χόρευσε δ' ἀμφὶ σὰν κιθάραν,
Φοῖβε, ποικιλόθριξ
νεβρὸς ὑψικόμων πέραν 585
βαίνουσ' ἐλατᾶν σφυρῷ κούφῳ,
χαίρουσ' εὔφρονι μολπᾷ.
τοίγαρ πολυμηλοτάταν στρ.
ἑστίαν οἰκεῖ παρὰ καλλίναον
Βοιβίαν λίμναν· ἀρότοις δὲ γυᾶν 590
καὶ πεδίων δαπέδοις
ὅρον ἀμφὶ μὲν ἀελίου κνεφαίαν
ἱππόστασιν αἰθέρα τὰν Μολοσσῶν ... τίθεται,
πόντιον δ' Αἰγαίων' ἐπ' ἀκτὰν 595
ἀλίμενον Πηλίου κρατύνει.

569 ὦ l] ἰώ r | πολύξεινος καὶ ἐλευθέρου Wecklein (πολυξείνου καὶ ἐλευθέρου Purgold)] πολύξεινος καὶ ἐλεύθερος MSS. 570 καὶ ὁ] χῷ L. 572 ἔτλα Matthiae] ἔτλη MSS. 574 νόμοις Pierson] δόμοις MSS. (δόμοισι B). 577 ποιμνήτας S. 579 βαλιαί L] βαλιαι r. 580 ὄθρυος L] ὀθρύος r. 582 χόρευσε Monk] ἐχόρευσε MSS. 588 τοιγάρ τοι B. 589 οἰκεῖ Purgold] οἰκεῖς MSS. 590 γυᾶν B] γυῖαν a (with the circumflex over υ deleted by a¹) γύαν L γυίαν P. 594 ὑπόστασιν B (with τ´ (= τὴν) written over the ν by B¹). 595 δ'] τ' S | Αἰγαίων' schol.] αἰγαῖον MSS.

ΑΛΚΗΣΤΙΣ. 29

καὶ νῦν δόμον ἀμπετάσας   ἀντιστρ.
δέξατο ξεῖνον νοτερῷ βλεφάρῳ,
τᾶς φίλας κλαίων ἀλόχου νέκυν ἐν
δώμασιν ἀρτιθανῆ·   600
τὸ γὰρ εὐγενὲς ἐκφέρεται πρὸς αἰδῶ.
ἐν τοῖς ἀγαθοῖσι δὲ πάντ' ἔνεστιν σοφίας. ἄγαμαι·
πρὸς δ' ἐμᾷ ψυχᾷ θάρσος ἧσται
θεοσεβῆ φῶτα κεδνὰ πράξειν.   605
ΑΔ. ἀνδρῶν Φεραίων εὐμενὴς παρουσία,
νέκυν μὲν ἤδη πάντ' ἔχοντα πρόσπολοι
φέρουσιν ἄρδην ἐς τάφον τε καὶ πυράν·
ὑμεῖς δὲ τὴν θανοῦσαν, ὡς νομίζεται,
προσείπατ' ἐξιοῦσαν ὑστάτην ὁδόν.   610
ΧΟ. καὶ μὴν ὁρῶ σὸν πατέρα γηραιῷ ποδὶ
στείχοντ', ὀπαδούς τ' ἐν χεροῖν δάμαρτι σῇ
κόσμον φέροντας, νερτέρων ἀγάλματα.

ΦΕΡΗΣ.

ἥκω κακοῖσι σοῖσι συγκάμνων, τέκνον·
ἐσθλῆς γάρ, οὐδεὶς ἀντερεῖ, καὶ σώφρονος   615
γυναικὸς ἡμάρτηκας. ἀλλὰ ταῦτα μὲν
φέρειν ἀνάγκη καίπερ ὄντα δύσφορα.
δέχου δὲ κόσμον τόνδε, καὶ κατὰ χθονὸς
ἴτω· τὸ ταύτης σῶμα τιμᾶσθαι χρεών,
ἥτις γε τῆς σῆς προύθανε ψυχῆς, τέκνον,   620
καί μ' οὐκ ἄπαιδ' ἔθηκεν οὐδ' εἴασε σοῦ
στερέντα γήρᾳ πενθίμῳ καταφθίνειν,

598 ξεῖνον Aldine] ξένον MSS.   599 φίλας Aldine] φιλίας MSS.   603 ἔνεστιν Barnes] ἔνεστι MSS. | in L ἄγαμαι has been deleted by l.   604 ἧσται S] ἦσται r.   608 ἐς] πρὸς S.   617 δύσφορα S (and a³)] δυσμενῆ r d.   622 καταφθίνειν Matthiae] καταφθινεῖν MSS.

πάσαις δ' ἔθηκεν εὐκλεέστερον βίον
γυναιξίν, ἔργον τλᾶσα γενναῖον τόδε.
ὦ τόνδε μὲν σώσασ', ἀναστήσασα δὲ   625
ἡμᾶς πίτνοντας, χαῖρε, κἀν Ἅιδου δόμοις
εὖ σοι γένοιτο. φημὶ τοιούτους γάμους
λύειν βροτοῖσιν, ἢ γαμεῖν οὐκ ἄξιον.

ΛΔ. οὔτ' ἦλθες ἐς τόνδ' ἐξ ἐμοῦ κληθεὶς τάφον,
οὔτ' ἐν φίλοισι σὴν παρουσίαν λέγω.   630
κόσμον δὲ τοῦτον οὔποθ' ἥδ' ἐνδύσεται,
οὐ γάρ τι τῶν σῶν ἐνδεὴς ταφήσεται.
τότε ξυναλγεῖν χρῆν σ' ὅτ' ὠλλύμην ἐγώ.
σὺ δ' ἐκποδὼν στὰς καὶ παρεὶς ἄλλῳ θανεῖν
νέῳ γέρων ὤν, τόνδ' ἀποιμώξῃ νεκρόν;   635
[οὐκ ἦσθ' ἄρ' ὀρθῶς τοῦδε σώματος πατήρ,
οὐδ' ἡ τεκεῖν φάσκουσα καὶ κεκλημένη
μήτηρ μ' ἔτικτε· δουλίου δ' ἀφ' αἵματος
μαστῷ γυναικὸς σῆς ὑπεβλήθην λάθρᾳ.]
ἔδειξας εἰς ἔλεγχον ἐξελθὼν ὃς εἶ,   640
καί μ' οὐ νομίζω παῖδα σὸν πεφυκέναι.
ἦ τἄρα πάντων διαπρέπεις ἀψυχίᾳ,
ὃς τηλικόσδ' ὢν κἀπὶ τέρμ' ἥκων βίου
οὐκ ἠθέλησας οὐδ' ἐτόλμησας θανεῖν
τοῦ σοῦ πρὸ παιδός, ἀλλὰ τήνδ' εἰάσατε   645
γυναῖκ' ὀθνείαν, ἣν ἐγὼ καὶ μητέρα
πατέρα τ' ἂν ἐνδίκως ἂν ἡγοίμην μόνην.
καίτοι καλόν γ' ἂν τόνδ' ἀγῶν' ἠγωνίσω

---

623 εὐκλεέστερον B] εὐκλεέστατον r.   625 τόνδ' ἐμὸν S | σώσασ'] σώσ' B.
626 πίτνοντας a] πιτνόντας B πιτνοῦντας S | κἂν S (written over an erasure in L)]
κεῖν r.   631 τοῦτον Earle] τὸν σὸν MSS.   635 ἀποιμώξῃ] ἀποιμώξῃ a ἀποιμώξεις S ἀποιμώξεις B. (ἀποιμώξει Matthiae).   636-39 rejected by Earle. See
Critical Notes.   643 τηλικόσδ' B a] τηλίκος L τ' ἡλίκος P.   647 τ' ἂν Elmsley] τ' B a τε γ' S. | μόνην S a] ἐμὸν B.

ΑΛΚΗΣΤΙΣ. 31

τοῦ σοῦ πρὸ παιδὸς κατθανών, βραχὺς δέ σοι
πάντως ὁ λοιπὸς ἦν βιώσιμος χρόνος. 650
[κἀγώ τ' ἂν ἔζων χἤδε τὸν λοιπὸν χρόνον,
κοὐκ ἂν μονωθεὶς ἔστενον κακοῖς ἐμοῖς.]
καὶ μὴν ὅσ' ἄνδρα χρὴ παθεῖν εὐδαίμονα
πέπονθας· ἤβησας μὲν ἐν τυραννίδι,
παῖς δ' ἦν ἐγώ σοι τῶνδε διάδοχος δόμων, 655
ὥστ' οὐκ ἄτεκνος κατθανὼν ἄλλοις δόμον
λείψειν ἔμελλες ὀρφανὸν διαρπάσαι.
οὐ μὴν ἐρεῖς γέ μ' ὡς ἀτιμάζοντα σὸν
γῆρας θανεῖν προύδωκας, ὅστις αἰδόφρων
πρὸς σ' ἦ μάλιστα, κἀντὶ τῶνδέ μοι χάριν 660
τοιάνδε καὶ σὺ χἠ τεκοῦσ' ἠλλαξάτην.
τοίγαρ φυτεύων παῖδας οὐκέτ' ἂν φθάνοις,
οἳ γηροβοσκήσουσι καὶ θανόντα σε
περιστελοῦσι καὶ προθήσονται νεκρόν.
οὐ γάρ σ' ἔγωγε τῇδε μὴ θάψω χερί· 665
τέθνηκα γὰρ δὴ τοὐπί σ'· εἰ δ' ἄλλου τυχὼν
σωτῆρος αὐγὰς εἰσορῶ, κείνου λέγω
καὶ παῖδά μ' εἶναι καὶ φίλον γηροτρόφον.
μάτην ἄρ' οἱ γέροντες εὔχονται θανεῖν,
γῆρας ψέγοντες καὶ μακρὸν χρόνον βίου· 670
ἦν δ' ἐγγὺς ἔλθῃ θάνατος, οὐδεὶς βούλεται
θνῄσκειν, τὸ γῆρας δ' οὐκέτ' ἔστ' αὐτοῖς βαρύ.
ΧΟ. Ἄδμηθ', ἅλις γὰρ ἡ παροῦσα συμφορά,
παῦσαι, πατρὸς δὲ μὴ παροξύνῃς φρένας.

651-2 rejected by Lenting. ἔξην α. 657 διαρπάσαι S διαρπάσειν r l. 658 ἀτιμάζοντα S] ἀτιμάζων τὸ r. 659 προύδωκας S] προύδωκά σ' r. 665 τῇδε μὴ Weil] τῇδ' ἐμῇ MSS. 671 ἔλθοι B. 672 θνῄσκειν] θανεῖν α. 673 Ἄδμηθ' Mekler] παύσασθ' MSS. 674 παῦσαι Mekler] ὦ παῖ MSS. (Elmsley pointed out that ὦ παῖ in 674 was probably a mistake of the copyist due to ὦ παῖ just below in 675). | φρένα S.

ΕΥΡΙΠΙΔΟΥ

ΦΕ. ὦ παῖ, τίν' αὐχεῖς, πότερα Λυδὸν ἢ Φρύγα   675
κακοῖς ἐλαύνειν ἀργυρώνητον σέθεν;
οὐκ οἶσθα Θεσσαλόν με κἀπὸ Θεσσαλοῦ
πατρὸς γεγῶτα γνησίως ἐλεύθερον;
ἄγαν ὑβρίζεις, καὶ νεανίας λόγους
ῥίπτων ἐς ἡμᾶς οὐ βαλὼν οὕτως ἄπει.   680
ἐγὼ δέ σ' οἴκων δεσπότην ἐγεινάμην
κἄθρεψ', ὀφείλω δ' οὐχ ὑπερθνῄσκειν σέθεν·
οὐ γὰρ πατρῷον τόνδ' ἐδεξάμην νόμον,
παίδων προθνῄσκειν πατέρας, οὐδ' Ἑλληνικόν.
σαυτῷ γὰρ εἴτε δυστυχὴς εἴτ' εὐτυχὴς   685
ἔφυς· ἃ δ' ἡμῶν χρῆν σε τυγχάνειν ἔχεις.
πολλῶν μὲν ἄρχεις, πολυπλέθρους δέ σοι γύας
λείψω· πατρὸς γὰρ ταῦτ' ἐδεξάμην πάρα.
τί δῆτά σ' ἠδίκηκα; τοῦ σ' ἀποστερῶ;
μὴ θνῇσχ' ὑπὲρ τοῦδ' ἀνδρός, οὐδ' ἐγὼ πρὸ σοῦ.   690
χαίρεις ὁρῶν φῶς· πατέρα δ' οὐ χαίρειν δοκεῖς;
ἦ μὴν πολύν γε τὸν κάτω λογίζομαι
χρόνον, τὸ δὲ ζῆν μικρόν, ἀλλ' ὅμως γλυκύ.
σὺ γοῦν ἀναιδῶς διεμάχου τὸ μὴ θανεῖν,
καὶ ζῇς παρελθὼν τὴν πεπρωμένην τύχην,   695
ταύτην κατακτάς· εἶτ' ἐμὴν ἀψυχίαν
λέγεις, γυναικός, ὦ κάκισθ', ἡσσημένος,
ἣ τοῦ καλοῦ σοῦ προύθανεν νεανίου;
σοφῶς δ' ἐφηῦρες ὥστε μὴ θανεῖν ποτε,
εἰ τὴν παροῦσαν κατθανεῖν πείσεις ἀεὶ   700
γυναῖχ' ὑπὲρ σοῦ· κᾆτ' ὀνειδίζεις φίλοις

679 ἄγαν μ' L.   680 ἄπει B.   682 ὀφείλω δ' B a] ὀφείλων S.   686 χρῆν B.
687 γύας L] γύιας B γυίας r.   689 ἠδίκησα S.   690 θνῇσχ' S] θνῇσκ' r.
692 ἦ S (with a²)] ἢ r.   693 σμικρόν a Γ.   694 σὺ γοῦν B L] σύ γ' οὖν r.
698 ἢ B.   699 δ' ἐφεῦρες B a δ' εὗρες S (but δέ γ' εὗρες l).   700 πείσεας ἂν S.
701 κατονειδίζεις B.

ΑΛΚΗΣΤΙΣ.

τοῖς μὴ θέλουσι δρᾶν τάδ', αὐτὸς ὢν κακός·
σίγα· νόμιζε δ', εἰ σὺ τὴν σαυτοῦ φιλεῖς
ψυχήν, φιλεῖν ἅπαντας· εἰ δ' ἡμᾶς κακῶς
ἐρεῖς, ἀκούσῃ πολλὰ κοὐ ψευδῆ κακά. 705
ΧΟ. πλείω λέλεκται νῦν τε καὶ τὸ πρὶν κακά·
παῦσαι δέ, πρέσβυ, παῖδα σὸν κακορροθῶν.
ΑΔ. λέγ', ὡς ἐμοῦ λέξαντος· εἰ δ' ἀλγεῖς κλύων
τἀληθές, οὐ χρῆν σ' εἰς ἔμ' ἐξαμαρτάνειν.
ΦΕ. σοῦ δ' ἂν προθνῄσκων μᾶλλον ἐξημάρτανον. 710
ΑΔ. ταὐτὸν γὰρ ἡβῶντ' ἄνδρα καὶ πρέσβυν θανεῖν;
ΦΕ. ψυχῇ μιᾷ ζῆν, οὐ δυοῖν, ὀφείλομεν.
ΑΔ. καὶ μὴν Διός γε μεῖζον' ἂν ζῴης χρόνον. 713
ΦΕ. μνήστευε πολλάς, ὡς θάνωσι πλείονες. 720
ΑΔ. φεῦ·
εἴθ' ἀνδρὸς ἔλθοις τοῦδέ γ' ἐς χρείαν ποτέ. 719
ΦΕ. ἀρᾷ γονεῦσιν οὐδὲν ἔκδικον παθών; 714
ΑΔ. μακροῦ βίου γὰρ ᾐσθόμην ἐρῶντά σε. 715
ΦΕ. ἀλλ' οὐ σὺ νεκρὸν ἀντὶ σοῦ τόνδ' ἐκφέρεις; 716
ΑΔ. σημεῖα τῆς σῆς γ', ὦ κάκιστ', ἀψυχίας. 717
ΦΕ. οὔτοι πρὸς ἡμῶν γ' ὤλετ'· οὐκ ἐρεῖς τόδε. 718
ΑΔ. σοὶ τοῦτ' ὄνειδος· οὐ γὰρ ἤθελες θανεῖν. 721
ΦΕ. φίλον τὸ φέγγος τοῦτο τοῦ θεοῦ, φίλον.
ΑΔ. κακὸν τὸ λῆμα κοὐκ ἐν ἀνδράσιν τὸ σόν.
ΦΕ. οὐκ ἐγγελᾷς γέροντα βαστάζων νεκρόν.
ΑΔ. θανῇ γε μέντοι δυσκλεής, ὅταν θάνῃς. 725
ΦΕ. κακῶς ἀκούειν οὐ μέλει θανόντι μοι.

706 τὸ Wakefield] τὰ MSS. 709 χρήν B. 711 ἡβῶντ' L (with b and a²) ἡμῶν τ' r. 713 ff. the arrangement in the text is that of Wecklein. See Critical Notes. 714 ἆρα B | παθών B P (corrected by p). 716 νεκρόν γ B. 717 τῆς σῆς γ' Herwerden] τῆς σῆς B a. σημεῖα γ' ὦ κάκιστε ταῦτ' ἀψυχίας S. 718 οὔτι S | γ' omitted in S. 723 λῆμμα B | ἀνδράσιν a L¹ p] ἀνδράσι r. 725 θανῇ S θάνῃ B θάνῃι a | θάνῃς S θάνῃι a θανῇ B. 726 μέλει S μέλλει r.

ΕΥΡΙΠΙΔΟΥ

ΑΔ. φεῦ φεῦ· τὸ γῆρας ὡς ἀναιδείας πλέων.
ΦΕ. ἥδ' οὐκ ἀναιδής· τήνδ' ἐφηῦρες ἄφρονα.
ΑΔ. ἄπελθε κἀμὲ τόνδ' ἔα θάψαι νεκρόν.
ΦΕ. ἄπειμι· θάψεις δ' αὐτὸς ὢν αὐτῆς φονεύς, 730
δίκας τε δώσεις σοῖσι κηδεσταῖς ἔτι.
ἦ τἄρ' Ἄκαστος οὐκέτ' ἔστ' ἐν ἀνδράσιν,
εἰ μή σ' ἀδελφῆς αἷμα τιμωρήσεται.
ΑΔ. ἔρρων νυν αὐτὸς χἠ ξυνοικήσασά σοι
ἄπαιδε παιδὸς ὄντος, ὥσπερ ἄξιοι, 735
γηράσκετ'· οὐ γὰρ τῷδ' ἔτ' ἐς ταὐτὸν στέγος
νεῖσθ'· εἰ δ' ἀπειπεῖν χρῆν με κηρύκων ὕπο
τὴν σὴν πατρῴαν ἑστίαν, ἀπεῖπον ἄν.
ἡμεῖς δέ — τοὖν ποσὶν γὰρ οἰστέον κακόν —
στείχωμεν, ὡς ἂν ἐν πυρᾷ θῶμεν νεκρόν. 740
ΧΟ. ἰὼ ἰώ. σχετλία τόλμης,
ὦ γενναία καὶ μέγ' ἀρίστη,
χαῖρε· πρόφρων σε χθόνιός θ' Ἑρμῆς
Ἅιδης τε δέχοιτ', εἰ δέ τι κἀκεῖ
πλέον ἔστ' ἀγαθοῖς, τούτων μετέχουσ' 745
Ἅιδου νύμφῃ παρεδρεύοις.

729 καί με S. 731 τε] δὲ S. | σοῖσι S a] τοῖσι σοῖσι B (but B¹ has deleted σοῖσι). 732 ἦ τἄρ'] ἤ τ' ἄρ' P a ἦ τ' ἄρ' L ἤ τ' ἄρ' B | ἄκλαυστος οὐκ ἔστ' ἐν ἀνδράσιν ἔτι B (b has written in the margin οὐκέτ' ἔστ' ἐν ἀνδράσιν). 734 ἔρρων schol. (τινὲς δὲ ἔρρων γράφουσι σὺν τῷ ν)] ἔρροις B a ἔρρου L p ἔρρο* P. | νυν Lascaris] νῦν MSS. 735 ὄντος S] ὄντες r (with l). 736 τῷδ' ἔτ' Elmsley] τῷδε γ' B a τῷδ' ἔτ' S. | ταυτό S. 737 χρῆν B] χρή L (with ν added by L¹) χρή r. 739 τοὖν ποσὶν L p] τοῦ ποσί P τοὔμποσίν a τουμποσί B. 741 ἰὼ ἰώ B a l] ἰώ S. | σχετλίη B. 742 ἄριστα S. 743-44 ᾅδης ἑρμῆς τε δέχηθ' B. 745 ἀγαθοῖσι B | μετέχουσ' a l] μετέχουσα P μετέχου B. 746 νύμφῃ B] νύμφα r. | προσεδρεύοις S.

ΑΛΚΗΣΤΙΣ.

ΘΕΡΑΠΩΝ.

πολλοὺς μὲν ἤδη κἀπὸ παντοίας χθονὸς
ξένους μολόντας οἶδ᾽ ἐς Ἀδμήτου δόμους,
οἷς δεῖπνα προύθηκ᾽· ἀλλὰ τοῦδ᾽ οὔπω ξένον
κακίον᾽ ἐς τήνδ᾽ ἑστίαν ἐδεξάμην.   750
ὃς πρῶτα μὲν πενθοῦντα δεσπότην ὁρῶν
ἐσῆλθε κἀτόλμησ᾽ ἀμείψασθαι πύλας.
ἔπειτα δ᾽ οὔτι σωφρόνως ἐδέξατο
τὰ προστυχόντα ξένια, συμφορὰν μαθών,
ἀλλ᾽ εἴ τι μὴ φέροιμεν, ὤτρυνεν φέρειν.   755
ποτῆρα δ᾽ ἐν χείρεσσι κίσσινον λαβὼν
πίνει μελαίνης μητρὸς εὔζωρον μέθυ,
ἕως ἐθέρμην᾽ αὐτὸν ἀμφιβᾶσα φλὸξ
οἴνου· στέφει δὲ κρᾶτα μυρσίνης κλάδοις
ἄμουσ᾽ ὑλακτῶν, [δισσὰ δ᾽ ἦν μέλη κλύειν·   760
ὁ μὲν γὰρ ᾖδε,] τῶν ἐν Ἀδμήτου κακῶν
οὐδὲν προτιμῶν, οἰκέται δ᾽ ἐκλαίομεν
δέσποιναν· ὄμμα δ᾽ οὐκ ἐδείκνυμεν ξένῳ
τέγγοντες· Ἄδμητος γὰρ ὧδ᾽ ἐφίετο.
καὶ νῦν ἐγὼ μὲν ἐν δόμοισιν ἑστιῶ   765
ξένον, πανοῦργον κλῶπα καὶ λῃστήν τινα,
ἡ δ᾽ ἐκ δόμων βέβηκεν, οὐδ᾽ ἐφεσπόμην
οὐδ᾽ ἐξέτεινα χεῖρ᾽, ἀποιμώζων ἐμὴν
δέσποιναν, ἣ 'μοὶ πᾶσί τ᾽ οἰκέταισιν ἦν
μήτηρ· κακῶν γὰρ μυρίων ἐρρύετο,   770

748 εἰς B.   749 ξένον Dobree] ξένου MSS.   750 ἐς S] εἰς r.   755 φέροιεν B. | ὤτρυνε B P.   756 χείρεσσι a] χείρεσι r.   759 μυρσίνης Canter] μυρσίνοις MSS.   760 δισσὰ — ᾖδε not in S (in L l has supplied 760 in the margin, and 761 in the text over an erasure). I have bracketed the words as an interpolation.   761 ᾖδε B.   765 ἑστιῶ B a.   767 ἐφεπόμην B.   769 ἣ 'μοὶ Wakefield] ἦ μοι MSS.   770 ἐρρύετο S] ἐρύετο r.

ΕΥΡΙΠΙΔΟΥ

ΗΡ.
ὀργὰς μαλάσσουσ' ἀνδρός. ἆρα τὸν ξένον
στυγῶ δικαίως, ἐν κακοῖς ἀφιγμένον;
οὗτος, τί σεμνὸν καὶ πεφροντικὸς βλέπεις;
οὐ χρὴ σκυθρωπὸν τοῖς ξένοις τὸν πρόσπολον
εἶναι, δέχεσθαι δ' εὐπροσηγόρῳ φρενί. 775
σὺ δ' ἄνδρ' ἑταῖρον δεσπότου παρόνθ' ὁρῶν,
στυγνῷ προσώπῳ καὶ συνωφρυωμένῳ
δέχει, θυραίου πήματος σπουδὴν ἔχων.
δεῦρ' ἔλθ', ὅπως ἂν καὶ σοφώτερος γένῃ.
τὰ θνητὰ πράγματ' οἶδας ἣν ἔχει φύσιν; 780
οἶμαι μὲν οὔ· πόθεν γάρ; ἀλλ' ἄκου' ἐμοῦ.
βροτοῖς ἅπασι κατθανεῖν ὀφείλεται,
κοὐκ ἔστι θνητῶν ὅστις ἐξεπίσταται
τὴν αὔριον μέλλουσαν εἰ βιώσεται·
τὸ τῆς τύχης γὰρ ἀφανὲς οἷ προβήσεται, 785
κἄστ' οὐ διδακτὸν οὐδ' ἁλίσκεται τέχνῃ.
ταῦτ' οὖν ἀκούσας καὶ μαθὼν ἐμοῦ πάρα,
εὔφραινε σαυτόν, πῖνε, τὸν καθ' ἡμέραν
βίον λογίζου σόν, τὰ δ' ἄλλα τῆς τύχης.
τίμα δὲ καὶ τὴν πλεῖστον ἡδίστην θεῶν 790
Κύπριν βροτοῖσιν· εὐμενὴς γὰρ ἡ θεός,
τὰ δ' ἄλλ' ἔασον ταῦτα καὶ πιθοῦ λόγοις
ἐμοῖσιν, εἴπερ ὀρθά σοι δοκῶ λέγειν·
οἶμαι μέν. οὔκουν τὴν ἄγαν λύπην ἀφεὶς
πίῃ μεθ' ἡμῶν [τάσδ' ὑπερβαλὼν τύχας, 795

771 ἆρα B P (corrected by P¹). **781** οἶμαι] δοκῶ Plutarch *Consol. ad Apollon.* 11, p. 104. **782** ἅπασιν ἀποθανεῖν Menander *Monostich.* 69. **783** ἔστιν αὐτῶν Plutarch *l. s. c.* **785** οἷ] οὗ S ἧ C. **787** τοῦτ' Orion *Anth.* viii. 4 p. 53. **788** πῖνε L p] πίνε r. **792** πιθοῦ Monk] πίθου P πείθου r. **794** οἶμαι μέν] these words are assigned to the servant in α. **795** τύχας] γρ. πύλας α¹ in the margin. The schol. mentions both readings. The words τάσδ'—πυκασθείς were rejected by Herwerden as interpolated from 829 and 832.

ΑΛΚΗΣΤΙΣ. 37

στεφάνοις πυκασθείς]· καὶ σάφ' οἶδ' ὁθούνεκα
τοῦ νῦν σκυθρωποῦ καὶ ξυνεστῶτος †φρενῶν
μεθορμιεῖ σε πίτυλος ἐμπεσὼν σκύφου.
ὄντας δὲ θνητοὺς θνητὰ καὶ φρονεῖν χρεών·
ὡς τοῖς γε σεμνοῖς καὶ συνωφρυωμένοις 800
ἅπασίν ἐστιν, ὥς γ' ἐμοὶ χρῆσθαι κριτῇ,
οὐ βίος ἀληθῶς ὁ βίος ἀλλὰ συμφορά.

ΘΕ. ἐπιστάμεσθα ταῦτα· νῦν δὲ πράσσομεν
οὐχ οἷα κώμου καὶ γέλωτος ἄξια.
ΗΡ. γυνὴ θυραῖος ἡ θανοῦσα·' μὴ λίαν 805
πένθει· δόμων γὰρ ζῶσι τῶνδε δεσπόται.
ΘΕ. τί ζῶσιν; οὐ κάτοισθα τἀν δόμοις κακά;
ΗΡ. εἰ μή τι σός με δεσπότης ἐψεύσατο.
ΘΕ. ἄγαν ἐκεῖνός ἐστ' ἄγαν φιλόξενος. 809
ΗΡ. μῶν ξυμφοράν τιν' οὖσαν οὐκ ἔφραζέ μοι; 812
ΘΕ. χαίρων ἴθ'· ἡμῖν δεσποτῶν μέλει κακά.
ΗΡ. ὅδ' οὐ θυραίων πημάτων ἄρχει λόγος.
ΘΕ. οὐ γάρ τι κωμάζοντ' ἂν ἠχθόμην σ' ὁρῶν. 815
ΗΡ. ἀλλ' ἦ πέπονθα δείν' ὑπὸ ξένων ἐμῶν; 816
ΘΕ. οὐκ ἦλθες ἐν δέοντι δέξασθαι δόμοις. 817
ΗΡ. οὐ χρῆν μ' ὀθνείου γ' οὕνεκ' εὖ πάσχειν νεκροῦ; 810
ΘΕ. ἦ κάρτα μέντοι καὶ λίαν οἰκεῖος ἦν. 811
[πένθος γὰρ ἡμῖν ἐστι· καὶ κουρὰν βλέπεις 818
μελαμπέπλους στολμούς τε. ΗΡ. τίς δ' ὁ κατ-
θανών;] 819

797 φρενῶν S] κακοῦ r. 803 ἐπιστάμεσθα L a] ἐπιστάμεθα r. 807 κάτοισθα L a²] κατοῖσθα r. 809 ff. The arrangement in the text follows Wecklein. See Critical Notes. 809 ἄγαν γ' S. 812 ἔφραξε B. 813 μέλλει B. 815 τι—σ' ὁρῶν] σε—ὁρῶν S (in P there is an erasure before ὁρῶν). 817 δόμους S. 810 οὐ χρῆν μ'] οὔκουν S. 811 θυραῖος a. 818-19 I have followed Kvičala and Wecklein in rejecting these two verses and retaining 820. See Critical Notes.

ΕΥΡΙΠΙΔΟΥ

ΗΡ. μῶν ἢ τέκνων τις φροῦδος ἢ γέρων πατήρ; 820
ΘΕ. γυνὴ μὲν οὖν ὄλωλεν Ἀδμήτου, ξένε.
ΗΡ. τί φής; ἔπειτα δῆτα μ' ἐξενίζετε;
ΘΕ. ᾐδεῖτο γάρ σε τῶνδ' ἀπώσασθαι δόμων.
ΗΡ. ὦ σχέτλι', οἴας ἤμπλακες ξυναόρου.
ΘΕ. ἀπωλόμεσθα πάντες, οὐ κείνη μόνη. 825
ΗΡ. ἀλλ' ᾐσθόμην μὲν ὄμμ' ἰδὼν δακρυρροοῦν
κουράν τε καὶ †πρόσωπον· ἀλλ' ἔπειθέ με
λέγων θυραῖον κῆδος ἐς τάφον φέρειν.
βίᾳ δὲ θυμοῦ τάσδ' ὑπερβαλὼν πύλας
ἔπινον ἀνδρὸς ἐν φιλοξένου δόμοις, 830
πράσσοντος οὕτω. κᾆτα κωμάζω κάρα
στεφάνοις πυκασθείς; ἀλλὰ σοῦ τὸ μὴ φράσαι,
κακοῦ τοσούτου δώμασιν προσκειμένου.
ποῦ καί σφε θάπτει; ποῦ νιν εὑρήσω μολών;
ΘΕ. ὀρθὴν παρ' οἶμον ἢ 'πὶ Λάρισαν φέρει 835
τύμβον κατόψει ξεστὸν ἐκ προαστίου.
ΗΡ. ὦ πολλὰ τλᾶσα καρδία καὶ χεὶρ ἐμή,
νῦν δεῖξον οἶον παῖδά σ' ἡ Τιρυνθία
Ἠλεκτρυόνος ἐγείνατ' Ἀλκμήνη Διί.
δεῖ γάρ με σῶσαι τὴν θανοῦσαν ἀρτίως 840
γυναῖκα κεἰς τόνδ' αὖθις ἱδρῦσαι δόμον
Ἄλκηστιν, Ἀδμήτῳ θ' ὑπουργῆσαι χάριν.

820 τίς φροῦδος ἢ S (τίς ἢ φροῦδος ἢ P] τι φροῦδον γένος ἢ B (but B¹ has deleted γένος) τι φροῦδον ἢ a. 825 μόνον L. 827 πρόσωπον is probably corrupt. | ἀλλ'] ἀλλ' ὅμως B (but B¹ has deleted ὅμως). 829 τύχας πύλας a (but a³ has erased πύλας and altered τύχας to πύλας). 831 κᾆτα (κᾶτα a²) κωμάζω a κατακωμάζω B κᾆτ' ἐκώμαζον L κἀπεκώμαζον P. 833 δώμασιν a] δώμασι S δόματος B | προσκειμένου Scaliger] προκειμένου MSS. 834 μολῶν B. 835 οἶμον B | Λάρισαν Nauck] λάρισσαν MSS. 836 προαστίου L p] προαστείου r. 837 καὶ χεὶρ] ψυχῇ τ' a (cf. Orest. 466). 839 ἠλεκτρυόνος C (Ἠλεκτρυόνος Blomfield)] ἠλεκτρύωνος r | ἐγείνατ' Blomfield] γείνατ' MSS. 841 ἱδρῦσαι P] ἱδρύσαι r. 842 θ'] δ S.

ΑΛΚΗΣΤΙΣ.

ἐλθὼν δ' ἄνακτα τὸν μελάμπτερον νεκρῶν
Θάνατον φυλάξω, καί νιν εὑρήσειν δοκῶ
πίνοντα τύμβου πλησίον προσφαγμάτων. 845
κἄνπερ λοχαίας αὐτὸν ἐξ ἕδρας συθεὶς
μάρψω, κύκλον δὲ περιβάλω χεροῖν ἐμαῖν,
οὐκ ἔστιν ὅστις αὐτὸν ἐξαιρήσεται
μογοῦντα πλευρά, πρὶν γυναῖκ' ἐμοὶ μεθῇ.
ἢν δ' οὖν ἁμάρτω τῆσδ' ἄγρας, καὶ μὴ μόλῃ 850
πρὸς αἱματηρὸν πέλανον, εἶμι τῶν κάτω
Κόρης ἄνακτός τ' εἰς ἀνηλίους δόμους
αἰτήσομαί τε· καὶ πέποιθ' ἄξειν ἄνω
Ἄλκηστιν, ὥστε χερσὶν ἐνθεῖναι ξένου,
ὅς μ' ἐς δόμους ἐδέξατ' οὐδ' ἀπήλασε, 855
καίπερ βαρείᾳ συμφορᾷ πεπληγμένος,
ἔκρυπτε δ' ὢν γενναῖος, αἰδεσθεὶς ἐμέ.
τίς τοῦδε μᾶλλον Θεσσαλῶν φιλόξενος,
τίς Ἑλλάδ' οἰκῶν; τοιγὰρ οὐκ ἐρεῖ κακὸν
εὐεργετῆσαι φῶτα γενναῖος γεγώς. 860

ΑΔ. ἰώ,
στυγναὶ πρόσοδοι, στυγναὶ δ' ὄψεις
χήρων μελάθρων. ἰώ μοί μοι. αἰαῖ.
ποῖ βῶ; πᾷ στῶ; τί λέγω; τί δὲ μή;
πῶς ἂν ὀλοίμαν;
ᾗ βαρυδαίμονα μήτηρ μ' ἔτεκεν. 865
ζηλῶ φθιμένους, κείνων ἔραμαι,

---

843 μελάμπτερον Musgrave (from the schol.)] μελάμπεπλον MSS. 846 λοχαίας Etym. Mag. (the Cod. Florentinus of that work has κἄν περ λοχαία σαυτὸν ἐξέδρας). The schol. says γράφεται λοχίας (probably a mistake for λοχαίας.)] λοχήσας MSS. 847 περιβάλω Monk] περιβαλῶ S περιβαλών r (with l). | ἐμὰ α ἐμὰν a² ἐμαῖν a³. 852 ἀνηλίου B. 859 ἑλάδ' B. 862 In L l has added a second ἰώ. | μοί μοι] μοι B | αἰαῖ] αἶ αἶ P αἶ ἆ L ἒ ἒ B ἒ ἒ a. 863 πᾷ Porson] πῇ l ποῖ r. 864 ὀλοίμ' ἄν B. 865 ᾗ βαρδαίμονα B | ἔτεκεν L] ἔτεκε P ἔτικτεν r.

κεῖν' ἐπιθυμῶ δώματα ναίειν.
οὔτε γὰρ αὐγὰς χαίρω προσορῶν
οὔτ' ἐπὶ γαίας πόδα πεζεύων·
τοῖον ὅμηρόν μ' ἀποσυλήσας 870
Ἅιδῃ Θάνατος παρέδωκεν.
ΧΟ. πρόβα πρόβα· βᾶθι κεῦθος οἴκων.   στρ.
ΑΔ. αἰαῖ.
ΧΟ. πέπονθας ἄξι' αἰαγμάτων.   ΑΔ. ἒ ἔ.
ΧΟ. δι' ὀδύνας ἔβας,
   σάφ' οἶδα, ΑΔ. φεῦ φεῦ. ΧΟ. τὰν νέρθε δ' οὐδὲν
      ὠφελεῖς. 875
ΑΔ. ἰώ μοί μοι. ΧΟ. τὸ μήποτ' εἰσιδεῖν φιλίας ἀλόχου
   πρόσωπον ⟨σ' ἔν⟩αντα λυπρόν.
ΑΔ. ἔμνησας ὅ μου φρένας ἥλκωσεν·
   τί γὰρ ἀνδρὶ κακὸν μεῖζον ἁμαρτεῖν
   πιστῆς ἀλόχου; μή ποτε γήμας 880
   ὤφελον οἰκεῖν μετὰ τῆσδε δόμους.
   ζηλῶ δ' ἀγάμους ἀτέκνους τε βροτῶν·
   μία γὰρ ψυχή, τῆς ὕπερ ἀλγεῖν
   μέτριον ἄχθος·
   παίδων δὲ νόσους καὶ νυμφιδίους 885
   εὐνὰς θανάτοις κεραϊζομένας
   οὐ τλητὸν ὁρᾶν, ἐξὸν ἀτέκνοις

871 παρέδωκε B. **872–77** are given to the chorus in L, while in P 872–76 (through μοί μοι) are assigned to the chorus and the rest from τὸ in 876 through διὰ παντός in 888 is given to Admetus. **873** αἰαῖ] αἲ αἲ B a αἲ αἲ L (omitted in P) | ἄξι' S] ἄξια r. **875** νέρθε δ' Hermann] νέρθεν MSS. **877** σ' ἔναντα Hartung] ἄντα MSS. For other conjectures see Critical Notes. **878** ἀδ. omitted in L (but it has been added by l). | ὁ μοῦ φρέν' ἥλκωσε B. **880** πιστῆς S a (with Stobaeus Flor. 69, 12)] φιλίας B. **883** μία γὰρ ψυχή B a] μιᾷ γὰρ ψυχῇ L ψυχῇ γὰρ μιᾷ P ψυχῇ δὲ μιᾷ l. | τῆς Stobaeus Flor. 68, 13. ὕπερ ἀλγεῖν Ed.] ὑπεραλγεῖν MSS. **887** sq. ἀτέκνοις and ἀγάμοις S] ἀτέκνους and ἀγάμους B a.

ΑΛΚΗΣΤΙΣ. 41

ἀγάμοις τ' εἶναι διὰ παντός.
ΧΟ. τύχα τύχα δυσπάλαιστος ἥκει. ἀντιστρ.
ΑΔ. αἰαῖ.
ΧΟ. πέρας δέ γ' οὐδὲν ἀλγέων τιθεῖς. ΑΔ. ἒ ἔ. 890
ΧΟ. βαρέα μὲν φέρειν,
ὅμως δὲ ΑΔ. φεῦ φεῦ. ΧΟ. τλᾶθ'· οὐ σὺ
πρῶτος ὤλεσας
ΑΔ. ἰώ μοί μοι. ΧΟ. γυναῖκα· συμφορὰ δ' ἑτέρους
ἑτέρα
πιέζει φανεῖσα θνατῶν.
ΑΔ. ὦ μακρὰ πένθη λῦπαί τε φίλων 895
τῶν ὑπὸ γαῖαν.
τί μ' ἐκώλυσας ῥῖψαι τύμβου
τάφρον ἐς κοίλην καὶ μετ' ἐκείνης
τῆς μέγ' ἀρίστης κεῖσθαι φθίμενον;
δύο δ' ἀντὶ μιᾶς Ἅιδης ψυχὰς 900
τὰς πιστοτάτας σὺν ἂν ἔσχεν, ὁμοῦ
χθονίαν λίμνην διαβάντε.
ΧΟ. ἐμοί τις ἦν στρ.
ἐν γένει, ᾧ κόρος ἀξιόθρηνος
ὤλετ' ἐν δόμοισιν, 905
μονόπαις· ἀλλ' ἔμπας
ἔφερε κακὸν ἅλις, ἄτεκνος ὤν,

889 ff. The verses are assigned in the text according to *a*. *B* gives αἶ αἶ (sic) to the chorus, πέρας — τιθεῖς to Admetus, and the following words through ὅμως δὲ to the chorus. *L* and *P* give 889-94 to the chorus. 889 αἶ αἶ] αἶ αἶ MSS. (*L* has αἶ αἶ). 890 δέ γ' a] δ' ἔγ' *B* δ' *S*. | ἀλγέων τιθεῖς *B S* ἀλγέων τίθης *a*. In *L l* has written *a* over τιθεῖς and β over ἀλγέων. 892 τλᾶθ' *B*. 894 θνατῶν *L*] θνητῶν *r*. 895 λῦπαι *L*] λύπαι *r*. 896 γαῖαν *B*. 897 ῥῖψαι Hermann] ῥίψαι MSS. 898 καὶ μετ'] κατ' *P*. In *L* three letters (doubtless κατ') have been erased here, and *l* has supplied καὶ μετ'. 901 σὺν ἂν ἔσχεν Lenting] συνανέσχεν *B P* ****νέσχεν *L* γε συνέσχεν *l* συνέχεν *a* (with σ written above the εχ by a¹). 902 λίμναν *S*. 904 κόρος *l*] κοῦρος *L r*. 905 ὤχετ' ἐν δόμοισι *S*.

πολιὰς ἐπὶ χαίτας
ἤδη προπετὴς ὢν
βιότου τε πόρσω.   910

ΑΔ. ὦ σχῆμα δόμων, πῶς εἰσέλθω;
πῶς δ' οἰκήσω μεταπίπτοντος
δαίμονος; οἴμοι.   πολὺ γὰρ τὸ μέσον·
τότε μὲν πεύκαις σὺν Πηλιάσιν   915
σύν θ' ὑμεναίοις ἔστειχον ἔσω,
φιλίας ἀλόχου χέρα βαστάζων,
πολυάχητος δ' εἵπετο κῶμος,
τήν τε θανοῦσαν κἄμ' ὀλβίζων,
ὡς εὐπατρίδαι καὶ ἀπ' ἀμφοτέρων   920
ὄντες ἀριστέων σύζυγες εἶμεν·
νῦν δ' ὑμεναίων γόος ἀντίπαλος
λευκῶν τε πέπλων μέλανες στολμοὶ
πέμπουσί μ' ἔσω
λέκτρων κοίτας ἐς ἐρήμους.   925

ΧΟ. παρ' εὐτυχῆ
σοὶ πότμον ἦλθεν ἀπειροκάκῳ τόδ'
ἄλγος· ἀλλ' ἔσωσας
βίοτον καὶ ψυχάν.
ἔθανε δάμαρ, ἔλιπε φιλίαν·   930
τί νέον τόδε; πολλοὺς
ἤδη παρέλυσεν
θάνατος δάμαρτος.

ΑΔ. φίλοι, γυναικὸς δαίμον' εὐτυχέστερον   935

910 πόρσω Gaisford] πρόσω MSS.   913 δ' S] not in r.   916 ἔσω L] εἴσω r l.   917 φιλίας] schol. γράφεται πιστῆς: cf. 876, 880.   920 κἀπ' L.
921 ἀριστέων Dobree] ἀρίστων MSS. | εἶμεν Heath] εἰμὲν a P ἦμεν r.   924 μ' ἔσω S] μ' εἴσω r.   626 ΧΟ. omitted in B.   929 After ψυχάν B has added ἄδμητ. ἔ ἔ χορ. ὦ ἄδμητε, and a has added ἔ ἔ.   932 πολλοὺς Canter] πολλοῖς MSS.   933 παρέλυσεν Matthiae] παρέλυσε MSS.   934 δάμαρτας B.

ΑΛΚΗΣΤΙΣ. 43

τοὐμοῦ νομίζω, καίπερ οὐ δοκοῦνθ᾽ ὅμως·
τῆς μὲν γὰρ οὐδὲν ἄλγος ἅψεταί ποτε,
πολλῶν δὲ μόχθων εὐκλεὴς ἐπαύσατο.
ἐγὼ δ᾽, ὃν οὐ χρῆν ζῆν, παρεὶς τὸ μόρσιμον
λυπρὸν διάξω βίοτον· ἄρτι μανθάνω. 940
πῶς γὰρ δόμων τῶνδ᾽ εἰσόδους ἀνέξομαι;
τίν᾽ ἂν προσειπών, τοῦ δὲ προσρηθεὶς ὕπο,
τερπνῆς τύχοιμ᾽ ἂν εἰσόδου; ποῖ τρέψομαι;
ἡ μὲν γὰρ ἔνδον ἐξελᾷ μ᾽ ἐρημία,
γυναικὸς εὐνὰς εὖτ᾽ ἂν εἰσίδω κενὰς 945
θρόνους τ᾽ ἐν οἷσιν ἷζε, καὶ κατὰ στέγας
αὐχμηρὸν οὖδας, τέκνα δ᾽ ἀμφὶ γούνασι
πίπτοντα κλαίῃ μητέρ᾽, οἱ δὲ δεσπότιν
στένωσιν οἵαν ἐκ δόμων ἀπώλεσαν.
τὰ μὲν κατ᾽ οἶκον τοιάδ᾽· ἔξωθεν δέ με 950
γάμοι τ᾽ ἐλῶσι Θεσσαλῶν καὶ ξύλλογοι
γυναικοπληθεῖς· οὐ γὰρ ἐξανέξομαι
λεύσσων δάμαρτος τῆς ἐμῆς ὁμήλικας.
ἐρεῖ δέ μ᾽ ὅστις ἐχθρὸς ὢν κυρεῖ τάδε·
ἰδοῦ τὸν αἰσχρῶς ζῶνθ᾽, ὃς οὐκ ἔτλη θανεῖν, 955
ἀλλ᾽ ἣν ἔγημεν ἀντιδοὺς ἀψυχίᾳ
πέφευγεν Ἅιδην· κᾆτ᾽ ἀνὴρ εἶναι δοκεῖ;
στυγεῖ δὲ τοὺς τεκόντας, αὐτὸς οὐ θέλων
θανεῖν. τοιάνδε πρὸς κακοῖσι κληδόνα
ἕξω. τί μοι ζῆν δῆτα κύδιον, φίλοι, 960
κακῶς κλύοντι καὶ κακῶς πεπραγότι;
ΧΟ. ἐγὼ καὶ διὰ μούσας στρ.

936 τοὐμοῦ B] τοὐμοῦ L a τοῦ μοῦ P. 939 χρῆν Elmsley] χρὴ MSS.
940 μανθάνων S. 944 ἐξελεῖ P ἐξελ* L ἐξελᾷ l]. 946 ἷζε S] ἷζε B ἷζε a p.
948 κλαίῃ S κλαίει r. | μητέρα B. 950 οἴκους S. 951 τ᾽ Wakefield] γ᾽ MSS.
953 λεύσων B. 955 ἰδοῦ L ἰδοὺ r. 957 κᾆτ᾽ S] εἶτ᾽ r. 960 ἕξω L b a³]
ἔξω r.

ΕΥΡΙΠΙΔΟΥ

καὶ μετάρσιος ᾖξα, καὶ
πλείστων ἁψάμενος λόγων
κρεῖσσον οὐδὲν Ἀνάγκας 965
ηὗρον, οὐδέ τι φάρμακον
Θρήσσαις ἐν σανίσιν, τὰς
Ὀρφεία κατέγραψεν
γῆρυς, οὐδ' ὅσα Φοῖβος Ἀσκληπιάδαις ἔδωκε 970
φάρμακα πολυπόνοις
ἀντιτεμὼν βροτοῖσιν.
μόνας δ' οὔτ' ἐπὶ βωμοὺς   ἀντιστρ.
ἔστιν οὔτε βρέτας θεᾶς
ἐλθεῖν, οὐ σφαγίων κλύει. 975
μή μοι, πότνια, μείζων
ἔλθοις ἢ τὸ πρὶν ἐν βίῳ.
καὶ γὰρ Ζεὺς ὅ τι νεύσῃ,
σὺν σοὶ τοῦτο τελευτᾷ.
καὶ τὸν ἐν Χαλύβοις δαμάζεις σὺ βίᾳ σίδαρον, 980
οὐδέ τις ἀποτόμου
λήματός ἐστιν αἰδώς.
καί σ' ἐν ἀφύκτοισι χερῶν εἷλε θεὰ δεσμοῖς.   στρ.
τόλμα δ'· οὐ γὰρ ἀνάξεις ποτ' ἔνερθεν 985
κλαίων τοὺς φθιμένους † ἄνω.
καὶ θεῶν σκότιοι φθίνουσι
παῖδες ἐν θανάτῳ. 990

964 ἀρξάμενος Stobaeus *Ecl.* I. 4, 3.   967 Θρήϊσσαις L a | σανίσιν Matthiae] σάνισι MSS.   968 κατέγραψεν Monk] κατέγραψε MSS.   970 ἔδωκε Musgrave] παρέδωκε MSS.   972 βροτοῖσιν P a] βροτοῖσι r.   974 ff. ἐλθεῖν — ἔστιν MSS. W. A. Wagner made the transposition.   978 νεύσῃ S νεύσει r.   980 χαλύβοισι S.   981 οὐ βίᾳ Γ.   In L l has written above γρ. οὐ βίᾳ. | σίδαρον L a] σίδηρον r.   984 ἀφύκτοις S.   985 τόλμα δ' S (l has written τὸ or τά above the a δ', but has deleted it afterwards)] τόλμα τάδ' B τόλμα τόδ' a.   986 φθινομένους B. | ἄνω is perhaps corrupt. See Critical Notes.   989 φθίνουσι S] φθινύθουσι r (with l).

ΑΛΚΗΣΤΙΣ. 45

φίλα μὲν ὅτ' ἦν μεθ' ἡμῶν,
φίλα δ' ἔ⟨τι⟩ καὶ θανοῦσα,
γενναιοτάταν δὲ πασᾶν
ἐζεύξω κλισίαις ἄκοιτιν.
μηδὲ νεκρῶν ὡς φθιμένων χῶμα νομιζέσθω ἀντιστρ. 995
τύμβος σᾶς ἀλόχου, θεοῖσι δ' ὁμοίως
τιμάσθω, σέβας ἐμπόρων.
καί τις δοχμίαν κέλευθον   1000
ἐμβαίνων τόδ' ἐρεῖ·
αὖτα ποτὲ **προύθαν'** ἀνδρός,
νῦν δ' ἐστὶ μάκαιρα δαίμων·
χαῖρ', ὦ πότνι', εὖ δὲ δοίης.
τοιαί νιν προσεροῦσι φᾶμαι.   1005
καὶ μὴν ὅδ', ὡς ἔοικεν, Ἀλκμήνης γόνος,
Ἄδμητε, πρὸς σὴν ἑστίαν πορεύεται.

HP. φίλον πρὸς ἄνδρα χρὴ λέγειν ἐλευθέρως,
Ἄδμητε, μομφὰς δ' οὐχ ὑπὸ σπλάγχνοις ἔχειν
σιγῶντ'. ἐγὼ δὲ σοῖς κακοῖσιν ἠξίουν   1010
ἐγγὺς παρεστὼς ἐξετάζεσθαι φίλος.
σὺ δ' οὐκ ἔφραζες σῆς προκείμενον νέκυν
γυναικός, ἀλλά μ' ἐξένιζες ἐν δόμοις
[ὡς δὴ θυραίου πήματος σπουδὴν ἔχων.]
κἄστεψα κρᾶτα καὶ θεοῖς ἐλειψάμην   1015
σπονδὰς ἐν οἴκοις δυστυχοῦσι τοῖσι σοῖς.
καὶ μέμφομαι μὲν μέμφομαι παθὼν τάδε,

992 δ' ἔτι καὶ θανοῦσα Portus (the Aldine has δέ τι, probably a misprint for δ' ἔτι) δὲ καὶ θανοῦσ' ἔσται B δὲ θανοῦσ' ἔσται a δὲ καὶ θανοῦσα ἐστὶν l' δὲ καὶ θανοῦσ' ἐστὶν L. See Critical Notes. 993 πασᾶν S] πᾶσαν r. 998 ὅμοιος B. 1001 ἐκβαίνων S. 1002 προύθαν' Monk] προύθανεν a P l προύθανεν r. 1004 πότνι' S] πότνια r. 1005 φᾶμαι Monk] φῆμαι MSS. 1006 χορ. is prefixed in L P a. 1009 μομφὰς L a] μορφὰς r. 1014 was rejected by Lachmann. Cf. 778.

οὐ μήν σε λυπεῖν ἐν κακοῖσι βούλομαι.
ὧν δ' οὕνεχ' ἥκω δεῦρ' ὑποστρέψας πάλιν
λέξω. γυναῖκα τήνδε μοι σῶσον λαβών, 1020
ἕως ἂν ἵππους δεῦρο Θρηκίας ἄγων
ἔλθω, τύραννον Βιστόνων κατακτανών.
πράξας δ' ὃ μὴ τύχοιμι — νοστήσαιμι γάρ —
δίδωμι τήνδε σοῖσι προσπολεῖν δόμοις.
πολλῷ δὲ μόχθῳ χεῖρας ἦλθεν εἰς ἐμάς· 1025
ἀγῶνα γὰρ πάνδημον εὑρίσκω τινὰς
τιθέντας, ἀθληταῖσιν ἄξιον πόνον,
ὅθεν κομίζω τήνδε νικητήρια
λαβών· τὰ μὲν γὰρ κοῦφα τοῖς νικῶσιν ἦν
ἵππους ἄγεσθαι, τοῖσι δ' αὖ τὰ μείζονα 1030
νικῶσι, πυγμὴν καὶ πάλην, βουφόρβια·
γυνὴ δ' ἐπ' αὐτοῖς εἵπετ'· ἐντυχόντι δὲ
αἰσχρὸν παρεῖναι κέρδος ἦν τόδ' εὐκλεές.
ἀλλ', ὥσπερ εἶπον, σοὶ μέλειν γυναῖκα χρή.
οὐ γὰρ κλοπαίαν, ἀλλὰ σὺν πόνῳ λαβὼν 1035
ἥκω· χρόνῳ δὲ καὶ σύ μ' αἰνέσεις ἴσως.

ΑΔ. οὔτοι σ' ἀτίζων οὐδ' ἐν ἐχθροῖσιν τιθεὶς
ἔκρυψ' ἐμῆς γυναικὸς ἀθλίου τύχας·
ἀλλ' ἄλγος ἄλγει τοῦτ' ἂν ἦν προσκείμενον,
εἴ του πρὸς ἄλλου δώμαθ' ὡρμήθης ξένου· 1040
ἅλις δὲ κλαίειν τοὐμὸν ἦν ἐμοὶ κακόν.
γυναῖκα δ', εἴ πως ἔστιν, αἰτοῦμαί σ', ἄναξ,
ἄλλον τιν' ὅστις μὴ πέπονθεν οἷ' ἐγὼ

1017 μὲν B a] δὴ L, δὲ Γ. 1021 θρήϊκας S (l has written lovs above the as).
1022 ἔλθω] ἔνθα B. | βιστονῶν B. 1024 σοῖσι] σοι B | πρόσπολον S. 1025 πολ-
λῶν δὲ μόχθων ἦλθε χεῖρας εἰς ἐμάς S. 1027 πόνον B] πόνων a πόνου S. 1030 αὖ
τὰ S] αὐτὰ Γ. 1034 μέλλειν B. 1036 μ'] γ' S. 1037 ἀτίζων cod. Har-
leianus 5743] ἀτιμάζων r. | ἐχθροῖσιν a] ἐχθροῖσι B αἰσχροῖσιν L αἰσχροῖσι Γ.
1038 ἀθλίους a. 1039 προκείμενον B Γ. 1040 εἰ τοῦ B εἴπερ S.

ΑΛΚΗΣΤΙΣ.

σώζειν ἄνωχθι Θεσσαλῶν, πολλοὶ δέ σοι
ξένοι Φεραίων· μή μ' ἀναμνήσῃς κακῶν. 1045
οὐκ ἂν δυναίμην τήνδ' ὁρῶν ἐν δώμασιν
ἀδακρυς εἶναι· μὴ νοσοῦντί μοι νόσον
προσθῇς· ἅλις γὰρ συμφορᾷ βαρύνομαι.
ποῦ καὶ τρέφοιτ' ἂν δωμάτων νέα γυνή;
νέα γὰρ ὥς, ἐσθῆτι καὶ κόσμῳ πρέπει. 1050
πότερα μετ' ἀνδρῶν δῆτ' ἐνοικήσει στέγην;
καὶ πῶς ἀκραιφνὴς ἐν νέοις στρωφωμένη
ἔσται; τὸν ἡβῶνθ', Ἡράκλεις, οὐ ῥᾴδιον
εἴργειν· ἐγὼ δὲ σοῦ προμηθίαν ἔχω.
ἢ τῆς θανούσης θάλαμον εἰσβήσας τρέφω; 1055
καὶ πῶς ἐπεσφρῶ τήνδε τῷ κείνης λέχει;
διπλῆν φοβοῦμαι μέμψιν, ἔκ τε δημοτῶν,
μή τίς μ' ἐλέγξῃ τὴν ἐμὴν εὐεργέτιν
προδόντ' ἐν ἄλλης δεμνίοις πίτνειν νέας,
καὶ τῆς θανούσης· ἀξία δέ μοι σέβειν· 1060
πολλὴν προνοίαν δεῖ μ' ἔχειν. σὺ δ', ὦ γύναι,
ἥτις ποτ' εἶ σύ, ταῦτ' ἔχουσ' Ἀλκήστιδι
μορφῆς μέτρ' ἴσθι, καὶ πρὸς ἥιξαι δέμας.
οἴμοι. κόμιζε πρὸς θεῶν ἐξ ὀμμάτων
γυναῖκα τήνδε, μή μ' ἕλῃς ᾑρημένον. 1065
δοκῶ γὰρ αὐτὴν εἰσορῶν γυναῖχ' ὁρᾶν

1045 μή μ' ἀναμνήσῃς S] μή με μι*μνήσῃς a μή με μιμνήσῃς d μή με μιμνήσκεις B. See Critical Notes. 1048 προσθεὶς S (corrected in L by l). | συμφοραῖς a. 1051 μετ' G. Hermann] κατ' MSS. | δή τιν' οἰκήσει a. 1052 στρωφωμένη (with ε written above the first ω and ο above the second by B¹). 1054 εἴργειν in B is written at the end of v. 1053 by a blunder of the scribe. | δέ σου MSS. 1055 ἢ B ἦ B¹. | θάλαμον εἰσβήσας a] εἰς θάλαμον βήσας r. 1058 ἐλέγχῃ B. 1059 ἄλλης S] ἄλλοις r. | πίτνειν Elmsley] πιτνεῖν r. 1060 δέ μοι S] δ' ἐμοὶ r. 1062 ταῦτ' Portus] ταῦτα MSS. (L¹ has written in the margin of L τὰ αὐτά). 1063 πρὸς ἥιξαι England] προσήιξαι B a προσήοιξαι L (with ι written over the οι by l) προσήιξε P. 1064 ἐξ] ἀπ' S. 1066 ὁρῶν B.

ΕΥΡΙΠΙΔΟΥ

   ἐμήν· θολοῖ δὲ καρδίαν, ἐκ δ' ὀμμάτων
   πηγαὶ κατερρώγασιν· ὦ τλήμων ἐγώ,
   ὡς ἄρτι πένθους τοῦδε γεύομαι πικροῦ.
ΧΟ. ἐγὼ μὲν οὐκ ἔχοιμ' ἂν εὖ λέγειν τύχην·   1070
   χρὴ δ', ἥτις εἴη, καρτερεῖν θεοῦ δόσιν.
ΗΡ. εἰ γὰρ τοσαύτην δύναμιν εἶχον ὥστε σὴν
   ἐς φῶς πορεῦσαι νερτέρων ἐκ δωμάτων
   γυναῖκα καί σοι τήνδε πορσῦναι χάριν.
ΛΔ. σάφ' οἶδα βούλεσθαί σ' ἄν. ἀλλὰ ποῦ τόδε;   1075
   οὐκ ἔστι τοὺς θανόντας ἐς φάος μολεῖν.
ΗΡ. μή νυν ὑπέρβαλλ', ἀλλ' ἐναισίμως φέρε.
ΛΔ. ῥᾷον παραινεῖν ἢ παθόντα καρτερεῖν.
ΗΡ. τί δ' ἂν προκόπτοις εἰ θέλεις ἀεὶ στένειν;
ΑΔ. ἔγνωκα καὐτός, ἀλλ' ἔρως τις ἐξάγει.   1080
ΗΡ. τὸ γὰρ φιλῆσαι τὸν θανόντ' ἄγει δακρυ.
ΛΔ. ἀπώλεσέν με, κἄτι μᾶλλον ἢ λέγω.
ΗΡ. γυναικὸς ἐσθλῆς ἤμπλακες· τίς ἀντερεῖ;
ΑΔ. ὥστ' ἄνδρα τόνδε μηκέθ' ἥδεσθαι βίῳ.
ΗΡ. χρόνος μαλάξει, νῦν δ' ἔθ' ἡβάσκει, κακόν.   1085
ΑΔ. χρόνον λέγοις ἄν, εἰ χρόνος τὸ κατθανεῖν.
ΗΡ. γυνή σε παύσει καὶ νέοι γάμοι πόθου.

1068 τλήμων *L a b*] τλῆμον *B Γ*.   **1071** ἥτις Monk] ὅστις MSS. | εἴη Hayley] εἰ σύ MSS. (σύ is omitted in *L*).   **1072** ὥστε σὴν omitted in *S*. (In *L L*¹ has written λειπ in the margin, but *l* has supplied ὥστε σὴν. In *P* another hand has supplied ἐκ θεοῦ to fill the lacuna.)   **1074** πορσῦναι *S*] πορσύναι *r*. **1077** μή νυν Monk] μή νῦν MSS. | ὑπέρβαλλ' Monk] ὑπέρβαλ' *a* ὑπέρβαιν' *r* | ἐναισίμως *S*] εἰνεσίμως *r*.   **1079** θέλεις MSS., with the Codex Hamiltonianus of Galen *De Plac. Hipp. et Plat.* V. p. 413 (p. 388 of Iwan Mueller's ed.)] θέλοις *C*, with the inferior MSS. of Galen. | στένειν ἀεί Galen *l. c.*   **1080** τις Galen] τίς μ' MSS.   **1082** ἀπώλεσε *B* | κἄτι *L* | καὶ ἔτι *r*.   **1083** ἀνταιρεῖ *B*. **1085** νῦν *S*] σε νῦν *B* σ' νῦν *a*: cf. v. 381 | ἡβάσκει Galen *op. cit.* p. 419 (p. 394 Mueller): cf. Photius *s. v.* ἡβάσκει] ἡβᾷ σοι MSS. The comma after ἡβάσκει was inserted by Bruhn.   **1087** νέοι γάμοι πόθου F. W. Schmidt (νέος γάμος πόθου Guttentag)] νέου γάμου πόθοι MSS. (*L* πόθος).

ΑΛΚΗΣΤΙΣ.

ΑΔ. σίγησον· οἷον εἶπας. οὐκ ἂν ᾠόμην.
ΗΡ. τί δ'; οὐ γαμεῖς γάρ, ἀλλὰ χηρεύσει λέχος;
ΑΔ. οὐκ ἔστιν ἥτις τῷδε συγκλιθήσεται. 1090
ΗΡ. μῶν τὴν θανοῦσαν ὠφελεῖν τι προσδοκᾷς;
ΑΔ. κείνην ὅπουπερ ἔστι τιμᾶσθαι χρεών.
ΗΡ. αἰνῶ μὲν αἰνῶ· μωρίαν δ' ὀφλισκάνεις.
ΑΔ. ὡς μήποτ' ἄνδρα τόνδε νυμφίον καλῶν.
ΗΡ. ἐπῄνεσ' ἀλόχῳ πιστὸς οὕνεκ' εἶ φίλος. 1095
ΑΔ. θάνοιμ' ἐκείνην καίπερ οὐκ οὖσαν προδούς.
ΗΡ. δέχου νυν εἴσω τήνδε γενναίων δόμων.
ΑΔ. μή, πρός σε τοῦ σπείραντος ἄντομαι Διός.
ΗΡ. καὶ μὴν ἁμαρτήσει γε μὴ δράσας τάδε.
ΑΔ. καὶ δρῶν γε λύπῃ καρδίαν δηχθήσομαι. 1100
ΗΡ. πιθοῦ· τάχ' ἂν γὰρ ἐς δέον πέσοι χάρις.
ΑΔ. φεῦ.
εἴθ' ἐξ ἀγῶνος τήνδε μὴ ᾿λαβές ποτε.
ΗΡ. νικῶντι μέντοι καὶ σὺ συννικᾷς ἐμοί.
ΑΔ. καλῶς ἔλεξας· ἡ γυνὴ δ' ἀπελθέτω.
ΗΡ. ἄπεισιν, εἰ χρή· πρῶτα δ' εἰ χρεὼν ἄθρει. 1105
ΑΔ. χρή, σοῦ γε μὴ μέλλοντος ὀργαίνειν ἐμοί.
ΗΡ. εἰδώς τι κἀγὼ τήνδ' ἔχω προθυμίαν.
ΑΔ. νίκα νυν. οὐ μὴν ἁνδάνοντά μοι ποεῖς.
ΗΡ. ἀλλ' ἔσθ' ὅθ' ἡμᾶς αἰνέσεις· πιθοῦ μόνον.

1089 χηρεύσῃ λέχος B χηρεύσει λέχος a χηρεύεις μόνος S. 1090 τῷδε] τῷδ' ἀνδρί B. 1093 μυρίαν B (b has written μω over the μυ). 1094 In L ἴσθι has been written above ὡς by L¹ | καλὸν B καλεῖν l (with ων written above by another hand). 1097 νυν L] νῦν r. | γενναίων] γενναίαν S. 1098 ἄντομαι S] αἰτοῦμαι r. 1101 πιθοῦ S] πείθου r. | τάχα γὰρ B. 1102 μὴ 'λαβες Tyrwhitt] μὴ 'λαβες C μὴ λάβες B μὴ λαβες a (μὴ λαβες a³) μὴ λάβῃς P μὴ λάβοις L (l has written in the margin γρ. μ' ἤλαβεν.) 1105 ἄθρει] ὅρα S. 1108 omitted in the text of B, but added in the margin by B¹ | νυν L] νῦν r. ποεῖς Wecklein] ποιεῖς MSS. In B from 1109 to 1113 the scribe has given the lines of Hercules to Admetus and vice versa. He prefixed to 1114 the sign indicating that the verse belonged to Admetus, but afterwards deleted it.

ΑΔ. κομίζετ', εἰ χρὴ τήνδε δέξασθαι δόμοις. 1110
ΗΡ. οὐκ ἂν μεθείην τὴν γυναῖκα προσπόλοις.
ΑΔ. σὺ δ' αὐτὸς αὐτὴν εἴσαγ', εἰ δοκεῖ, δόμους.
ΗΡ. ἐς σὰς μὲν οὖν ἔγωγε θήσομαι χέρας.
ΑΔ. οὐκ ἂν θίγοιμι· δῶμα δ' εἰσελθεῖν πάρα.
ΗΡ. τῇ σῇ πέποιθα χειρὶ δεξιᾷ μόνῃ. 1115
ΑΔ. ἄναξ, βιάζῃ μ' οὐ θέλοντα δρᾶν τάδε.
ΗΡ. τόλμα προτεῖναι χεῖρα καὶ θιγεῖν ξένης.
ΑΔ. καὶ δὴ προτείνω, Γοργόν' ὡς καρατομῶν.
ΗΡ. ἔχεις; ΑΔ. ἔχω. ΗΡ. ναί, σῷζε νυν, καὶ τὸν Διὸς
  φήσεις ποτ' εἶναι παῖδα γενναῖον ξένον. 1120
  βλέψον πρὸς αὐτήν, εἴ τι σῇ δοκεῖ πρέπειν
  γυναικί· λύπης δ' εὐτυχῶν μεθίστασο.
ΑΔ. ὦ θεοί, τί λέξω; θαῦμ' ἀνέλπιστον τόδε·
  γυναῖκα λεύσσω τὴν ἐμὴν ἐτητύμως,
  ἢ κέρτομός μ' ἐκ θεοῦ τις ἐκπλήσσει χαρά; 1125
ΗΡ. οὐκ ἔστιν ἄλλη· τήνδ' ὁρᾷς δάμαρτα σήν.
ΑΔ. ὅρα γε μή τι φάσμα νερτέρων τόδε.
ΗΡ. οὐ ψυχαγωγὸν τόνδ' ἐποιήσω ξένον.
ΑΔ. ἀλλ' ἣν ἔθαπτον εἰσορῶ δάμαρτ' ἐμήν;
ΗΡ. σάφ' ἴσθ'· ἀπιστεῖν δ' οὔ σε θαυμάζω τύχην. 1130
ΑΔ. θίγω, προσείπω ζῶσαν ὡς δάμαρτ' ἐμήν;

1111 μεθείμην σοῖ γυναῖκα a.   1112 εἰσάγαγ' B | δοκεῖ S] βούλει r. | δόμους Cod. Marc. IX. 10] δόμοις L r.   1114 δῶμα δ' S] δώματ' r.   1117 προτεῖναι B] προτείνειν S πρότεινε a. | θιγεῖν Elmsley] θίγειν B S θίγε a.   1118 δή] μὴν S | καρατομῶν Lobeck] καρατόμῳ MSS.   1119 ἔχω ναί is given to Admetus in the MSS. Wakefield was the first who gave ναί to Heracles, but he altered it to καί. Monk restored the true reading. | νυν] νῦν MSS.   1120 παῖδα was omitted in B, but B¹ has written above λείπει τὸν παῖδα.   1121 πρὸς B] δ' ἐς r. | σῇ Musgrave] σοι MSS.   1122 δ' is omitted in B. | εὐτυχῶν B P.   1123 λέξω S] λεύσω B λεύσσω a.   1124 λεύσσω a] λεύσω B λεύσσων P λεύσων L. | τὴν] τήνδ' S.   1125 ἢ a] ἦ r. | μ' ἐκ Buecheler] με MSS. | ἐμπλήσσει P.   1126 ἄλλη Radermacher] ἀλλὰ MSS.   1127 τόδε Herwerden] τόδ' εἰσορῶ B (γρ. τόδ' ἢ has been written above by B¹ when writing the scholia) τόδ' ἢ r.

ΑΛΚΗΣΤΙΣ.

ΗΡ. πρόσειπ'. ἔχεις γὰρ πᾶν ὅσονπερ ἤθελες.
ΑΔ. ὦ φιλτάτης γυναικὸς ὄμμα καὶ δέμας,
ἔχω σ' ἀέλπτως, οὔποτ' ὄψεσθαι δοκῶν.
ΗΡ. ἔχεις· φθόνος δὲ μή γένοιτό τις θεῶν. 1135
ΑΔ. ὦ τοῦ μεγίστου Ζηνὸς εὐγενὲς τέκνον,
εὐδαιμονοίης, καί σ' ὁ φιτύσας πατὴρ
σῴζοι· σὺ γὰρ δὴ τἄμ' ἀνώρθωσας μόνος.
πῶς τήνδ' ἔπεμψας νέρθεν ἐς φάος τόδε;
ΗΡ. μάχην συνάψας δαιμόνων τῷ κυρίῳ. 1140
ΑΔ. ποῦ τόνδε Θανάτῳ φῂς ἀγῶνα συμβαλεῖν;
ΗΡ. τύμβον παρ' αὐτὸν ἐκ λόχου μάρψας χεροῖν.
ΑΔ. τί γὰρ ποθ' ἥδ' ἄναυδος ἕστηκεν γυνή;
ΗΡ. οὔπω θέμις σοι τῆσδε προσφωνημάτων
κλύειν, πρὶν ἂν θεοῖσι τοῖσι νερτέροις 1145
ἀφαγνίσηται καὶ τρίτον μόλῃ φάος.
ἀλλ' εἴσαγ' εἴσω τήνδε· καὶ δίκαιος ὢν
τὸ λοιπόν, Ἄδμητ,' εὐσέβει περὶ ξένους.
καὶ χαῖρ'· ἐγὼ δὲ τὸν προκείμενον πόνον
Σθενέλου τυράννῳ παιδὶ πορσυνῶ μολών. 1150
ΑΔ. μεῖνον παρ' ἡμῖν καὶ ξυνέστιος γενοῦ.
ΗΡ. αὖθις τόδ' ἔσται, νῦν δ' ἐπείγεσθαί με δεῖ.
ΑΔ. ἀλλ' εὐτυχοίης, νόστιμον δ' ἔλθοις δρόμον.
ἀστοῖς δὲ πάσῃ τ' ἐννέπω τετραρχίᾳ
χοροὺς ἐπ' ἐσθλαῖς συμφοραῖσιν ἱστάναι 1155
βωμούς τε κνισᾶν βουθύτοισι προστροπαῖς.

1132 πανθ' ὅσαπερ S. 1134 οὔποθ' B. 1137 φιτύσας B] φυτεύσας r.
1138 σὺ γὰρ τἀμ' ὤρθωσας S (σὺ γὰρ δὴ τἀμά γ' ὤρθωσας l). 1140 κυρίῳ a d,
with the schol.] κοιράνῳ B S. 1143 ἔστηκε B. 1150 τυράννῳ B P L¹] τυράννου a L. | πορσυνῶ L] πορσύνω r | μολών S] μολῶν r. 1151 ξυνέστιος S] συνέστιος r. 1153 δρόμον Wilamowitz] δόμον S πόδα a (a¹ has written in the margin γρ. δόμον γρ. καὶ ὁδόν) d ὁδόν B. 1154 πάσῃ τ' a πᾶσι τ' r (πᾶσιν l).
1155 συμφοραῖς συνιστάναι a. 1156 κνισᾶν C] κνισσᾶν r | προστροπαῖς L a] προτροπαῖς r.

νῦν γὰρ μεθηρμόσμεσθα βελτίω βίον
τοῦ πρόσθεν· οὐ γὰρ εὐτυχῶν ἀρνήσομαι.
XO. πολλαὶ μορφαὶ τῶν δαιμονίων,
πολλὰ δ' ἀέλπτως κραίνουσι θεοί·   1160
καὶ τὰ δοκηθέντ' οὐκ ἐτελέσθη,
τῶν δ' ἀδοκήτων πόρον ηὗρε θεός.
τοιόνδ' ἀπέβη τόδε πρᾶγμα.

1157 μεθηρμόσμεσθα *l*] μεθηρμόμεσθα *B* μεθηρμόσμεθα *r*.   1163 τόδε] τόδε τὸ *B*.
At the end stands in *B* a *P* τέλος εὐριπίδου ἀλκήστιδος, in *L* εὐριπίδου ἄλκηστις.

SELECT CONJECTURES.

The conjectures which have been made as to readings in the text of the *Alcestis* number more than four thousand. From this great mass I have selected the following as worthy of mention, either from their plausibility and ingenuity or from the influence which they have exerted upon the history of the text. Among them will be found nearly all* of Nauck's and Wecklein's, and many of those made by F. W. Schmidt and Kviçala.

Verse 16 πατέρα τε γραῖάν θ᾽ Monk, καὶ πατέρα γραῖάν θ᾽ Nauck. 17 οὐχ εὗρε· πλὴν γυναικὸς οὔτις ἤθελε (rejecting v. 16) Kviçala. 19–20 ἢν νῦν κ.ο.ε.χ. βαστάζεται | ψυχορραγοῦσαν Usener. Kirchhoff thinks a line has been lost after v. 19. 23 Earle suggests μελάθρων τήνδε φιλτάτων στέγην. 30 τιμῶν ἐνέρους Maass. 31 νοσφιζόμενος Wecklein. 34 Monk suggested σφήλαντα. 36 τόδ᾽: τόθ᾽ Elmsley. 44 βίαν σ᾽: βίαν γ᾽ Earle. 45 χθονὸς κάτω Matthiae. 49 Von Holzinger would punctuate with a colon after χρῇ. 51 καὶ προθυμίαν: Wecklein suggests τῆς προθυμίας. 63 ἇ: χᾶ Herwerden. 64 πείσει Schmidt (παύσῃ the MSS). 66–7 Perhaps these two lines should be rejected as an interpolation. 70 κᾆτ᾽ οὐ for κοὔθ᾽ ἡ Steup. 71 δράσει G. Hermann, δράσω Weil. Zacher would insert 70 and 71 after 62, giving 70 to Thanatos (with a period after χάρις) and reading δ᾽ for θ᾽ in 71. 79 φίλων ⟨τοι⟩ πέλας Dobree, φίλων ⟨οὐ⟩ πέλας Nauck (formerly), φίλων ⟨που⟩ πέλας Heiland. 81 βασίλειαν χρὴ πενθεῖν ἢ ζῶσ᾽ Lascaris (with ἰ), βασίλειαν πενθεῖν χρή μ᾽ ἢ ζῶσ᾽ Kirchhoff. 83 πᾶσί τ᾽: πλεῖστον Naber. ἀεὶ πᾶσιν for ἐμοὶ πᾶσί τ᾽ Schmidt. 85 Ἡελίου θυγάτηρ (omitting τόδε) Dindorf.

---

* Except, of course, such as have been received into the text.

91 μετακύμιον Kviçala (with one schol.) μετακοίμιος Zacher. Hartung conjectured that an anapaestic dipody has been lost after 96. Kirchhoff sets the lacuna before πῶς. 99 ὡς: ἡ Tournier. 101 ἐπὶ: ἐνὶ Tournier. 103 νεολαία: νεαλὴς Dindorf. 116 Ἀμμωνίδας Musgrave. 117 παραλύσει Wakefield. 119 θεῶν δέ γ' ἐσχάραν Reiske, θεῶν δ' ἔτ' ἐσχάρας Ribbeck. 120 ἔτι for ἐπὶ Weil. 122 μούνως δ' Wakefield. 125 ἦλθ' ἂν Monk. 126 Ἄιδα: Ἄιδαο Monk. πύλας: πυλῶνας Hermann, πύλας ⟨καὶ⟩ Dindorf. Kirchhoff marks a lacuna after Ἄιδα τε. 132 ff. Mekler restores thus:

πάντα γὰρ ᾖ	χρῆν	δὴ τετέλεσται
βασιλεῦσι	τέλη	
πάντων δὲ θεῶν	εἰσ'	ἐπὶ βωμοῖς, κ. τ. λ.,

supposing a tear in the archetype. Nauck brackets τετέλεσται βασιλεῦσι. Kirchhoff marks lacunas after ἤδη, τετέλεσται, βασιλεῦσι, θεῶν, βωμοῖσι, supposing that these words began five lines the ends of which have been lost. 134 Dindorf conjectures that six anapaests have fallen out either before or after πλήρεις. 136 ἐκ δόμων: γὰρ δόμων Usener. 148, 149 Tournier would insert these two lines after 143. 153 οὐ μὴ γενέσθαι τήνδ' Reiske, τίς, μὴ γενέσθαι Matthiae. 160 δόμων: δοκῶν Herwerden, δοχῶν Lenz. 180 ὅλην for (MSS.) μόνην Schmidt. 187 θαλάμων Nauck. Earle transposes 204 and 205. 208 Lachmann would reject this line only, retaining 207. 213 τίς ἂν πῶς Aldine, τίς ἂν πᾷ Lascaris, 'alii aliter.' Nauck reads bacchiacs, thus: ἰὼ Ζεῦ, τίς ἂν πῶς πόρος πᾷ γένοιτ' ἂν τύχαις ἃ πάρεστιν τυράννοις and 227 παπαῖ φεῦ, ἰὼ παῖ Φέρητος, παπαῖ, οἷ' ἔπραξας δάμαρτος στερηθείς. 215 ἔτ' εἰσί τις Herwerden. 223 τοῦδ' ἐφεῦρες (MSS.): τῷδ' ἐφηῦρες ⟨τοῦτο⟩ Hermann, τοῦτ' ἐφηῦρες ⟨τῷδε⟩ Hadley, τόνδ' ἐφρούρεις Schmidt. Dindorf regards τοῦδ' ἐφεῦρες as an interpolation; τοιόσδε (sc. ἦσθα), καὶ νῦν Wecklein, τοῦδ' ἦσθα (sc. λυτήριος), καὶ νῦν Weil. 227 σᾶς: ἃς Weil. 230 οὐρανίῳ: οὐρανίαν Lenting, ἀρτανίῳ Herwerden, ἀγχονίῳ Wecklein, οὐλομένῳ Hayley. 231 ἐπόψει: ἔτ' ὄψει Schmidt. 243 βίον: χρόνον Schmidt. 245 οὐράνιαι: οὐράνιοι Earle. 247 ἀνθ' οἷον θανεῖν Wecklein. 252 f. Allen restores the text of this and the antistrophic passage thus:

ὁρῶ δίκωπον ὁρῶ σκάφος, ἄγει μ' ἄγει μέ τις, οὐχ ὁρᾷς;
νεκύων δὲ πορθμεὺς ἔχων νεκύων ἐς αὐλάν, βλέπων
χέρ' ἐπὶ κοντῷ με δὴ καλεῖ ὑπ' ὀφρύσιν κυαναυγέσιν·
"τί μέλλεις; σὺ κατείργεις." τί ῥέξεις; ἄφες. οἵαν
τάδε τοί με σπερχόμενος ταχύνει. | ὁδὸν ἁ δειλαιοτάτα προβαίνω.

254 χέρ': χέρας Paley* (omitting μ' ἤδη). 249 πατρίας the Aldine.
254–5 Earle reads καλεῖ μ' ἐπείγων· | τί μέλλεις; σὺ κατείργεις. 260
Kirchhoff marks a lacuna before νεκύων. εἰς αὐλὰν νεκύων Nauck.
261 κυαναυγὲς Kirchhoff.* αἴδαν Wilamowitz. ᾅδας πτέροις. μέθες
με Kirchhoff. 262 τί ῥέξεις; μέθες Nauck. 272 ὀρῶτον: ὀρώτην
Elmsley. 273 ἀκούειν (or ἀκοῦσαι) Monk. 274 μεῖζον: χεῖρον Stadtmueller. 278 ἐν σοὶ δ' ἔστιν Schmidt. 282–3 Nauck rejects κἀντὶ
— καταστήσασα. 284 ff. Earle would read θνῄσκω, παρόν μοι μὴ
θανεῖν, ὑπὲρ σέθεν. | ἀλλ' ἄνδρα τε σχεῖν Θεσσαλῶν ὃν ἤθελον | καὶ δῶμα
ναίειν ὄλβιον τυραννίδι | οὐκ ἠθέλησα ζῶσ' ἀποσπασθεῖσα σοῦ | ξὺν παισὶν
ὀρφανοῖσιν· οὐδ' ἐφεισάμην | ἥβης, ἔχουσ' ἐν οἷς ἐτερπόμην ἐγώ (289
with a). 287 οὐκ: κοὐκ Lenting. ἀλλ' οὐ γὰρ ἠθέλησ' (omitting ζῆν)
Gomperz. Heiland rejects 287–9. 291 ἥκον ἐκλιπεῖν βίον Hartung.
καταλιπεῖν ἥκον βίον Bauer, καταλύειν ἥκον βίον Weil. καταφρονεῖν ἥκον
βίον Mekler. ἥκον ἐκστῆναι βίου? 304 ἐμῶν: νέμων Mekler, σέβων
Earle, μοι τῶν Kviçala, ὄντας Tournier. διαδόχους for δεσπότας
Schmidt. 308–10 are rejected by Hirzel. 313 Hermann and
Kirchhoff put the comma after τέκνον, Nauck and most edd. after
μοι. 314 πικρᾶς τυχοῦσα συζύγου Hartung. Kviçala rejects 314–16.
318 τόκοισι τοῖσι σοῖς σε Nauck. 321 is rejected by Mekler. τρίτην: ἔνην Weil. μηνὸς: φέγγος (and τρίτον for τρίτην) Herwerden.
μέλλον Kviçala, who also suggested μὴν ἐσέρχεται. οὐδ' εἰς τριταῖον
ἦμαρ Wecklein. σμῆνος ἔρχεται κακῶν Naber. σοι μητρὸς for μοι μηνὸς
Schneider. 325 παῖδες: Prinz conjectures κεδνῆς. 330 ποτε: πόσιν
Mekler. 332–3 Nauck believes to be an interpolation. 333 ἄλλη
σοῦ 'κπρεπεστέρα Bothe. ἄλλη 'στ' (Schmidt) εὐπρεπεστέρα (Lenting)
is suggested by Prinz. ἄλλως ⟨τ'⟩ Weil. 340 μ' ἔσωσας Herwerden.
346 ἐξάραιμι Wakefield. 353 οἶμαι: οἶδα Elmsley. 355 φίλους:

* Cf. Monk's note on 262 of his edition (= 254 Prinz) where he suggested
χέρας and κυαναυγές (though apparently he had given them up).

φίλος Musgrave. 360 κατῆδον ἄν Weidner. 361 Χάρων: γέρων Cobet. 362 βίον: δέμας Nauck. 363 ἐκεῖσε: ἐκεῖ σὺ Prinz, ἐκεῖ γε Wecklein. 372 ἔσχον (MSS.): εἶχον Nauck, εἶργον Schmidt. 373 ἐφ' ὑμῖν: ἐφ' ἡμῖν Nauck. 374 γέ: δέ Nauck. Lenting would give 393–403 to Perimele. 394 οὐκέτ': οὐκ Wecklein. 401 σ' ἔγωγ' ὦ μᾶτερ, ἐγὼ and 413 ἔβας σὺν τᾷδε τέλος are suggested by Nauck. Wilamowitz would read ἐγώ σ' ἐγὼ μᾶτερ σὸς ποτὶ σοῖσι (omitting 402 καλοῦμαι ὁ), and omit 414 ἔφθιτο γὰρ πάρος. 403 γόνασιν for στόμασιν Herwerden. 404 τὴν οὐ: τήν γ' οὐ Hermann. 407 Wecklein omits τε. 409 Hermann conjectured that τλάμων is to be supplied after ἔργα. 423 μένοντες: μέλποντες Schmidt. 433 τοῦδ': Monk suggests τῆσδ'. 434 ἐπεί γ' ἔθνησκεν ἀντ' ἐμοῦ μόνη Usener, τιμᾶν λίαν ἐπεὶ τέθνηκεν ἀντ' ἐμοῦ Kvičala. 448 κύκλος: κυκλὰς Scaliger (with ὥρα), κύκλον Hadley. 450 μηνὸς: φέγγος Wecklein. 452 παννύχου: πάννυχον Wecklein. 458 Κωκυτοῦ τε ῥεέθρων Matthiae, Κωκυτοῖό τε ῥείθρου Earle. 461 αὐτᾶς Wecklein. 464 ἔμοιγ': ἐμοί τ' Hermann. 473 Nauck considers συνδυάδος corrupt. He is inclined to reject ἀλόχου, and γύναι in 463 above. 474 ἦ μάλ' ἂν Tournier. 476 χθονός: πόλεως Nauck. 487 τοι πόνους Nauck, μὴν πόνους Weil (μ' ἦν πόνους L). 505 ὃς τὸν: ὅστις Koster. 514 σῶν: Earle suggests σοι. 526 τότ' Wakefield. 527 κοὐ θανὼν οὐκ ἔστ' ἔτι Weil. κοὐκέτ' ἔστ' οὐ κατθανών Bruhn. 528 τό τ' εἶναι: τό γ' εἶναι Earle. 531 μεμνήμεθα: τητώμεθα Wecklein, λελείμμεθα Schmidt, μεθείμεθα Metzger. 533 ἄλλως: ἁμοῖς Schmidt. 537 ὑπορρίπτεις Tournier. 540 εἰ μόλοι: ἂν μόλοι Schmidt, ἢν μόλῃ Heiland. 542 αἰσχρὸν παρὰ κλαίουσι: αισχρόν ⟨τι⟩ π. κ. Elmsley, αἰσχρὸν ⟨τὸ⟩ π. κ. Erfurdt, αἰσχρὸν ⟨δὲ⟩ π. κ. Porson, αἰσχρὸν γάρ ἐν κλαίουσι Weidner. αἰσχρὸν παρὰ πταίουσι Mekler, α. π. στένουσι Mueller. αἰσχρὸν φίλοις κλαίουσι θοινᾶσθαι πάρα Tate. 552 τί: ἦ Reiske. 555 ἐπεί μοι: ἐπείτοι Naber. 557–8 Herwerden rejects. 565 καὶ τῷ: καί τῳ Heath, καὐτῷ Schmidt, καὶ σοὶ Earle. 566 αἰνέσεις Earle. 576 ποιμνίτας ⟨τινὰς⟩ ὕμνους Herwerden. 580 δὲ: τε Musgrave. 585 πέραν: πέρι Herwerden. 594 Bauer conjectured that ὀρέων should be supplied after Μολοσσῶν to fill the lacuna. 596 ἀλίμενον: ἀλιμένου Reiske. 624 δυσμενῆ: δυσπετῆ Schmidt, δυσχερῆ Nauck, δυστυχῆ Kirchhoff, δυσφερῆ Kvičala. δύσλοφα (for δύσφορα) Mekler. 630 λέγω: νέμω

SELECT CONJECTURES. 57

Schmidt. 632 Nauck thinks spurious. He suggests δώρων for τῶν σῶν, and Mekler τιμῶν. φανήσεται for ταφήσεται Weil. 635 γέρων ὤν: γεραιός Earle. Badham rejects 636–41, Nauck 638-9, Weil 637–41, Schenkl 637–42. 641 Wagner and Dobree reject (and Nauck is inclined to do so). 644 ἠθέλησας : ἠμέλησας Weil. 646 ὀθνείαν: ὀθνεῖον is suggested by Earle. 645-7 Badham rejects. 647 καὶ πατέρα πανδίκως ἂν Schmidt, καὶ πατέρ' ἂν ἐνδίκως ἂν Weil. (καὶ πατέρα was suggested by Hartung.) μόνην: ἐμοί Nauck (ἐμόν B), νέμων Kviçala, ὁμοῦ Schmidt, θανεῖν Kirchhoff. Wecklein suggests πατέρα τ' ἂν ἡγοίμην ἂν ἐνδικώτατα. 655 ἦν δ' ἐγώ σοι: ἢ γεγώς σοι Nauck. δόμων: θρόνων Schmidt. 668 Nauck rejects, and in 667 would read κείνου λέγω, κείνου τόδε or κεῖνον σέβω: κείνου γ' ἐγώ Kviçala, κείνου γ' ἐρῶ or κείνου μέλω Schmidt, κείνου μ' ἐρῶ Weil. Badham rejects 666-8, Hartung 669-72. 674 ὦ παῖ (MSS.) : ὦναξ Monk, ἅλις Kviçala, παλαιοῦ Hense. 679 καὶ: παῖ Weil (who puts a colon after ἡμᾶς in 680). 680 οὐ: κού Wecklein. Nauck would strike out 688 and read in 687 πολυπλέθρους δ' ἔχεις γύας. Schmidt conjectures that 690 should be put after 691. 697 λέγεις : ψέγεις second Hervagian ed. 708 λέξαντος : λέξοντος Reiske, 'λέγξοντος Hermann. 711 Bauer would punctuate with a period, not a sign of interrogation. 713 μάσσον' for μεῖζον' Schmidt. μείζονα (omitting ἂν) Schaefer. 714 and 715 Nauck places after 719. 716 ἀλλ' οὐ νεκρὸν σύ γ' ἀντὶ σοῦ Nauck. 717–18 Wecklein rejects. 719 τοῦδε γ': τοῦδ' ἔτ' Kirchhoff. 724 γέροντα: γέροντι Weil. 732 ἦ: ἢ Kviçala. 739 τοὔμπεσὸν for τοὐν ποσὶν Weil. 756 ποτήριον δ' ἐν χερσὶ Musgrave, ποτῆρα δ' εὐθὺς χερσὶ Nauck, ποτῆρα δ'· ἐν ταῖς χερσὶ Cobet, ποτῆρα δ' ἐ(ὐρὺ)ν χερσὶ Weil. ποτῆρα δ' εἶτ' ἐν χερσὶ ? 780 οἶδας: οἶσθας Nauck. 785 ᾗ 'ποβήσεται Lenting, οἷ 'ποβήσεται Wecklein. 792 ταῦτα: πάντα Markland. 797 φρενῶν: τρόπου Nauck. 798 σκύφου : σκύφῳ Heiland. 807 τί: πῶς Tournier. οὐ κάτοισθα: οὐκ ἄρ' οἶσθα Cobet. 808 τι: γε Elmsley. 810 εὖ πάσχειν: εὖ πράσσειν Nauck. Prinz thinks 810 and 811 spurious. Nauck removes them and inserts them after 813. Nauck rejects 816–19, Kirchhoff 818–20, Kviçala 818-19. Hannemueller rejects 817–20 (reading πέποιθε δεινά τις in 816). Mekler rejects 820, and the words καὶ κουρὰν στολμούς τε in 818–

19, reading ὑμῖν for ἡμῖν in 818. 820 τέκνων: γένους Kirchhoff. γέρων πατήρ: πατὴρ γέρων Hermann. 822 δῆτά με ξενίζετε Heiland. 827 πρόσωπον: πρόσωθεν Weil, πεπλώματ' Stadtmueller. πρόσοψιν? κουράν τε δυσπρόσωπον Herwerden, κουράν τ' ἄχει προσῳδόν Schmidt. 832 μή: μοι Matthiae. τόδ' ἦν for τὸ μὴ Schmidt. τοῦτο for σοῦ τὸ Kviçala. 834 ποῦ: ποῖ Monk. 836 ξεστὸν: χωστὸν Nauck. 838 μ' for σ' Tournier. 839 Ἠλεκτρυώνη 'γείνατ' Wilamowitz. 845 πίνοντα: πεινῶντα Schmidt. 847 δὲ: τε Nauck. He suspects ἐμαῖν; and Wecklein suggests περιβαλὼν χεροῖν τύχω. 851 τὴν κάτω Aldine. 852 δόμους: μυχούς Nauck. 857 Schmidt believes to be an interpolation. 862 Hermann doubles αἰαῖ, Wecklein omits it. 873 πέπονθας: πεπονθὼς Hermann (reading πέρας δ' οὐδὲν τίθης ἀλγέων in 890). 876 μήποτ': μηκέτ' Metzger. 879 τί γὰρ: τίνος Tournier. 877 ⟨μ' ἐν⟩αντα Hermann, ⟨τιν'⟩άντα Musgrave. ⟨σε π⟩άντα Hadley. Dindorf rejects ἄντα λυπρόν and marks a lacuna; σ' ἂν ἦν ἄλυπον Wecklein. 885 νόσους: μόρους Naber. 890 Perhaps δ' ἔτ' for δέ γ'. 901 ψυχὰ τὼ πιστοτάτα Wecklein. 907 ἄτεκνος ὤν: ἀπότεκνος Weil. 921 ἀριστῶν Hermann. 930 ἔλιπε, φιλία a writer in the Quarterly Review XV. p. 123, ἔλιπέ σε φίλα Schmidt. 934 δάμαρτα Dindorf (reading πολλοῖς 931). 943 εἰσόδου: ἐξόδου Lenting, εἰσδοχῆς Earle. Nauck thinks the verse an interpolation. 948 πίπτοντα: πίτνοντα Wecklein. 960 κύδιον: κέρδιον Purgold. 971 ἀντιτεμὼν: ἀντίτομον Kvičala. 975 μέλει for κλύει Wecklein. 984 Nauck prefers καί σέ γ' ἀφύκτοισι. 986 ἄνω: βροτῶν Earle. ἄναξ? 992 φίλα δὲ θανοῦσ' ἔτ' ἔσται Prinz, φ. δ. θανοῦσα κεῖται Wecklein, φ. δ. θανοῦσ' ἐς ἀεί Nauck, φ. δ. καὶ ἐν θανοῦσιν Weil. 1005 φᾶμαι: φωταί Schmidt. 1009 ἔχειν: στέγειν Schmidt. 1015 ἐλειψάμην: ἐσπεισάμην Aldine. 1018 λυπεῖν ⟨γ'⟩ Monk. 1036 Nauck suspects ἴσως. 1045 μὴ 'μέ· μιμνήσκεις κακῶν Kirchhoff (following B). 1055 θάλαμον ἐμβήσας Schmidt. 1060–61 ἀξίως δέ νιν σέβειν | πολλὴν πρόνοιαν δεῖ μ' ἔχειν Rassow. 1062 ἔχουσ': ἔχεις (with comma before and after ἴσθι) Weil. 1063 Nauck rejects προσήιξαι and conjectures καὶ δέμας προσεμφερές (προσεικαστόν Schmidt). Prinz suggests that 1062 and 1063 should be combined, so as to read μορφῆς μέτρ' ἴσθι ταῦτ' ἔχουσ' Ἀλκήστιδι. 1070 οὐ λέγοιμ' ἂν εὖ σ' ἔχειν τύχης Schmidt. 1071 ἥτις ἐστί Monk(?),* ὅστις εἶσι Hermann; Wecklein suggests ἥτις εἶσι.

ὅσιος εἰ σύ Schmidt. Bauer would put a comma after λέγω, not a period. 1086 χρόνον: ὀρθῶς is suggested by Nauck. 1090 ἥτις: ἣ Kirchhoff (reading τῷδ᾽ ἀνδρί). 1093 αἰδῶ μὲν αἰνῶ Prinz. 1094 ἴσθ᾽ οὔποτ᾽ — καλῶν Wakefield, ὡς οὔποτ᾽ — καλεῖς Herwerden, οὐ μήποτ᾽ — καλεῖς Kvičala, ὡς μήποτ᾽ ἴσθι τόνδε νυμφίον καλῶν Weidner (rejecting ἄνδρα). Kirchhoff conjectures that two verses have fallen out before this line. 1097 γενναίων: γενναίως Lenting, γ᾽ ἐνναίειν Schmidt. 1101 ἐς δέον: Nauck suggests εἰς καλόν. 1107–8 Nauck considers spurious. Prinz suspects εἰδώς τι. 1115 μόνῃ: μόνου Nauck. 1118 Weil gives the second half of the line to Heracles. 1119 νυν: νιν Monk. 1123 θαῦμ᾽: φάσμ᾽ Nauck. 1124 λεύσσω: λέξω Earle (reading φάσμ᾽ and λεύσσω in 1123). 1125 χαρά: χάρις Kvičala. Nauck suspects ἐκπλήσσει χαρά. ἢ κερτόμῳ με θεῶν τις ἐκπλήσσει χαρᾷ Wheeler. 1126 οὐκ ἔστιν ἄλλως· τήνδ᾽ Nauck. 1127 ἀλλ᾽ ἦ τι φάσμα νερτέρων τόδ᾽ εἰσορῶ; Kirchhoff. 1129 Mekler proposes ξυνάορον for δάμαρτ᾽ ἐμήν. 1130 τύχῃ Reiske. 1131 ὡς ⟨ἐτητύμως⟩ Earle. 1134 οὔποθ᾽ ἅψεσθαι Stadtmueller. 1141 φῄς: Prinz suggests ᾽τλης. 1143 ὧδ᾽ for ἧδ᾽ Earle. 1154 τετραρχίᾳ: τετραπτόλει Nauck. 1157 μεθηρμόσμεσθα: μεθωρμίσμεσθα Wakefield.

* Prinz ascribes this conjecture to Monk, but it is not in Monk's edition. Tyrwhitt suggested ὅστις ἐστί.

CRITICAL AND EXEGETICAL NOTES.

[In citing from the dramatists Kirchhoff's edition of Aeschylus (Berlin, 1880), Mekler's Sophocles (Leipzig, 1889), Kirchhoff's smaller edition of Euripides (Berlin, 1867), and for the fragments Nauck's *Tragicorum Graecorum Fragmenta* (second ed. Leipzig, 1889) have been used.]

VERSE 1. Scene Pherae in Thessaly, in front of the palace of King Admetus. Apollo, armed with bow and quiver (vv. 35, 39–40), comes out of the palace-door and speaks the prologue. ᾿Ω δώματ' ᾿Αδμήτει': the address serves at once to fix the locality and to lend impressiveness to the opening of the play. The *Andromache* and *Electra* open with a similar apostrophe. — The use of the adjective derived from a proper noun instead of the possessive genitive is too common in the tragedians to need illustration.

2. θῆσσαν τράπεζαν: so *El.* 205 θῆσσαν ἑστίαν. αἰνέσαι: Schol. εὐαρεστῆσαι, καταδέξασθαι.

4. φλόγα: here unqualified by an adjective; although when the flame meant is the lightning (as here) the usual phrase is φλὸξ κεραυνία or οὐρανία.

8. Wakefield and Earle read δ' ἐς αἶαν with Athenagoras. But (1) it is a well-known principle of criticism that variant readings found only in quotations made by one classical writer from another should be regarded with great suspicion, as the ancients so often quoted from memory: (2) as has been repeatedly pointed out (recently by Wecklein *Berliner Woch. f. klass. Phil.* 1895, No. 40, p. 1255), the tragedians do not use the form αἶα where γαῖα is metrically possible.

9. Cf. *Phoen.* 425 οὐ μεμπτὸς ἡμῖν ὁ γάμος εἰς τόδ' ἡμέρας: *Hippol.* 1003, Soph. *O. C.* 1138. ἐσῴζον: as to the evidence for the iota subscript, see note on 292.

10. This line has given some difficulty. Wuestemann objects that Apollo would not call himself ὅσιος, especially when he was still laden with blood-guilt from the slaughter of the Cyclopes. Wheeler (*De Alcest. et Hippol. interp.* p. 11) goes so far as to say of the verse: 'spurium esse certis argumentis docuit me vir illustrissimus mihi hoc loco non nominandus. Menda non sanabilia duo sunt.' Nevertheless, I cannot help believing the line to be perfectly sound. If ὅσιος means 'outwardly pure,' there is a real difficulty; for according to the prevailing Delphian form of the legend (symbolized by the festival called *Stepteria*) Apollo was not purified until his servitude was over, though there was another form of the story according to which he was purified in Crete *before*

he went to Thessaly (see the 3d. hypoth. to Pindar *Pyth.*, vol. II. p. 298 Boeckh). I do not believe, however, that the objection occurred to Euripides at all. Cf. Aesch. *Suppl.* 204 ἁγνόν τ' Ἀπόλλω φυγάδ' ἀπ' οὐρανοῦ θεόν, where Apollo is called ἁγνός, though his punishment is mentioned in the same breath. Besides, ὅσιος usually denotes *inward piety* rather than *ceremonial purity* (Schmidt *Synonymik* s. v. ἱερός). Apollo merely means that being himself pious by nature he found a congenial spirit in his master. The fact that there are two resolved feet in the line does not militate against its genuineness; see note on v. 802. The verse cannot be detached from its context without injuring the connection; the play on words in ὁσίου γὰρ ἀνδρὸς ὅσιος ὤν is characteristic *; indeed, it would be hard to find a more Euripidean line.

12. Μοίρας δολώσας: cf. Aesch. *Eum.* 713 ff. τοιαῦτ' ἔδρασας καὶ Φέρητος ἐν δόμοις · | Μοίρας ἔπεισας ἀφθίτους θεῖναι βροτούς . . . σύ τοι παλαιὰς διανομὰς καταφθίσας | οἴνῳ παρηπάτησας ἀρχαίας θεάς. Wilamowitz (*Isyllos* p. 66) with great plausibility conjectures that Aeschylus and Euripides are here following Phrynichus (see Introd. p. xv). ᾔνεσαν: cf. αἰνέσαι in v. 2. In both uses there is the underlying idea of concession or acquiescence.

13. ᾄδην: here a common noun, 'death,' as often; e.g. *Hippol.* 1047 ταχὺς γὰρ ᾄδης ῥᾷστος ἀνδρὶ δυσσεβεῖ, Aesch. *Ag.* 667 ᾄδην πόντιον πεφευγότες. It is very difficult to determine at what point the *personal* element in such words ceases to be felt.

16. This line was rejected by Dindorf, and is bracketed by Prinz and Nauck. Earle rejects it altogether. As it stands in the MSS. (πατέρα γεραιάν θ' ἥ σφ' ἔτικτε μητέρα), Nauck's objection (*Euripideische Studien* II. p. 49) : " Die Worte πατέρα γεραιάν τε μητέρα können nach dem Zusammenhange nur als Apposition zu πάντας φίλους genommen werden; dass es aber vollkommen sinnlos ist πάντας φίλους durch πατέρα καὶ μητέρα zu erläutern, wird jeder zugeben müssen " is unanswerable. Hermann, with his usual positiveness, observes: " Non tria, amici, et pater, et mater commemorantur, sed omnes comprehenduntur amicorum nomine, quorum deinde exempla afferuntur"; but this is unsatisfactory. We should in that case at least have an intensive particle, " even his own father and mother." Dr. Verrall has recently argued (*Euripides the Rationalist* pp. 27 ff.) that the MSS. reading is sound because " according to the bargain none was admissible except the *family of Admetus*," so that the πάντες φίλοι are necessarily the father, mother and wife of Admetus (the children being too young to be accepted as substitutes). This position seems quite untenable. (1) The writer in the *Bibliotheca* of Apollodorus, I. 9, 15, 2 Hercher (probably following the Hesiodic account; see Wilamowitz *Isyllos* pp. 57 ff.) says: ᾐτήσατο παρὰ Μοιρῶν ἵνα, ὅταν Ἄδμητος μέλλει τελευτᾶν, ἀπολυθῇ τοῦ θανάτου, ἂν ἑκουσίως τις ὑπὲρ αὐτοῦ θνῄσκειν ἕληται. The words πατὴρ ἢ μήτηρ ἢ γυνή, which follow in the MSS., have ever since Heyne's time been justly regarded as '*interpretamentum miselli grammatici*':

---

* See Weber's article (in *Comment. Wolfflinianae*, p. 99 f.) on " Nominalparataxen " in the tragedians.

Hercher omits them in his text. Hyginus (*Fab.* 51), who probably drew from the same source (Wilamowitz *l. s. c.* p. 68), says "*et illud ab Apolline accepit ut pro se alius voluntarie moreretur.*" The schol. on v. 12 observes: οἴνῳ γὰρ ταύτας, φασί, τῶν λογισμῶν ἀπαγαγὼν ἐξῃτήσατο Ἄδμητον, οὕτω μέντοι ὥστε ἀντιδοῦναι ἑαυτοῦ ἕτερον τῷ Ἅιδῃ. The schol. on v. 34 says: μεθύσας γὰρ αὐτὰς ᾔτησε παρ' αὐτῶν ἀντὶ Ἀδμήτου ἄλλον ἀποθανεῖν. So too the first hypothesis to the play: Ἀπόλλων ᾐτήσατο παρὰ τῶν Μοιρῶν ὅπως ὁ Ἄδμητος τελευτᾶν μέλλων παράσχῃ τὸν ὑπὲρ ἑαυτοῦ ἑκόντα τεθνηξόμενον. In none of these cases is any restriction spoken of such as Dr. Verrall assumes to have existed (if we except the worthless gloss in Apollodorus mentioned above). And if Euripides meant to restrict the substitution to the family of Admetus, why did he use such phrases as ἄλλον νεκρόν and πάντας φίλους, which, taken apart from v. 16, would certainly be understood otherwise? (2) Again, Dr. Verrall, understanding τοῖς κάτω (v. 14) as meaning *the dead of Admetus's family*, observes: "The death of a person of another family, who would be buried with *his* 'loved ones,' in a different burying-place, and worshipped with other and alien rites, would be no compensation at all." But surely it is more natural to take τοῖς κάτω (sc. θεοῖς) as meaning the deities of the underworld (cf. v. 75, v. 851 ff.). According to the *Eoeae* (Wilamowitz *l. s. c.*) the deity whose wrath made the sacrifice necessary was the Pheraean Artemis Βριμώ (cf. Apollod. *Bibl.* I. 9, 15, 2); and this very Βριμώ was identified with the chthonian Hecate (Lycoph. *Alex.* 1176, Apollon. Rhod. III. 860) or Persephone (Lycoph. *Alex.* 698 and schol.), the queen of the underworld. Euripides doubtless was familiar with this fact. Hence Dr. Verrall's argument loses much of its force. (3) Again, could there be a more glaring instance of bathos than after the fine line πάντας δ' ἐλέγξας καὶ διεξελθὼν φίλους (with its emphatic πάντας) to suddenly inform the reader that these πάντες φίλοι were only *three* in number? The question then arises whether the line should be emended or rejected as an interpolation. Nauck's καὶ πατέρα γραῖάν θ' ἡ σφ' ἔτικτε μητέρα is probably the best emendation that has yet been suggested; but he himself was inclined in his later years to reject the line. The omission of the verse restores a clear and simple connection, and leaves to πάντας φίλους its proper and natural sense. I believe the line to be an interpolation, made by some one who wished, like Dr. Verrall, to restrict the substitution to the family of Admetus.

17, 18. ὅστις, Reiske's certain and necessary emendation for ἥτις, is accepted by almost all modern editors of the play. Kvíçala's οὐκ ηὗρε· πλὴν γυναικὸς οὗτις ἤθελε is elegant, but not convincing. With regard to 17, however, there is a wide difference of opinion. One class of editors (Dindorf, Kirchhoff, Prinz, Weil, Nauck) reads θανεῖν and (with C) μηδ' ἔτ'. Another (Monk, Wecklein, Earle, with Wilamowitz *Hermes* XVII. p. 364) reads θανὼν (with Reiske) and μηκέτ' (with all the best MSS.). To read θανεῖν and retain μηκέτ' is out of the question, as the asyndeton is too harsh. In behalf of the reading θανεῖν . . . μηδ' ἔτ' may be urged the frequent parallelism in such expressions, e.g. v. 21, *Heracl.* 969 χρῆν τόνδε μὴ ζῆν μηδ' ὁρᾶν φάος ἔτι, *El.* 349 ἀνήρ ἐστι καὶ λεύσσει φάος; etc. But the arguments of Wilamowitz in favor of θανών ... μηκέτ' seem conclusive (see *Hermes l. s. c.*). μηκέτι has the support of the best MSS. of both classes, while μηδ' ἔτ' is attested only by the comparatively worthless Codex Havniensis. Moreover, if θανών ... μηκέτ' was the original reading, when some 'intelligent reader' changed ὅστις in 17 to ἥτις, thinking that γυναικός should be its antecedent, θανών in 18 could not be changed to θανοῦσα for metrical reasons, and hence would naturally be altered to θανεῖν. This would leave exactly that form of the two lines which is found in the best MSS. Then some one, thinking to better matters, would change μηκέτ' to μηδ' ἔτ' to avoid the asyndeton, exactly as we find in C. But if θανεῖν ... μηδ' ἔτ' was the original reading, the change of μηδ' ἔτ' to μηκέτ' was quite uncalled-for. Besides, the expression θανών ... μηκέτ' εἰσορᾶν φάος can easily be paralleled, e.g. *Ion* 853 ἀποδοὺς θανεῖν τε ζῶν τε φέγγος εἰσορᾶν, *Hel.* 530 φησὶ δ' ἐν φάει | πόσιν τὸν ἀμὸν ζῶντα φέγγος εἰσορᾶν, etc. — κείνου: the use of the demonstrative instead of the indirect reflexive changes the point of view from that of Admetus to that of Apollo and the audience, as Earle well puts it. Besides, πρὸ οὗ or αὑτοῦ would have given hiatus. For a still bolder use of the demonstrative instead of the reflexive, see Xen. *Hellen.* I. 6, 14 ἑαυτοῦ γε ἄρχοντος — εἰς τοὐκείνου δυνατόν.

19. Usener (*Fleckeisen's Jahrb.* vol. 139 [1889] p. 364) says of this line: "quoniam quis tandem mulierem moribundam sustentet plane obscurum est, ferri nequit." He would therefore emend (see Select Conjectures). But ἐν χεροῖν is purposely left indeterminate, the poet not caring to specify whether Alcestis is being carried by Admetus himself, or the attendants, or both. Cf. v. 201 ἄκοιτιν ἐν χεροῖν ἔχων (but 266 μέθετε, μέθετε ... κλίνατ'). The dual (χεροῖν) is, of course, no proof that Admetus alone is meant.

20. ψυχορραγοῦσα: cf. v. 141, and *Herc. F.* 324. The schol. explains by ἐγγὺς τοῦ ἀποθανεῖν οὖσα. Hesychius has ψυχορ(ρ)αγεῖ· ἀποθνῄσκει, and the schol. on Apoll. Rhod. II. 835 explains ψυχορραγέοντα by ἀποψυχοῦντα (*sic*). The word is not uncommon in late writers. The edd. from Monk down point out the analogy with στημορραγεῖν (Aesch. *Pers.* 827).

22. Cf. *Hippol.* 1437 ff., where Artemis withdraws to avoid pollution from the dying Hippolytus. The Greeks thought not only that a person was polluted by touching, seeing, or being under the same roof with a corpse, but also that the house in which there was a dead body was itself rendered impure; a belief which is attested not only by numerous passages in ancient writers, but also by inscriptions (e.g. Dittenberger *Sylloge* nos. 379, 468, 469) and by the custom of placing the ὄστρακον or ἀρδάνιον at the door (see note on vv. 98 ff.).

23. The question arises whether Apollo is conceived as just quitting the service of Admetus, or whether his servitude has ceased some time before and he has merely been revisiting his former master. The language of the text is not in itself decisive (cf. vv. 8–9), but on the whole favors the former alternative, which I am strongly inclined to accept. The tone of lingering affection in which Apollo speaks in v. 23 is certainly appropriate to one leaving a kind master after a long term of service. τῶνδε φιλτάτην : so the schol. on *Hippol.* 1437. This is probably right : τῶνδε φιλτάτων, the reading of one class of MSS., and τήνδε φιλτάτην, that of the other, are both due to that tendency to assimilate the constructions and forms of adjacent words which has been so pernicious to our classical texts.*

24. As to the genuineness of vv. 24-76, see Introd. p. xxxvii f. If the passage is an interpolation, it is at least an early one. — Enter Thanatos. He carries a sword (v. 76), and we may perhaps infer from v. 843 that he has black wings (or black *garments* if we read μελάμπεπλον). On the conception of Thanatos in this play, see notes on 261 and 845.

25. ἱερέα: the MSS. have ἱερῆ (though in *L* the first hand has written ερέα above the ερῆ). The question whether the acc. sing. in η from nouns in ευς is allowable in the tragedians is disputed. The evidence seems to be as follows. In Homer the forms Τυδῆ (Δ 384, cf. Herodian, vol. II. pp. 676-7 Lenz) and Μηκιστῆ (Ο 339) are found in the most and best of the MSS.; though in both passages there are some variants, and in both emendation is easy. The form 'Οδυσῆ is said by the schol. to have been read by Aristarchus in τ 136, though the MSS. have ὀδυσσῆα or ὀδυσῆα. Whether these forms in ῆ should be retained or not is matter of high dispute, and editors are very evenly divided. The present writer is inclined, with Nauck (*Bulletin de l'Académie imp. de St. Pétersbourg* 17 pp. 190 ff.), Christ, Van Leeuwen and others, to reject them. See Menrad *De contractionis usu Homerico*, pp. 60 ff. Hesiod has no instance of the form in ῆ. In Pindar, too, it is surprisingly rare; I have noted but three cases, 'Αλκυονῆ *Isth.* V. (VI.) 33 and *Nem.* IV. 27, and 'Οδυσσῆ *Nem.* VIII. 26. In the other lyric poets there seems to be no instance of the form in ῆ ('Ερετρῆ Crates fr. 5 is Bergk's emendation, the MSS. having 'Ερέτρην). In Herod. VII. 220 in an oracle the form βασιλῆ occurs (so most MSS., βασιλεῖ C, βασιλῆα dz). Aeschylus seems not to have the form in ῆ, and I have found no instance in Sophocles. In Euripides I have noted four cases, *El.* 439 'Αχιλῆ, *Rh.* 708 'Οδυσσῆ, fr. 781, 24 Nauck βασιλῆ (βασιλεῖ M. Schmidt), all lyric, and the one in our text. Aristophanes has ξυγγραφῆ in a chorus, *Achar.* 1150 (but there the soundness of the text is doubtful on other grounds, and many editors read τὸν μέλεον τῶν μελέων with Elmsley). The Attic inscriptions do not have the form in ῆ (Meisterhans p. 109, Wecklein *Cur. Epigr.* p. 21), though it is not rare in the κοινή and common in the later Doric (Kühner-Blass I. p. 451, 3). In view of these facts I doubt whether Euripides ever used the contracted form in ῆ in trimeters, and am inclined to read ἱερέα with Monk. For the synizesis cf. Γηρυονέα Hesiod *Th.* 982 (so Rzach with M), Πηλέα Soph. fr. 447, 1, 'Οδυσσέα Soph. *Aj.* 104, Μενοικέα Eur. *Phoen.* 913, 'Αχιλλέα *Rhes.* 977, *I. A.* 1341,

* On the frequent interchange of pronominal forms in the MSS., see Wecklein *Beiträge zur Kritik des Euripides* p. 479 f.

Πηλέα Aristoph. *Ran.* 863, etc. φθινόντων : so Wecklein for θανόντων of the MSS. Thanatos is the ἱερεύς of the *dying* (cf. 74 ff.), not of those *already dead;* hence the emendation seems necessary. The resemblance both in form and meaning between φθινόντων and θανόντων would facilitate the change. Weil thinks that θανόντων is used by a kind of prolepsis : but *Herc. F.* 454 ἀγόμεθα ζεῦγος οὐ καλὸν νεκρῶν, which he quotes, is scarcely a parallel to this passage.

26. σύμμετρος, which Nauck conjectured to be the true reading (the adjective, not the adverb, being regularly used in such cases), is actually found in *P*, the other MSS. having συμμέτρως. Nauck compares Soph. *Antig.* 387 ποίᾳ ξύμμετρος προύβην τύχῃ;

27. φρουρῶν τόδ' ἦμαρ : the figure is that of one watching a prisoner who is liable to escape him. I know of no other instance of φρουρεῖν ἦμαρ or ἡμέραν in Euripides, Aeschylus or Sophocles.

29. πολεῖς : cf. *Or.* 1269 τίς ὅδ' ἄρ' ἀμφὶ μέλαθρον πολεῖ σὸν ἀγρότας ἀνήρ;

30-31. This passage has given rise to much discussion. Nauck (*Eur. Stud.* II. p. 50) rejected v. 31 as a useless and inappropriate addition. He pointed out that v. 30 ἀδικεῖς αὖ τιμὰς ἐνέρων makes complete sense by itself (cf. *Phoen.* 958 ἀδικεῖ τὰ τῶν θεῶν), and thought that 31 was added by some one who did not understand the construction ἀδικεῖς τιμάς. The line has a very Byzantine look, and is actually wanting in *P*. Nauck's objections to ἀφοριζόμενος do not, however, appear conclusive. The verb ἀφορίζειν signifies "to mark off with bounds" (ὅροι), and hence "to circumscribe, limit, define," the usual meaning of the word; and in the middle it may mean "to mark off for oneself" as one's own property, and hence to "appropriate," as in the passage from our text and Isocr. *Phil.* 120 χώραν ὅτι πλείστην ἀφορίσασθαι. Another way of explaining the latter usage is to assume that ἀφορίζειν sometimes meant "to *remove* the bounds," and in the middle "to appropriate by removing the bounds"; cf. the Scriptural injunction not to move a neighbor's landmark. But I know of no passage where ἀφορίζειν is used with the meaning "to remove the bounds" from a piece of property. On ὁρίζειν and its compounds, see Pollux IX. 8. But though ἀφοριζόμενος may be defended, its juxtaposition with καταπαύων ("appropriating and suppressing") is certainly harsh, and I am inclined to think that Nauck's critical insight guided him aright in rejecting the line.

33-4. Μοίρας δολίῳ | σφήλαντι τέχνῃ : see note on v. 12.

35. τοξήρη : proleptic. Cf. *Ion.* 980 ξιφηφόρους σοὺς ὁπλίσας ὀπάονας for the construction, and for the word *Rhes.* 226 Ἄπολλον . . . μόλε τοξήρης, *Herc. F.* 188 τοξήρη σάγην, ib. 1062 τοξήρει ψαλμῷ τοξεύσας.

36. τόδ' : i.e. πόσιν ἐκλύσασ' αὐτὴ προθανεῖν. The τόδε is used because Thanatos wishes to make his statement just as *explicit* as possible, and remind Apollo of the exact terms of the agreement. Hence it is needless to read τόθ' with Elmsley.

38. θάρσει: the form in ρσ is commonly said to be early Attic, but this has not thus far been confirmed by the inscriptions. See Meisterhans[2] p. 76, 5. **λόγους κεδνούς**: cf. *Rhes.* 272 φέρω κεδνοὺς λόγους.

39. τί ... τόξων ἔργον: cf. *Hippol.* 911 σιωπῆς δ' οὐδὲν ἔργον, and the Latin *opus est*.

40. Monk aptly compares Hor. *Odes* III. 4, 60 *nunquam humero positurus arcum ... Apollo.* **αἰεί**: so L. Porson, relying upon insufficient evidence, denied that the tragedians used this form; but in the words of Mr. Rutherford (*New Phrynichus* p. 112), "no one would now venture to dispute that in the old Attic of Tragedy forms like καίω, κλαίω, αἰετός, αἰεί, ἐλαία, were retained when κάω, κλάω, ἀεί ἐλάα had replaced them in ordinary speech." Cf. Wecklein *Cur. Epigr.* p. 64: "Nulla causa est cur formam αἰεί ubi prior longa requiritur a diverbio tragicorum abiudicemus: comprobatur illa titulis, libris, testimonio Marcellini" (*vit. Thucyd.* 52). The Medicean MS. of Sophocles and Aeschylus generally has αἰεί where the metre requires a long penult. The Attic inscriptions show ἀεί and αἰεί side by side down to about 360 B.C., after which (except in the decrees of θιασῶται) ἀεί is the form in regular use. Hence the statements of the grammarians (see Voemel *Dem. Contr.* pp. 28 ff., Wecklein *l. s. c.* pp. 63 ff.) that ἀεί was the Attic form are correct as to the later Attic usage, but should not be understood as excluding αἰεί from the tragedians. See also Ellendt's Lex. to Sophocles *s. v.* ἀεί, Meisterhans[2] pp. 24–5, Kühner-Blass I. p. 137. In the passage from our text the penult is long and has the ictus, and besides αἰεί, as being the older and rarer form, is more likely to be right than the later and more familiar ἀεί. A copyist might easily change αἰεί to ἀεί, but would scarcely have changed ἀεί to αἰεί. Hence I have followed the reading of L.

43. νοσφιεῖς: cf. *Suppl.* 153 ἢ πού σφ' ἀδελφὸς χρημάτων νοσφίζεται; ib. 539. Euripides seems not to have used the double-accusative construction with this verb.

44. πρὸς βίαν σ': Earle's conjecture, γ' for σ', is very plausible, and may well be right; but it does not seem necessary to alter the reading of the MSS.

45. κάτω χθονός: so the best MSS. (except P, which has κατὰ χθονός). Matthiae read χθονὸς κάτω, and so Hermann, Dindorf and Earle (see his pref. p. VI note). It is true, as Hermann observes, that the chiastic order (ὑπὲρ γῆς ... χθονὸς κάτω) is more effective; and the inferior MSS. c, d, (also a?) are said to have that reading; but Euripides did not always put things in the most effective way, and it seems most prudent to follow the best MSS. Cf. *Troad.* 1243 εἰ δ' ἡμᾶς θεὸς | ἔστρεψε τἄνω περιβαλὼν κάτω χθονός. κατὰ χθονός in P is doubtless due to κατὰ χθονὸς in 75 (cf. 103). Cf. *Heraclid.* 592, where Stobaeus read κάτω χθονός, but our MSS. have κατὰ χθονός.

47. νέρτεραν: this reading (that of P and l) is certainly right, and is accepted by all the edd. Cf. *Herc. F.* 335 νερτέρᾳ ... χθονί, and from the *Cresphontes* (fr. 450 Nauck) εἰ μὲν γὰρ οἰκεῖ νερτέρας ὑπὸ χθονός. Weil compares Aesch. *Pers.* 839 ἄπειμι γῆς ὑπὸ ζόφον κάτω.

48. Cf. *Med.* 941 οὐκ οἶδ᾽ ἂν εἰ πείσαιμι, πειρᾶσθαι δὲ χρή. It is curious that the Greek οὐκ οἶδ᾽ εἰ so often indicates a leaning toward the *negative* side of a question, while the Latin *nescio an* usually implies a leaning toward an *affirmative* view. On the position of ἂν see Goodwin *M. and T.* 220, 2.

50. This is a very troublesome line. Two principal questions arise: (1) what does τοῖς μέλλουσι mean, and (2) whether we should read ἐμβαλεῖν with the MSS. or ἀμβαλεῖν with Bursian. Τοῖς μέλλουσι (sc. θνῄσκειν) might mean (α) "those who *are destined* to die." But *all* are destined to die, and Alcestis with the rest; hence this interpretation seems impossible here, particularly if we read ἐμβαλεῖν. Some editors (Jerram, and Earle if I rightly understand his note) explain the phrase as meaning (β) "those who in the natural course of things will die," i.e. *the old*, and retain ἐμβαλεῖν. But this is surely very forced, and would be liable to be misunderstood, as Alcestis herself μέλλει θνῄσκειν in another sense. The words may also mean (γ) "those who are delaying," or "hesitating to die," i.e. *the aged*, who are ripe for death but fain would linger, possibly with special reference to the father and mother of Admetus. Cf. the schol.: τοῖς γεγηρακόσι, τούτοις γὰρ λέγει ⟨τῷ⟩ μέλλουσι. βραδύνουσι γὰρ ἐν τῇ ζωῇ. In this case we must obviously read ἐμβαλεῖν. Lastly (δ) the words may mean "those who are about to die," "are at the point of death," with special reference to Alcestis. Bursian's emendation will then be necessary. The choice clearly lies between (γ) and (δ). Both interpretations are supported by eminent authorities, but a question of this kind cannot be settled by "counting heads." Explanation (γ) has the support of the schol., and requires no change of text; but (δ), to which I strongly incline, gives to τοῖς μέλλουσι a simpler and more natural sense, while an unusual form like ἀμβαλεῖν would be extremely liable to be altered to a more familiar one. Cf. *Hec.* 1263 ἀμβήσει, where a L G have ἀμβήσῃ but A B E ἐμβήσῃ. Bauer thought that the line contained an intentional "*double entendre*," τοῖς μέλλουσι being capable of meaning *either* "the aged" or "those who are about to die," i.e. Alcestis (retaining ἐμβαλεῖν); but this would have given Thanatos a chance to make a very effective retort, taking the words in the latter sense, and Apollo would have no object in thus "laying himself open" to his adversary. Thanatos is here said θάνατον ἀμβαλεῖν, just as Lyssa *Herc. F.* 866 (quoted by Monk) says πρὶν ἂν ἐμὰς λύσσας ἀφῇ, and as the chorus say of Ares *Iph. Aul.* 775 (quoted by Jerram) κυκλώσας Ἄρει φονίῳ. For other ancient and modern parallels see Monk and Jerram *ad h. loc.*

51. This line, too, has occasioned much discussion. The plain and simple meaning is, "I understand, of course, your meaning and your zeal," ἔχω being used in its colloquial meaning of "comprehend," "grasp," like the Lat. *teneo*, the Elizabethan "take" ("D'ye take me") and the "catch on" of modern slang. Cf. *Orest.* 1120 ἔχω τοσοῦτον, τἀπίλοιπα δ᾽ οὐκ ἔχω, *Hippol.* 1436 ἔχεις γὰρ μοῖραν ᾗ διεφθάρης, etc., and the ἔχεις τι; of comedy. Apollo has expressed his wish somewhat vaguely, and Thanatos, who has an uneasy con-

CRITICAL AND EXEGETICAL NOTES.

sciousness of his own mental inferiority, wishes to show that he is aware what the former is aiming at. The δή gives at the same time a sneering tone to the remark. Some think that the line has a double sense, (1) that given above, and (2) "I understand you and am ready" (σέθεν in the second case being taken with λόγον only) or "I cherish regard for you (ἔχω λόγον σέθεν) and goodwill toward you," and that Thanatos means (1) while Apollo pretends to understand him as meaning (2). But the order shows that σέθεν is to be taken with *both* λόγον and προθυμίαν. If ἔχω προθυμίαν σέθεν could really mean "I am eager to serve your interests," "feel good-will toward you," this objection would be obviated; but what evidence is there of such a usage? Cf. *Heracl.* 410 ἔχω... προθυμίαν | τοσήνδ' ἐς ὑμᾶς. Προθυμίαν ἔχειν τινός, "to desire a thing," is, of course, a common construction. Weil boldly alters ἔχω to ἔκχει, on the ground that if Thanatos perfectly understood Apollo's words he would immediately protest. But the sneer is protest enough.

52. ἔστ᾽ οὖν ὅπως... μόλοι: On the omission of ἄν after ἔστιν ὅπως see Goodwin *M. and T.* 241. V. 51 is so worded that though Thanatos does not mean to spare Alcestis, Apollo can draw from it the opposite inference, or at least *pretend* to do so. The sneer he purposely overlooks.

55. ἄρνυμαι γέρας: cf. *Hec.* 40 αἰτεῖ δ᾽ ἀδελφὴν τὴν ἐμὴν Πολυξένην | τύμβῳ φίλον πρόσφαγμα καὶ γέρας λαβεῖν. The reading of *L* and *P*, κλέος, is either a gloss on γέρας which has crept into the text, or possibly a slip of some early copyist who was thinking of the Homeric κλέος ἀρέσθαι. Mistakes of the latter sort are especially common at the end of a line; and, as Bruhn has ably shown in his "*Lucubrationes Euripideae*," this is due, at least in part, to the fact that the scribe in copying first fixed a number of words in his mind and then wrote them out, and as he did so the grasp of his memory became weaker as he neared the end; so that he often would get the last word wrong, or substitute for it some other of kindred meaning which happened to be in his mind. The scholiast read γέρας.

56. Schol.: ὁ δὲ Ἀπόλλων καίτοι νοήσας τὸ λεχθὲν παραλογίζεται τὸν Θάνατον, φάσκων ὅτι κἂν γραῦς ὄληται ἡ Ἄλκηστις ἀξίως ταφήσεται, τὸ μεῖζον γέρας λέγων ἐπὶ πολυτελοῦς ταφῆς.

57. πρὸς τῶν ἐχόντων: "in the interest of the rich." For this use of πρός cf. Soph. *O. T.* 1434 πρὸς σοῦ γάρ, οὐδ᾽ ἐμοῦ, φράσω, Herod. VIII. 60, 2 τὸ ἐν στενῷ ναυμαχέειν πρὸς ἡμέων ἐστί, Thuc. II. 86, 5 νομίζοντες πρὸς ἐκείνων εἶναι τὴν ἐν ὀλίγῳ ναυμαχίαν, etc. The use of πρός in expressions like πρός τινος εἶναι, "to side with one," is analogous. Euripides often employs ὁ ἔχων, οἱ ἔχοντες = ὁ πλούσιος, οἱ πλούσιοι, e.g. *Suppl.* 240 ff. οἱ δ᾽ οὐκ ἔχοντες καὶ σπανίζοντες βίου... εἰς τοὺς ἔχοντας κέντρ᾽ ἀφιᾶσιν κακά, fr. 326, 8 κακὸς δ᾽ ὁ μὴ ἔχων, οἱ δ᾽ ἔχοντες ὄλβιοι, fr. 462, 2 τῶν ἐχόντων πάντες ἄνθρωποι φίλοι, etc.; and many examples might be cited from other writers. τιθείς: *P* has τιθεῖς, and hence Prinz, Bauer-Wecklein and Weil read τιθεῖς. The question as to whether τιθεῖς is good Attic cannot be said to be settled as yet. Porson condemned the form, and Brunck defended it. It has more recently found vigorous champions in Cobet (*Misc. Crit.* pp. 282 ff.) and Mr. Rutherford (*New Phrynichus* pp. 316–17), though Kühner-Blass (II. p. 193) seem inclined to decide against it. Wecklein-Bauer go so far as to say "τιθεῖς ist die attische Form der 2. Pers. Präsens" (see their note *ad loc.*). The Attic inscriptions unfortunately are silent on this point, but the evidence of the MSS. is *very* strong in favor of the Atticity of τιθεῖς (see for the evidence Von Bamberg in *Ztsch. f. Gymn.* W. XXVIII. pp. 27–8, Kühner-Blass *l. s. c.*). I have noted the following cases from Euripides: *Alc.* 57 (τιθεὶς P, τίθης r), 890 (τιθεῖς B L P, τίθης a), *Androm.* 210 (τίθης A, τιθεῖς B, τίθης E, τιθεῖς with η written over the ει P, τίθης a), *Cycl.* 545 (τιθεῖς P, τίθεῖς with η written above ει L), *Hel.* 550 (προστιθεῖς), *Heracl.* 690 (προστιθεὶς P, προστίθεις with ῇ written above ει L), *Herc. Fur.* 710 (προστιθεῖς), *Ion* 741 (τιθεὶς P, τιθεῖς L), 1525 (προστιθεὶς P, προστιθεῖς L), *Orest.* 1187 (ὑποτιθεῖς A, ὑποτίθεις B, ὑποτιθεῖσα E, ὑποτίθεις F, ὑποτίθης L e).

When the inscriptions are silent, the testimony of the best MSS. becomes doubly important. The cod. Laurentianus of Sophocles, the Ravennas and Venetus of Aristophanes and the Clarkianus of Plato all have instances of the form in question. Hence, while I should not dare (like Cobet, and apparently Wecklein) to assert that τιθεῖς is *the* Attic form, it seems probable that it was in good use. A change from τιθεῖς to τίθης would be far more apt to be made by copyists than one in the other direction; hence I have followed P (except as to accent) in this passage. Cf. 890.

59. An extremely troublesome line. L has ὠνοῖντ' (ω rewritten), P and a ὠνοιντ', B ὄνοιντ', l ὄναιντ'. L and P have οἷς, the rest apparently οὓς. All have γηραιούς. The passage clearly puzzled the scholiasts; one says: παρὰ τῶν πολυχρονίων ἀγοράσειαν ἂν οἱ πλούσιοι τὸν ἐκείνων χρόνον ὥστε αὐτοὺς βραδέως ἀποθανεῖν; another has (perversely) ἀγοράσειαν ἂν γηραιοὺς οἷς πάρεστι τὸ θανεῖν, ἐὰν τοῦτο συγχωρήσω. The reading ὄνοιντο we may dismiss at once, as it gives no appropriate sense and ὄνομαι does not occur in the tragedians. The editors fall into two great classes, (I) those who read ὠνοῖντ' and (II) those who prefer ὄναιντ', and these again have their subdivisions.

I. *Those who read* ὠνοῖντ'.

(a) Lascaris, Monk, Hermann, Woolsey, Jerram and others read (with L, and P except as to the accent of ὠνοῖντ') ὠνοῖντ' ἂν οἷς πάρεστι γηραιοὺς θανεῖν. The sense will then be, as Hermann puts it: "*emerent, quibus opes suppetunt, grandaevos mori quos vivere cupiunt, sive semet ipsos, sive quos amant alios.*" This reading, taken as a whole, has better MSS. authority than any of the others.

(b) Dindorf and Earle, feeling that the exemption of *the rich themselves* from death is what should be especially emphasized, read ὠνοῖντ' ἂν οἷς πάρεστι γηραιοὶ θανεῖν. This gives a clear sense, and one suited to the context, and I believe it to be the true reading. The nom. γηραιοί might very easily be changed to γηραιούs by some copyist or reader who did not understand the construction and thought that an accus. was needed with the infinitive, or wished to make the adjective the object of ὠνοῖντ' (as one of the scholiasts seems to have done).

II. *Those who read* ὄναιντ'.

(a) Kirchhoff, Nauck, Prinz, Bauer-Wecklein, Weil and others read ὄναιντ' ἂν οὓς πάρεστι γηραιοὺς θανεῖν. This is usually rendered: "those would be benefited who could afford to purchase long life" ("die wegen ihres Reichthums in der Lage wären etc." Bauer-Wecklein). But (1) the "wären" begs the question. The true rendering would be "those whose living to old age is (*now*) possible," not "those who (*in that case*) *would be able* to live to old age." Weil saw this; but even his version, "les riches auraient un avantage, puisqu'ils ont le moyen de mourir vieux (si des funerailles somptueuses peuvent procurer une longue vie)," does not meet the difficulty. If ὄναιντ' ἄν is a "less vivid future" apodosis, it does not harmonize with the pres. ind. πάρεστιν. If, however, ὄναιντ' ἄν be regarded as "potential optative," "those can obtain advantage who (under your new νόμος) have the power to reach old age" (cf. νόμον τιθεῖς in 57), the construction becomes at least a possible one. But (2) the reading ὄναιντ' has only the authority of *l*. The reading of B, ὄνοιντ', is probably a mistake for ὠνοῖντ', not for ὄναιντ', as *a* has ὤνοιντ'. (3) The reading ὄναιντ', as Earle points out, could easily arise through the influence of πρὸς τῶν ἐχόντων.

(β) It would also be grammatically possible to read ὄναιντ' ἂν οἷς πάρεστι γηραιοὺς θανεῖν (or γηραιοῖς θανεῖν with Heiland), with the same meaning as (a) but a somewhat easier construction. These readings are liable to the same objections as (a), and γηραιοῖς has no MSS. authority.

On the whole, the choice seems to lie between I (a) and I (b), and of these the second is the clearer and simpler. οἷς πάρεστι will then = οἱ πλούσιοι (not, as Matthiae understood it, οἷς πάρεστι sc. τὸ ὠνεῖσθαι).

62. The sigmatism of the line expresses anger and contempt; cf. *Ion* 386 σὺ δ' οὔτ' ἔσωσας τὸν σὸν ὃν σῶσαί σ' ἐχρῆν.

63. πάντ': Prinz's conjecture ταῦτ' is quite needless; Thanatos means, "You cannot have *everything* to which you have no right, though you *have* defrauded me in *one* case" (cf. v. 43).

64. κλαύσῃ: so Earle, who suggests that παύσῃ of the MSS. is due to contamination of κλαύσῃ with a gloss πείσῃ. παύσῃ clearly will not do (stop doing what?); πείσει (better πείσῃ), F. W. Schmidt's emendation, makes good sense, but is rather weak, while κλαύσῃ seems admirably suited to the tone of the dialogue. Apollo begins in a tone of studied though ironical courtesy; as the conversation goes on he begins to lose patience, and finally answers Thanatos in his own rough way (cf. 62). Wecklein calls κλαύσῃ an "unpassender Ausdruck" (*Woch. f. klass. Philol.* 1895 p. 1255), but Euripides uses the verb in this sense some fifteen times, chiefly in angry dialogues of just this character.

It is noticeable that here the MSS. all have the form in -ῃ, which is now recognized to be preferable to that in -ει. The latter is probably a mere "graphic variant," due to the confusion between ῃ and ει which began in the fourth century B.C., and the grammarians of the Roman period preferred it (see Voemel *Dem. Cont.* p. 84) because it enabled them to distinguish the subjunctive in -ῃ from the indicative in -ει. See Meisterhans p. 131, Kühner-Blass II. p. 60, Blass *Aussprache des Griech.*[3] p. 47, etc. Earle takes ἄγαν as modifying κλαύσῃ, comparing *Hel.* 1398 ἄγαν γὰρ αὐτὸν οὐ παρόνθ' ὅμως στένεις: but there no one would think of taking ἄγαν with παρόνθ', while in the passage from the text it is surely more natural to take it with ὠμός, "you will certainly come to grief ('catch it'), very savage though you are."

66-7. I formerly suspected these lines to be an interpolation, as they are not essential to the construction, and the addition of the detail seems at first sight to weaken rather than strengthen the statement. But Euripides often errs in this direction, and, as Earle points out, the lines have a certain ὄγκος which may help to lend impressiveness to the prediction. It is hard in studying a work of this kind to avoid contracting what some one has wittily called the *delirium delens.* Wheeler (*De Alc. et Hipp. Interp.* pp. 12 ff.) rejects in this one scene vv. 30-31, 58-9, 66-71, 73-6! ἵππειον ὄχημα: so ὄχημ' ἵππειον *Hippol.* 1355, νάϊον ὄχημα *Iph. T.* 410, ὄχημα πωλικόν *Rhes.* 621, 797, ἱππικῶν ὀχημάτων Soph. *El.* 740, etc. Cf. v. 483 Θρηκὸς τέτρωρον ἅρμα Διομήδους μέτα. Ἅρμα is a less pretentious word. μέτα: a case of so-called tmesis (πέμψαντος . . . μέτα = μεταπέμψαντος). So most edd. Weil and Wecklein read μετὰ "having sent (him) to fetch the team from," etc., the addition of ἐκ δυσχειμέρων τόπων being possible because of "the verbal idea contained in μετά." Weil compares 483 and *Phoen.* 1317 ἥκω μετὰ | . . . ἀδελφήν: but these are not parallel to such a construction as πέμπω (τινὰ) μετά τι ἐκ τόπου τινός. On the other hand, cf. for the "tmesis" *Hec.* 504 Ἀγαμέμνονος πέμψαντος, ὦ γύναι, μέτα, and for the construction Arist. *Vesp.* 679 παρ' Εὐχαρίδου τρεῖς ἀγλίθας μετέπεμψα, Thuc. IV. 30 στρατιάν τε μεταπέμπων ἐκ τῶν ἐγγὺς ξυμμάχων. The active is, of course, less common than the middle, but is perfectly classical and Euripidean.

71-2. Kirchhoff, Nauck and Prinz follow Dindorf in rejecting these two lines, rightly as it seems to me. The MSS. show no variant, but the schol., who says καὶ οὔτε ἡμεῖς ἕξομέν σοι(ἔχομέν MSS.) χάριν, ἀλλὰ καὶ ὃ βουλόμεθα πράξομεν, appears to have read δράσω (Weil suggests that he read πράξω θ' ὁμοίως τἄμ', which seems improbable). As the lines stand ταῦτ' is not clear, δράσεις is strange (as Thanatos is to take a passive rather than an active part in the transaction), and ὁμοίως is suspicious. Hermann's δράσει (sc. Heracles) does not help matters; for, as Dindorf observes, "hoc si voluisset poeta, dixisset saltem δράσει τ' ἐκεῖνος ταῦτα, quo pronomine multo magis opus erat quam illo ὁμοίως: ne quid de verbis ἀπεχθήσει τ' ἐμοὶ dicam, ubi potius σύ τ' ἀπεχθήσει ἐμοὶ dici debebat." This last objection remains if we read δράσω, which besides emphasizes Apollo's share in the transaction too much. Nowhere else in the play are we told that Heracles is merely his instrument. Zacher's suggestion (see Select Conjectures) is ingenious but not convincing; in short the lines have never been satisfactorily emended. I am inclined to hold, with Dindorf, that they were composed and added to the text by some grammarian who thought the close of Apollo's speech too abrupt.

72. The first ἄν points out the participle as conditional (Goodwin *M. and T.* 224), and at the same time helps to emphasize πόλλ' (ib. 223).

73. ἡ δ' οὖν γυνὴ: cf. Soph. *Antig.* 769 τὼ δ' οὖν κόρα τώδ' οὐκ ἀπαλλάξει μόρου.

74. στείχω δ' ἐπ' αὐτήν: it is not quite right, I think, to say that ἐπί here = μετά of 46. True, ἐπί with the accus. is often so used, as in *Androm.* 73, 81 (which Earle cites), *Rhes.* 28, etc. But why should Thanatos "*go after her*" (to fetch her) in order to cut off the lock of hair? To do that he need only enter the room where she is lying. Probably ἐπ' here means merely "to" (cf. *Orest.* 88 ἥκετον ἐφ' ἡμᾶς ἀθλίως πεπραγότας). In *Ion* 1043 ἐχθρὸν δ' ἐπ' ἄνδρα στεῖχε, ἐπ' clearly means "against," and in our passage there may be a slight implication of hostility. ὡς κατάρξωμαι ξίφει: from Homer down κατάρχεσθαι is the technical word for performing the rites preliminary to a sacrifice, and particularly for the operation of cutting off hair from the victim's head and placing it on the fire. Hesychius says κατάρξασθαι τοῦ ἱερείου· τῶν τριχῶν ἀποσπάσαι (Photius has κατάρξασθαι τῶν τριχῶν· ἀπάρξασθαι τοῦ ἱερείου). For the literature on κατάρχεσθαι, see Mr. Blaydes's very elaborate note on Aristoph. *Aves* 959, and for Greek offerings of hair and their significance, see Wieseler *Philologus* IX. 711 ff., esp. 714–15.

75. ἱερὸς ... θεῶν: Monk compares Aristoph. *Plut.* 937 μὴ δῆθ', ἱερὸν γάρ ἐστι τοῦ Πλούτου πάλαι. So Plat. *Leges* V. 741 C γῆς ἱερᾶς οὔσης τῶν πάντων θεῶν, etc. The dative with ἱερός is less frequent.

76. ἔγχος: = ξίφει in v. 74. Euripides uses the word in the same way in *Elect.* 696 and *Phoen.* 1413 (cf. 1404); cf. Soph. *Aj.* 287, *Antig.* 1236, etc. Some of the ancient critics, misunderstanding Homer *Il.* VII. 255 τὼ δ' ἐκσπασσαμένω δολίχ' ἔγχεα χεροῖν ἅμ' ἄμφω | σύν ῥ' ἔπεσον, thought that ἔγχεα there meant *swords*, an opinion which was refuted by Aristarchus (see the *Scholl. Aristonic.* on *Il.* VII. 255, 273). Whether the loose tragic use of ἔγχος is due to the same misunderstanding (so Blass in Mueller's *Handbuch d. Alt.-Wiss.* I.² p. 151) or is merely a poetic inexactness (cf. the use of "blade," "glaive," etc. in English poetry) I will not undertake to say. ἁγνίσῃ: the "relative general condition" without ἄν (or κέ) in the protasis is more common in Homer than the regular form (Goodwin *M. and T.* 538), and is doubtless older. On the use of the form without ἄν in later poets see Goodwin 540. In this passage Euripides is following Phrynichus; Servius on Virg. *Aen.* IV. 694 says: "*Alii dicunt Euripidem Orcum in scenam ducere gladium ferentem, quo crinem Alcesti abscindat, Euripidem hoc a Phrynicho* (so O. Jahn; poenia F, phenico T) *antiquo*

tragico mutuatum." Euripides in his turn was imitated by Virgil *Aen.* IV. 698-9 "*nondum illi flavum Proserpina vertice crinem | abstulerat Stygioque caput damnaverat Orco,*" as is pointed out at length by Macrobius V. 19, 1–5, *q. v.* There is a similar allusion in Hor. *Carm.* I. 28, 19, "*nullum | saeva caput Proserpina fugit,*" where see the edd. — With this line closes the prologue, in the ancient sense of that word. Apollo probably withdraws at v. 69, Thanatos enters the main door of the palace at 76.

77-140. The πάροδος. We are told in the hypothesis ὁ δὲ χορὸς συνέστηκεν ἔκ τινων πρεσβυτῶν ἐντοπίων, and the schol. on v. 77 says ἐκ γερόντων Φεραίων ὁ χορός. It has been pointed out by Bendixen (*De Alcest. Eur. Comment.*, cited by Ritter *De Eur. Alcest.* p. 32) and Arnoldt (*Chorische Technik des Eur.* pp. 52 ff.) that several things in the play seem inconsistent with this view. The wish in vv. 473 ff. certainly would sound strangely in the mouth of gray-haired men ; and the chorus make no allusion to, or complaint of, their own old age. But the statement in the hypothesis probably goes back to Aristophanes of Byzantium, who lived less than two centuries after Euripides, and who doubtless had seen the *Alcestis* performed ; it scarcely seems probable, therefore, that he would have made a mistake in the matter. Moreover, the wish in 473 ff. must not be taken too strictly as applying to the chorus themselves; it may be the poet who is speaking (cf. 962 ff.). V. 212, too, though it does not *necessarily* imply that the coryphaeus is an old man, is certainly more natural if the person addressed is a man of age and position. On the whole, I strongly incline to the traditional view. There is great danger that, in analyzing the information which has come down to us from antiquity, we may prune away the true together with the false.

As to the division of this πάροδος and the distribution of the parts there has been great difference of opinion. All recent editors accept the statement of the schol. on v. 77 (which is confirmed by the MSS.) that the chorus is divided into two semi-choruses. They disagree, however, as to the amount sung by these semi-choruses, some (e.g. Kirchhoff, Nauck, Weil, Wecklein) assigning them only 93–7 and 105-111, while others (Arnoldt, Prinz, Earle, etc.) extend the division into semi-choruses through nearly the whole of the πάροδος. In a matter of this kind, where we have so little evidence, the MSS. are the safest guide, as the division which they offer us may well go back to early acting-copies of the play. Hence in the text I have followed them as closely as practicable. The introductory anapaestic system has χορ. prefixed to it in *L* and *P*, and I have assigned it (with most edd.) to the chorus. Whether it was sung by the whole chorus or by the coryphaeus I will not undertake to decide, as in the present state of our knowledge it is useless to dogmatise on such points. The other MSS. have ἡμιχ., but it does not seem probable that the division into semi-choruses took place at the very beginning of the πάροδος. At 86 and 89 I have prefixed ἡμιχ. with *all* the MSS. At 89 the sudden change from a question to a direct statement points clearly to a change of speakers. As to

93-7 there is now substantial agreement among editors, and I have followed the usual arrangement. The same is true of 105-111. At 98 I have prefixed ἡμιχ. with the MSS., and at 101 have added it, following Hartung. A comparison with 89 shows that symmetry requires the addition. At 112 I have prefixed χορ. with B and a (L and P have no sign, doubtless through a copyist's error). At 132 I have added a παράγραφος, to show that (as I believe) the following lines were delivered by the coryphaeus. 132-5 *may* have been sung by the whole chorus, but 136-40 were clearly spoken by the coryphaeus, and it seems most natural to suppose that he also sang the preceding anapaests. See for other arrangements Arnoldt *Chorische Technik des Eur.* pp. 153 ff., and the edd. *ad loc.* Cf. also Schmidt *Kunstformen d. griech. Poesie* III. p. 11 and Westphal-Rossbach *Griechische Metrik*[3] pp. 165, 149, 494 for the metrical treatment.

77. πρόσθεν : πρόσθε the MSS., but the metre requires a spondee.

78. σεσίγηται : Wecklein compares *Iph. T.* 307 αὐλεῖται μέλαθρον. The use of the perfect ("lies hushed in silence") is very picturesque.

79. This dimeter as it stands in the MSS. has lost a long syllable either before or after πέλας. The τις of *l* is a mere guess of the scribe. For some of the conjectures which have been made see Select Conj. The best suggestion that has yet been offered is probably that of Monk, πέλας ⟨ἔστ'⟩ οὐδείς, as the copula so frequently falls out. This line has ἡμιχ. prefixed to it in the MSS. But it seems very improbable that the division into semi-choruses took place at or near the beginning of the πάροδος. The natural place for that division is at 86, at the close of the anapaestic system, where both the construction and metre change. Hence I have followed Kirchhoff in striking out the ἡμιχ. The only recent editor, so far as I know, who retains it is Mr. Jerram.

80. ὅστις ἂν εἴποι : so B a L ; ὅστις ἂν ἔνεποι (so *l* ; ἔννεποι P) is incorrect because an anapaest cannot immediately follow a dactyl, as four shorts must not come together unless they belong to the same foot. See Christ, *Metrik*[2] p. 242 (§ 282). The variant probably arose thus : ενεποι was written by mistake for ἂν εἴποι, and then changed to ἔνεποι to give sense. Then ἂν was inserted because the construction required it, thus giving the reading of *l* and (with a slight change in the spelling) P. The letters a and ε are very often confused in the MSS.

81. βασίλειαν πενθεῖν χρή, ἢ ζῶσ', the reading of the MSS., is certainly wrong, as the hiatus is objectionable and there is not the customary caesura after the second foot. Kirchhoff would insert μ' after χρή, which obviates the first difficulty but not the second (cf. Nauck *Eur. Stud.* II. p. 51). Probably a transposition is necessary. Two different arrangements of the line have been proposed : (1) βασίλειαν χρὴ πενθεῖν ἢ ζῶσ' (so *l*), (2) χρὴ βασίλειαν πενθεῖν ἢ ζῶσ' (so Blomfield and Nauck). (1) has the (slight) authority of *l*, and requires merely the transposition of χρή and πενθεῖν : but (2), though the change is slightly bolder, certainly sounds much better to the ear, and is probably right. Nauck remarks: " Die überlieferte falsche Wortstellung ist dadurch veranlasst dass man βασίλειαν an φθιμένην heranrückte, zu dem es dem Sinne nach gehört. Ganz ähnlich im folgenden Verse, wo ebenfalls die Caesur fehlt, weil man τόδε unrichtig zu φῶς zog." Weil retains the MSS. reading both here and in 79 and 82 by dividing the cola differently, thus: ἀλλ' οὐδὲ φίλων πέλας οὐδείς, | ὅστις ἂν εἴποι | πότερον φθιμένην βασίλειαν | πενθεῖν χρή, | ἦ ζῶσ' ἔτι φῶς τόδε λεύσσει | Πελίου παῖς | Ἄλκηστις, ἐμοὶ πᾶσί τ' ἀρίστη | δόξασα γυνὴ | πόσιν εἰς αὐτῆς γεγενῆσθαι. He thus obtains in 79-82 three catalectic dimeters, the first followed by an acatalectic monometer, the other two each by a catalectic monometer. But a system of eleven lines of which four are paroemiacs and *four monometers* is surely an almost unparalleled anomaly.

82. The MSS. have the order ἔτι φῶς τόδε λεύσσει Πελίου παῖς, which lacks the customary caesura after the second foot. Here again a transposition is probably necessary. Blomfield's ἔτι παῖς Πελίου λεύσσει τόδε φῶς is too violent; words are not to be shuffled in this way like cards. The reading ἔτι φῶς λεύσσει τόδε παῖς Πελίου will not do on account of the hiatus. Bothe's ἔτι φῶς λεύσσει Πελίου τόδε παῖς is the best that has hitherto been suggested, and is probably right; though the position of τόδε is certainly hard. Some editors (e.g. Wuestemann, Dindorf) follow the Aldine in omitting τόδε. This leaves a paroemiac, which seems out of place here. Earle, following a hint of Dindorf's, drops τόδε and reads Πελίου θυγάτηρ (thinking that Πελίου παῖς owes its origin to v. 37). But he seems inclined to over-estimate the influence which similar passages have had upon the text of each other; and in the absence of all MSS. evidence for θυγάτηρ Bothe's transposition is on the whole more likely to be right.

83. πᾶσί τ' has been suspected, without adequate reason. See Select Conj.

86. I believe that Arnoldt and Prinz are right in making the dialogue between the semi-choruses begin here. Probably it was carried on by the leaders only, not by the semi-choruses each as a whole. As to the arrangement of the semi-choruses and the evolutions which they went through speculation is worse than useless; for we have absolutely no evidence.

87. χειρῶν: so Nauck for χερῶν, as the corresponding verse of the antistrophe (98) has a long first syllable (πη-).

88. ἢ γόον: so L, rightly, as the antistrophe (v. 99) has a dactyl (χέρνιβ' ἐ-); γόων, the reading of the other MSS., is either due to the wish to have the usual genitive construction after κλύειν, or (more probably, as two accusatives precede it) is a simple mistake of some early scribe. The letters ω and ο are constantly confused in Greek MSS., as every scholar knows. It is not many years since such cases as the one in the text were explained on the theory that the tragedians wrote in the old Attic alphabet, in which O stood for both *omicron* and *omega*; but the researches of Köhler and others have made it probable that Euripides, at any rate, used the Ionic alphabet. See Meisterhans pp. 3 ff. In our passage the mistake must have been made quite early, as B a P all have γόων; and γόον of L is probably a correction of the scribe (who was evidently a man of some learning, as is clear from his corrections and emendations in other places) rather than an independent variant. ὡς πεπραγμένων: on the omission of the noun see Goodwin *M. and T.* 848.

90. στατίζεται: so Hermann for στατίζετ'. The elision of αι in the 1st and 3d pers. sing. was probably not allowed by the tragedians, as the examples are few and suspicious (see Kühner-Blass I. p. 238); and comparison with the antistrophe (τομαῖος ἅ v. 102) shows that another syllable is needed. On the shortening of the final diphthong before an initial vowel see Seidler *De Dochm.* pp. 95 ff., Christ *Metrik*³ p. 26 and Kühner-Blass I. p. 197, 5. For the word itself cf. *El.* 315 πρὸς δ' ἕδραισιν Ἀσίδες | δμωαὶ στατίζουσ', where the active is used intransitively in the same sense.

91. μετακύμιος ἄτας: a troublesome phrase. The four scholia on the passage show that it occasioned difficulty even in ancient times. Four explanations may be distinguished : (1) most editors and the third schol. take the word μετακύμιος to mean "among" or "between the waves" (cf. μεταδήμιος, μεταίχμιος, μετακόσμιος, μεταμάζιος, μεταπόντιος, μεταστήθιος, etc.). The sense will then be : "Would that thou wouldst appear amid the waves of ἄτη" to still them. This I believe to be the true meaning; the language would almost inevitably call up to the mind of a Greek the image of Poseidon amid the waves of the sea, quelling their fury. (2) Earle, taking μετακύμιος in the same sense as above, thinks that the figure is that of a beacon-light appearing amid the waves. This is ingenious, but would be much less likely to occur to a Greek hearer than to a modern ~~one~~, as lighthouses, though not unknown in antiquity, were far from common. (3) Some hold, with one of the scholiasts, that the word means "after the waves," bringing calm after the storm. Analogies for this meaning of μετά in the compound are hard to find. Μεταδόρπιος apparently sometimes means "after supper" (see L. & S. *s. v.*), though this is disputed. Cf. also μεταχρόνιος. (4) The fourth scholiast says: ὥσπερ λέγομεν μεταίχμιον τὸ μεταξὺ δύο στρατευμάτων, οὕτως μετακύμιον τὸ μεταξὺ δύο κυμάτων (cf. Hesych. *s. v.* μετακύμιον). Hence, as Kvičala (*Studien zu Eur.* II. p. 6) points out, he probably read μετακύμιον ἄτας, i.e. (as Kvičala explains it), "the respite from misfortune." But surely to call a *person* "die Ruhepause des Unglücks" is a strange mode of expression. On the whole it seems much the wiser course to adopt explanation (1) and take ἄτας as dependent upon the substantive (κύματα) implied in μετακύμιος.

93-7. It is disputed whether these lines metrically correspond to 105-11. Westphal-Rossbach observe (*Gr. Metrik*³ p. 165) : "Dreimal beginnen die Anapaeste nach Vollendung der Strophen mit zwei Paroemiaci und einer dazwischen stehenden katalektischen Dipodie, welche metrisch mit einem Ionicus a minore übereinkommt ... Eine antistrophische Responsion aber, die bereits Seidler dochm. p. 81 versucht hat, findet nicht statt." On the other hand Kirchhoff and most recent editors hold that the lines in question do respond, and (as it appears to the present writer) with good reason. True, the verses as they stand in the MSS. do not accurately respond (see Apparatus Criticus); but Kirchhoff's elegant restoration of v. 94 is necessary to the sense. Vv. 93-7 are a dialogue between two parties in opposite states of mind, the expressions of hope *alternating* with those of despondency. Hence v. 93, which has a hopeful tone, should be followed by an utterance of the *opposite* kind, not by one of the *same* character. The words νέκυς ἤδη (sc. ἐστίν) should therefore precede, not follow, οὐ δὴ φροῦδός γ' ἐξ οἴκων. The transposition was due to some scribe or grammarian who wished to make νέκυς the subject of φροῦδός (ἐστιν); and the γάρ which the MSS. have after οὐ was inserted to connect 93 with 94, the latter being thus made a reason for the statement in 93. But as soon as νέκυς ἤδη was restored to its proper place the γάρ became not only needless but objectionable, and Kirchhoff struck it out. Again in 96 the very baldness of the language shows that something is gone, whether the lacuna is after Ἄδμητος (as Hartung conjectured) or after ἔρημον (as Earle thinks). Ἔρημον of what? But these very changes, which are necessary to the sense, restore the responsion; and the chances are a hundred to one that this coincidence is not accidental. Seeing that a responsion was intended, some early scholar (after the transposition in 94 had been made) tried to restore it by transposing 106 and 107 (as in *L* and *P*), thus making a bad matter worse. There can be little question that Kirchhoff has restored the true reading. Christ (*Metrik*[2] p. 263) says: "Strophische Responsion scheint den anapaestischen Systemen von Hause aus fremd gewesen zu sein und kann namentlich in den Einzugsliedern schon desshalb nicht erwartet werden, weil hier der Chor beim Vortrag der Anapaeste sich weder in Halbchöre theilte noch in zurücklaufenden Linien bewegte." But as in our passage (which he seems to have overlooked) there *is* a division into semi-choruses, this objection clearly will not apply.

93. οὐ τἄν: i.e. οὐ τοι ἄν. The scribes who wrote our MSS. (or their sources) did not understand the crasis, and divided wrongly, οὔτ' ἄν. **φθιμένης**: so Monk for φθιμένας. The Doric forms should probably be excluded from the anapaests.

94. **φροῦδος**: feminine, as in *Iph. T.* 154, Soph. *Elect.* 807. The fem. in -η is more common.

95. πόθεν: sc. τοῦτ' οἶσθα, or the like. Cf. 781, and *Phoen.* 1620. οὐκ αὐχῶ: the verb αὐχέω from its regular meaning of "to boast" readily passes into that of "feel confident," as here and Aesch. *Prom.* 338 αὐχῶ γαρ αυχῶ τηνδε δωρεὰν ἐμοὶ | δώσειν Δί'. It then becomes still weaker, = "think" or "expect," as in 675, *Heracl.* 931 οὐ γάρ ποτ' ηὔχει χεῖρας ἕξεσθαι σέθεν, *Tro.* 770 οὐ γάρ ποτ' αὐχῶ Ζηνά γ' ἐκφῦσαί σ' ἐγώ, etc.

96. ἔρημον: this word was probably followed by two words in the genitive (Wecklein suggests τῶν θρηνούντων), which have fallen out. To be sure, it *might* be used absolutely, as in ἐρήμη δίκη (so Earle); but this seems very bald, and it is probable that the two lost words made the meaning of ἔρημον more explicit.

98 ff. On the custom of placing the ὄστρακον or ἀρδάνιον full of water before the door of the house in which there was a dead body, cf. the schol.: ὁπότε τις ἀποθάνοι, πρὸ τῶν πυλῶν ὄστρακα πληροῦντες ὕδατος ἐτίθεσαν καὶ κλάδους δάφνης, ἵνα οἱ ἐξιόντες περιρραίνοιντο. The water had to be brought from another house (Pollux VIII. 65, Hesych. s.v. ὄστρακον). Cf. Aristoph. *Eccles.* 1033 (and Blaydes *ad loc.*), and see Bekker-Göll *Charikles* I. p. 252; Hermann-Blümner *Griech. Privatalterthümer* p. 365; Rohde *Psyche* p. 203 (with note 2).

100. φθιτῶν (so L and P) is clearly the true reading, as the responsion shows; φθιμένων, the reading of the other family of MSS., is a gloss on φθιτῶν which has crept into the text. It is singular that φθιτός is never used with the article. πύλαις: Prinz reads φύλαις, doubtless a misprint. Wecklein conjectured that we should read ἐπὶ φθιτῶν φορᾷ. But does Euripides ever use φορά in this way? I believe the text to be perfectly sound; the expression ὡς νομίζεται ἐπὶ φθιτῶν πύλαις, "as is customary at the portals of the dead," is not quite logical here, as ὡς νομίζεται does not refer to δρῶ but to the placing of the water at the door, and Tournier's ἢ νομίζεται would be easier; but the sense is clear, and there does not seem to be sufficient ground for any change.

101-2. Apparently clipped hair was placed at the entrance of a house in which there had been a death, just as we tie up the door-handle with crape. But (like previous editors) I have not been able to find another allusion to this custom in any Greek classical writer (though references to offerings of hair at tombs are, of course, very frequent). Cypress-twigs, however, were used for a similar purpose; cf. Servius on *Aen.* III. 681: *apud Atticos funestae domus huius* (i.e. *cupressi*) *fronde velantur.* To escape the difficulty Lascaris read χαίτας τ' οὔτις . . . τομαῖος, "no one with shorn hair," and one scholiast seems to have found χαίταν or χαίτας in his text, for he paraphrases by οὐδεὶς δὲ ἐν τοῖς προθύροις ἄνθρωπος τετμημένος ἐστὶ τὴν τρίχα : but Aesch. *Cho.* 160 ὁρῶ τομαῖον τόνδε βόστρυχον τάφῳ supports the reading of the MSS. Weil ingeniously reads χαῖτα τ' οὔτις ἐπὶ προθύροις | τομαῖος, ἃ δὴ νεκύων | πένθη (sc. ἐστίν), πίτνει, thus making χαῖτα the subject of πίτνει. But is it probable that the cutting of the hair was done in front of the house rather than within it? Passers-by should certainly have been spared such a barbarous spectacle! As the strophe has a short syllable, ἅ must be neuter plural, not a Doric feminine singular. If the text is sound, the plur. is generic. Weil compares *Orest.* 920 αὐτουργός, οἵπερ καὶ μόνοι σῴζουσι γῆν: add *Hel.* 440, *Suppl.* 868. For this use, see Hadley-Allen 629 a, and for the neuter after a feminine antecedent Hadley-Allen 630, Goodwin 1022. But it must be confessed that the combination of the two irregularities is hard; and though I have not ventured to change the text, I am much inclined to read πένθη ("signs of mourning") with Weil, in which case ἅ would be "attracted" into the gender of πένθη. πένθεσι and πένθει, the readings of the MSS., would then be conjectures by persons who wished to make ἅ fem. sing., and πένθεσι seems to point to an original plural. (πένθει might also be due to iotacism.) Still, the text *may* be sound, though I know of no exact parallel in Euripides. The nearest seems to be

Andром. 271-2 ἃ δ' ἔστ' ἐχίδνης καὶ πυρὸς περαιτέρω, | οὐδεὶς γυναικὸς φάρμακ' ἐξηύρηκέ πω, but there the poet has just been speaking of ἑρπετὰ ἄγρια and the neuter plural is still in his mind.

103. πίτνει: "falls," i.e. "is cut off." So in English the phrase "his head fell" is used of persons executed by the axe or guillotine. Some (e.g. Musgrave and Jerram) take the word as meaning "happens"; but though πίπτω, πίτνω may be used of a chance occurrence ("to turn out," "befall"), they are rarely if ever used of what *customarily* or *regularly* takes place. For the shortened ultima of πίτνει, see the note on στατίζεται in v. 90. οὐ: so the Aldine. The MSS. have οὐδέ, which gives one short syllable too many if we retain νεολαία. The question therefore is, whether to keep νεολαία and read οὐ or to emend νεολαία and retain οὐδέ. All the MSS. have οὐδέ: B P l have νεολαία, the rest νεολαῖα. The schol. says: νεολαία · ἡ νέα, κυρίως δὲ ὁ ἐκ τῶν νέων ὄχλος. Hesychius says: νεολαία · νέων ἄθροισμα. ἢ νεότης. ἢ νέος λαός. Photius has: νεολαίαν (νεολέαν cod.); τὴν νεότητα τετρασυλλάβως οἱ Ἀττικοί · Βαβυλωνίοις (Aristoph. fr. 67 Kock); Ὦ Ζεῦ τὸ χρῆμα τῆς νεολαίας ὅσον. Add Pollux II. 11, τὸ δὲ τούτων (sc. νεανίσκων) πλῆθος νεολαία, and Bekker's *Anecd.* 52, 25, νεολαία · ἔστι νέος λαὸς ἡ (leg. ἢ) νεότης, παρ' ὃ γέγονεν ἡ νεολαία. The lexicographers, therefore, clearly knew the word only as a noun; and (with the possible exception of our passage) it is always so used by classic writers. See Aesch. *Pers.* 663, *Suppl.* 655; Theocrit. XVIII. 24; Lucian *Anachar.* 38, *Phal.* 1, 3, in all of which passages the word clearly means "youth" or "young people." Hence in the place in our text various changes have been suggested to avoid taking νεολαία as an adjective, e.g. νεολαίᾳ, νεολαίας, νεαλής (W. Dindorf). Of these the last is the best, as it gives an adjective to agree with χείρ, makes good sense and renders it unnecessary to alter οὐδέ: and νεαλής may well be right. But νεολαία may be the fem. of an adj. νεολαῖος (Doric?) from a noun νεόλαος (cf. ἀκρόπολις, etc.). Photius has νεολέος · ἔφηβος: and this νεολέος (mistake for νεολαῖος?) looks like the masculine of the said adjective. Like so many other adjectives, these words have become nouns through the omission of the nouns with which they once agreed. It is possible, not to say probable, that in the passage from our text there is a survival of the early adjectival use.* Moreover, οὐ would be extremely apt to be changed to οὐδέ by some one who wished to remove the asyndeton. Hence it seems, on the whole, wisest to read οὐ νεολαία with Matthiae. Νεολαία χεὶρ γυναικῶν = χεὶρ νέων γυναικῶν by *Enallage*. Cf. *Hippol.* 394 θυραῖα... φρονήματ' ἀνδρῶν, *Herc. Fur.* 450 γραίας ὄσσων ἔτι πηγάς, ib. 468 πεδία τἀμὰ γῆς, *Phoen.* 1351 λευκοπήχεις κτύπους χεροῖν, and the like.

105. κύριον ἦμαρ: cf. *Or.* 1035 τόδ' ἦμαρ ἡμῖν κύριον, also ib. 48, *Alc.* 158.
109. διακναιομένων: cf. *Med.* 164. The word is a very expressive one.
111. ἀπ' ἀρχῆς: "from the first," as in *Phoen.* 1595. Wecklein is wrong, I think, in rendering it "überhaupt," which would be ἀρχήν.

* See also Zacher *De nominibus in -αιος* p. 73 (in *Dissert. philol. Halenses* vol. III.).

112 ff. A very involved passage. The construction is: ἀλλ' οὐδέ ἐστιν ὅποι αἴας τις στείλας ναυκληρίαν ἢ Λυκίαν εἴτε ἐπὶ τὰς ἀνύδρους Ἀμμωνιάδας ἕδρας δυστάνου ψυχὰν παραλύσαι.

112. ναυκληρίαν: this word seems to mean here "expedition"; cf. *Med.* 527 Κύπριν νομίζω τῆς ἐμῆς ναυκληρίας | σώτειραν εἶναι. In *Hel.* 1519 τίς δέ νιν ναυκληρία | ἐκ τῆσδ' ἀπῆρε χθονός; it almost = ναῦς. In *Alc.* 257 it means simply "voyage."

114. Λυκίαν: the MSS. have Λυκίας, which many edd. retain, some regarding it as a noun, others as an adjective. So far as the form goes, it might be either. By those who retain Λυκίας the following explanations of its construction have been suggested: (1) that it is an adjective agreeing with αἴας (so apparently Woolsey); but the order of the words is strongly against this, and it is much more forcible to take αἴας = "the world"; (2) that it is the genitive of the noun and is in a kind of "partitive apposition" with αἴας (so Jerram); but the sudden change of construction to ἐφ' ἕδρας is then very harsh; (3) that it is an adjective agreeing with αἴας understood, which is in apposition with αἴας (so Bauer-Wecklein); an explanation which is liable to the same objection as the preceding; (4) that it is an adjective agreeing with ἕδρας understood, the preposition being expressed with the second member only; which is possible but hard; (5) that it is the genitive of the noun and depends on ἕδρας understood (so Wuestemann); which is still harsher, as one ἕδρας will then be modified by a genitive and the other by an adjective, thus destroying still further the parallelism of the construction. Another alternative is to read Λυκίαν with Monk (though this has no MSS. authority). Λυκίαν may then be "accus. of limit of motion," followed by a change of construction to the accus. with ἐπί: or we may regard the preposition as expressed with one member and understood with the other (so Monk, who compares *Phoen.* 284, *Heracl.* 755, Soph. *O. T.* 734, 761, etc.). Λυκίαν could very easily have been altered to Λυκίας through the influence of αἴας just above it, and certainly gives a clearer and simpler construction. On the whole, I incline to Monk's view, though explanation (3) *may* be right after all. This instance shows how many possibilities the critic is obliged to weigh against each other even in fairly plain passages. And yet the *Alcestis* is called an "easy" play! For ἢ ... εἴτε = ἢ ... ἢ, cf. Soph. *Aj.* 177 ἦ ῥα κλυτῶν ἐνάρων ψευσθεῖσα δώροις εἴτ' ἐλαφαβολίαις;

115-16. The text follows Nauck, whose elegant restoration of these lines is one of his finest critical achievements. See his *Eur. Stud.* II. pp. 51 ff. The order of the words in the MSS. looks like the work of some schoolmaster who wished to make the construction plain to his pupils; and the same may be said of vv. 81-2. ἀνύδρους: the Libyan desert in which the temple and oasis of Jupiter Ammon were situated was without water, though in the oasis itself there is a fountain. Cf. *El.* 734 f. ξηραί τ' Ἀμμωνίδες ἕδραι | φθίνουσ' ἀπειρόδροσοι, and see Herodot. IV. 81 with Rawlinson's note. Arrian (*Anab.* III. 4) says: ὁ δὲ χῶρος ἵναπερ τοῦ Ἄμμωνος τὸ ἱερόν ἐστι τὰ μὲν κύκλῳ πάντα ἔρημα καί ψάμμον τὸ πᾶν ἔχει καὶ ἄνυδρον. The temple of Apollo at Patara in Lycia and that of Jupiter Ammon in Libya are mentioned both as famous oracular shrines and as widely distant from Greece and from each other (cf. ὅποι αἶας in 113).

117. παραλῦσαι: so *B*, the other MSS. having παραλῦσαι. The optative is perfectly correct (see Goodwin *M. and T.* 241), and Wakefield's παραλύσει, which many editors have adopted, is a quite unnecessary change. Cf. v. 52. The origin of this curious use of the optative without ἄν is doubtful. I cannot, however, agree with Earle that the optative was originally one of desire (see his note on 52). It seems much more probable that it is a survival of the early potential use of the optative without ἄν (Goodwin *M. and T.* 240; cf. 13). Suppose, for example, the paratactic construction ἔστ' οὖν; ὅπως Ἄλκηστις ἐς γῆρας μόλοι; "Is it possible then? How (ὅπως in its old interrogative use) can Alcestis reach old age?" From a construction of this kind the hypotactic one might easily arise. But the origin of the usage is very uncertain, and Goodwin is wise in not attempting an explanation.

118. ἀπότομος: so Blomfield. The change is necessary, as the antistrophe has Διόβολον (128): and ἄποτμος (the reading of the MSS. except *L*), though a good Euripidean word (*Hippol.* 1144), is weaker and less appropriate than ἀπότομος. Moreover, it looks as though *L* once had ἀπότομος (see Critical Apparatus), and the double accent of ἀπότμος in *B* points in the same direction. Cf. 981, Soph. *O. T.* 877 ἀπότομον ὤρουσεν εἰς ἀνάγκαν, and the Homeric αἰπὺς ὄλεθρος. So in English the expression "a rugged fate," i.e. a harsh, inexorable one, is sometimes heard.

119. πλάθει: this rare poetic word is used with the accus. (*Rhes.* 13-14 τίνες... τὰς ἀμετέρας | κοίτας πλάθουσ'?) and with the dat. (Soph. *Phil.* 726 ἵν' ὁ χαλκάσπις ἀνὴρ θεοῖς | πλάθει πᾶσιν). It is commonly said to be a by-form of πελάζω, but is really a distinct formation in θ°/ε from the root πλα-. Cf. πελάθω. θεῶν ff.: a difficult sentence. Vv. 120-21 read thus in the MSS.: οὐκ ἔχω ἐπὶ τίνα | μηλοθύταν πορευθῶ, and the antistrophic lines 130-31 thus: νῦν δὲ τίν' ἔτι βίου | ἐλπίδα προσδέχομαι. All editors agree that for προσδέχομαι we should read (with Musgrave) προσδέχωμαι, as both sense and metre require. When this change is made, the metrical correspondence becomes pretty close. Vv. 130-31 give perfectly good sense as they stand; but with 119-21 the case is otherwise. As Monk long ago pointed out, ἐπ' ἐσχάραις followed so closely by ἐπὶ τίνα μηλοθύταν is very harsh. Moreover μηλοθύτης in the sense of a "sacrificer," "priest," is attested only by this passage; and the analogy of *Iph. T.* 1116 βωμούς τε μηλοθύτας and of phrases like βούθυτος ἑστία or ἐσχάρα (see for the passages Nauck *Eur. Stud.* II. pp. 52-3) favors Reiske's emendation ἐσχάραν. Μηλοθύταν will then be an adjective agreeing with ἐσχάραν. Reiske, Nauck and Earle would also change μηλοθύταν to μηλόθυτον; but in the passage from *Iph. T.* quoted above all the MSS. have μηλοθύτας (though a noun in -ους precedes), and it is audacious (to say the least) to alter the word in *both* of the *two* passages where it occurs in classical Greek. Μηλοθύτης may perfectly well have been used as an adjective, like so many other nouns of agency in -της. Suidas (*s. v.* βουτύπος) and perhaps Athenaeus (XIV. 660 A) have βουθύτης (as a noun). What now is to be done with vv. 120 and 130? Weil and Wecklein-Bauer change the ἐπί in 120 to ἔτι, which palaeographically is almost no change at all, and retain the order of words found in the MSS. Ἔτι will then correspond in position with the ἔτι in 130. (A still closer correspondence might be obtained by striking out δέ in 130 and reading νῦν βίου ἔτι τίνα, but the asyndeton is too harsh, to say nothing of other objections.) But if Weil's reading is correct, we have *syllaba anceps*, and in 130 hiatus, at the end of the colon (to say nothing of the shortening ἔχω ἔτι in 120, which, to be sure, is possible enough). These difficulties would not be insuperable if taken singly, but occurring as they do *together* they militate strongly against the soundness of the text. Moreover βίου in 130 is suspicious and could well be spared. It may be an interpolation or gloss which has crowded out some other word. If so, the true reading is probably lost past recovery. The best of the emendations that have been suggested is that of Hartung, which I have adopted in the text. It involves, however, the changing of both strophe and antistrophe, which is always a serious objection; and besides if in 120 the original reading was οὐκέτι it is hard to see why οὐκ and ἔτι should ever have been separated.* I doubt if any really satisfactory restoration of the text can be made with the evidence now at our command.

122. μόνος: this word is, I think, sound, though it has been suspected by Nauck and others. It is put first because strongly emphatic, and ἄν has, as so often, attached itself to the emphatic word. Hence μόνος need not be taken as belonging to the apodosis, and there is no real anacoluthon. The thought is clear: "the son of Phoebus, if he were now alive, is the only person who could restore Alcestis"; but this is expressed a trifle loosely: "if the son of Phoebus, and he alone, were now alive, Alcestis would return to the upper world." The position of ἄν, as Weil observes, is no more strange than in the familiar idiom οὐκ οἶδ' ἄν εἰ (cf. v. 48). That the poet started to write μόνος δ' ἄν ἀνήγαγεν (or ἔσωσεν) αὐτήν and then deliberately changed the construction, leaving μόνος hanging, as it were, is to my mind incredible. The first syllable of μόνος does not correspond with ἀλλ' of 112; but in the anacrusis this inaccurate responsion is allowed. Wakefield conjectured μούνως, but there is no certain instance of μοῦνος or μούνως in Euripides, though Sophocles uses μοῦνος. ἦν ... δεδορκώς: as the perfect of δέρκομαι has a present sense, the periphrastic form is nearly equivalent to a true imperfect, though giving still greater prominence to the *state* or *condition*.

123. ὄμμασιν: the ν movable was added by Barnes to restore the correspondence with ἔσθ' ὅπα (113).

125. ἦλθεν: as in long sentences ἄν is so often repeated, Monk's ἦλθ' ἄν

---
* Cf. however the reading of *B* in l. 732.

has much in its favor. In the absence of MSS. testimony for it, I have not ventured to introduce it into the text; but it may well be right, particularly as a and ε are so often confused in the MSS. The use of the *aorist* here is very singular (see Goodwin *M. and T.* 414). Cf. the condition εἰ ... παρῆν ... κατῆλθον ἄν in 357 ff. In both cases the protasis is clearly contrary to fact in present time; but what is the time of the apodosis? It is clearly not past, nor even, strictly speaking, present, for Alcestis is not yet dead. We may perhaps state the usage thus: a contrary-to-fact protasis in present time may have an apodosis referring to the *immediate future*, which apodosis then takes the aorist indicative with ἄν. (The optative with ἄν could not be used, or the contrary-to-fact implication would at once be lost.) For other examples of this usage of the aorist, see Goodwin *l. s. c.* (add to his list *I. A.* 1214). The only other alternative to this view that I can see is to suppose that in the apodoses of these conditions the speaker or writer by a kind of "mental prolepsis" projects himself into the future and looks back from that stand-point, so that the aorist really refers to the past; as one might say in English, "were the son of Phoebus alive, he would have rescued her; but as it is, no one can save her." This, however, seems less probable. σκοτίους: *B* has σκοτίας, but Euripides has a well-known predilection for the two-ending declension, and uses with two endings many adjectives which in other writers commonly have three. The parallelism of ἀνύδρους in 115, to which Earle calls attention, is also in favor of the form in *-ους*.

126. This line has been emended in various ways (see Select Conjectures) by those who read Ἀμμωνιάδας (or with Musgrave Ἀμμωνίδας) ἕδρας in 116; but Nauck's arrangement of the strophe (see note on 115) renders change unnecessary here.

127. δμαθέντες: i.e. those overcome by death. Cf. *Troad.* 175 καὶ ζῶντες καὶ δμαθέντες, *Iph. T.* 190 τῶν πρόσθεν δμαθέντων | Ταντάλιδᾶν, etc.

128. πρὶν αὐτὸν εἷλε: on the indicative after πρίν in the Attic poets (seven cases only in Euripides) see Goodwin *M. and T.* 633. Διόβολον | πλῆκτρον: this seems to be the only passage where πλῆκτρον is used of the thunder-bolt. For the epithet Monk compares Soph. *O. C.* 1464 κτύπος ἄφατος ὅδε διόβολος.

130-31. See the note on 119 ff. If the text is sound, τίνα βίου ἐλπίδα must mean "what hope of her living"; but the expression seems vague and forced, and βίου may be an unskillful addition by some one who wished to define ἐλπίδα, or a mere gloss which has crept into the text.

132 ff. This is indeed a "locus desperatissimus," and has long been a battle-ground of critics. The MSS. show no variants, except that *L a* have βασιλεῦσιν for the form without ν in 132, and all the MSS. but *L P* have an (obviously interpolated) ἀλλ' before οὐδ' in 135. The schol. has merely the following note on 132: ἃ ἔδει ποιεῖν τετέλεσται τῷ Ἀδμήτῳ· τί δέ; τὸ εὔξασθαι ⟨καὶ⟩ τὸ θῦσαι τοῖς θεοῖς.

The principal objections made by Nauck and others to the soundness of the text as it stands in the MSS. are the following: (1) the first line violates the rules of anapaestic verse; (2) the words πάντα γὰρ ἤδη τετέλεσται βασιλεῦσι are too vague; (3) the paroemiac πάντων δὲ θεῶν ἐπὶ βωμοῖς is out of place; (4) θυσίαι has no verb; (5) πλήρεις seems an unsuitable epithet to apply to θυσίαι, and its meaning, too, is not clear. Let us examine these one by one.

The first objection is easily obviated by making πάντα γὰρ ἤδη τετέλεσται the first line, and βασιλεῦσιν (adopting the reading of L and a) the second. The system will then begin with a paroemiac followed by a monometer, like the two systems in 93 ff. and 105 ff. As to the vagueness of 132, it is not so great as has been represented, for τὰ τέλη is easily supplied with πάντα, being implied in τετέλεσται. The paroemiac 133 is perhaps sufficiently defended by those in the two preceding systems (93 ff. and 105 ff.) already mentioned; but as a verb seems needed with θυσίαι and the copula can so easily fall out, I have followed Mekler in inserting εἰσ' after θεῶν, thus forming an acatalectic dimeter. The main difficulty is with πλήρεις, which, however, can fairly be rendered "full," "abundant"; cf. fr. 912, 5 (Nauck) σὺ δέ μοι θυσίαν ἄπυρον παγκαρπείας δέξαι, πλήρη προχυθεῖσαν,* and Hel. 1411 ὡς ἂν τὴν χάριν πλήρην λάβω. It would also be possible to render it "in full tale," so that no altar lacks its sacrifice; cf. the analogous use in passages like Hec. 521-2 παρῆν μὲν ὄχλος πᾶς Ἀχαικοῦ στρατοῦ | πλήρης προτύμβου, Aristoph. Eccl. 95 εἰ πλήρης τύχοι | ὁ δῆμος ὤν. I see no sufficient reason, therefore, for assuming a series of lacunas with Kirchhoff and others, or for making any violent alteration of the text. The scholiast's explanation of 132 (see above) is no proof that his text contained anything which is not in our MSS.; his ἃ ἔδει ποιεῖν is merely an attempt to supply the ellipsis after πάντα.

132. βασιλεῦσιν: the so-called "*pluralis maiestatis.*" The scholiast's note shows that he understood it as meaning Admetus alone.

134. αἱμόρραντοι: for the formation the edd. compare κυμοδέγμονος *Hippol.* 1173. So, too, αἱμοβαφῆ Soph. *Aj.* 219, etc. Cf. σπερματολόγος and σπερμολόγος, αἱματόρρυτος and αἱμόρρυτος. See for a list of similar formations Kühner-Blass II. p. 331 n. 4. In Bekker's *Anecdota* III. p. 1308 the words αἱματόρραντοι (sic) θυσίαι are said to be found in the Oxford Codex Baroccius of Choeroboscus; but I have been unable to find the passage in Hilgard's edition of Choeroboscus.

136-434, first ἐπεισόδιον.

136. Usener (*Jahrb. f. Phil.* vol. 139 p. 369) would read γάρ for ἐκ. Probably, however, no change should be made. The *Alcestis* abounds in *asyndeta*, which are not to be emended away but are due to the desire to produce a rhetorical effect by the very abruptness thus secured. Weil compares for the omission of γάρ *Phoen.* 99-100 ἀλλ' οὔτις ἀστῶν τοῖσδε χρίμπτεται δόμοις, | κέδρου παλαιὰν κλίμακ' ἐκπέρα ποδί, which is still more daring.

138-9. The sense of these lines seems clear enough: "Your weeping is excusable, to be sure; but I wish you would (stop and) tell me whether Alcestis

---

* The order is against taking παγκαρπείας with πλήρη, as do some.

is alive or not," or as Bauer-Wecklein put it: "Das Weinen ist dir zwar nicht zu verargen; ich möchte aber, dass du jetzt meine Frage beantwortetest." What there is obscure or difficult about this I confess myself unable to see. Weil, however, reads πένθει μεν, ὥς τι δεσπόταισι τυγχάνει, εὔγνωστον κ.τ.λ., and observes: "J'ai corrigé la leçon πενθεῖν μέν, εἰ (juste au-dessus de εἰ au vers suivant) τι ... συγγνωστόν, dont le sens ne s'accorde ni avec les sentiments du chœur ni avec la suite des idées"! In this, as in some other cases, the brilliant French critic has been led astray by his own over-acuteness. The words are merely a courteous request to the domestic to stop weeping and give the desired information.

141. Even in her grief the servant cannot resist the temptation to quibble. What Johnson says of Shakespeare is peculiarly true of Euripides: "His persons, however distressed, have a conceit left them in their misery, a miserable conceit."

144-5. I have followed H. Mueller in placing these two lines after 149. As they stand in the MSS. the sudden apostrophe to Admetus is needlessly abrupt, but when 144 follows 149 the address is adequately motived by the mention of him in ᾧ σφε συνθάψει πόσις. Any one who has copied out a long στιχομυθία will realize how easy it is to get the lines transposed by mistake. Tournier (followed by Weil) would place 148-9 after 143, less happily, as it seems to me. πάθῃ: here P has preserved the true reading at the end of the line, while at the end of 142 and 140 L a have the correct form of the text. These, like hundreds of other instances, show how extremely liable the last part of a line is to suffer change.

146. μέν: Weil reads νυν, which seems a needless alteration. For the use of μέν, cf. *Hippol.* 316 ἀγνὰς μέν, ὦ παῖ, χεῖρας αἵματος φέρεις: The particle serves both to lend emphasis to the preceding word and to indicate that the asker of the question expects an affirmative answer. It may be well rendered by our "I suppose." σῴζεσθαι: σώσασθαι L P; but, as Earle points out, the present is preferable as denoting continuance, "be kept in safety," "preserved," βίον being subject, not object. All recent edd. read σῴζεσθαι.

148. ἐπ' αὐτῇ: ἐπ' αὐτοῖς, the reading of L P, was known to the schol., who observes: ἐπὶ τοῖς εἱμαρμένοις ὁ ἀνὴρ τὰ προσήκοντα ποιεῖ, ἢ ἐπ' αὐτῇ τῇ Ἀλκήστιδι. Ἐπ' αὐτοῖς, "in view of the circumstances," gives fairly good sense, and Hermann (who daringly read ἠλπισμέν' for ἐλπὶς μέν in 146) preferred it; but ἐπ' αὐτῇ is clearer and more probable. The variant αὐτοῖς may have come from αὐτῆς = αὐτῇ being mistaken for αὐτς = αὐτοῖς, or possibly the last letters of the word had been lost in the archetype and were variously supplied from conjecture by early scholars or copyists. πράσσεται: not an "old-Attic" form, for the Attic inscriptions show ττ from the earliest times (Meisterhans p. 75). The use of σσ in the tragedians and Thucydides is probably an Ionism (Cauer in *Curtius' Studien* VIII. pp. 283 ff.). Aristophanes and the Attic prose writers have regularly ττ.

153. The reading of the MSS., which Monk and Earle retain, would be satisfactory if it really admitted of the former's rendering "what must the woman be that has surpassed her?"; but unfortunately, as Hermann pointed out, the true version would be "what must become of the woman who has surpassed her" (or, if the article is generic, "of the supremely excellent woman"). Cf. e.g. Aesch. *Sept.* 297 τί γένωμαι; Thuc. II. 52, 3 οὐκ ἔχοντες ὅ τι γένωνται. Hence some emendation is necessary, and I have adopted that of Lenting. The reading in the MSS. looks like a clumsy attempt at emendation by some one who was puzzled by the construction τὸ μὴ οὐ γενέσθαι after the verb of denial (see Goodwin *M. and T.* 811). For other suggestions see Select Conjectures.

159. Earle's notion that λευκόν is proleptic appears to me, I must confess, horribly prosaic, though defended by the analogy of *Hel.* 676 ff. But perhaps I am biased by our modern prejudices. England, who is a high authority, seems inclined to agree with Earle.

160. δόμων, which had been suspected (see Select Conjectures), has recently been ably defended by Radermacher (*N. Jahrb. f. Phil.* 1895 p. 235), who accepts the old explanation of Graevius, that δόμοι here = *cista*, and compares *El.* 870 φέρ,' οἷα δὴ 'χω καὶ δόμοι κεύθουσί μου | κόμης ἀγάλματ' ἐξενέγκωμαι, Soph. *Trach.* 578 δόμοις γὰρ ἦν (sc. ὁ χιτών) . . . ἐγκεκλημένον καλῶς. Add Hesiod. *Op.* 96 ff. μούνη δ' αὐτόθι Ἐλπὶς ἐν ἀρρήκτοισι δόμοισιν | ἔνδον ἔμιμνε (cited by Earle). Δόμοι (δόμος being properly "anything built," from δέμω) can be applied as well to the compartments of a chest or wardrobe as to the apartments of a house. Lenz's conjecture δοχῶν, which Bauer-Wecklein accept, seems to me distinctly bad, as Hesychius has δοχούς, δοχεῖα, λουτῆρας, implying that the word was commonly used of vessels to contain *liquids*.

162. κατηύξατο : this, not κατεύξατο, is the regular Attic form. The statement of Moeris p. 161 : ηὐξάμην διὰ τοῦ η Ἀττικῶς, διὰ δὲ τοῦ ε Ἑλληνικῶς is confirmed by the Attic inscriptions. See Meisterhans p. 136, 14.

163. δέσποιν' : it is not certain what goddess is here meant. πρόσθεν ἑστίας is not decisive, as the statues of various deities (θεοὶ ἑστιοῦχοι) were placed near the hearth. The epithet δέσποινα is often applied to Persephone and sometimes to Hecate; and the Pheraean Artemis also might be thus addressed by Alcestis. But it seems far more probable that the deity here meant was Hestia than that she was one of the chthonian divinities. The grim Pheraean Artemis Βριμώ in particular was scarcely a goddess to whom such a prayer would be offered by an anxious mother.

165. ὀρφανεῦσαι : this rare word is used at least five times by Euripides, here and v. 297 in the active in the sense of "to rear" or "care for orphans," and 538, *Hippol.* 847, *Suppl.* 1132 in the middle with the meaning of "to live in orphanhood." It is a distinctively Euripidean word. τῷ μέν : the boy was Eumelus who afterward led his father's forces in the Trojan war (*Il.* II. 712). The schol. on Aristoph. *Vesp.* 1239 mentions another son, Hippasus.

166. τῇ δέ: the daughter's name was Perimele. She married Argus and bore him Magnes, after whom Magnesia in Thessaly was named (Antonin. Liberal. 23).

167. ἀπόλλυμαι: this reading is more elegant and idiomatic than ἀπόλλυται, and is clearly right. Some one wished to have a verb in the third person, of which ἡ τεκοῦσα could be directly the subject, and so altered ἀπόλλυμαι to ἀπόλλυται, the reading of L and P.

168. θανεῖν: precative infinitive (Goodwin *M. and T.* 785). This seems a more probable explanation than that of Jerram, who holds that the clause καὶ τῷ μὲν ... γενναῖον πόσιν forms a parenthesis, after which the infinitive construction dependent on αἰτήσομαι in 164 is resumed.

170. οἱ κατ' Ἀδμήτου δόμους: a good example of something which is very rare indeed — the omission of the copula in a relative clause. Bauer-Wecklein compare *Odyssey* XX. 298, δμώων, οἱ κατὰ δώματ' Ὀδυσσῆος θείοιο.

173. μυρσίνης: this is preferable to μυρσινῶν, the reading of L P, as the adjective μυρσινός or μυρρινός is very rare (though Callimachus *ad Dian.* 202 has μυρρινὸς ὄζος). Cf. 757 and note. A purifying power was attributed to the myrtle; hence it was used in lustrations and funeral solemnities, and was consecrated to the deities of the lower world.

173. ἄκλαυστος: ἄκλαυτος L. About the true orthography of this word there is much uncertainty. In Homer the form without σ seems best attested, and is adopted by nearly all recent editors, though in all the four passages where it occurs (*Il.* XXII. 386; *Odyss.* IV. 494; XI. 54 and 72) there is considerable MS. authority for the sigmatic form. In Aeschylus (*Septem* 683 and *Eum.* 564) the Laurentian has the form with σ (but κλαυτόν *Septem* 320). In Sophocles the Laurentian has the sigmatic form once (*El.* 912; cf. κλαυστά *O. C.* 1360), the non-sigmatic four times (*Ant.* 29, 847, 876, *O. C.* 1708). In Euripides, besides the passage from our text, we have *Androm.* 1235, where all the MSS. have the form without σ, *Phoen.* 1634, where the MSS. except L b c have the sigmatic spelling, and *Hec.* 30, where all the MSS. but L have the non-sigmatic form. In view of these facts I see no reason why the statement of Eustathius (1673, 17), τὸ δὲ ἄκλαυτον οἱ μεθ' Ὅμηρον καὶ ἄκλαυστον, should not be true of Euripides. Probably both forms existed side by side, and the poet used now one, now the other, as he saw fit. Hence I have followed the majority of the MSS. in reading ἄκλαυστος. The fact that both B and P have this form is much in its favor. It is noticeable that ἄκλαυστος is here coupled with another adjective beginning with a privative. Cf. the Homeric ἄκλαυτος ἄταφος (*Il.* XXII. 386; *Odyss.* XI. 54 and 72), and *Hec.* 30, *Phoen.* 1634, Soph. *Ant.* 29, 876, Aesch. *Eum.* 555. For the active sense, cf. *Odyss.* IV. 494 οὐδέ σέ φημι δὴν ἄκλαυτον ἔσεσθαι, Aesch. *Sept.* 683 ἀκλαύστοις ὄμμασιν.

174. φύσιν: here = "complexion." Φύσις, being in itself a colorless word, requires "to be filled with meaning from the context to the requisite amount," as some one has well put it.

175 ff. Sophocles probably had this passage in mind when he wrote *Trach.* 912 ff.: ἐπεὶ δὲ τῶνδ' ἔληξεν, ἐξαίφνης σφ' ὁρῶ | τὸν 'Ηράκλειον θάλαμον εἰσορμωμένην | ... καθέζετ' ἐν μέσοισιν εὐνατηρίοις, | καὶ δακρύων ῥήξασα θερμὰ νάματα | ἔλεξεν, ὦ λέχη τε καὶ νυμφεῖ' ἐμά, | τὸ λοιπὸν ἤδη χαίρεσθ', ὡς ἔμ' οὔποτε | δέξεσθ' ἔτ' ἐν κοίταισι ταῖσδ' εὐνήτριαν. No Sophoclean play shows so strong an affinity in style with the *Alcestis* as the *Trachiniae*.

176. 'δάκρυσε: the copyists, who doubtless did not find the aphaeresis indicated in their sources save by the omission of the augment, have written δάκρυσε: but the unaugmented form is not admissible in trimeters. In such cases as this it is now the fashion not to mark the aphaeresis at all, but to write δὴ ἐδάκρυσε and the like. But convenience certainly requires that it be indicated; and though the ancients often did not mark it, I see no reason why we should not.*

177-8. There can be no doubt that Nauck is right in rejecting 178. The use of κορεύματ', ἐκ and πέρι is alone enough to condemn it, and a more clumsy "Anhängsel" it would be hard to find. Two plausible reasons may be suggested, either of which would account for the interpolation: (1) the interpolator may have inserted a line in order to supply a substantive with which παρθένει' could agree, or (2) κορεύματα may be a gloss on παρθένει', which was subsequently filled out so as to make a complete trimeter. The instances in which glosses, παρεπιγραφαί and the like have led to wholesale interpolations are not rare; how great their influence upon the text has been is ably shown by Mr. Rutherford in his editions of Thucydides and the scholia to Aristophanes. The question next arises, whether παρθένει' ἔλυσ' ἐγώ in 177 is sound. The use of the active form ἔλυσ' as Nauck (*Eur. Stud.* II. 54) pointed out, is defended by *Tro.* 501 οἵαις ἔλυσας συμφοραῖς ἄγνευμα σόν, and Pindar *Isthm.* VII. 94 (VIII. 45) λύοι κεν χαλινὸν ὑφ' ἥρωι παρθενίας, both of the woman. For παρθένεια in the sense of "virginity" I know no parallel from classical writers, though the Septuagint has τὰ παρθένεια for the tokens of virginity. Still, the expression seems possible enough, and the text probably needs no further change; though it would be easy to read παρθένευμ' with Hannemueller (cf. *Ion* 1472).

179-80. A much disputed passage. The question turns on the first word in 180. We may distinguish the following views:

A. Those who retain the MSS. reading μόνην.

(1) Some editors retain μόνην and take ἀπώλεσας in the sense of "destroy." The rendering will then be: "Farewell; for I do not hate thee; but thou hast destroyed me only; for because I shrink from betraying thee and my spouse I am about to die." This makes fairly good sense, but the exact force of μόνην is not clear. Woolsey says: "μόνην, *me only*, i.e. no other woman has perished in a similar manner, destroyed by marriage in this way." But Alcestis is addressing her own particular λέχος, not speaking of marriage in general.

* For inscriptional cases of aphaeresis, see Lucius in *Diss. phil. Argentor.* IX. p. 396.

Jerram says: "'you have destroyed me, but you will destroy no other woman,' for no one will do for a husband what I have done for him." Weil explains: "c'est moi seule que tu fais mourir (mon époux vivra)." These different explanations show how vague the sense is if we read μόνην. And what is the force of δέ after ἀπώλεσας? To render it by *nam*, as Hermann does, is surely bold.

(2) Earle and others render ἀπώλεσας by "lost," a meaning which the word not infrequently has. The sense will then be: "thou hast lost me only (but not Admetus)." But in that case why δέ? We can scarcely suppose that the particle here = γάρ, though it sometimes has nearly the same force.

B. Reiske wished to put the stop after με and read μόνη προδοῦναι γάρ σ' ὀκνοῦσα κ.τ.λ. This gives very good sense, and the position of γάρ can, of course, be easily paralleled. Still, though the change is slight, I prefer Blomfield's emendation.

C. Others read μόνον with Blomfield. The sense will then be clear: "Farewell; for I do not hate thee; but thou, and thou alone, hast destroyed me; for it is because I shrink from betraying thee and my spouse that I am about to die." To one who believes that in Greek, as in Latin, the emphatic position is usually at or near the beginning of the sentence or clause, the order of the words (especially the position of προδοῦναί σ') is, I think, decisive in favor of this view. The δέ, too, thus receives its proper force. If this view is the right one, we should read δέ με (with the MSS.) in 179; those who prefer μόνην should, of course, read δ' ἐμέ.

181-2. These lines are wittily parodied by Aristophanes in the well-known passage of the *Equites*: ὦ στέφανε, χαίρων ἄπιθι, καί σ' ἄκων ἐγὼ | λείπω· σὲ δ' ἄλλος τις λαβὼν κεκτήσεται, | κλέπτης μὲν οὐκ ἂν μᾶλλον, εὐτυχὴς δ' ἴσως. For the elliptic use of ἄν (sc. οὖσα) see Goodwin *M. and T.* 227 and 483.

183. προσπίτνουσα: the long controversy as to the correct accentuation of this by-form of πίπτω may, I think, be said to have been pretty definitely decided in favor of Elmsley and against Hermann; and nearly all recent editors prefer πίτνω to πιτνῶ. The MSS. waver between the two spellings; even the Medicean of Aeschylus and Sophocles is not consistent.

184. ὀφθαλμοτέγκτῳ: this word is apparently of Euripidean coinage; at all events it seems to occur nowhere else in classic Greek. πλημμυρίδι: the edd. from Monk down point out that Euripides is here following Aeschylus, who says (*Choeph.* 177-8): ἐξ ὀμμάτων δὲ δίψιοι πίπτουσί μοι | σταγόνες ἄφαρκτοι δυσχίμου πλημμυρίδος. The grandiloquence of the description contrasted with the simple language of Alcestis herself is very effective. Δεύεται, which Porson restored *ex conj.*, is confirmed by the MSS. of the first class; the early edd. had δεύετο (with *L* and *P*), and κύνει above in 182 (with the same MSS.).

185. δακρύων: I cannot agree with Professor Earle that this is genitive of source or cause. πολλῶν is not decisive against the ordinary view: "when she had had her fill of many tears" is certainly a possible and natural poetic expression. Cf. *Phoen.* 1750 κόρον ἔχουσ' ἐμῶν κακῶν, and expressions like μεστὸς πολλῶν ἀγαθῶν, etc., where the πολλῶν is seemingly pleonastic.

187. Two questions arise in regard to this line — what does ἐπιστράφη mean, and should we read θάλαμον with the MSS. or θαλάμων with Nauck?

(1) Many editors, including Monk, render ἐπεστράφη "returned." There seems, however, to be no passage where it is *certain* that ἐπιστρέφομαι has this meaning, either in Euripides or elsewhere. The alleged instances of this use are all susceptible of a different interpretation.

(2) Others (with Liddell and Scott *s. v.*) render the verb "turned round" (to look back). This meaning of ἐπιστρέφομαι is well attested, e.g. Xen. *Sympos.* 9, 1 καὶ ὁ Λύκων ὁ πατὴρ αὐτῷ συνεξιὼν ἐπιστραφεὶς εἶπε, Herod. I. 88, etc. Cf. also the figurative use in *Rhes.* 400 οὐκ ἦλθες οὐδ' ἤμυνας οὐδ' ἐπεστράφης and similar passages. But this translation seems weak; for the next line shows that Alcestis not only looked back but actually went and threw herself upon the bed again. We should expect a verb of *going* rather than one of mere *turning about*.

(3) Euripides himself has *Hel.* 83 πόθεν γῆς τῆσδ' ἐπεστράφης πέδον; ib. 89 τί δῆτα Νείλου τούσδ' ἐπιστρέφει γύας; ib. 768 Κρήτης τε Λιβύης θ' ἃς ἐπεστράφην πόλεις. In these cases the meaning of the verb seems to be "wander to," "visit." Cf. *Andr.* 1031 θεοῦ νιν κέλευσμ' ἐπεστράφη. The closest parallel to our passage, however, is *Ion* 352 καίτοι πόλλ' ἐπεστράφη πέδον, where ἐπεστράφη (though it *may* be rendered "returned to," "visited ") probably means "roamed over," "wandered through" (in the search for traces of the child), as in the Hesiodic γαῖαν ἐπιστρέφεται. In all these instances the notion of *roaming* or *wandering* seems to lie in the word. Hence in our passage, as the participle ἐξιοῦσα may have a future sense, I am inclined to render: "and oft she wandered through the chamber about (or intending) to go out," i.e. went about to take a last look before leaving. If this view is correct, θάλαμον requires no change. Those, however, who accept (1) or (2) must read θαλάμων with Nauck, as the word for "chamber" is naturally expected with the verb of leaving, which logically comes first, not with that of returning or looking round. The order of the words and the frequent use of the plural of θάλαμος by Euripides favor Nauck's emendation (*Eur. Stud.* II. 54); but on the whole I think no change is necessary. The order may be due to metrical reasons.

188. αὖθις ... πάλιν: a common pleonasm. Sophocles even goes so far as to end a line (*Oed. Col.* 364) with αὖθις πάλιν. Cf. also *Hel.* 932 πάλιν ... αὖθις αὖ.

190. ἐς ἀγκάλας: ἐν ἀγκάλαις *L P*, which is perfectly possible, and may be right*; cf. *Hippol.* 1431 λαβὲ | σὸν παῖδ' ἐν ἀγκάλαισι. With λαβεῖν sometimes the idea of motion predominates, sometimes that of rest.

193. οἰκτίροντες: the Attic inscriptions show that οἰκτίρω, not οἰκτείρω, is the correct spelling. See Meisterhans p. 142; Kühner-Blass II. p. 498.

---

* Wecklein prefers it; see his *Beiträge zur Kritik des Euripides* p. 539.

195. This line is here in place; but in 312 (where see note) it appears in a distorted form and is inappropriate to the context. From ὅν, ὑφ' οὗ is to be understood with προσερρήθη.

197. γ': so the second Hervagian edition. The τ' of the MSS. is probably due to confusion between T and Γ. The intensive particle "seems demanded by the sense," as Earle justly observes. ὤλετ': ᾤχετ', F. W. Schmidt's emendation, is quite needless, and was subsequently withdrawn by Schmidt himself. δ': τ', the reading of P, which Prinz and Weil accept, is probably due to some grammarian who, after γ' had become corrupted to τ', was offended by τ' ... δ', and wished to have a second τ' coördinate with the first one. This constant effort to plane away all that seemed irregular and reduce everything to one "dead level" of monotony was one of the worst failings of the Byzantine scholars, as it is of some modern critics.

198. οὔποθ' οὗ: Nauck's brilliant and certain emendation. The various readings of the MSS. (see Critical App.) show that the scribes were misled by the unusual position of the negative. This position is due to the desire to give it special emphasis, and perhaps also to metrical reasons.

199. τοισίδ': the emphatic form is clearly preferable to τοῖσιν of L P.

200. εἰ: here, on the other hand, L and P are almost certainly right. ἧς of B perhaps came from a carelessly written ἧι (C for a crooked iota) or it may have been a deliberate emendation; and ἧι (so a) in its turn is doubtless a mistake for εἰ, due to iotacism. It would be *possible*, but much less elegant, to read ἧς and take γυναικός as gen. of cause. σφε: that this reading is correct is shown by the agreement of L P a; γε, the reading of B, is either a perverse emendation or a blunder of the scribe.

201. ἄκοιτιν: a formal word, "consort," like ἄλοχος.

204. χειρὸς ἄθλιον βάρος: (1) Some take βάρος as accus. of specification with παρειμένη, and understand by χειρός the hand of Alcestis. So the schol., who paraphrases by τὴν ἰσχὺν τῆς χειρὸς παραλελυμένη.

(2) Others (better, I think) make βάρος refer to Alcestis herself, "a hapless burden of the hand," helpless and unable to move.

Elmsley, Kirchhoff, Prinz, Weil, Bauer-Wecklein, Earle and others hold that a line has been lost after 204. This is quite needless. There is no lacuna, and with the punctuation given in the text the sense is perfectly clear: — "and all relaxed, a piteous burden for the hand, but yet with life still left in her, albeit but little, she wishes," etc. The true punctuation and meaning were first pointed out by F. D. Allen.

207 8. These two lines (with προσόψομαι instead of προσόψεται) occur also in *Hec.* 411-12. In our passage they are unnecessary, and ἀκτῖνα κύκλον θ' ἡλίου is displeasing after πρὸς αὐγὰς ... τὰς ἡλίου. Valckenaer rejected them, and nearly all modern editors have followed his example. Probably some early reader wrote the parallel passage from the *Hecuba* in the margin of his MS. and it was then copied into the text of the *Alcestis* by mistake.

212. Exit maid-servant. The choral dialogue which follows is differently divided by different editors. The MSS. give very little guidance. The arrangement in the text is substantially that of Prinz, except that I have assigned 220–25 and 232–7 to the whole chorus, and have prefixed a παράγραφος to 238 to indicate that 238–43 were delivered by the coryphaeus. But the details of the distribution are, and probably always will be, uncertain.

213. The text of this line is extremely uncertain; πῶς πᾶ is suspected, and some editors omit πῶς, others πᾶ, while Musgrave would strike out both words. But B and P have both words, and L seems to have once had them, though the second has been erased. In the face of this evidence the fact that a omits πῶς is of little weight, as that MS. is full of arbitrary changes. Hence I have retained both.* The accumulated questions mark the extreme excitement of the chorus. Nauck's restoration of bacchiacs (see Sel. Conj.) is elegant but daring, and the changes which it requires are too sweeping. Unfortunately the antistrophic line 226 is lacunose, and gives little help. In 214 the MSS. show no variant, and as the sense of the two lines 213–14 is clear, there does not seem to be good reason for change.

215. ἔξεισί τις: i.e. "will any one come out of the palace to give us directions, or shall we put on mourning at once on our own responsibility?" Herwerden's ἔτ' εἰσί τις seems unnecessary. As the servant has gone in to inform her master of the presence of the chorus, they have good reason to expect that some one will come out and tell them what to do. The words are doubtless spoken after a short pause. τέμω: the deliberative subjunctive was restored by Hermann. The copyists, who perhaps did not know ἔτεμον, took the form to be future and accented it τεμῶ. Ἔτεμον, not ἔταμον, is the Attic form of the aorist; see Meisterhans p. 146, and the authorities there cited.

216. στολμὸν πέπλων: so *Andr.* 148 στολμόν τε χρωτὸς τόνδε ποικίλων πέπλων, Aesch. *Choeph.* 29 πρόστερνοι στολμοὶ πέπλων.

218. δῆλα μέν: i.e. that Alcestis is dead and the mourning should be put on; or we may understand ὅτι οὐκ ἂν γένοιτο πόρος κακῶν (so Earle). It is hard to tell whether 218–19 is an answer to 215–17, or a continuation of 213–14 without regard to the intervening words of the other semi-chorus.

219. εὐχώμεσθα: here the scribe of a, who was evidently a man of some learning, has the right form; L is next in point of accuracy, then P, while B, which has ἐχώμεθα, is farthest from the truth. The correspondence is not perfect, as the antistrophe has κατθάνουσαν (232), but -μεσθα is required to = -νοῦσαν. γὰρ δύναμις: so B. The other MSS. have γὰρ ἁ δύναμις, and it is possible that not ἁ but γάρ should be omitted, thus giving another of the asyndeta so common in this play. Hermann omitted both γάρ and ἁ, scanning θεῶν without synizesis. μεγίστη: so the best MSS. C d a have μεγίστα, but these are comparatively untrustworthy. The agreement of B L P makes it probable that the archetype had μεγίστη. Many edd., however, prefer the Doric form.

* Possibly, however, we should read ἰὼ Ζεῦ τίς ἂν πόρος πᾶ κακῶν, a dochmiac dimeter.

223. A very difficult place. The strophe has — ᴗ — — — —, the antistrophe (235) — — ᴗ — —, and it is clear that some change is necessary to restore the responsion. The principal MSS. show no variant in either the strophic or antistrophic line. Editors have treated this passage in the most various ways. They may be roughly divided into three groups:

A. Those who with W. Dindorf reject τοῦδ' ἐφηῦρες. To fill the lacuna thus left various substitutes, τοιόσδε, παρῆσθα, etc. have been suggested; see Sel. Conj.

B. Those who with Erfurdt and Monk reject καὶ νῦν, and τάν in the antistrophic line. These I believe to be in the right.

C. Those who adopt other measures: e.g. Hermann, who read τῷδ' for τοῦδ' with Heath, inserted τοῦτο after ἐφηῦρες, and in 235 στέναξον after χθών; and so Earle. Weil proposed τοῦδ' ἦσθα (sc. λυτήριος), καὶ νῦν. See also Sel. Conj.

On examining 223 the first thing which appears suspicious is τοῦδ'. If it is genitive after πάρος the construction is clearly very unusual, as πάρος with the genitive is very rarely used of *time* (though there is an instance in *Andr.* 1208). If, on the other hand, it depends on μηχανάν understood, "(a means of escape) from this (evil)," the ellipsis seems harsh in the extreme. We feel that ἐφηῦρες needs an object that is *expressed*. Moreover τοῦδ' is not found in all MSS., for (according to Hermann, Kirchhoff and Dindorf: Prinz does not mention the reading) *C*, the Copenhagen MS., has τοῦτ', and the Florentinus of Voss had τῶν δ'. These are probably conjectures, not independent variants; but they show that τοῦδ' was felt to be wrong quite early. We note also that ἐφηῦρες, if its ultima is long by position, corresponds in the number and quantity of its syllables with ἄρισταν. Ἐφευρίσκω is a favorite word with Euripides, occurring at least ten times in the plays (and again v. 699 of the *Alcestis*). It seems to me, also (though here opinions differ), that καὶ νῦν, occurring as it does at the end of the line and being clearly implied in the context, looks very like an interpolation, and can well be dispensed with. If so, by striking out τάν in 235 (which may easily have been inserted by some later hand) the complete responsion is restored, as Erfurdt long ago pointed out. Cf. Westphal-Rossbach *Gr. Metrik* p. 286 note. Hence I am strongly inclined to read τοῦτ' (i.e. τὸ λυτήριον ἐκ θανάτου εἶναι) with *C* and Monk, and to reject καὶ νῦν and τάν with Erfurdt. Hermann, to be sure, says in his curt way "parum norunt morem tragicorum, qui καὶ νῦν putant abesse posse": but to *say* this is one thing, to *prove* it another.

224. ἐκ: λυτήριος is usually followed by the gen. of separation without a preposition, as in Aesch. *Eum.* 294, Soph. *El.* 635, etc. Euripides probably used the preposition here for metrical convenience. See note on 983.

226. The lacuna in this line was first marked by W. Dindorf. The reading of *L* and *P* is obviously a mere attempt to fill up the gap in the line with interjections. What the original reading was it is quite impossible to say.

CRITICAL AND EXEGETICAL NOTES. 95

227. ὦ παῖ: this does not accurately correspond to γένοι- of 214; but in the anacrusis a short may answer to a long, and hence no change is necessary. See Metrical Appendix. οἷα πράξεις: I have accepted Jacob's emendation, as Alcestis is not yet dead, and in 232 (which was probably spoken by the same semi-chorus) we have the future ἐπόψει. It may be urged that in 218 the death of Alcestis is assumed; but it is not certain to what δῆλα refers (see note *ad loc.*). δάμαρτος: as the ultima is long by position, this does not correspond to πάρεστι of the strophe (214). Perfect responsion may be restored by reading πάρεστιν in the strophic line, or ᾶς for σᾶς (with Weil) in the antistrophe; but probably no change should be made. Responsion in logaoedic strophes is usually pretty strict, but exceptions certainly sometimes occur. στερείς: so Monk for στερηθείς, as the strophic line has ⏑ —, not ⏑ — —. The conjecture is supported by *Bacch.* 1363 (στερεῖσα Barnes, στερηθεῖσα P), *Suppl.* 793 (στερεῖσα Markland, στερεῖσθαι MSS.), *Iph. T.* 474 (στερεῖσα Scaliger, στερηθεῖσα MSS.).

228. ἆρ': so Hermann. The letters ι and ρ are often extremely alike in Greek MSS., both in literary and cursive writing; hence ἆρ' was mistaken for αἶ. Then, as the interjection usually occurs twice or four times, it was doubled as in L P or quadrupled as in B a. — For the sentiment cf. *Bacch.* 246, *Heracl.* 246, Soph. *O. T.* 1373, Aristoph. *Achar.* 125, etc. (cited by Monk).

229. πλέον: this is the classical form of the neut. sing.; see Meisterhans pp. 119–20, Wecklein *Cur. Epigr.* p. 27.

230. οὐρανίῳ: the epithet seems unduly extravagant, and the word has been suspected by Lenting, Prinz, Wecklein and others. The soundness of the text has been defended by Earle, who compares *Hipp.* 1207 κῦμ' οὐρανῷ στήριζον, *Andr.* 830 ἐρρ' αἰθέριον πλοκάμων ἐμῶν ἄπο, λεπτόμιτον φάρος. Add *El.* 860 ὡς νεβρὸς οὐράνιον πήδημα κουφίζουσα, ib. 1158 οὐράνια τείχεα, *Tro.* 1087 τείχεα... οὐράνια, ib. 325 πάλλε πόδ' αἰθέριον, *Bacch.* 1064 ἐλάτης οὐράνιον ἄκρον κλάδον, etc. Euripides even goes so far as to say of a horse *Tro.* 519 ἵππον οὐράνια | βρέμοντα. But these uses, bold as they are, do not seem to me to justify the expression in the text, and I have marked the word as corrupt. For some of the emendations that have been proposed see Sel. Conj.; but the "inevitable word" has not yet been suggested. πελάσσαι: Erfurdt's emendation is necessary, as the strophic line ends with ἤδη. The tragedians sometimes allow themselves the Epic license of doubling the σ of the first aorist after a short vowel; cf. *Iph. A.* 1051 ἀφύσσε, Soph. *Phil.* 1163 πέλασσον, etc.

232. εἰν: so Dindorf, the MSS. having ἐν. A long syllable is required, as the strophe (219) has θεῶν. The Epic and Doric form εἰν is found also in 436 εἰν Ἅιδα δόμοισιν, and in Soph. *Antig.* 1241 εἰν Ἅιδου δόμοις (in an iambic trimeter; Heath and Jebb read ἐν γ'). Jerram objects that these are not parallel to our passage, as both are imitations of the Homeric εἰν Ἀΐδαο δόμοισιν *Il.* XXIII. 19, 179; but εἰν ἤματι τῷδ' is probably also an Epic reminiscence. Cf. also Aesch. *Suppl.* 839 εὑρείαις εἰν αὔραις, where, however, the soundness of the text is very doubtful. It is *possible* to retain ἐν by rejecting both γάρ and ἅ in 219 with Hermann; but γάρ stands in all the MSS. ἤματι: that this form stood in the archetype is made probable by the agreement of B L P; the authority of d and a is slight in comparison. The limits of Dorism in the tragic choruses are not well defined, and in cases like the present the wisest course is to follow the best MSS. τῷδ' ἐπόψει: L and P have τῶδε γ' ὄψει, a reading obviously due to a II mistaken for Γ. The two are often extremely alike in the MSS., particularly when (as often) the II has its second leg shorter than the first.

233. The dying Alcestis is slowly borne upon the stage. Admetus and the two children accompany her. ἰδοῦ ἰδοῦ, which is not in L and P, had probably been omitted in their common source by a mere error of the copyist. The imperatives are, at all events, appropriate, though it is to be noted that the correspondence with 220 is not exact ($- - - - = \cup - \cup -$).

234. L and P have στέναξον ὦ βόασον ὦ (P βόησον), but στέναξον as the more explicit word should probably come second.

235. [τὰν]: see note on 223.

236. μαραινομέναν: pregnant, "wasting away (and going)." Cf. 363 ἔκεισε προσδόκα μ'. Woolsey aptly compares the words of the Scotch song "I am wearing awa' to the land of the leal."

237. χθόνιον: I have followed Weil in transposing this word, as it is clear that χθόνιον ..."Αιδαν was meant to answer φόνιον ..."Αιδαν of 225. The Greek dramatists delighted in subtle correspondences of this sort; see for numerous instances Christ Metrik[2] pp. 642 ff. γᾶς, which Monk restored ex conj., is found in B, the other MSS. having γᾶν. When κατά means "under," "down beneath" (either of motion or rest), the genitive is the regular construction. Cf. 107, El. 144, Ion 1441, Hippol. 836, 1366, Suppl. 1024, Rhes. 831, An. 503, Iph. T. 170, etc.; and on the other hand for the use of κατὰ γᾶν Or. 832, 1398, Bacch. 371, Hippol. 194, etc.

238 ff. This anapaestic system was in all probability sung by the coryphaeus.

241. λεύσων καὶ L P. The insertion of καί, which disturbs the metre, was evidently due to some one who read τᾶσδε for τάσδε in 240.

242. ἀπλακών: the MSS. here and in Iph. A. 124 λέκτρων ἀπλακών have ἀμπλακών, but the metre requires a short first syllable. Cf. Aesch. Eum. 915 (ἀπλακήματα Pauw, ἀμπλακήματα MSS.). In these cases some would retain the spelling of the MSS. (e.g. Clemm Rhein. Mus. 32 pp. 466 ff.; Kühner-Blass I. p. 286, II. p. 307 note 3), supposing the μ to have been so faintly sounded as not to count toward "making position." But we have one clear case of απλ, Soph. O. R. 472, where the Laurentian by the first hand, Triclinius, the schol., Zonaras and Suidas all support the reading ἀναπλάκητοι. (Kühner-Blass l. s. c. are wrong in saying "ἀναμπλάκητος codd., ἀναπλ. die Neueren Soph. O. R. 472"; the μ in L has been added above the word by a later hand.) Hence I have preferred, with most edd., to spell with απλ where the metre requires a short syllable. The formation of ἀμβλακεῖν, ἀμπλακεῖν, ἀπλακεῖν is

very doubtful. Curtius and Jebb hold the π to be original, the verb being cognate with πλάζω; while Kühner-Blass hold the π to be an euphonic insertion, π being used instead of β because βλ commonly makes position, so that ἀμβλακών could not = ‿ ‿ —. Cf. ἄμβροτος, ἄβροτος, (μ)βλίττω etc. — Note the alliteration in ἀρίστης ἀπλακὼν ἀλόχου ... ἀβίωτον ... βιοτεύσει. ἀβίωτον ... βιοτεύσει: a favorite oxymoron. Cf. *Hippol.* 821, 868, Aristoph. *Plutus* 969, Demos. XXI. 132 ἀβίωτον ᾤετ' ἔσεσθαι τὸν βίον ἑαυτῷ, etc. F. W. Schmidt's suggestion to read βίον for χρόνον is tempting, and may be right; but I suspect that Euripides thought that ἀβίωτον βίον βιοτεύσει would be "too much of a good thing."

245. Some, absurdly enough, have seen in this line an allusion to the theory of Anaxagoras respecting the revolution of the heavens. It has often been noted that Euripides is especially fond of references to the sky, clouds, upper air, etc., and his references to the sea and figures drawn from it are also very numerous (see E. Schwartz *De metaphoris e mari et re navali petitis quaest. Eurip.*). Probably no ancient poet had a keener eye for natural phenomena.

246 ff. The alternation of the iambic trimeters with the more impetuous lyric metres is very effective.

247. θανῇ: here all the MSS. but L have the better form in ῃ.

249. νυμφίδιοι: this seems preferable to νυμφίδιαι, the reading of L and P; see note on 125 σκοτίους. πατρῴας: I have retained the reading of the MSS., though most edd. follow the Aldine in reading πατρίας. Musgrave, Matthiae, Wuestemann, Kirchhoff and Jerram retain πατρῴας. If we may trust the MSS., Euripides often shortens the second syllable of πατρῷος in lyric and anapaestic passages; so *Bacch.* 1368, *El.* 1315, *Hec.* 82 (most MSS.), *Me.* 431, *Tro.* 162; cf. Soph. *Phil.* 724, Pind. *Nem.* IX. 14, etc. Many editors follow Porson in substituting πάτριος in such cases; but the *number* of instances is against the change. The distinction in meaning between πάτριος and πατρῷος which Hermann and others have striven to establish certainly was very frequently neglected, if indeed it really existed. Porson's words "Attici πάτριος et πατρῷος promiscue usurpant" are abundantly borne out by the usage of Euripides; thus, for example, he constantly uses πατρία and πατρῴα γᾶ without any perceptible difference of meaning. See Beck's index for abundant examples. — The mention of the νυμφίδιοι κοῖται in Iolcus, as the schol. and Weil point out, does not agree with vv. 177 and 911 ff., which represent the marriage as having taken place in Pherae. This is probably a mere piece of carelessness on the part of the poet.

252 ff. With this passage the edd. compare Aristoph. *Ran.* 181 ff. (which is not, I think, an intentional parody of this scene), *Lysist.* 605 ff. (which is clearly a real parody of our passage), and Athenaeus VIII. 341 *C*, where Machon uses for comic purposes part of the *Niobe*, a dithyramb of Timotheus, which was apparently very similar in tone to this passage from the *Alcestis*.

252. δίκωπον σκάφος: Wuestemann compares Lucian *Charon* 1 ἐγὼ δὲ τὴν δικωπίαν ἐρέττω μόνος: and the boat which Dionysus rows in the *Ranae* seems to have been two-oared. For antique representations of Charon and his boat, see Roscher *Lex. d. Mythologie* p. 886, Baumeister *Denkmäler des klass. Alt.* s. v. Charon. [ἐν λίμνᾳ] : these words disturb the responsion, add little to the sense, and are almost certainly a gloss (perhaps suggested by the mention of the λίμνη in Aristoph. *Ran.* 137 and 181). They were omitted in the Aldine, and are rejected by most editors.

254. This line, with the antistrophic line 261, forms one of the worst *cruces* of the play. The two cannot well be treated separately. Editors have disagreed widely as to the constitution of the text, the kind of metre, and the division into cola. We may roughly distinguish the following classes :

(1) Those who retain the reading of the MSS. except as to χεῖρ' in 254, which they change to χέρ' (with the Aldine), as the antistrophic line has a short syllable. So Monk, Hermann, Dindorf, Pflugk, Nauck, Prinz, Woolsey, Jerram. With this reading H. Schmidt (*Kunstformen* vol. III.) gives the following scheme of the lines (logaoedic-trochaic) :

∪ | — ∪ | ∪ ∪ ≳ | — ∪ | — ≳ ‖ — ∪ | — ∪ | ∟ | — ∧

But the apparent anapaest in the second foot of 254 is awkward, and it is very doubtful whether Euripides ever admits an anapaest in logaoedic verse (see Groeppel *De Eurip. versibus logaoedis,* p. 84). It is much better to scan as iambic, thus :

∪ — | ∪ ∪ ∪ | ≳ — | ∪ — ‖ ≳ — | ∪ — | ∪ ∟ | —

The lines give good sense as they stand, and I believe no further change to be necessary. The strophe and antistrophe will then be "iambo-logaoedic"* (see Westphal-Rossbach *Metrik*³ p. 720).

(2) Others, following a suggestion of Paley, omit μ' ἤδη in 254, and read κυαναυγές with Kirchhoff in 261. Of these some, e.g. Bauer-Wecklein, read χέρ' in 254; in which case the first syllable of ὀφρύσι will be short (ἔχων, ∪ — = ὑπ' ὀφρυ-, ∪ ∪ ∪): others read χέρας (suggested by Paley), thus restoring exact responsion,

∪ | — ∪ | ∪ ∪ ∪ | ∟ | — ∪ | — ∧ ‖ ∪ | — ∪ | ∟ | — ∧

But μ' ἤδη cannot well be spared, for we miss the personal object with καλεῖ: and surely the epithet κυαναυγής suits the hair of the eyebrows better than it does the eyes or the look. I know of no other place in any classic writer where the phrase κυαναυγὲς βλέπειν occurs; while the Homeric κυανέῃσιν ἐπ' ὀφρύσι and κυανοχαίτης are familiar to every reader, and were probably in the mind of Euripides.

* I.e. logaoedic with iambic elements.

(3) Others still resort to bolder expedients. For example, Weil reads in 261 (with χέρ' in 254) ὑπ' ὄφρυσι κυαναυγὲς βλέπων, πτερωτός. ⟨ἁ⟩ μέθες με, dropping Ἀίδας and bringing up μέθες με from the next line. This reading does not seem likely to meet with much acceptance. Earle has in the strophe ἔχων χέρας ἐπὶ κοντῷ | Χάρων καλεῖ μ' ἐπείγων· | τί μέλλεις; σὺ κατείργεις. τάδε τοί με | σπερχόμενος ταχύνει, and in the antistrophe ὑπ' ὄφρυσι κυαναυγὲς | βλέπων πτερωτὸς Ἀίδας. | τί ῥέξεις; μέθες. οἵαν ὁδὸν ἁ δει- | λαιοτάτα προβαίνω, thus establishing a very elegant parallelism. But the changes, are, I fear, too sweeping. Still neater is F. D. Allen's restoration (see " Select Conjectures ").

256. τάδ' ἕτοιμα, the reading of *L P*, makes good sense if τάδ' is taken as the object of κατείργεις ; but in that case the clause σπερχόμενος ταχύνει is left with nothing to connect it with what precedes, and ταχύνει (which must be transitive or it would be awkwardly tautological with σπερχόμενος) is deprived of an object. Hermann, who accepted τάδ' ἕτοιμα, changed σπερχόμενος to σπερχομένοις, putting a colon after the latter word, and altered ταχύνει to τάχυνε. But τάδε τοί με, the reading of the other class of MSS., calls for no alteration of the text, and is clearly preferable. Τάδ' ἕτοιμα is probably an emendation of some early scholar who divided the words wrongly. Elmsley and Monk read τάδε· τοῖα *ex conj*. Τάδε and με are probably both objects of ταχύνει = λέγων ταχύνει : Klotz and Jerram compare Soph. *Aj.* 1107 τὰ σέμν' ἔπη κόλαζ' ἐκείνους. Cf. also Soph. *Aj*. 1404 ἀλλ' οἱ μὲν κοίλην κάπετον χερσὶ ταχύνατε for the transitive use. It is possible to take τάδε as "accus. of inner content" with σπερχόμενος : but it is more probable that σπερχόμενος is used absolutely, " in haste," as it so often is in Homer.

259. ἄγει μ' ἄγει μέ τις : the repetition has led to haplography, most MSS. omitting the first με, while *B* omits the second. The reading of α (ἄγει μ' ἄγει τις ἄγει μέ τις) looks like a conflation : see note on 1045. The μ' is clearly necessary, as without it there would be hiatus or shortening, neither being possible here.

260. νεκύων = νεκύων of 253. Note the subtle parallelism that runs through strophe and antistrophe.

261. κυαναυγέσι : see note on 254. κυαναυγές, which Kirchhoff and others receive into the text, was first suggested by Monk (see his note on 262). πτερωτὸς Ἀίδας : these words have given much trouble. The main difficulties are two : (1) it was not Hades but Hermes or Thanatos whose function it was to conduct the dead down to the lower world, and in this play (cf. v. 24 ff.) it is Thanatos who comes to fetch Alcestis ; (2) Thanatos is represented as having wings, but neither on the monuments nor in the literature is Hades so represented, save in *very* few instances (one in Kaibel *Epigr. Grace.* 89 ; see Robert *Thanatos* pp. 34 ff.; where our passage is discussed at length). Several ways of escaping these difficulties have been suggested :

A. Some scholars alter the text. Weil, as we have seen, omits Ἀίδας altogether : but the knife of the critic, like that of the surgeon, should be used only as a last resort. Wilamowitz would read αἴδαν, which Robert (*l. s. c.*) accepts; but, elegant as the emendation is, the position of πτερωτός is distinctly against it.

B. Some hold that here and elsewhere in the play Hades and Thanatos are treated as identical. So Rohde, who says (*Psyche* p. 540 note): "Eigentlich ist er (Thanatos) nur ein Diener des Hades; aber da doch ᾅδης schon ganz gewöhnlich = θάνατος gebraucht wurde, so wird Thanatos auch selbst geradezu "Αἰδης genannt (271: so oben p. 491, 3); nur als identisch mit Hades kann er ἄναξ νεκρῶν heissen 855 (δαιμόνων κοίρανος 1143)." But the whole conception of Thanatos in this play, his coming to fetch the souls of the dying, his lurking about the tomb and drinking of the sacrificial blood (843 ff.), appears so inconsistent with the Greek idea of the god Hades that this explanation seems impossible. The words ἄνακτα νεκρῶν (843) are too general to be decisive, especially as the ἄναξ νεκρῶν seems to be distinguished from τῶν κάτω | Κόρης ἄνακτός τ' (851-2); and as if to make us sure of the distinction Euripides says in 870-71 τοῖον ὅμηρόν μ' ἀποσυλήσας | Ἅιδῃ Θάνατος παρέδωκεν: while in 1140 κυρίῳ, not κοιράνῳ, is probably the true reading (see note *ad loc.*).

C. Others still hold that the word "Ἀίδας is here used loosely, so that πτερωτὸς "Ἀίδας means merely "a winged shape from the under-world." Hermann observes: τις "Ἀίδας est *nescio quis Orcus*, i.e. nescio quod simulacrum Orci." (He makes τις agree directly with "Ἀίδας: but it is also possible to take τις as subject of ἄγει, and "Ἀίδας as in apposition with τις, and the distance between the words favors the latter view; hence I have put a comma after βλέπων.) Though decision is hard, I strongly incline to this view. A dying woman in her agony does not speak by the card. Moreover, words like "Death," "the grave," etc. may be loosely used in almost all languages; and Euripides need not mean by "Ἀίδης *the god* Hades any more than, for example, Mr. Kipling when he speaks of a cobra as "the hooded Death" means to identify the animal with the unseen power.

262. In *a* and *B* the words μέθες με stand before τί ῥέξεις. These words are not found in *L P*, disturb the responsion, and are probably a gloss on ἄφες which has crept into the text. Nauck omits μέθες με, but reads μέθες for ἄφες. But ἄφες, which is the rarer word in this sense and is found in all the MSS., is more likely to be the true reading. Πράξεις of *B* is a gloss on ῥέξεις: cf. Hesych. τί ῥέξεις· τί πράττεις, which *may* refer to this passage, though the difference of tense makes it doubtful.

264. τῶν: the article has here its old demonstrative force; see Hadley-Allen 653 a.

266. *B* and *a* have μέθετε με μέθετε μ', *L P* omit με. Either reading is *possible*, but the repetition of *both* μέθετε and με seems wooden, and probably *L P* are right. A dittography would be all the easier as μέθετε begins with με. Kirchhoff, as usual, follows the reading of the first class.

267. ποσίν: Hermann's certain emendation. *L*, which has ποσί, is here nearer right than the other MSS., which read πόσι. The scribes evidently took the word to be vocative of πόσις.

271. οὐκέτι: this time L P have the dittography, reading οὐκέτι δή. ἔστιν: cf. *Hel.* 279 οὗτος τέθνηκεν, οὗτος οὐκέτ' ἔστι δή. It is quite possible, however, to read ἐστίν with Weil, taking σφῷν as "dative of possessor." He compares Soph. *O. C.* 1612 οὐκ ἔστ' ἔθ' ὑμῖν τῇδ' ἐν ἡμέρᾳ πατήρ. The MSS. favor Weil's reading, as all but L have ἐστί (L has ἐστιν); but in matters of accent they are very untrustworthy.

272. ὁρῶτον: so all the MSS. Elmsley wished to read ὁρῴτην, in accordance with the principle which he laid down (see his notes on *Med.* 1041 and Aristoph. *Ach.* 733) that in the 2d person dual of the historical tenses and the optative -την, not -τον, is the true ending, the form in -τον being an invention of the Alexandrian grammarians. But, though some scholars still hold Elmsley's view, the weight of evidence is distinctly against him; and few critics now uphold the sweeping changes which he made in order to carry out his theory. In the optative, in particular, there is not a single well-attested instance of the form in -την (Kühner-Blass II. p. 69). See Fritsche on Aristoph. *Thesm.* 1159, Von Bamberg in *Zeitschr. f. Gymn.-W.* 1874 p. 622 f., Kühner-Blass *l. s. c.*, and on the other side Wecklein *Cur. Epigr.* p. 18.

273. ἀκούω: as Monk points out, one would rather expect ἀκούειν; but probably no change should be made.

275. σε: this word was inserted by Porson, in accordance with the regular idiom; cf. 1098, *Hippol.* 607, *Med.* 324 πρός σε γονάτων, Soph. *Phil.* 468 πρός νύν σε πατρός, etc., and in Latin Terence *Andria* 538 *per te deos oro*, Hor. *Od.* I. 8, 1 *per te deos oro*. The metre shows that the addition of a short syllable was necessary to complete the anapaest.

276. ἀλλ' ἄνα: cf. *Il.* XVIII. 178 ἀλλ' ἄνα, μηδ' ἔτι κεῖσο, *Od.* XVIII. 13, and the like; and Soph. *Aj.* 194 ἀλλ' ἄνα ἐξ ἑδράνων. All the MSS. but B have ἀνατόλμα, and so the edd. before Porson; but the verb ἀνατολμάω is found only in late writers. See Porson's note on *Med.* 325.

279. A very troublesome line. Either ἐσμέν (so the MSS.; the text follows Wecklein, who reads ἡμῖν) is corrupt, or there is a very daring admixture of two idioms, ἐν σοί ἐσμεν and ἐν σοί ἐστι καὶ ζῆν ἡμᾶς καὶ μὴ ζῆν. Such an admixture seems possible enough, but I have not been able to find a real parallel in Euripides or in other classic writers; though cases like Soph. *O. T.* 314 ἐν σοὶ γάρ ἐσμεν and *Phil.* 963 ἐν σοὶ καὶ τὸ πλεῖν ἡμᾶς, ἄναξ, | ἤδη 'στὶ καὶ τοῖς τοῦδε προσχωρεῖν λόγοις (cited by Valckenaer and Monk) are not very rare. Hence I am on the whole inclined to regard ἐσμέν as corrupt, and have accepted Wecklein's emendation. F. W. Schmidt's ἔστιν would be an easy change, but does not bring out so well the *personal* interest of Admetus in his wife's recovery.

282. σε πρεσβεύουσα: "putting you first," deeming your welfare of more importance than my own. Cf. Aesch. *Eum.* 1. From this signification the verb easily passed into the more common one of "to honor," "worship." This use bears striking indirect testimony to the respect which the Greeks paid to old age.

283. καταστήσασα φῶς τόδ' εἰσορᾶν: καταστήσασα here = ποιήσασα. Kvičala compares Thuc. II. 84, 3 καὶ κατέστησαν ἐς ἀλκὴν μὲν μηδένα τρέπεσθαι αὐτῶν ἀπὸ τῆς ταραχῆς: ib. VI. 16, 6 Λακεδαιμονίους... κατέστησα ἐν Μαντινείᾳ περὶ τῶν ἀπάντων ἀγωνίζεσθαι: Herod. V. 25 καταστήσας τὸν ἀδελφεὸν ὕπαρχον εἶναι.

285. Θεσσαλῶν, the reading of α, is clearly right; the partitive construction is the more elegant, and the jingle Θεσσαλὸν ὃν ἤθελον would be intolerable. The reading Θεσσαλὸν is due to the influence of the following ὅν.

287. οὐκ ἠθέλησα: the attempts which have been made to remove the asyndeton are, in my opinion, one and all futile. The asyndeta which abound in this play are not to be emended away, but in the words of Professor von Wilamowitz "revocanda sunt a purum culta arte rhetorica."

288. οὐδ' ἐφεισάμην: sc. τῶν δώρων ἥβης.

291. A "locus desperatissimus." The case is very similar to that of l. 278. The idiom εὖ (καλῶς) ἥκω βίου, "I am well situated, well off, in respect to life," is perfectly good; cf. Elect. 751 πῶς ἀγῶνος ἥκομεν, Heracl. 213 γένους μὲν ἥκεις ὧδε τοῖσδε, Herod. I. 30 τοῦ βίου εὖ ἥκοντι, ib. V. 62 χρημάτων εὖ ἥκοντες, etc. (I have not been able to find an instance of this idiom with καλῶς instead of εὖ, if we except the passage in the text; but one can scarcely doubt that the two adverbs might be used interchangeably.) The expression ἥκει μοι θανεῖν, "it beseems me to die," is also possible; cf. Soph. O. C. 738 οὕνεχ' ἧκέ μοι γένει | τὰ τοῦδε πενθεῖν πήματ' εἰς πλεῖστον πόλεως. (I do not find any instance of εὖ or καλῶς used with this impersonal construction, though there seems to be no reason why they should not have been so employed; Herod. I. 30 πόλιος εὖ ἡκούσης and the like are, of course, different.) The question now arises, whether in our passage there is an admixture of the two constructions καλῶς αὐτῶν ἡκόντων βίου and ἧκον αὐτοῖς κατθανεῖν, or the text is corrupt.

A. Many editors, including Monk, Hermann, Kirchhoff, Christ, Nauck, Weil, Earle, Woolsey, Jerram, retain the MSS. reading. The schol. says ἀντὶ τοῦ ἥκοντος· ὅ ἐστιν· καιροῦ αὐτοῖς ἥκοντος εἰς τὸ ἀποθανεῖν ἀπογεγηρακόσιν. Woolsey renders the line "while it was highly proper for them in point of age to die"; Jerram "though they had reached a fit time of life for dying gloriously" or "with credit to themselves"; Earle "though they are come to a point of life at which it were a fitting thing for them to die," and Weil "quand ils sont arrivés dans la vie à un point où il serait opportun d'en sortir." These are all attempts to "attain the unattainable" by combining two conflicting forms of expression. Ἧκον cannot mean at the same time "though they had arrived" = ἡκόντων and "though it became them" = καθῆκον or προσῆκον, and any rendering which gives it both senses, however skilfully disguised, simply begs the question. Even Woolsey, whose rendering is the most justifiable of the number, though he translates καλῶς ἧκον "while it was highly proper," goes on to speak of the use of ἥκειν with an adverb and the genitive in a way which shows the same confusion of ideas.

B. Some critics, with whom I must agree, hold that κατθανεῖν is either corrupt or a gloss which has displaced some verb governing βίου. The latter alternative seems extremely probable; but as we cannot restore the lost verb with certainty I have marked κατθανεῖν with a dagger. For some of the readings that have been suggested, see Select Conjectures. The *sense* doubtless was "though it was highly fitting (καλῶς ἧκον) for them to depart from life." The chief objection to this is the use of καλῶς with ἧκον; but as ἥκει itself is very rare in this sense, it is not strange that no other example of the use of καλῶς with it happens to occur.

292. σῶσαι: that in the present σῴζω is the correct orthography is now generally agreed; see Meisterhans p. 142 note and the authorities there cited, and Usener in Fleckeisen's *Jahrb. f. Philol.* 1865 pp. 238 ff. The question as to the first aorist is much more difficult; see Kühner-Blass II. p. 544, Usener *l. s. c.*, Meisterhans p. 145 note (with the references there given). Doubtless ἔσωσα from σαόω and ἔσωσα from σῴζω existed side by side. The verb σαόω being epic and poetic, we ought probably in prose of the classical period to write ἔσωσα. The Attic inscriptions show the form with ι: so C. I. A. 1675, 4 (4th cent.) ἔ(σ)ωσεν, 605, 6 (early part of 2d cent.) ⟨ἔ⟩σωσεν. Cf. also Dittenberger's *Sylloge* 330, 15 (Cos, 3d cent.) διέσωσε, ib. 316, 10 (Dyme, 3d cent.) συνδιασώσαντες, Tabl. Heracl. I. 51 κατεσώσαμες, ib. II. 31 κατεσώξαμες, and the Laconian form κατέσοιξα mentioned by Hesychius (cited by Blass *l.c.*). The MSS., as might be expected, favor ἔσωσα (though in Soph. *Philoct.* 919 the Laurentian has σῶσαι: see Usener *l. s. c.*). The testimony of the inscriptions, however, is clearly much more reliable; and were our passage *prose* I should be strongly inclined to write σῶσαι. But as it is *verse*, the form may come from σαόω; hence I have not ventured to add an ι against the MSS. The question of the forms of the perfect middle and passive space will not permit me to discuss here.

294. φιτύσειν: this must be the true reading, as the metre requires that the antepenult be long and φυτεύω has ῠ.

295. ἔζων: so B. The other MSS. have ἔζην (but in L ω has been written over the η by the first hand), and so the *Etymol. Magnum* 413, 9. But ἔζην (as if from ζῆμι) was formed after the analogy of ἔζης, ἔζη, and is probably a late word (though the MSS. have it in Demos. XXIV. 7). Cf. Thomas Magister *s. v.* ἔζων: ἔζων, οὐκ ἔζην, ὥς οἴονταί τινες ... ἔζης δὲ καὶ ἔζη: and Herodian II. 315, 6 Lenz. Moeris says ἔζην Ἀττικῶς. ἔζων Ἑλληνικῶς: but ἔζην and ἔζων should undoubtedly be transposed in his text.

301. This line passed into a proverb, and is found also among the Menandrian monosticha (552).

304. ἐμῶν: this word seems inappropriate here; Alcestis would not have been likely to emphasize her ownership so strongly, especially when making

such a request of her husband. Hence ἐμῶν has been suspected by Prinz and others. L and P have τῶν ἐμῶν, which *might* be a mistake for τῶν σῶν, especially as C and Є are so easily confused in the MSS. But τῶν is far more probably a mere interpolation, the article having been inserted as in 227, 318, 731. Ἀνάσχου, too, gives trouble; the schol. explains it by ἀνάγαγε, ἀπόδειξον, probably with the underlying idea of holding up a torch; cf. *I. A.* 732, *Med.* 482, etc. But one almost instinctively wishes to take the word in the usual sense of the middle, "suffer," "allow," with a participle; and it is highly probable that a participle, e.g. ὄντας (Tournier), has dropped out and ἐμῶν been inserted to fill the lacuna, or that ἐμῶν is itself a corruption of the participle. For the suggestions that have been made see Select Conj.; none of them is entirely satisfactory, but Wecklein's τρέφων, which I have received into the text, gives far the best sense.

305. ἐπιγήμῃς : for the force of ἐπί, cf. ἐφ' ὑμῖν 373. Weil compares Herod. IV. 154 ἐπὶ θυγατρὶ ἀμήτορι . . . ἔγημε ἄλλην γυναῖκα. Orest. 589 οὐ γὰρ ἐπεγάμει πόσει πόσιν and Andoc. 1, 128 ἐπέγημε τῇ θυγατρὶ τὴν μητέρα are different, ἐπιγαμεῖν there meaning "to take a second spouse in addition to the first"; but Plutarch *Compar. Aristid. et Cat.* 6 and *Cat. Maj.* 24 has the verb in the same sense in which it is used in our passage.

310. ἐχίδνης : with the Greeks, as with us, the viper was an emblem of malice and cruelty. Cf. Aesch. *Choeph.* 249, Soph. *Ant.* 531, etc.

311. πύργον μέγαν : so *Od.* XI. 556 of Ajax, τοῖος γάρ σφιν πύργος ἀπώλεο: *Med.* 390 ἦν μέν τις ἡμῖν πύργος ἀσφαλὴς φανῇ, Soph. *O. T.* 1201 θανάτων δ' ἐμᾷ | χώρᾳ πύργος ἀνέστα.

312. This line, which is clearly out of place here, = 195 with the change of καί for οὐ. The question as to the way in which it came to be inserted here is very interesting. Probably (cf. Earle's edition pp. 65 ff.) v. 195 began a page and 311 ended one in the archetype, so that the scribe, mistaking the page, copied 195 instead of 313. If so, we have 312 – 195 = 117 = three pages of 39 lines each. Now curiously enough Wilamowitz (*Analecta* p. 51) had noted that the end of *Troad.* 193, 194, 195 and the beginning of 232, 233, 234 were mutilated, and hence he inferred that the archetype had 38 or 39 lines on a page, a conclusion which our passage strikingly verifies. Hence Mekler's defense of 312 is quite needless (see his *Euripidea* pp. 21 ff.).

313. τέκνον μοι : this, not τέκνον μου, is the regular idiom. κορευθήσει : παρθενεύσῃ schol., "wie wird dein Tochterloos sein?" Kvičala. The word probably means, not "grow up to maidenhood" (Liddell and Scott), but (with καλῶς) "pass your maidenhood in good repute." Some would render it "be wedded" (cf. διακορεύομαι).

314. τοίας : so Reiske and Herwerden. Many edd. retain ποίας, the MSS. reading, regarding the second question as a kind of explanation of πῶς in 313. But the difference between τ and π is very slight, and the sentence gains immensely in force and clearness by the change. Τοίας means of course "such as I have described," ἐχίδνης οὐδὲν ἠπιωτέρα. Kviçala thinks 314-16 interpolated, as Alcestis has already urged Admetus in the most pressing way (305 ff.) not to marry again. But nothing can be more natural than for the mother, who knows the weak nature of Admetus, to hark back in her anxiety to the point about which she feels special uneasiness. Indeed, this passage alone would show that Euripides was a close student of the workings of the female mind.

315-16. μή ... διαφθείρῃ: a beautiful example of the independent subjunctive with μή expressing "apprehension coupled with a desire to avert the object of fear" (Goodwin *M. and T.* 261 ff., esp. 264).

317. νυμφεύσει: the active is here used as in *I. A.* 885 ἵν' ἀγάγοις χαίρουσ' Ἀχιλλεῖ παῖδα νυμφεύσουσα σήν.

318. Here the two families of MSS. diverge widely, the first having τοῖσι σοῖσι θαρσυνεῖ, the second σοῖσι θαρσυνεῖ τέκνον. Kirchhoff observes "οὔτ' ἐν τόκοισι σοῖσι θαρσυνεῖ, τέκνον [*B*] *C* manifesta interpolatione." But why may not τοῖσι be an interpolation just as well as τέκνον? Nothing is more common than the insertion of the article where it does not belong, as every scholar knows. Moreover the reading τόκοισι τοῖσι σοῖσι is far from euphonious, and Nauck makes the matter even worse by reading σοῖς σε for σοῖσι. On the other hand τέκνον is distinctly fine; one can easily imagine the tone of fond affection with which the mother lingers on the word.

320-22. A famous *crux*. The MSS. show no variant, except that *L* and *P* have οὐκέτ' instead of μηκέτ'. In *L* 321-2 are omitted from the text, but have been added by the first hand on the lower margin. The schol. says only: οὐκ εἰς τὴν αὔριον τοῦ μηνὸς τούτου οὐδὲ εἰς τὴν μεταύριον.

The difficulty centres around μηνός in 321. The older commentators tried in vain to explain it. "Musgrave says that he can find no reason why μηνὸς should be used. Monk supposes an allusion in these words to a custom at Athens, of making those who were to be capitally punished drink the hemlock within three days. But this had nothing to do with the third day of the *month*, nor does such a custom seem to have existed. The reviewer of Monk in the Quarterly thinks that the appointed day for the death of Alcestis was the first of the month. The scholiast's paraphrase ... makes μηνὸς idle. Some find a reference to days of grace granted by the creditor to the debtor, and to the payment of monthly interest, the time for which may have been the day of the new moon. *But for all this, there is, so far as I know, no evidence of facts*" (Woolsey). If μηνός is retained, the only possible explanation seems to be that of the reviewer of Monk, that the κύριον ἦμαρ on which Alcestis was to die was the νουμηνία, on which (as well as on the ἔνη καὶ νέα) debts were customarily paid. The τρίτη μηνός will then be mentioned simply to strengthen the statement (cf. χθὲς καὶ πρώην, χθὲς καὶ τρίτην ἡμέραν). But though ἐς τρίτην μηνός, "on (or rather "against") the third of the month," *may* be a possible poetic expression, I know no example of it; the usual phrase is, of course, εἰς τρίτην ἱσταμένου. Hesychius s. v. φθινὰς ἀμέρα (*Heracl.* 779) says τὴν ἱσταμένου τρίτην τριμήνιον λέγει, which, if it refers to Euripides, might suggest the reading οὐδ' ἐς τριμηνιαῖον ἔρχεται κακόν (but τριμήνιον seems not to occur, and τριμηναῖος is late).

It seems more probable, therefore, that 321 is corrupt. For some of the emendations that have been proposed, see Select Conj. Herwerden would read ἐς τρίτον μοι φέγγος; and it is noteworthy that in 450, where μηνός again gives trouble, Wecklein would read φέγγος. But palæographically the two words are not very much alike. Weil conjectured ἔνην for τρίτην; but, as I have pointed out (*Harvard Studies in Class. Phil.* VII. p. 221), "τρίτην might well be a gloss on ἔνην: but if ἔνην = τρίτην the difficulty with μηνός remains; while if it = ἔνην καὶ νέαν, the Hesiodic ἔς τ' αὔριον ἔς τ' ἐννηφιν (*Works and Days* 410) and phrases like αὔριον καὶ τῇ ἕνῃ (Antiphon 143, 44) and εἰς ἔνην (Aristoph. *Achar.* 172) are distinctly against the conjecture." Νηλές (i.e. ΝΗΛΕϹ for ΜΗΝΟϹ), which I had supposed to be my own conjecture (see *Harvard Studies l. s. c.*), I find to have been anticipated in a dissertation by Hoefer, which, however, I have been unable to consult at first hand. It seems as probable as any; but certainty is impossible.

Another alternative is to reject 321 with Mekler and Earle, or 321-2, which two lines, as we have seen, are omitted in the text of *L*, it is uncertain for what reason. But emendation seems preferable to excision. — μηκέτ': οὐκέτ' of *L* and *P* is probably due to the influence of the following οὐ in οὔσιν. λέξομαι: passive in sense, as in *Her.* 906, *Herc. F.* 582, *I. T.* 1047, and Soph. *O. C.* 1186; see Goodwin *Gr. Gram.* 1248 n., Hadley-Allen 496.

325. μητρὸς: sc. ἀρίστης. The ellipsis seems harsh; παῖδες may be a gloss on ὑμῖν which has displaced some adjective agreeing with μητρός.

326. οὐχ ἅζομαι: schol. οὐκ εὐλαβοῦμαι, οὐκ ἀπέχομαι. καὶ Ὅμηρος· μηδ' ἅζεο θοῦρον Ἄρηα (*Il.* V. 830). Cf. Hesych. s. v. οὐχ ἅζομαι: οὐ σέβομαι, οὐκ ἐντρέπομαι, and *Heracl.* 600 δυσφημεῖν γὰρ ἅζομαι θεάν, *Orest.* 1116 δὶς θανεῖν οὐχ ἅζομαι (οὐ χάζομαι MSS.).

327. εἴπερ ... ἁμαρτάνει: this is preferable to the reading of the other class, ἤνπερ ... ἁμαρτάνῃ, though the apodosis is future. The indicative is more courteous to Admetus, implying that the condition is merely a *pro forma* one, "if he is in his right senses" (as of course he is).

331. τόνδ' ἄνδρα = ἐμέ, as usual. Some take ἄνδρα as the second accus. with προσφθέγξεται, "shall call me husband"; but Euripides never elsewhere uses προσφθέγγομαι with two accusatives, and surely the words "no Thessalian bride shall ever greet me in your stead" are explicit enough. Or, with Hermann, we may take νύμφη as in apposition with Θεσσαλίς, "no Thessalian woman shall ever address me as bride in your stead." Earle takes ἄνδρα with both τόνδε and προσφθέγξεται; while Mekler quite needlessly alters ποτε to πόσιν.

332-3. These lines have given much trouble, and Nauck and Kirchhoff regard them as an interpolation.

332. Cf. *Heracl.* 409 ἥτις ἐστὶ πατρὸς εὐγενοῦς, 513 πατρὸς οὖσαν εὐγενοῦς (cited by Earle).

333. The first class of MSS. have εὐπρεπεστάτη (L and P ἐκπρεπεστάτη), which is certainly wrong. Such a use of the superlative cannot be justified by any amount of argument. Wecklein's εὐπρεπὴς οὕτω seems to me very brilliant and convincing. For other emendations, see Sel. Conj. It is hard to determine whether we should read εὐπρεπής or ἐκπρεπής, as both give good sense and each is favored by the reading of one family of MSS. Ἐκπρεπής may be right, and in *Hec.* 269 the Cod. Marcianus has εἶδος ἐκπρεπεστάτη: but it is impossible to be certain, as the two words are perpetually confused in the MSS. For the position of οὕτω see L. and S. *s.v. B*, and cf. *Heracl.* 413 κακῶς οὕτω. The exact force of ἄλλως is well brought out by Bauer-Wecklein: "εἶδος ἄλλως, sonst, in anderer Hinsicht, nämlich in Hinsicht auf Schönheit." A good parallel is Herod. I. 60 γυνὴ ... μέγεθος ἀπὸ τεσσέρων πηχέων ἀπολείπουσα τρεῖς δακτύλους καὶ ἄλλως (i.e. in other respects, as well as in her height) εὐειδής. The statement so often made that ἄλλως in such cases = "besides" is not quite accurate.

340. τὰ φίλτατα not merely = τὴν ψυχήν but includes the ties that bind husband and wife together. Cf. *Med.* 16 νοσεῖ τὰ φίλτατα. These ties will be in part severed by her death.

341. ἔσωσας: Herwerden's μ' ἔσωσας is very plausible, though the object can easily be supplied from the context. ἆρα = *nonne*, as in 228.

344. κατεῖχ': Monk compares *Tro.* 555 φοινία δ' ἀνὰ πτόλιν βοὰ κατεῖχε Περγάμων ἕδρας, and Aesch. *Pers.* 424 οἰμωγὴ δ' ὁμοῦ | κωκύμασιν κατεῖχε πελαγίαν ἅλα.

345. βαρβίτου: the βάρβιτος was an instrument resembling the lyre, but longer and narrower. See K. von Jan *Die griech. Saiteninstrumente* pp. 20 ff.

346. ἐξαίροιμι: ἐξάροιμι L P. Wakefield conjectured ἐξάραιμι, which the schol. seems to have read, and which Wecklein (*Beiträge zur Kritik des Eur.* p. 528) prefers. I have followed *B a* with most edd., as the verb seems to denote a *process* rather than the mere occurrence of an act.

351. Λίβυν ... αὐλόν: "We find Λίβυς αὐλὸς in *H. F.* 684: Λίβυς λωτός in *Hel.* 170 sq., *Troad.* 544, *I. A.* 1036" (Earle). The flute was called Libyan because flutes were made from the wood of the lotus, a tree which grew in Libya; cf. Theophrastus Περὶ φυτῶν IV. 3, 1. See on the αὐλός the very thorough and careful article by Howard *Harvard Studies in Class. Phil.* IV. 1 ff. λακεῖν here = "sing." The word is generally used of harsher sounds. Aristophanes makes Euripides himself say τί λέλακας (*Achar.* 410).

348–56. These lines could well be spared, and are probably an interpolation. They are offensive to modern taste; but this is of itself a very unsafe criterion; for, as Paley pertinently observes, "the Greeks had a deeper feeling for sculptured forms than we can pretend to realize." But they are awkwardly expressed (especially 355–6), and, as was pointed out to me years ago by Prof.

F. D. Allen, they are both preceded and followed by a *reference to music*, so that the context gains very much in continuity by their excision.

353. ψυχράν: ψυχρός, like the Lat. *frigidus*, often means "empty," "insipid," "unsatisfactory." Hermann wickedly observes on 348 δέμας τὸ σόν: "ψυχρὸν παραγκάλισμα (Soph. *Ant.* 650), nec *minus frigidum poetae inventum*." Some one has even gone so far as to suggest that the poet in using ψυχρὰν τέρψιν is hinting at the ψυχρότης of the lines! He might have adduced οἶμαι (taking it as ironical) in support of his notion. οἶμαι: "no doubt," "to be sure," without ironical force. Οἶδα has been suggested for οἶμαι both here and in 565; but probably no change should be made, although the palæographical difference between the two words is not so very great.

354. ἀπαντλοίην, a very expressive word, "draw off," as one draws off the bilge-water from a ship's hold. Cf. *Ion* 927, *Or.* 1641, Aesch. *Prom.* 84. Euripides is exceedingly fond of such metaphors; see note on 245.

355-6. A very awkward passage; if we retain χρόνον, the sudden change from the dative with ἐν to the *accusative* (which seems quite out of place here) is very harsh, and the asyndeton is also troublesome. But though in the text I have adopted Wecklein's χῶντιν' and Prinz's τρόπον, I suspect the trouble is due to the unskilfulness of the interpolator rather than to textual corruption. Render: "for 'tis a pleasant thing to see one's friends, both at night and in whatever way one may come" (lit. "be present"). The change from the plural φίλους to the sing. παρῇ is rather abrupt, and Musgrave's φίλος would be easier; but the *constructio ad sensum* is possible enough. I doubt, however, if the lines are worth the trouble that commentators have taken about them.

357 ff. Cf. *I. A.* 1211 ff. εἰ μὲν τὸν Ὀρφέως εἶχον, ὦ πάτερ, λόγον ... ἐνταῦθ' ἂν ἦλθον (cited by Monk), both for the sense and for the use of the aorist ἦλθον (as to which see note on ἦλθεν 125). κατῆλθον has been emended in various ways (see Sel. Conj.), but no change is needed.

361. Χάρων: Cobet's emendation γέρων is very plausible, as Χάρων might so easily be a gloss on οὑπὶ κώπῃ ψυχοπομπὸς γέρων, and the substitution would be facilitated by the resemblance between the words Χάρων and γέρων. Glosses which resemble in *outward form* the words which they explain (e.g. πράξεις for ῥέξεις 262) are especially liable to oust the true reading. But as Χάρων may be right, I have not ventured to alter the text.

362. ἔσχεν: so Earle, in accordance with the regular usage. Porson defended the MSS. reading ἔσχον, and many editors have followed him; but, as Earle points out, *Hec.* 88 f. ποῦ ποτε θείαν Ἑλένου ψυχὰν | καὶ Κασάνδραν ἐσίδω, Τρῳάδες, ὥς μοι κρίνωσιν ὀνείρους, which Porson urged in favor of ἔσχον, is not really parallel. Such a *constructio ad sensum** is very different from a case like the present, in which two subjects in the singular separated by οὔτε ... οὔτε are supposed to be used with a plural verb. Besides Є and O are constantly confused in MSS. βίον: δέμας Cobet and Nauck; but βίον is supported by *Bacch.* 1339 μακάρων τ' ἐς αἶαν σὸν καθιδρύσει βίον (cited by Pflugk).

---

* Porson read ἢ instead of καὶ in *Hec.* 88, with some MSS.

363. ἐκεῖσε προσδόκα μ': *constructio praegnans*; see note on μαραινομέναν παρ' "Αιδαν 236. Neither Prinz's ἐκεῖ οὔ nor Wecklein's ἐκεῖ γε seems necessary. The verb of motion is expressed with προσδοκᾶν in Aesch. *Ag.* 653 Μενέλεων ... προσδόκα μολεῖν.

365. κέδροις: the wood of the cedar was much used for coffins because it preserved the bodies of the dead from decay. Cf. *Orest.* 1053, *Tro.* 1141. On the coffins of the Greeks see Becker-Göll *Charikles* III. pp. 139 ff. That in the historical period the custom of burning the bodies of the dead and that of burying them existed side by side among the Greeks is now generally admitted: see Becker-Göll *l. s. c.* pp. 132–41; Rohde *Psyche* p. 208 and note. The Homeric poems speak only of burning the dead; but recent excavations at Mycenae and elsewhere have shown that (as one might expect on *a priori* grounds) the practice of burying the bodies of the deceased is older than that of burning them. — It has been repeatedly asserted that this passage is inconsistent with other places in the play which imply that the body of Alcestis was to be burned; but (1) Admetus is speaking under great excitement, and his words must not be taken too literally; and (2) there is no passage in the play which *necessarily* implies that the *body itself* was to be burned (see note on v. 608).

367–8. The ridiculous parody in Aristoph. *Acharn.* 893–4, where Dicaeopolis says to the eel μηδὲ γὰρ θανών ποτε | σοῦ χωρὶς εἴην ἐντετευτλανωμένης, will occur to every reader.

372. γαμεῖν: the regular Attic form; γαμήσειν is late. τινά: L and P have ποτέ, which is doubtless due to ποτε in 367, the eye of the copyist having caught the wrong line. The mistake must have been already made in their common source.

373. ἐφ' ὑμῖν: see note on ἐπιγήμῃς, 305. Nauck would read ἐφ' ἡμῖν, comparing *Mel.* 694 γυναῖκ' ἐφ' ἡμῖν δεσπότιν δόμων ἔχει: but no change is necessary.

374 ff. A στιχομυθία follows, broken at the end by the short, gasping utterances of the dying woman and the cries and entreaties of her despairing husband. The sudden change in 390 from the even flow of the monostich is very effective.

381. This line is omitted in L and P (though in L it has been added by a later hand), and the omission has caused confusion in the assignment of the lines. Note that both 380 and 381 commence with an anapaest. In the case of *proper names* the tragedians admit the anapaest not only in the first foot of the trimeter, but sometimes, though less frequently, in the second, third, fourth and fifth. A word which is not a proper name can stand as an anapaest only in the first foot. In Aeschylus (with two exceptions) and the earlier plays of Sophocles an anapaest which begins a line must always be a word, or a part of a word, which is anapaestic according to its natural prosody, e.g. κορυφαῖς, ἀδάμαν|τίνων; in the later tragedy we also find initial anapaests that consist of two words (usually a particle and substantive or preposition and its object (e.g. ἐπὶ τοῖσ|δε), or of a word which is naturally a tribrach but has become an anapaest by position), as ἑκατὸν | προσῆγε. See C. Fr. Mueller *De pedibus solutis in dialog. senariis Aesch. Soph. Eurip.*, and Christ *Metrik*² p. 325 f., Westphal-Rossbach *Metrik*³ pp. 225–6. Mr. Jerram says in his note on 375 that the anapaest in the first foot of an iambic line is freely employed by Euripides but *never* by Sophocles or Aeschylus, *except when the foot consists of a single word*. But cf. Soph. *Phil.* 795 τὸν ἴσον | χρόνον τρέφοιτε τήνδε τὴν νόσον.

383. πολλή μ' ἀνάγκη : sc. μητέρα γενέσθαι : μ' is Monk's certain emendation for γ'. Some of the forms of γ and μ look much alike, and they are not infrequently confused in the MSS. Here the mistake may have been facilitated by the fact that there is a γ' just beyond in the same line.

384. χρῆν μ' : this, the reading of one MS. (c) is certainly right ;* μ' ἐχρῆν of L and P does not suit the metre, and χρή μ' of B and a, though more nearly right in form, has not the necessary contrary-to-fact implication. Ἄν is not used, as the chief stress falls on the infinitive (Goodwin *M. and T.* p. 407) ; and the antithesis between ζῆν and ἀπέρχομαι is thus emphasized still more. The combination ζῆν χρῆν, cacophonous as it seems, recurs in v. 939, and ζῆν ἐχρῆν *Orest.* 1030. Euripides often offends in this way ; he even has γυνή γένῃ *Hel.* 1298.

381. μαλάξει : cf. 744, 1085, *Or.* 1201, Soph. *Aj.* 594. The meaning of "soften" easily passes into those of "soothe," "assuage," "appease," "alleviate."

383. προθνῄσκοντες : masculine, though referring to Alcestis, on account of the generalizing plural ἡμεῖς. See Hadley-Allen 639.

385. σκοτεινόν : proleptic.

386. ἀπωλόμην : "anticipating aorist," referring vividly to the future. See Goodwin *M. and T.* 61.

388. ὀρθὸν πρόσωπον : cf. *Heracl.* 635 ἔπαιρέ νυν σεαυτόν, ὄρθωσον κάρα.

393 ff. A monody ἀπὸ σκηνῆς, supposed to be sung by the child Eumelus. In reality the words were sung by some one behind the scenes, while the person taking the rôle of the child merely acted out the song. Cf. the Latin *cantare ad manum*. Young children appear and speak in several of the plays of Euripides: see *Androm.* 504 ff. ; *Suppl.* 1122 ff. This was only in accordance with the practice criticised by Aristophanes *Ran.* 949–50 ἀλλ' ἔλεγεν ἡ γυνή τέ μοι χὠ δοῦλος οὐδὲν ἧττον, | χὠ δεσπότης χἠ παρθένος χἠ γραῦς ἄν. μαῖα : usually "nurse," here "mother," as in Aesch. *Cho.* 44 γαῖα μαῖα.

394. Cf. *Suppl.* 1139 βεβᾶσιν, οὐκέτ' εἰσί μοι, πάτερ, | βεβᾶσιν, *Orest.* 971 βέβακε γὰρ βέβακεν, οἴχεται τέκνων | πρόπασα γέννα. Wecklein reads οὐκ for οὐκέτ', and omits τε (which is found only in L P) in 407.

399. παρατόνους : "stretched at her side," "hanging at her side." The word seems not to occur elsewhere in writers of the classical period.

---

* See on the frequent interchange of χρή and χρῆν in the MSS. Wecklein *Beiträge zur Kritik des Euripides* p. 531, and cf. his *Studien zu Eur.* p. 366 f.

401. A very difficult place. The responsion shows that ἐγώ σ' ἐγώ μᾶτερ of P is preferable to σ' ἐγώ, μᾶτερ, ἐγώ of B a; but the hiatus ἀντιάζω—ἐγώ is awkward. It may, however, be easily removed by reading in 400 ἀντιάζω σ' with Monk. If ἀντιάζω σ' · | ἐγώ σ' ἐγώ, μᾶτερ is the true reading, we can account for the text of B a thus: in this source σ' was omitted before the second ἐγώ by an easy haplography; then to obviate the hiatus thus left μᾶτερ was transposed, and the remaining σ' was removed from its place after ἀντιάζω and put in 401 before the first ἐγώ to furnish καλοῦμαι with an object. Kirchhoff, to be sure, with his usual prejudice against L P, says of the reading of P "nescio an non correctori metrico debeantur"; but it is most unfair to point out all the mistakes of a class of MSS. and then whenever they offer a really plausible reading to attribute it to a Byzantine grammarian or a "corrector metricus." L has ἐγώ σε γάρ μᾶτερ, which is clearly an arbitrary attempt at emendation. Nauck would read σ' ἔγωγ' ὦ μᾶτερ, ἐγώ and in 413 ἔβας σὺν τᾷδε τέλος: but why alter both strophe and antistrophe when (with so slight a change in 400) the reading of P gives good sense and accurate responsion?

402. If καλοῦμαι ὁ is sound, a trochee has been lost before it corresponding to ἔφθι- in 414; νῦν γε (so the Aldine), νῦν σε, ὅς σε, ὧδε, etc. have been suggested to fill the lacuna. Wilamowitz (accepting the reading of P in 401) would omit 402 altogether, and strike out ἔφθιτο γὰρ πάρος in 414. This is very plausible, and *may* be right; the true reading is far from certain. In B and a a σ' stands before ὁ, but the antistrophic line shows that the ultima of καλοῦμαι must be shortened.

403. στόμασιν: the ν is required by the responsion. Herwerden's γόνασιν is worse than needless; Alcestis is dead and her corpse is *lying*, not sitting or standing up; and hence there is no reason for the child to clasp his mother's knees. He would naturally kneel at her head and clasp her about the neck and try to rouse her with his kisses, as young children will in such cases. Even were this otherwise, στόμασιν might still be defended; cf. *Herc. F.* 1208 ἀμφὶ σὰν γενειάδα . . . προσπίτνων, *Hec.* 274. νεοσσός: Euripides has this word in the sense of "child" some half a dozen times. Cf. Aesch. *Choeph.* 488, etc. The way in which this use arose may be seen from the similes in *Herc. F.* 71-2, *Troad.* 750-51.

406. λείπομαι . . . μονόστολος: with λείπεσθαι and similar verbs a seemingly pleonastic μόνος is often joined, e.g. *Med.* 51 πῶς σοῦ μόνη Μήδεια λείπεσθαι θέλει, etc.; and μονόστολος is here used in the same way. The word properly means "without convoy," of vessels; schol. ἀπὸ μεταφορᾶς τῶν μόνων στελλομένων πλοίων· μονόστολος οὖν ἀντὶ τοῦ ἔρημος. Cf. *Phoen.* 742 μονοστόλου δορός.

409 ff. The lacunas were first marked as in the text by Hermann, who also transposed μοι in 410, which in the MSS. stands just before σύγκασι. In 409 a spondee (τλάμων?) has been lost after ἔργα corresponding to ἀμόν in 396.

410. σύγκασί μοι κούρα: cf. *I. T.* 800 ὦ ξυγκασιγνήτη. The schol. explains by συνόμαιμε, συναδελφέ.

412. In this line five short syllables are wanting to complete the responsion, and in 413 a long and three shorts are lacking. The lacuna is probably due to a tear in the archetype.

413. ἀνόνατ' ἀνόνατ': adverbial accusative. Cf. *Hec.* 766 ἀνόνητα (sc. ἔτεκον) . . . τόνδ' ὃν εἰσορᾷς: *Her. F.* 716 ἀνόνητά γ' ἱκετεύουσαν ἐκσῶσαι βίον: *Hippol.* 1145 ἔτεκες ἀνόνητα. γήρως τέλος: the "period" or "term of old age"; cf. βίου τέλος, θανάτου τέλος. "End" or "goal" would be a more literal rendering; cf. the Scriptural phrase "fullness of years."

417. λοίσθιος: a poetic word.

419. Cf. 782, *Orest.* 1245 ἢ ζῆν ἅπασιν ἢ θανεῖν ὀφείλεται, *Andr.* 1272 and fr. 10 κατθανεῖν ὀφείλεται, etc. Euripides is very fond of certain cadences, and repeats them again and again almost *ad nauseam*.*

421. προσέπτατ': προσπέτεσθαι is used of the swift and sudden coming of evils, as here and Aesch. *Prom.* 643, Soph. *Aj.* 282. "The metaphor was apparently originally derived from the swooping of birds, particularly carrion-birds, upon their prey" (Earle).

422. ἐκφοράν: on the ἐκφορά, see Becker-Göll *Charikles* III. pp. 128 ff.; Hermann-Blümner *Gr. Privatalt.* pp. 367 ff.

423. μένοντες: F. W. Schmidt's μέλποντες is very plausible, and *may* be right; but μένοντες, "while you are waiting" (before the procession starts), makes good sense, and probably no change should be made. ἀντηχήσατε: Jerram suggests that the ἀντί refers to the answering of strophe by antistrophe in the following chorus.

424. παιᾶνα: the word παιάν may be used of any solemn song or chant, even of one in honor of the gods of the lower world: cf. *Troad.* 578 τί παιᾶν' ἐμὸν στενάξεις; ib. 126 αὐλῶν παιᾶνι στυγνῷ, Aesch. *Choeph.* 145 παιᾶνα τοῦ θανόντος ἐξαυδωμένας, *Sept.* 847 'Άιδα τ' ἐχθρὸν παιᾶν' ἐπιμέλπειν, *Ag.* 623 πρέπει λέγειν παιᾶνα τόνδ' 'Ερινύων (Monk).

424. ἀσπόνδῳ: the schol. read ἀσπονδον (which is clearly inferior), for he says θρῆνον ἐφ' ᾧ οὐ σπένδουσιν ὥσπερ ἐν τοῖς παιᾶσιν. Monk and others compare the well-known fragment of the *Niobe* of Aeschylus (161 Nauck) μόνος θεῶν γὰρ Θάνατος οὐ δώρων ἐρᾷ, | οὐδ' ἄν τι θύων οὐδ' ἐπισπένδων ἄνοις, | οὐδ' ἔστι βωμὸς οὐδὲ παιωνίζεται· | μόνου δὲ Πειθὼ δαιμόνων ἀποστατεῖ, and *Il.* IX. 158 'Άιδης τοι ἀμείλιχος.

425 ff. Rohde (*Psyche* p. 511 note 1) observes: "Diese ausschweifenden Trauerkundgebungen wohl nach dem in thessalischen Dynastengeschlechtern Ueblichen."

426. πένθος κοινοῦσθαι: so *L P*; πένθους the other family of MSS. The accus. is preferable as the "*difficilior lectio*"; Matthiae pointed out that Euripides has two other cases of the accus. with κοινοῦσθαι, *Ion* 608 κοινουμένη τὰς συμφοράς σοι, ib. 857 συμφορὰν . . . κοινουμένη τήνδε. Add *Troad.* 61 κοινώσῃ λόγους, Xen. *Vect.* 4, 32 κοινουμένους τὴν τύχην, Thuc. 8, 8, 1 ὁ μὲν οὖν Καλλίγει-

* See Schroeder *De iteratis apud. trag. Graec.* p. 8 f. (in *Diss. phil. Argent.* vol. VI.).

τος καὶ Τιμάγορας . . . οὐκ ἐκοινοῦντο τὴν στόλον, ib. 8, 82, 3 ἵνα δὴ δοκῇ πάντα μετ' ἐκείνου κοινοῦσθαι. In these cases κοινοῦσθαι means "to make common to one's self," and so "share," the transitive force predominating; while in κοινοῦσθαι τινος the genitive-construction of κοινός predominates. It is *possible*, of course, that πένθος is merely a copyist's blunder for πένθους: but the probabilities seem to me to lie in the other direction.

427. As to signs of mourning among the Greeks, see Becker-Göll *Charikles* III. pp. 156 ff., and cf. 215-17, *Hel.* 1087 f., *I. A.* 1347-8, *Phoen.* 322-6, etc. The text of the line is extremely doubtful, *B* and *L P* diverging widely. It is clear (see Critical Apparatus) that in the common source of *a* and *d* stood only κουρᾷ ξυρ, followed by a lacuna. If this lacuna goes back to the common ancestor of all our MSS., as seems probable, the readings of *B* and *L P* are merely different attempts to fill out the gap, and the disagreement between them is accounted for. Μελαμπέπλῳ στολῇ was then probably suggested by 216 (cf. the suspected line 819, and *Orest.* 457-8), and μελαγχίμοις πέπλοις by some Aeschylean passage (cf. Eustath. p. 1254 οὕτω Αἰσχύλος πέπλους μελαγχίμους φησίν), perhaps *Cho.* 11 φάρεσιν μελαγχίμοις. (It is quite *possible*, however, that the lacuna in the source of *a d* was due merely to inability or unwillingness to decide between two readings of nearly equal authority.) In the *Phoenissae* (l. 372) we have the interpolated line κάρα ξυρῆκες καὶ πέπλους μελαγχίμους, probably suggested by our passage and *El.* 335 κάρα τ' ἐμὸν ξυρῆκες. This, so far as it goes, supports μελαγχίμοις πέπλοις: but though *Phoen.* 372 is at least as old as the time of the schol. *ad loc.*, its source may perfectly well have been merely a MS. of the same family as *B*, and hence it is not at all decisive. Hesychius has μελάμπεπλος· πενθήρης, which may or may not refer to our passage. I incline, on the whole, to follow *L P*, simply as a matter of taste; that Euripides wrote either μελαμπέπλῳ στολῇ or μελαγχίμοις πέπλοις we have no certain means of proving.

428. μονάμπυκας: the ἄμπυξ was a band passing horizontally across the horse's forehead; see Daremberg and Saglio *Dict. des Antiquités* s. v. *Ampyx*. Μονάμπυξ is properly "having a single head-band," hence "single," not hitched to a chariot. Schol. ἀζύγους. κέλητας.

429. Monk compares Plutarch *Vit. Alex.* 72 εὐθὺς μὲν ἵππους τε κεῖραι πάντας ἐπὶ πένθει καὶ ἡμιόνους ἐκέλευσε, and *Pelop.* 33. The Persians had the same custom; see Herod. IX. 24.

434. τιμᾶν: τιμῆς, the reading of *L P*, gives equally good sense and metre; but the infinitive construction is the less common-place one. τέτληκεν ἀντ' ἐμοῦ θανεῖν: Nauck's very plausible conjecture. The MSS. have τέθνηκεν, and as the last word μόνη, μόνην or λίαν, variants which seem to point to a lacuna in the archetype at the end of the line. The true reading is far from certain.

435-75. First Stasimon.

435-6. A reminiscence of *Il.* XXIII. 179 χαῖρέ μοι, ὦ Πάτροκλε, καὶ εἰν Ἀίδαο δόμοισιν.

437. οἰκετεύοις: ἅπαξ εἰρημένον in classic Greek. Hesychius has οἰκετεύεται· συνοικεῖ. Though so rare, the word is regularly formed, and there seems to be no ground for questioning the soundness of the text.

442. πολὺ δὴ πολὺ δή: "the present (or a similar) passage seems to be parodied in Aristoph. *Av.* 539 πολὺ δὴ πολὺ δὴ χαλεπωτάτους λόγους" (Earle).

444. λίμναν ... πορεύσας: a daring construction after the analogy of πόρον or ὁδόν πορεύειν. Cf. Soph. *Trach.* 559 ὃς τὸν βαθύρρουν ποταμὸν Εὔηνον βροτοὺς | μισθοῦ 'πόρευε χεροῖν, on which Mr. Jebb observes: "Here the second acc. denotes the space traversed; it would more usually denote the place *to* which, as in Eur. *Tro.* 1085 ἐμὲ ... σκάφος | ... πορεύσει | ... Ἄργος." Πορεύσας properly applies only to Charon, the more remote subject Ἀίδας being lost sight of. ἐλάτᾳ δικώπῳ: ἐλάτη, properly the fir, often means "oar," but is here used in the sense of "boat": cf. *Phoen.* 208 Ἰόνιον κατὰ πόντον ἐλάτᾳ πλεύσασα. So in Latin *abies* and *pinus* often = *navis*.

446. ὀρείαν χέλυν, because the shell of the land-tortoise, which loves the high ground, was used for this purpose.

447. κλέοντες: the tragedians probably do not use the form κλείω, though the MSS. have it here. Cf. *I. A.* 1046 (κλέουσαι Monk, κλύουσαι MSS.), fr. 369, 7 (Stob. *Flor.* 55, 4; κλέονται Gaisford, κλέωνται SM, καλέσονται Λ), Soph. *Trach.* 639 (κλέονται Musgrave; καλέονται MSS.).

448–51. An extremely troublesome passage. The difficulty centres about ὥρας in 449 and μηνός in 450. The MSS. vary between ὥρα (P l a) and ὥρᾳ (B); L has ὥρ with an erasure after ρ. All have μηνός, and all but a l (παννύχου) have παννύχους. Hesychius has περιίσσεται (leg. περινίσσεται) ὥρας· περιέρχεται τὰς ὥρας, which shows that the author of the gloss read ὥρας and took it as acc. plural. We may distinguish four principal ways of dealing with the passage:

A. Barnes, Musgrave and others accept Scaliger's κυκλάς for κύκλος. Καρνείου will then agree with μηνός, and ἀειρομένας will be intransitive; so that the rendering will be: "at Sparta when the circling season (κυκλὰς — ὥρα) of the Carnean month comes round, when the moon is on high all night long." This gives good sense; but we have no proof that Aeschylus, Sophocles or Euripides ever used κυκλάς; nor do I find any instance in which they use ἀείρεσθαι in this way of heavenly bodies, though, to be sure, the scholiast takes it as intransitive. Sophocles has the *active* αἴρῃ of the sun, *Phil.* 1331.

B. Monk reads ὥρᾳ, and puts a comma after Σπάρτᾳ and one after σελάνας. He observes "editum defendit. *Iph. A.* 717 Ὅταν σελήνης εὐτυχὴς ἔλθοι κύκλος": whence it would appear that he made σελάνας depend on κύκλος, and Καρνείου ... μηνός on ὥρᾳ. But this makes the construction (κύκλος ... ἀειρομένας παννύχου σελάνας) very clumsy, and σελάνας is too far from κύκλος.

C. Earle and others (with Hesychius) read ὥρας and take it as acc. with περινίσσεται. The rendering will then be: "at Sparta when the circle of the Carnean month comes the round of the seasons, when the moon hangs high in the heavens all night long." This may well be right; cf. *Ion* 1486 δεκάτῳ μηνὸς ἐν κύκλῳ. But the intransitive use of ἀειρομένας is still an objection. I cannot find an instance of σελήνη ἀείρεται or the like in the tragedians.

D. Wecklein and others take ὥρας as gen. sing., and Καρνείου as agreeing with it. To this view I strongly incline, believing μηνός to be a gloss on Καρνείου ὥρας, which gloss has ousted from the text some noun which was the object of ἀειρομένας. This noun may have been φέγγος (Wecklein), or some other word of like meaning. That μηνός is itself a corruption of φέγγος I do not believe; though in 321 Herwerden suggests φέγγος for μηνός. But the two words are not very much alike, and φ preserves its characteristics pretty stubbornly.

452. λιπαραῖσι: the epithet which so pleased the Athenians when applied to their city (see Aristoph. *Achar.* 639 and Blaydes' learned note, where the examples of this use of the adjective are given at length). Pindar (*Nem.* IV. 29, *Isthm.* II. 30, fr. 76 Bergk) seems to have inaugurated the practice of calling Athens λιπαραί, and even Aristophanes himself follows suit in no less than three passages (*Nub.* 299, *Eq.* 1329, fr. 110 Kock)! Does Euripides hint in *Troad.* 801–3 at the reason why the term was especially appropriate to Athens?

457. φάος: poetic accus. of the limit of motion. τεράμνων: a favorite word with Euripides, who always uses it in the plural. It is not found in Sophocles or Aeschylus. The spelling varies in the MSS. between τέραμνα and τέρεμνα; but on the whole the weight of authority is on the side of τέραμνα. It is noteworthy that in two passages (*Phoen.* 333, *Orest.* 1371) the Marcianus has the form with α while most of the other MSS. have that with ε. Hesychius has τέρεμνα · οἰκήματα.

458. Some (e.g. Bothe and Wecklein) regard this line as spurious, as there is no corresponding line in the antistrophe. But an examination of the antistrophe shows that something has been lost after 468, unless we assume a violent anacoluthon. The text of 458 is in doubt; I have given Κωκυτοῖό τε (with Earle) ῥείθρων. Κωκυτοῖς of L P points to κωκυτοῖο (C for O), and L actually has κωκυτοῖο by a later hand and ῥείθρων. Earle reads ῥείθρου; but Sophocles, except perhaps in *Ant.* 1124 (ῥέεθρον L, ῥείθρων Hermann), and Euripides always use the plural. Κωκυτοῦ τε ῥεέθρων (so B and α) also is possible. All the MSS. have before κωκύτου (or κωκύτοις) an interpolated καί, which was struck out by Matthiae.

459. ποταμίᾳ νερτέρᾳ τε κώπᾳ: the adjectives take the place of adverbial phrases. For the expression, cf. *Hel.* 526 εἰναλίῳ κώπᾳ, *Heracl.* 82 ἁλίῳ πλάτᾳ, *I. T.* 140 κλεινᾷ σὺν κώπᾳ χιλιοναύτᾳ, *Rhes.* 53 νυκτέρῳ πλάτῃ, etc.

460. I have accepted Wilamowitz's excellent emendation of this line; ὦ φίλα γυναικῶν occurs *Hippol.* 848, but ὦ μόνα γυναικῶν is not, I think, Euripidean.

462. αὑτᾶς: Erfurdt's emendation, which the antistrophic line (471) shows to be necessary. For the use of the reflexive of the third person, where we should expect the second, see Goodwin *Gr. Gram.* 995 note, Hadley-Allen 686 a. For the sentiment, cf. Kaibel *Epigr. Graec.* 551, 4 κούφη σοι κόνις ἥδε πέλοι: Tibullus II. 4, 50 *terraque securae sit super ossa levis;* the Latin formula frequent on tomb-stones, S. T. T. L., i.e. *sit tibi terra levis;* and especially the last two lines of that most dainty and pathetic epigram, Martial V. 34, *mollia non rigidus cespes tegat ossa, nec illi | Terra, gravis fueris: non fuit illa tibi.* Such prayers can be traced back to the primitive belief that the earth did actually discommode the dead by its pressure.

469. Some, e.g. Wecklein, believe that no verse has been lost here and assume an anacoluthon, regarding ὃν ἔτεκον -- χαίταν as parenthetic, and σὺ δ' ἐν ἥβᾳ κ.τ.λ. as following just as though the parenthesis were an independent clause preceding. But this is difficult for several reasons. The transition from 468 to 469 is singularly abrupt; moreover if Wecklein is right we must reject 459, which is at least as old as the time of the scholiast of *B*, and for the insertion of which-(supposing it to be spurious) no adequate reason has been suggested.

472. νέᾳ: so *B a*; *L* and *P* have νέα νέου, which the responsion will not allow. The way in which the reading νέα νέου arose is doubtful. It may be a conflation of two readings νέᾳ and νέου (ι subscript is often omitted in the MSS.), or perhaps νέου was written beside νέᾳ (or *vice versa*) as a variant lection and then was copied into the text by mistake, or possibly the common source of *L* and *P* may have had νέου, and νέα be a gloss on ἐν ἥβᾳ. Νέᾳ is probably right; it is the youthfulness of Alcestis, not that of Admetus, that the poet wishes to emphasize.

473. κῦρσαι: κυρῆσαι MSS., but the strophic line shows Musgrave's correction to be necessary. Euripides has both ἔκυρσα (cf. *Ion* 1105) and ἐκύρησα (cf. *Her.* 215). Κύρω and κυρέω are said not to occur either in classic Attic prose or in comedy.

474. συνδυάδος: ἅπαξ εἰρημένον. It is probably a noun, though many lexx. give it as an adjective. Nauck (*Eur. Stud.* II. 62) regards the word as corrupt. He thinks that in its place should stand some word meaning "wife," to which ἀλόχου was added as a gloss. Hence he would strike out ἀλόχου, and γύναι in 464. But συνδυάδος has been ably defended by Zacher (*Philologus* L. l. p. 542). He points out that συνδυάζεσθαι presupposes συνδυάς, and that the word is a regular formation from σύνδυο after the analogy of πεμπάς, δεκάς, etc. It differs from δυάς because the two members of the pair belong together as a whole. Render "such union with a loving consort."

476-567. Second Epeisodion. Heracles enters from the left, doubtless wearing the lion-skin and carrying his club. His costume enables the chorus and spectators to recognize him at once; hence no introductory words are necessary.

476. κωμῆται: the word κώμη was often used of a neighborhood or district; cf. Aristotle *Poet.* 3, 6 οὗτοι μὲν (sc. οἱ Πελοποννήσιοι) κώμας τὰς περιοικίδας καλεῖν φασιν, Ἀθηναῖοι δὲ δήμους. Hence as Suidas says (s. v. κωμῆται), κωμήτας οἱ παλαιοὶ τοὺς ἐκ τοῦ αὐτοῦ ἀμφόδου καὶ τόπου ἔλεγον. The word is peculiarly appropriate here, as Thessaly contained few large towns, and these were mostly independent of each other, each being surrounded by its own group of dependent villages. χθονός: Nauck would read πόλεως, as the repetition χθονός — χθόνα (479) — χθόνα (485) is suspicious. He might have adduced in favor of his view Hippol. 34, 36, in one of which lines χθόνα has probably displaced πόλιν. But Nauck's conjecture seems far from certain.

479. χθόνα: here L P have πόλιν, but χθόνα seems preferable on account of ἄστυ in the following line. πόλιν may be a conjecture, or a slip of the kind described in the note on v. 55.

480. προσβῆναι: see Goodwin M. and T. 772 a.

481. Eurystheus was king of Tiryns as well as of Argos and Mycenae.

482. Here L and P have συνέζευξαι: cf. Ion 243 εἰ θεῷ συνεζύγη, Hel. 255 τίνι πότμῳ συνεζύγην, Andr. 98 στερρὸν δαίμον' ᾧ συνεζύγην, and Hippol. 1389 οἵαις συμφοραῖς συνεζύγης (where the Aldine has προσεζύγης). B a have in our passage προσέζευξαι: but, as Nauck (Eur. Stud. II. p. 63) pointed out, the verb προσζεύγνυμι does not occur in the early literature; though in late Greek it is not uncommon.

487. τοὺς πόνους: so Monk; P has only πόνους, the article having fallen out in the source of L and P. L has μ' ἦν πόνους, an obvious attempt to fill out the lacuna ex conj. B a have τοῖς πόνοις, which many edd. adopt; ἀπειπεῖν will then mean "say no to," and the πόνοι be personified (so Earle). Cf. Hec. 942 ἀπεῖπον ἄλγει. But it seems simpler and more natural to take ἀπειπεῖν in its usual sense, "renounce," and read πόνους: cf. Herc. F. 1354 ὧν (sc. πόνων) οὔτ' ἀπεῖπον οὐδέν' οὔτ' ἀπ' ὀμμάτων κ.τ.λ.

489. ἀγών has here, as often, the double sense of "athletic contest," "race," and "danger," "peril." Cf. Herod. VIII. 102 πολλοὺς πολλάκις ἀγῶνας δραμέονται περὶ σφέων αὐτῶν οἱ Ἕλληνες: also I. A. 1456 δεινοὺς ἀγῶνας διὰ σὲ δεῖ κεῖνον δραμεῖν, Or. 878 ἀγῶνα θανάσιμον δραμούμενον, El. 883 ἥκεις γὰρ οὐκ ἀχρεῖον ἔκπλεθρον δραμὼν | ἀγῶν' ἐς οἴκους.

491. ἀπάξω: the fut. indic. (as compared with ἂν λάβοις in 494) shows the confidence with which Heracles looks forward to the result.

492. εὐμαρές: cf. fr. 176, 2 N. μαθεῖν δὲ πᾶσίν ἐστιν εὐμαρές: also I. A. 519, 969, Hel. 1227, fr. 382, 10, fr. adesp. 11. Sophocles has the word once (El. 179), Aeschylus twice (Ag. 1280, Suppl. 325), Pindar thrice (Ne. XI. 33, Py. III. 105, Ne. III. 21). The schol. on Il. XV. 137 says: μάρη γὰρ ἡ χεὶρ κατὰ Πίνδαρον, ὅθεν καὶ εὐμαρές. If he is correct, the word closely resembles εὐχερής both in origin and meaning. Hesychius says εὐμαρές· εὐχερές. ὑγιές. ῥᾴδιον. ἀσφαλές, and Suidas εὐμαρής εὔκολος, εὐχερής.

494. ἀρταμοῦσι: a rare word. Cf. El. 816 ὅστις ταῦρον ἀρταμεῖ καλῶς. It properly means "to cut in pieces like a butcher" (ἄρταμος). The schol. explains by μαγειρεύουσιν. ἄρταμος γὰρ λέγεται ὁ μάγειρος.

496. αἵμασιν: "clots" or "gouts of blood." Cf. for this use of the plural *El.* 1172, *I. T.* 73, Aesch. *Ag.* 1247 (αἱμάτων = "streams of blood"), Soph. *Ant.* 120, etc.

497. Cf. *Herc. F.* 64 ὃς οὕνεκ' ὄλβου μέγας ἐκομπάσθη ποτέ.

498. ζαχρύσου: probably a reference to the celebrated gold-mines near Scapte Hyle, which were leased by the historian Thucydides. πέλτης: the πέλτη was a small, light shield of wood, often covered with goat-skin and shod with iron. The word is here used collectively = πελταστῶν: cf. *Rhes.* 410 ἔρρηξα πέλτην. "In Greek the weapon often stands for the person armed with it" (Wecklein). Others, with Monk, regard πέλτης ἄναξ as = πελταστής, and compare Aesch. *Pers.* 376 κώπης ἄναξ: a view which to me seems less probable. The Thracian targeteers enjoyed a reputation similar to that of the Rhodian and Balearic slingers and the Cretan bowmen.

499. δαίμονος: here, as often = "fortune," "destiny." But to the mind of the Greek hearer of the play was present the idea of a personal δαίμων.

500. σκληρός: "a metaphor from a hard and stony road, as πρὸς αἶπος from a steep one. There is doubtless a reference here to the words of Hesiod (*Op.* 287-292) about the rugged path of virtue, — words that formed, as it were, the text of Prodicus' apologue of Heracles at the cross-ways (Xen. *Mem.* 2, 1, 21-34), which was doubtless familiar to Euripides" (Earle).

501. πᾶσιν (παισὶν MSS.) is Wecklein's brilliant emendation, which certainly adds greatly to the force of the sentence.

502. Λυκάονι: this seems to be the only passage where a son of Ares named Lycaon is mentioned.

503. Κύκνῳ: according to Apollodorus (*Bibl.* 2, 5, 11, 3 and 2, 7, 74 Hercher) Heracles fought with two different Cycni, one the son of Ares by Pelopeia and the other the son of the same god by Pyrene. The contest with the former, which took place near Iton in Thessaly, was the more celebrated, and is doubtless the one referred to here. Cf. *Herc. F.* 389 ff. and Hesiod *Scut. Her.* 345 ff. ἔρχομαι συμβαλῶν: see for the construction Goodwin *M. and T.* 895. This is better than to take ἔρχομαι literally, "am on my way," as do some editors. The phrase is nearly equivalent to a fut. indic., or μέλλω with the infin.

506. τρέσαντα: see for the tense *M. and T.* 148. πολεμίαν, which Dobree had conjectured for πολεμίων, is actually found in *B* and *a*, and is almost certainly right. Nauck compares *Med.* 1322, *Hec.* 1153, *Orest.* 271, fr. 705, 2. Add *Rhes.* 286.

507. καὶ μήν, as often, marks the entrance of a character.

508. πορεύεται, like Lat. *incedere*, the appropriate word for the stately advance of the monarch.

509. Πέρσεως τ' ἀφ' αἵματος: Alcmene, mother of Heracles, was the daughter of Electryon, one of the sons of Perseus and Andromeda. See the schol., and Hesiod *Scut. Her.* 3, etc.

511. θέλοιμ' ἄν: sc. χαίρειν, a *double-entendre*. ἐξεπίσταμαι: "I am well assured," stronger than ἐπίσταμαι.

512. τί χρῆμα: like the simple τί: see L. and S. *s. v.* χρῆμα II. 2 for parallels.

513. ἐν τῇδ' ἡμέρᾳ: nouns denoting *day, night, month* and *year* generally are put in the dative of time without a preposition if an adjective word is joined with them; but exceptions sometimes occur, especially when the time *within which* an action takes place is to be indicated. See Hadley-Allen 782 a.

514 ff. Note the order in which Heracles mentions the members of his host's family (children, father, wife); cf. *Hippol.* 794 ff. (father, children, wife).

516. ὡραῖος, "ripe in age," ready for the grave. Cf. *Phoen.* 968 αὐτός δ', ἐν ὡραίῳ γὰρ ἔσταμεν βίῳ | θνῄσκειν ἕτοιμος, Aristoph. *Vesp.* 1365 ὡραῖας σοροῦ.

520. πέρι: all the MSS. save L and P have ἔτι. For the simple genitive with the meaning of "concerning," "in respect of which" see Hadley-Allen 733 a, Sonnenschein 413 and the examples there cited; but the present writer, for one, cannot believe that Euripides used that rare and difficult construction in a passage like the one in the text. Nauck is quite wrong, however, when he alleges that ἔτι is "überflüssig und störend." On the contrary, the use of ἔτι with ζῆν is almost stereotyped; cf. *Bacch.* 8, *I. T.* 771, *Or.* 1147, *Suppl.* 454, *Hel.* 56, 293, etc.

523. μοίρας: a striking instance of "attraction." The verse would not allow the order ἧς μοίρας.

524. ὑφειμένην, like ὑπέστη, v. 36. "Perhaps the figure is here that of a victim bowing to receive the death-stroke" (Earle).

526. εἰς τόδ', i.e. until she dies, a euphemism. Wakefield's τότ' is tempting, but not, I think, necessary. ἀμβαλοῦ: so Nauck for ἀναβαλοῦ, to avoid the tribrach in the fifth foot. Euripides sometimes admits three shorts in the fifth, but very rarely in his earlier plays. There is no certain instance in the *Alcestis*. Hence it seems better to substitute the apocopated form in this place. See note on ἀμβαλεῖν, l. 50, and cf. *Hec.* 1281 (ἀμμένει l, ***μένει L ἀναμενεῖ A ἀναμένει r), *Andr.* 444 (ἀναμένει MSS., ἀμμένει Nauck), Soph. *El.* 1397 (ἀμμένει MSS.). See Nauck's learned note in his *Eur. Stud.* II. p. 64 f.

527. A troublesome line, and one about which there probably will always be difference of opinion. I conceive the history of the text to have been this: in 521 Admetus has made about Alcestis the ambiguous statement ἔστιν τε κοὐκέτ' ἔστιν. This Heracles naturally does not understand. Admetus tries to explain (523, 525), but his visitor still fails to comprehend. Finally the king states his meaning in words which are seemingly most explicit, though chosen so as to conceal the fact of the queen's death: τέθνηκ' ὁ μέλλων, καὶ θανὼν οὐκ ἔστ' ἔτι, i.e. "the person who is soon to die is (to all intents and purposes) already dead, and, being dead, no longer exists." But this sentence, simple as it seems, had two peculiarities which led to corruption of the text, viz. the separation of οὐκ and ἔτι and the use of the two participles side by side in different constructions. Some scholar reconstructed the verse in the form τέθνηχ' ὁ μέλλων κοὐκέτ' ἔσθ' ὁ κατθανών, thus removing both peculiarities and producing a very tolerable trimeter. This version has come down to us in *B a*. In *L*, on the other hand, τέθνηκε (and in *P* τέθνηκεν) has been written for τέθνηχ' (probably their common source had τέθνηκε, the ν in *P* having been added to remove hiatus), and the article inserted before θανών. In *P* a further change has been made, the clumsy and unmetrical transposition οὐκέτ' ἐστιν. Thus in *P* has been accomplished, though in a very awkward way, *precisely* the same result which in *B* and *a* has been attained by a clever reconstruction. Many edd. prefer to follow *B a*; but the most obvious course is not necessarily the right one. For other readings, see Sel. Conj. The one in the text is due to Schwartz, the editor of the scholia.

528. τ': γ' Earle; but cf. Aesch. *Prom.* 926 ὅσον τό τ' ἄρχειν καὶ τὸ δουλεύειν δίχα, Soph. *O. C.* 808 χωρὶς τό τ' εἰπεῖν πολλὰ καὶ τὰ καίρια, Plato *Protag.* 336 B χωρὶς ᾤμην εἶναι τὸ συνεῖναί τε διαλεγομένους καὶ τὸ δημηγορεῖν.

531. γυνή, γυναικός: intentionally ambiguous, "the woman" or "my wife."

532. ὀθνεῖος: this word (from † ὄθνος, old by-form of ἔθνος?) was the Athenian term for ἀλλότριος (Bekker's *Anecd.* p. 1095). Hesychius has ὀθνεῖα· μάταια. ἀλλότρια, ἀλλοεθνῆ, ξένα, ἀλλογενῆ. Cf. Plato *Legg.* 629 E, *Rep.* 470 B. Suidas says: ὀθνεῖος οὐχ ὁ ἐκ τῆς ἀλλοδαπῆς ἀφιγμένος ὥς τινες ἀπέδοσαν, ἀλλοεθνής, ἀλλ' ὁ ἀπὸ πόλεως τῆς αὐτῆς ὢν καὶ ἄλλως ἐπιτήδειος, οὐ μέντοι κατὰ γένος προσήκων, which looks as though he were misled by the use of the word in our passage. Ὀθνεῖος does not occur in Aeschylus or Sophocles, and Euripides has it only in the *Alcestis* (cf. 646, 810).

533. ἄλλως: in a double sense, "otherwise" and "notwithstanding." See L. and S. *s.v.* 1 and 2, b. ἀναγκαία: cf. Latin *necessaria*. Admetus, while his words are literally true, contrives to give a false impression throughout.

536. εἴθ' ηὕρομεν: a typical instance of an unfulfilled wish referring to a past object. See *M. and T.* 732.

537. ὑπορράπτεις: very rare in classic Greek, though it occurs not infrequently in late writers. It is properly a tailor's term, "to stitch underneath," "patch up." Here it is used figuratively, like ῥάπτειν, ὑφαίνειν and Lat. *suere*, *consuere*. It is not found in Aeschylus or Sophocles, and occurs only here in Euripides.

540. εἰ μόλοι: see *M. and T.* 501 c. παρὰ κλαίουσι: if the text is sound -ρα is here lengthened before κλ. Usually in trimeters a short final syllable ending in a vowel is not lengthened before a mute and liquid, except in the case of γμ, γν, δμ, δν, and sometimes βλ and γλ. But cf. *El.* 1058 ἆρά κλύουσαν, Aesch. *Pers.* 773 νέα φρονεῖ. Cases of this kind of lengthening in lyric passages are much more frequent. The truth seems to be, that while the rule as laid down by Porson (see his note on *Orest.* 64) generally holds good, exceptions sometimes occur. Almost all such rules of usage, e.g. the "Canon Davesianus" and "Porson's rule of the fifth foot," are subject to some exceptions, which should not be emended or explained away. Elmsley and Earle insert τι after αἰσχρόν, thus obtaining a tribrach instead of the suspicious iambus. See Christ *Metrik*[2] p. 14; Kühner-Blass I. p. 306; Goebel *De Correptione Attica*, pp. 19 ff. and Kopp *Rhein. Mus.* 1886 p. 256.

544. μυρίαν χάριν: as we might say "I will be infinitely obliged to you."

546. δωμάτων: for the gen. with ἐξώπιος and other adjs. of separation, see G. 1140, H. 753 g. Ἐξώπιος (ἐξ and ὤψ) is properly "out of sight of," and hence "apart from," "away from." Cf. *Suppl.* 1038 ἦ δόμων ἐξώπιος βέβηκε, *Med.* 628 χρονίζων δωμάτων ἐξώπιος, and the line parodied by Aristoph. *Thesm.* 881 αὐτὸς δὲ Πρωτεὺς ἔνδον ἔστ', ἦ 'ξώπιος; (cf. *Hel.* 468). The word is not used by Aeschylus and Sophocles.

547. ξενῶνας: guests were usually lodged under the same roof as their hosts, the upper story (ὑπερῷον) being often used for this purpose. But large and luxurious dwellings sometimes had separate apartments for guests, at a little distance from the main building and connected with it by a passage-way, in which was a door (θύραι μέταυλοι 549). See Bekker-Göll *Charikles* II. p. 140; Hermann-Blümner *Privatalt. d. Griech.* p. 495 note 3. As Earle has pointed out (see the introd. to his ed. p. xl.), Heracles must have gone in at a side-door of the back-scene, for he and the servant can scarcely have retired through one of the πάροδοι. But the presence of two doors occasions no difficulty; for though the permanent stone προσκήνια of Hellenistic times often show only one door (sometimes none at all), the theaters of the fifth and fourth centuries probably had προσκήνια with three doors. See Doerpfeld *Gr. Theater*, pp. 67, 377-8, 552.

548. εὖ: so England for ἐν of the MSS. Those who retain ἐν either take it with κλῄσατε as a case of so-called "tmesis," or as equivalent to ἔνδον (so Earle).

549. θύρας μεταύλους: here not of the door between the *andronitis* and *gynaeconitis*, but of a door in the passage between the ξενῶνες and the palace proper. θοινωμένους: a poetic word.

551. προσκειμένης: the MSS. have προκειμένης: but as the calamity has *already come*, Wakefield's emendation is necessary.

552. ξενο|δοκεῖν: in the iambic trimeter "resolutions are by far most frequent in the third foot. This fact stands in connection with the fact that in that part of the line, after the caesura, begins a new trochaic series, with the first thesis strongly accentuated. For in trochaic verse it is the first long that is most frequently resolved" (Christ).

553. Admetus, stung by the censure of the chorus, retorts with an impassioned speech. σφε: the tragedians sometimes use this form as singular; see Goodwin *Gr. Gram.* 394, Hadley-Allen 261 D, a.

558. The MSS. except L and P (ἐχθροξένους) have κακοξένους. The sense is much the same with either reading; but ἐχθροξένους, as the rarer and stronger word, is more likely to be right than the more colorless κακοξένους, especially as κακόν stands at the end of the preceding line. Aeschylus has ἐχθρόξενος repeatedly (*Prom.* 725, *Sept.* 589, 604).

560. διψίαν: the commentators compare *Il.* IV. 171 καί κεν ἐλέγχιστος πολυδίψιον Ἄργος ἱκοίμην. But the epithet is by no means a mere epic reminiscence; for the plain of Argos is very dry and dusty still. Jerram aptly quotes Wordsworth (*Hist. of Greece*), who says: "The higher parts of this plain suffer from want of water, whence the epithet applied to it by Homer (πολυδίψιον), indicative of the thinness of the soil."

561. τὸν παρόντα δαίμονα: cf. *Andr.* 974.

565–6. I keep τῷ and αἰνέσει with the MSS.; Heracles is clearly meant. Schmidt's καὐτῷ would give the same sense. Some editors read καί τῳ (the indefinite) with Heath. This might be a more polite form of expression than the direct address, or it might be sarcastic, like φοβεῖταί τις Aesch. *Cho.* 52, and the like. But the emphatic position of τῷ is against this reading. Earle has the conjectures καί σοί and αἰνέσεις: but the fact that the chorus do at once proceed to praise Admetus is a fatal objection. The difficulty lies, I think, in φρονεῖν δοκῶ: I have given in the text Herwerden's δόξω φρονεῖν. If φρονεῖν δόξω were once written by mistake, δόξω might easily have been changed to δοκῶ for metrical reasons, as the last foot cannot be a spondee. Moreover when this idiom occurs at or near the end of a trimeter δοκῶ usually comes first: cf. fr. 188, 3 N. δόξεις φρονεῖν, Soph. *Aj.* 594 δοκεῖς φρονεῖν, *O. C.* 1666 and *El.* 550 δοκῶ φρονεῖν, Critias fr. 4 δοκῇ φρονεῖν, etc.; though this is not a very safe criterion (Aesch. *Prom.* 389 φρονεῖν δοκεῖν).

566. ἐπίσταται: the meaning "to know how" to do a thing readily passes into that of "to be able" to do it. Cf. *Il.* XXI. 320 οὐδέ οἱ ὀστέ᾽ ἐπιστήσονται Ἀχαιοί | ἀλλέξαι, Soph. *Trach.* 543 ἐγὼ δὲ θυμοῦσθαι μὲν οὐκ ἐπίσταμαι | νοσοῦντι. So in French "il ne saurait faire ce que vous voulez."

567. Admetus now enters the palace, and the chorus sing the second Stasimon (568–605).

568. πολύξεινος καὶ ἐλευθέρου: Wecklein for πολύξεινος καὶ ἐλεύθερος (see his *Studien zu Euripides* p. 364). Purgold had already proposed πολυξείνου καὶ ἐλευθέρου: but the epithet πολύξεινος suits the *house*, while ἐλεύθερος (here = ἐλευθέριος, Lat. *liberalis*) is better adapted to the *man*.

570. "In thee did Pythian Apollo, lord of the tuneful lyre, deign to dwell." εὐλύρας: cf. Aristoph. *Thesm.* 969, where the epithet, as here, is applied to Apollo. The word is very rare.

573. μηλονόμας: Doric for μηλονόμης. The word is very rare, if not indeed ἅπαξ εἰρημένον.

574. νόμοις: so Pierson for δόμοις. Those edd. who retain δόμοις either hold that in σοῖσι there is a sudden transition of the address from the house to Admetus (so Monk, Woolsey, Jerram, Earle), or that there is no such transition, but that δόμοις refers to the different apartments of the palace. But νόμοις agrees far better with the following lines. We need not suppose that in σοῖσι Admetus is addressed, for the pastures and herds attached to the palace are meant. In the heroic age the home of a king (e.g. that of Odysseus) had its own pastures, stalls and cattle.

575. δοχμιᾶν: "slanting," "sloping." Schol. τῶν πλαγίων καὶ ἀνακεκλιμένων ὀρῶν. κλιτύων: κλιτύς is from κλίνω: cf. Lat. *cli-vus.* συρίζων: i.e. "playing on the shepherd's pipe" (σῦριγξ). See as to the σῦριγξ Howard in *Harvard Stud. in Class. Phil.* IV. pp. 18 ff. — This passage shows very clearly the poet's power of sketching a charming picture in a few words. Earle aptly compares *I. A.* 573 ff.

576. ποιμνίτας: Pollux 7, 185 has ποιμνῖται κύνες. The word seems to be always used as an adjective, though a noun in its formation. So ἱππότης, πρυμνητής, etc., are sometimes used as adjs., e.g. *Suppl.* 660 ἱππότην ὄχλον. Cf. *victor exercitus* and the like in Latin. ὑμεναίους, properly "marriage-songs," is doubtless used here in a general sense, "strains"; though the schol. somewhat coarsely explains it by ποιμενικὰς ᾠδὰς δι' ὧν ἦγεν τὰ βοσκήματα εἰς τὸ ἀλλήλοις μίγνυσθαι, and so Aelian *II. A.* 12, 44.

579. σὺν ... ἐποιμαίνοντο, a case of so-called "tmesis." It is really, of course, a survival of the early adverbial use of the preposition. βαλιαί: "dappled"; cf. Vergil's *lynces variae, Georg.* III. 264.

580. Ὄθρυος: this important mountain-range of Thessaly forms the watershed between the Peneius and Spercheius. It rises at its highest point to a height of about 5500 feet, and is still covered with forests to a large extent. λεόντων: Herodotus (VII. 126) asserts, and Aristotle (*II. A.* VI. 31) confirms the statement, that in Europe lions were found only between the Nestus and the Achelous; but Dio Chrysostom (*Orat.* XXI. p. 269 C, cited by Rawlinson in his note on Herod. *l. s. c.*) says that in his time they were extinct in Europe. The story of the attack made by lions upon the baggage-camels of Xerxes (Her. VII. 125) is well known. Cf. the graphic representation of a lion-hunt on one of the Mycenaean swords.

581. δαφοινός: "tawny," of the color of the hide. So also *Il.* X. 23 δαφοινὸν ... δέρμα λέοντος: cf. *Il.* XI. 474, where the epithet is applied to jackals; *Il.* II. 308, where it is used of a snake; Aesch. *Prom.* 1022 of an eagle, and Hom. *Hymn* 19, 23 of the skin of a lynx. In all these cases the animal to which the term is applied is a beast of prey. Was this because with the meaning of "red" or "tawny" was associated to some extent the other meaning of "blood-thirsty" or "cruel"? Both significations arose logically enough from the original one of "all bloody," "wholly blood-red." Sophocles does not use the word.

582. χόρευσε: so Monk for ἐχόρευσε, to restore correspondence with ἔτλα δέ of the strophe (573). For the omission of the augment, see Goodwin 549, Hadley-Allen 354 D.

585. νεβρός: for νεϝρός, from the root νεϝ; cf. Skt. *navas*, Lat. *novus*, Eng. "new." The word must originally have been applied to any young animal.

ὑψικόμων πέραν ἐλατᾶν: i.e. beyond the limits of the forest. For the use of πέραν = πέρα, cf. *Hippol.* 1053, Pindar *Nem.* V. 21. Herwerden would read πέρα. ὑψικόμων: so Tertullian (*Jud. Dom.* 8) uses the epithet *alticomae* of cypresses.

586. σφυρῷ: properly the ankle; here by "synecdoche" for the foot in general.

588. πολυμηλοτάταν: a Homeric epithet, applied to Orchomenos (*Il.* II. 605) and to persons (e.g. *Il.* II. 705). Earle compares Pindar *Ol.* I. 16 ff., to which may be added *Pyth.* IX. 11 (cited by Monk). The neighborhood of Pherae still abounds in flocks.

589. οἰκεῖ: the necessary emendation of Purgold and Markland for οἰκεῖς. The third person is required both because Phoebus, not Admetus, has just been addressed and because of τίθεται, κρατύνει, which follow. The subject of οἰκεῖ is, of course, a pronoun understood referring to Admetus. παρὰ ... λίμναν: so *Il.* II. 711 οἱ δὲ Φέρας ἐνέμοντο παραὶ Βοιβηΐδα λίμνην κ.τ.λ. Cf. Strabo c. 436 Meineke. The lake was called Βοιβηΐς or Βοιβία λίμνη from the town of Boebe which was situated upon it. The epithet καλλίπαον is puzzling, especially as the lake is said to have no outlet, though several streams flow into it. When applied to a river or fountain (e.g. *Med.* 835 καλλινάου ... Κηφίσου) the term is appropriate enough; but why use it of a *lake?* Woolsey suggests that it refers to the water moved to and fro by the wind, but probably the poet is not speaking by the card.

590 ff. We may render: "And for his tilth and the level stretches of his fields he sets as limit on the side toward the sun's evening resting-place the clime of the Molossian mountains"; ἀρότοις γυᾶν refers to the rich arable lands as distinguished from the πεδίων δαπέδοις, the upland pastures with their broad expanses. ἱππόστασιν: properly the *stable* where the Sun puts up his steeds at night. For the expression, cf. fr. 771, 5 N. ἕω φαεννὰς Ἡλίου θ' ἱπποστάσεις, and Pollux I. 184. After Μολοσσῶν two shorts and a long are needed to correspond to σοφίας of 602. Probably some anapaestic word has dropped out; Bauer and Earle suggest ὀρέων, which may well be right. The response might also be restored by striking out ἄγαμαι in 602, and so *l* actually reads; but this would spoil the antithesis in 602–3.

595. Αἰγαίων': the schol. takes this word as an adj. agreeing with ἀκτήν, for he paraphrases: κρατεῖ δὲ καὶ ἐπὶ τὴν Αἰγαίωνα ἀκτὴν τὴν πόντιον καὶ ἀλίμενον. He is probably right; though some edd. regard the word as a noun. There are at least three possibilities: (A) Αἰγαίων' may be an adj. = Αἰγαῖον; (B) it may be the name of the sea-giant put for the sea itself by "metonymy" (so Jerram, Earle), or (C) it may be a substantive meaning "the Aegean sea"; cf. Hesych. s. v. Αἰγαιῶν· ἐνάλιος θεός. καὶ τὸ περὶ τὰς Κυκλάδας πέλαγος. If it is a noun, it is the object of κρατύνει: but if, as seems more probable, it is an adjective, κρατύνει is used absolutely, "he rules as far as the harbourless Aegean sea-strand of Pelion." The MSS. have αἰγαῖον; but the schol. certainly read

Αἰγαίων', and the antistrophe (604) has — — —. For the phrase Monk compares *Troad.* I ἥκω λιπὼν Αἰγαῖον ἁλμυρὸν βάθος | πόντου.

596. Reiske would read ἀλιμένου for ἀλίμενον, which is an easy change and may be right. Πηλίου: the mention of Pelion would naturally recall to a Greek the fearful shipwreck of the Persians on the Magnesian coast in 480 B.C. The name Ἴπνοι or "Ovens" was given to a part of the Πηλιὰς ἀκτή, either because of the seething of the waters there (so Earle) or more probably because of the oven-like caves in the cliffs which may still be seen there. Cf. Herod. VII. 128 and Strabo IX. p. 443 M.

597. δόμον ἀμπετάσας: short-hand expression for πύλας δόμου ἀμπετάσας.

598. νοτερῷ βλεφάρῳ: i.e. "in spite of his grief." ξεῖνον: the correspondence requires this form; the MSS. have ξένον.

599. φίλας: so the Aldine. The MSS. have φίλιας, but the strophic line (589) has ∪ —.

600. ἀρτιθανῆ: an extremely rare word.

601. Render: "for natural nobility of soul is impelled too far toward respect for others' rights": ἐκφέρεται strictly means "is carried out of the proper course," the figure being that of a race-horse or runner who swerves out of the bounds of the race-course. Hence it implies a mild censure of the excessive hospitality of Admetus. Cf. Soph. *El.* 628 ὁρᾷς; πρὸς ὀργὴν ἐκφέρει. Αἰδώς is a word almost as untranslatable as the τὸ τί ἦν εἶναι of Aristotle.

602. πάντα σοφίας = πᾶσα σοφία. ἔνεστιν: so Barnes for ἔνεστι, to restore the responsion. ἄγαμαι: "I am filled with awe and wonder." The word is not in *l*, and many editors omit it (see note on 594). But without it the antithesis between 602 and 603 is lost, and δ᾽ of 603 becomes merely connective.

604. Many edd. compare Aesch. *Ag.* 945 θάρσος εὐπειθὲς ἵζει φρενὸς φίλον θρόνον. The sense then is: "Confidence sits (enthroned) at my heart." This seems better than to render ἧσται "lurks" with Liddell and Scott.

605. φῶτα: here, as in 472, without contemptuous force. κεδνὰ πράξειν = καλῶς πράξειν. As Monk acutely observes, "ea vox (κεδνός) usum habet non minus late patentem quam ἀγαθός vel ἐσθλός." He compares *Troad.* 683 πράξειν τι κεδνόν, and for the idiomatic use of the neut. plu. of the adj. with πράσσειν *Orest.* 538 θυγάτηρ δ᾽ ἐμὴ θανοῦσ᾽ ἔπραξεν ἔνδικα, *I. A.* 346 πράσσοντα μεγάλα, *El.* 1359 εὐδαίμονα πράσσει. To these may be added *Heracl.* 438 (τάδε πράσσειν = οὕτως πράσσειν, a nearly similar case), Aesch. *Ag.* 1397 ἄτιμα δ᾽ οὐκ ἐπραξάτην, etc.

606-962. Third Epeisodion. The king comes out of the palace, followed by his attendants carrying the bier on which lies the body of Alcestis. See note on l. 422.

606. ἀνδρῶν Φεραίων εὐμενὴς παρουσία = ἄνδρες Φεραῖοι εὐμενῶς πάροντες, but the use of the abstract gives the address a certain dignity and formality.

607. πάντ᾽: sc. τὰ πρόσφορα.

608. ἄρδην: for the testimonies of the ancient grammarians as to this word, see Ellendt *Lex. Soph. s. v.* It is used once by Aeschylus, three times by Sophocles, and at least half a dozen times by Euripides. ἐς τάφον τε καὶ πυράν: cf. *Suppl.* 1058 τύμβῳ καὶ πυρᾷ φαίνει πέλας. Monk and others long ago pointed out that this passage of our play and 740 seems to imply that the body of Alcestis was to be burned, and are therefore inconsistent with 365 f. and 897 f., which clearly imply that it was to be buried. Hence they have reproached the poet for carelessness. Dr. Verrall, on the other hand (see his *Euripides the Rationalist* pp. 122 ff.), holds that "the sort of *pyra* which he (i.e. Admetus) has in view is a *grave-pyre, in* which, as he says, not *on* which, the corpse would be placed. It is a mortuary kiln, a chamber in the royal tomb, opening from the floor of it. Here the body would be laid; here that of Alcestis was laid and left by the performers of the funeral. Afterwards — at night we should probably suppose, since one object of the whole arrangement was to achieve a sanitary purpose without insulting the majesty of the dead or affronting the eyes of the living — fire would be put to the fuel with which the chamber had been provided, and the chamber closed." He then compares the so-called "grave of Agamemnon" discovered by Schliemann at Mycenae, and the "fiery rock-chamber" of *I. T.* 626 (πῦρ ἱερὸν ἔνδον χάσμα τ' εὐρωπὸν πέτρας). But this solution, ingenious as it is, is not, I fear, wholly correct. Dr. Dörpfeld, probably the highest living authority, holds (cf. Schuchhardt *Schliemann's Ausgrabungen*[2] p. 194) that there is no trace of cremation in the "shaft-graves" at Mycenae; the ashes found in them (and in other tombs at Volo, etc.) have probably come from burnt-offerings. In the words of Rohde (*Psyche* p. 31), "Den Fürsten ist reicher Vorrath an kostbarem Geräth und Schmuck mitgegeben, unverbrannt, wie ihre eigenen Leichen nicht verbrannt worden sind; sie ruhen auf Kieseln, und sind mit einer Lehmschicht und Kiesellage bedeckt; Spuren von Rauch, Reste von Asche und Kohlen weisen darauf hin, dass man die Körper gebettet hat auf die Brandstelle der *Todtenopfer*, die man in dem Grabraume vorher dargebracht hatte." If this "Brandstelle der Todtenopfer" is the πυρά of the *Alcestis*, the difficulty is in great part removed; the body is laid upon it (cf. 740), but not burned. I find no proof in the *Alcestis* that the queen's corpse was to be cremated. The case of Capaneus in the *Supplices* 980 ff. is quite different; there the body is burned on a pyre in the open air. As to the passage from the Iphigenia, that refers to a barbarian country; and the custom there spoken of was felt to be so un-Greek that Diodorus (XX. 14) actually suggests that Euripides had in mind the human burnt-offerings of the Carthaginians! — Instead of ἐς L P have πρὸς, which Wecklein (*Beiträge zur Kritik des Eur.* p. 538) prefers. Either reading gives good sense; but ἐς is peculiarly appropriate if the tomb and πυρά were of the character just described, as the body would be carried to and *into* the burial-chamber.

609. It was a religious duty to take a last, solemn farewell of the deceased before the body was burned or buried. This was commonly done by exclaiming χαῖρε (among the Romans *vale*), adding the name of the dead person. See Hermann-Blümner *Privatalt. d. Griech.* p. 370 note 3. The chorus are prevented from at once complying with the king's command by the coming of Pheres; but they take their farewell in vv. 741 f. after the old man's departure.

610. Cf. the English "to take the last journey," to the grave.

611. Enter the aged Pheres, followed by attendants bearing rich ornaments for the dead. γηραιῷ ποδί: cf. *Hec.* 64 γηραιᾶς χειρός, Soph. *O. C.* 200 γεραιὸν σῶμα, and the like.

613. νερτέρων ἀγάλματα: ἄγαλμα may be used here as often in Homer, = πᾶν ἐφ' ᾧ τις ἀγάλλεται, the idea being that the dead actually rejoiced in the offerings and honors bestowed upon them. This belief is a very wide-spread one among primitive peoples, and survives even at the present day to a much greater extent than most persons probably imagine. The word may, however, mean simply "ornaments."

617. δύσφορα: δυσμενῆ, the reading of all the MSS. but *L P*, has been defended as being the "*difficilior lectio*"; but I fear that it *is* "difficilior" in another sense of the Latin comparative. As Jerram and others observe, δυσμενής is *very* rarely used of *things*; and the σχῆμα ἐτυμολογικόν (φέρειν . . . δύσφορα) is too Euripidean to be lost. As Earle points out, δυσμενῆ may be due to the μέν just above at the end of 616; or it may be merely an unskilful attempt to fill out a lacuna by some one who found only δυσ . . . legible in his MSS. For some of the numerous emendations that have been suggested, see Sel. Conj.

618. κατὰ χθονὸς ἴτω: i.e. be buried with her.

620. ἥτις γε: causal relative. "It is to be observed that either ὅστις or ὅς γε generally represents this causal sense (expressed in Latin by the subjunctive), but that we sometimes find both combined, precisely in the same way" (Paley).

623. εὐκλεέστερον: so *B*. The other MSS. have the superlative, which would be too extravagant, especially as the tone of the speech is a trifle cold and perfunctory.

624. ἔργον τλᾶσα: cf. *Med.* 796 τλᾶσ' ἔργον ἀνοσιώτατον: ib. 1328, etc. It is hard in such cases to decide whether the verb is really transitive or whether there is an ellipsis of δρᾶν or ποιεῖν: but instances like *Hec.* 1251 τὰ μὴ καλὰ | πράσσειν ἐτόλμας, etc. seem to point in the latter direction.

627-8. The edd. compare a proverb quoted by the rhetor Aristides, ἢ τοιαύτην χρὴ γαμεῖν ἢ μὴ γαμεῖν. λύειν: ἀντὶ τοῦ λυσιτελεῖν Schol. Cf. *Med.* 566 ἐμοί τε λύει τοῖσι μέλλουσιν τέκνοις | τὰ ζῶντ' ὀνῆσαι, ib. 1112, 1362.

629. ἦλθες: "the aorist, expressing simply a past occurrence, is sometimes used where we should expect a perfect" (Goodwin *M. and T.* 58). ἐξ ἐμοῦ: source passing into agency. This use of ἐξ is especially common with verbs of giving, and perhaps originated with them; though even in Homer occur such cases as *Il.* II. 33 ἐφῆπται ἐκ Διός, ib. 669 ἐφίληθεν ἐκ Διός, etc. In Attic prose the preposition is rarely used to denote agency.

630. φίλοισι : probably masculine (cf. 1037), though some take it as neuter. σὴν παρουσίαν = σέ παρόντα. Cf. 606.

631. τοῦτον: so Earle. The MSS. have τὸν σὸν, which is highly suspicious, as we have σήν in 630 and τῶν σῶν in 632. The change from τὸν σὸν to τοῦτον is really very slight.

632. Nauck would reject this line as an interpolation; he says (*Eur. Stud.* II. p. 65 f.) : "Die im zweiten Verse gegebene Begründung für das Zurückweisen der Schmucksachen ist unpassend schon an sich und zumal in dieser Situation; kein Todter bedarf des Schmuckes, und nicht darum weil Alcestis schon hinlänglich versorgt ist, sondern weil Pheres sein Leben mehr geliebt als seinen Sohn und weil er somit den Tod der Alcestis verschuldet, werden seine Gaben verschmäht. Es scheint daher unzweifelhaft das v. 632 dem Dichter fremd ist; vermuthlich haben wir in den Worten τῶν σῶν ἐνδεής einen Doppelgänger zu τὸν σὸν ἐνδύσεται." But according to the Greek conception the dead *did* need the clothes, etc. that were buried with them; had Nauck forgotten the story of Periander and his wife Melissa (Herod. V. 92), the money that was put in the mouth of the corpse, etc.? It is clear from his words that he has lost the point of the taunt; Admetus means "When I bury her she will have enough ornaments from *me*, and will not be at all in need of gifts from such as *you*." One can easily imagine what a world of scorn a good actor would infuse into the words τῶν σῶν. Ἐνδεής is saved from ambiguity by the context; otherwise the sense might be "she will have plenty of your possessions when she is buried." Cf. *Troad.* 906 μὴ θανῇ τοῦδ' ἐνδεής.

633. τότε : the asyndeton and emphatic position are very effective. ὠλλύμην : a fine example of the imperf. denoting likelihood or danger. Cf. *Herc. F.* 537.

635. γέρων ὤν is certainly awkward, and Earle's conjecture γεραιός is very plausible. He compares *Phoen.* 103 γεραιὰν νέᾳ χεῖρ' κ.τ.λ. Still Euripides may have written γέρων ὤν, harsh as it sounds. See note on ζῆν χρῆν, 379.

636 ff. These lines have been suspected by many commentators, and with good reason. Admetus has far too strong a sense of "the divinity that doth hedge a king" to make such a damaging admission in regard to himself. The only question is how many lines are to be rejected. G. A. Wagner wished to reject 641, and Nauck 638 and 639. Badham and Prinz regard 636–41 as spurious. For other opinions see Sel. Conj. Earle retains 640–41, and suggests that 634–9 is a parallel passage (from an *Oedipus?*) which was written in the margin and has crept into the text. This seems, on the whole, the most probable view. Admetus would never have admitted that he was the son of a *slave*, but might very well in his anger go so far as to say that Pheres was not his father.

636. ἦσθ' ἄρα: "the imperfect ἦν (generally with ἄρα) may express a *fact* which is just recognized as such by the speaker or writer, having previously been denied, overlooked, or not understood" (Goodwin *M. and T.* 39).

639. ὑπεβλήθην: this passage shows how ὑποβάλλειν came to be the technical word for substituting a child, like Lat. *supponere, subdere.* Cf. ὑποβολιμαῖος.

640. εἰς ἔλεγχον ἐξελθών: ἐξέρχεσθαι, like κατέρχεσθαι, is used of one who engages in a task, trial or conflict. Cf. *Hec.* 226 μήτ' ἐς χερῶν ἅμιλλαν ἐξέλθῃς ἐμοί. Woolsey compares Soph. *Phil.* 98 εἰς ἔλεγχον ἐξιών, which, however, is not quite parallel. ὅς εἶ: not "who you are" (which would be τίς or ὅστις εἶ), but "what sort of man you are" (= οἷος εἶ). So in Latin in indirect questions *qui sis = qualis sis.*

642. τἄρα = τοι ἄρα. πάντων: διαπρέπειν here is followed by the gen. after the analogy of verbs of superiority and comparison: some, however, regard πάντων as partitive genitive. The genitive-construction with this verb is very rare.

644. ἠθέλησας: in Attic prose ἐθέλω, not θέλω, is the usual form, and in Attic inscriptions θέλω does not appear until about 250 B.C. In the tragedians both forms occur in lyric passages, while in trimeters the pres. ἐθέλω is excluded for metrical reasons. The aorists ἠθέλησα and ἤθελον, according to Veitch, belong only to ἐθέλω.

645. ἐάσατε: because the mother is included, the plur. is used.

646. ὀθνείαν: see note on 532.

647. The καί is probably intensive, not correlative with τ'. Good writers never, or almost never,* employ καί ... τε like τε ... καί: and in passages like fr. 328, 3, Aesch. *Suppl.* 708, *Septem* 558-9, *Eum.* 75-7, etc. which some have regarded as exceptions to this rule, a close examination shows that καί and τε are not correlative. Hermann regards the καί ... τε in our passage as a kind of anacoluthon instead of καί μητέρα καί πατέρα, and renders *quam ego et matrem, — patremque adeo duco solam,* the use of τε for καί thus giving greater emphasis to πατέρα.

647. The ἄν was inserted by Elmsley, B and a having only τ' ἐνδίκως. L and P have τε γ', the γ' being clearly "*metricorum supplementum.*" μόνην: so L P a. B has ἐμόν, whence Nauck conjectured ἐμοί. Probably in the MS. from which B was derived μόνην had lost the last two letters, and ἐμόν was an attempt of the scribe to restore the text by filling out the word. 434 (see note) is not a parallel case, as there B, L P and a disagree; while in our passage the agreement of a with the other family makes it probable that μόνην stood in the archetype.

648-9. Note the emphatic position of καλόν and τοῦ σοῦ πρὸ παιδός. Earle would read κατθανεῖν, quite needlessly. The participle is conditional.

650. πάντως: to be taken with βραχύς.

651-2. These lines, which are obviously an imitation of 295-6, are rejected by Lenting, Nauck, Paley, Prinz, Weil, Wecklein and Earle. They are very weak and inept, and are certainly an interpolation. ἔζων: see note on 295.

---

* Cf. however, *Andr.* 59 εὔνους δὲ καὶ σοὶ ζῶντί τ' ἦν τῷ σῷ πόσει.

653. καὶ μήν: "and what is more," introducing a new point of special importance.

655. παῖς δ' ἦν ἐγώ σοι: Nauck's conjecture ἢ γεγώς σοι is ingenious but not convincing. The emphatic pronoun of the first person is quite in keeping with the self-esteem which belongs to the character of Admetus. διάδοχος: "perhaps a substantive, as in Aesch. *Prom.* 1027" (Earle). This view is probably correct, though Euripides generally uses διάδοχος as an adj. Cf. *Andr.* 743, 803, *Hec.* 588, *Suppl.* 72. δόμων is suspicious, as the next line ends with δόμον. F. W. Schmidt's θρόνων for δόμων is very plausible, though I have not ventured to receive it into the text.

657. λείψειν ἔμελλες: for the periphrasis see Goodwin *M. and T.* 428 (a). ἔμελλες: in the indic. with ὥστ' to express actual result (*M. and T.* 601). διαρπάσαι may be inf. of purpose, but is better taken as inf. limiting the meaning of ὀρφανόν (*M. and T.* 763). The order distinctly favors the latter view. All MSS. but *L P* have διαρπάσειν, which reading is clearly due to the influence of λείψειν just before.

658, 659. ἀτιμάζοντα, προὔδωκας (*sic*) *L P*. With this reading the sense will be: "You will not say, either, that you gave me up to death because I did not pay respect to your old age." The rest of the MSS. have ἀτιμάζων τὸ σὸν and προὔδωκά σ', which gives the meaning: "You won't say, either, that it was from disrespect for your old age that I gave you up to death." The former reading is clearly better suited to the connection. Admetus is arguing that his father has no reasonable excuse for being unwilling to die in his stead. Pheres has enjoyed sovereign power; he has a son to take his place, and that son has always shown him due respect, so that the old man cannot plead ill-conduct on the part of Admetus as a pretext for unwillingness to make the sacrifice. This is clear and consistent. On the other hand, the other reading makes an abrupt transition to the defense of Admetus himself against a possible accusation from his father. The schol. must have had προὔδωκας and ἀτιμάζων τὸ σόν in his text; for he observes, oddly enough: οὐ μὴν ἐρεῖς γε ὡς θανεῖν με προὔδωκας ἀτιμάζοντα τὸ σὸν γῆρας. τὸ γὰρ ἀτιμάζων ἀντὶ τοῦ ἀτιμάζοντα. Or is the last clause of the scholium a later addition by one who had ἀτιμάζων in his text and was trying to reconcile it with the scholiast's explanation? οὐ μὴν ἐρεῖς: cf. Aristoph. *Nub.* 53 οὐ μὴν ἐρῶ γ' ὡς ἀργὸς ἦν. For the proleptic μ' Monk compares Soph. *El.* 552 ἐρεῖς μὲν οὐχὶ νῦν γέ μ' ὡς ἄρξασά τι | λυπηρὸν εἶτα σοῦ τάδ' ἐξήκουσ' ὕπο. αἰδόφρων: only here in Euripides. Sophocles has it once (*O. C.* 237 ὦ ξένοι αἰδόφρονες), Aeschylus not at all. It seems not to occur elsewhere.

660-61. χάριν ἠλλαξάτην: cf. *El.* 89 φόνον φονεῦσι πατρὸς ἀλλάξων ἐμοῦ.

662. οὐκέτ' ἂν φθάνοις: for this use of φθάνω with a participle see *M. and T.* 894.

663. γηροβοσκήσουσι: cf. *Med.* 1032 ff. εἶχον ἐλπίδας | πολλὰς ἐν ὑμῖν γηροβοσκήσειν τ' ἐμὲ | καὶ κατθανοῦσαν χεροῖν εὖ περιστελεῖν.

664. περιστελοῦσι, προθήσονται: technical words; see Hermann-Blümner *Griech. Privatalt.* pp. 302 ff.

666-68. These three lines were rejected by Badham; Nauck, too, rejects 668 as absurd, and proposes to read τόδε instead of λέγω. But it is not necessary to reject or change anything. It is perfectly true that Admetus cannot *logically* call himself the γηροτρόφος of his dead wife. But who is strictly logical under such circumstances? Almost every impassioned speech of this kind, when closely analyzed, shows inconsistencies and absurdities. Admetus means: "I will not cherish you in your old age nor bury you; those duties I owe to the one who has preserved my life, and who is therefore my real parent." The fact that Alcestis is dead is for the moment left out of sight. τοὐπὶ σ': ὅσον τὸ κατὰ σέ schol. So *Hec.* 514. ἡμεῖς δ' ἄτεκνοι τοὐπὶ σ', and *Rhes.* 397. αὐγάς: sc. ἡλίου. So 808 αὐγὰς προσορῶν, and *Hel.* 1373 αὐγὰς εἰσορᾶν.

669 ff. Euripides loves to close a long speech with a maxim or moral apophthegm. μάτην: note the emphatic position.

671. The edd. call attention to the fact that this line violates the so-called "rule of Porson." This celebrated rule, as stated by Porson himself (*Suppl. ad Praef. ad Hecubam*), is as follows: 'Nempe hanc regulam plerumque in senariis observabant Tragici, ut, si voce quae Creticum pedem efficeret terminaretur versus, eamque vocem hypermonosyllabon praecederet, quintus pes iambus vel tribrachys esse deberet.... Res eadem est, si Creticus in trochaeum et syllabam dissolvitur, vel si, Cretico in syllabam longam et iambum dissoluto, syllaba longa est aut articulus, aut praepositio, aut quaevis longa denique vox, quae ad sequentia potius quam praecedentia pertineat.' It is clear that in the first sentence quoted Porson has either made an error or is using 'Creticum pedem' in its wider sense, to include the Fourth Paeon ($\cup \cup \cup -$); otherwise, if the fifth foot were a *tribrach*, the line could not end in a true Cretic ($- \cup -$). Just below he is evidently using 'Creticus' in the narrower sense. Porson's rule has been frequently misstated by grammarians. The principle is perhaps best expressed thus (cf. Hadley-Allen 1091, 5): "if the fifth foot of a tragic trimeter is divided by a caesura, the syllable immediately preceding that caesura must be short or a monosyllable." To this there are two principal exceptions. One is thus stated by Porson himself: 'Verum si secunda quinti pedis pars ejus sit generis, ut praecedenti verbo adhaereat (i.e. an enclitic or ἄν after an elision), et ambo quasi unam vocem simul efficiant, non jam amplius necesse erit, ut verbum praecedens brevi syllaba terminetur.' For a list of cases of this kind, see Wecklein *Studien zu Aeschylus* p. 130. The other exception is when the main caesura falls in the fourth foot (see Wecklein *l. s. c.*, who gives a list of cases; cf. Hermann *El. Doct. Met.* p. 22), as in the line in the text.

673-4. Ἄδμηθ', παῦσαι: so Mekler for παύσασθ' and ὦ παῖ. παύσασθ' is clearly wrong, as Pheres has thus far taken no part in the dispute. and the sing. παροξύνῃς immediately follows. ὦ παῖ was doubtless written by mistake under the influence of the ὦ παῖ just below, and has probably displaced an imperative. Then some one, seeing the need of an imperative, inserted παύσασθ' in place of the first word of 673. Ἄδμηθ' is supported by the analogy of 416, 552, 1007, and παῦσαι by the parallelism with 707. Mekler, however, (*Euripidea* pp. 14 ff.) gives a more artificial explanation of the origin of the corruption. He suggests that a strip containing the first four letters of 673 and 674 had been torn out, and that some one in filling up the lacuna from another copy made a mistake of a line and filled up the gap in 673 with the first six letters of 674 and that in 674 with the first two letters of 675, thus:

[ΠΑΥϹΑϹ]Θ.
[Ω Η]ΑΙ

(But if his restoration of the text is right, the sixth letter of 674 would have been I, not C, and we should have had in 673 not [ΠΑΥϹΑϹ]Θ but [ΠΑΥϹΑΙ]Θ.) **φρένας**: φρένα *L P*, "under the influence of Φρύγα" (Earle).

675. αὐχεῖς: here, as usual, in a bad sense. **Λυδὸν ἢ Φρύγα**: cf. Aristoph. *Aves* 1244 φέρ' ἴδω, πότερα Λυδὸν ἢ Φρύγα | ταυτὶ λέγουσα μορμολύττεσθαι δοκεῖς; The proverb marks the contempt of the free Greeks for the servile Asiatics very forcibly.

676. κακοῖς ἐλαύνειν: cf. *Androm.* 31 κακοῖς πρὸς αὐτῆς σχετλίοις ἐλαύνομαι, *Ion* 1619 ὅτῳ δ' ἐλαύνεται | συμφοραῖς οἶκος (which is slightly different). **ἀργυρώνητον**: a rare word; cf. Aesch. *Ag.* 913 ἀργυρωνήτους ὑφάς.

677-8. These two lines are an echo of a favorite formula of Attic law. **γεγῶτα γνησίως**: really a *figura etymologica*, as γνησίως is from the root γεν-, γνη-.

679. νεανίας: adj. as in *Hel.* 209, 1562, *Herc. F.* 1095 and often. It has here a bad sense, "insolent." Jerram well observes: "This use of the word would be familiar at Athens, where the fashionable young men of the day were in the habit of committing assaults upon respectable citizens."

680. A difficult place. Most editors since the time of Elmsley take οὐ with οὕτως, and render "not so easily" or "not with impunity," comparing *Heracl.* 374 οὐχ' οὕτως ἃ δοκεῖς κυρήσεις. They either take βαλών absolutely, "having fired your shot," or supply with it λόγους, κακοῖς or the like. Probably this is right; but it is at least *possible* to take οὐ with βαλών, "without hitting (your mark)"; cf. *Bacch.* 1179 τίς ἁ βαλοῦσα πρῶτα; This use of βάλλω is by no means rare from Homer down. Οὕτως would then mean "as you came," i.e. without accomplishing your object. The order of the words seems to me to favor this interpretation; but it is undeniably less effective than the direct threat. Weil would read παῖ for καὶ in 679, and Wecklein would change οὐ in 680 to κοὐ, thus bringing ῥίπτων into agreement with the subject of ὑβρίζεις. The conjunction of the two participles is certainly awkward, and the emendations are tempting; but I have not ventured to receive them into the text. Render "and since you keep flinging at me words full of the insolence of youth, you shall not get away with impunity after firing your shot."

687–8. Nauck (*Eur. Stud.* II. 69 ff.) says of this passage: "Der begründende Satz πατρὸς — πάρα ist höchst nüchtern und nicht einmal passend für den Zweck des Pheres, der zeigen will dass er für seinen Sohn genug gethan habe. Das Futurum λείψω scheint sich mit πολλῶν ἄρχεις nicht zu vertragen; wenn Admetus König ist, so hat er nicht auf den Tod des Vaters zu warten, um in den Besitz der πολύπλεθροι γύαι zu gelangen. Die Stelle würde somit gewinnen, wenn V. 688 fehlte, d. h. wenn man vorher schriebe πολλῶν μὲν ἄρχεις, πολυπλέθρους δ' ἔχεις γύας." This reasoning is most sophistical. I quite agree with Kviçala (*Stud. zu Eur.* p. 80), who points out that the words πατρὸς — πάρα were intended to stand in strong contrast with 683 οὐ γὰρ πατρῷον τόνδ' ἐδεξάμην νόμον, and that the future λείψω shows that Pheres, while giving up the sovereignty, had reserved for life the use of the royal estates. And what could be more "nüchtern" than Nauck's proposed reading?

691. This line is quoted by Aristoph. *Thesm.* 194, and amusingly parodied in *Nub.* 1415. Cf also *Hec.* 1256 (a similar cadence).

697. λέγεις: "talk about," "tell of," probably a colloquial use; ψέγεις is an old conjecture which was revived by Cobet, and which Earle adopts; but no change is necessary. Cf. Xen. *Cyropaed.* I. 3, 10 λέγων δὲ ἕκαστος ὑμῶν τὴν ἑαυτοῦ ῥώμην, and the like; also the Latin use of *narro*, e.g. *vigilantiam tuam tu mihi narras?* Terence *Adelphoe* 398. This use of λέγω may have been developed from the poetic use in the sense of "sing of," "celebrate."

700 f. εἰ τὴν παροῦσαν ... γυναῖχ': a most biting taunt. τοῖς μὴ θέλουσι, "any who are unwilling"; the μή, of course, gives the participle a conditional force.

704–5. Monk aptly compares Terence *Andria* 920 *si mihi perget quae volt dicere, ea quae non volt audiet.*

706–7. Note the parallelism with 673–4. τό: Wakefield for τά of the MSS. πλείω will then mean "more (than is fitting)" as often. The reading τά probably arose because some early copyist was thinking of the construction πλείω ἢ τὰ πρὶν κακά. κακορροθῶν: so *Hippol.* 340 ξυγγόνους κακορροθεῖς.

708. λέξαντος: so the MSS. With this reading the sense will be: "Speak on, assuming that I have spoken (ill of you). But if you don't like to hear the truth (about yourself), you ought not (on that account) to wrong me." Admetus means to imply that he did not abuse Pheres but merely told the truth about him, though the latter chooses to assume that the case is otherwise. There is no need of changing λέξαντος to λέξοντος with Reiske or to 'λεγξοντος with Hermann. The latter based his emendation on the schol., which says: λέγε ὡς καὶ ἐμοῦ κακῶς λέξαντος, δι' ὧν οὐκ ἠθέλησας ὑπὲρ ἐμοῦ ἀποθανεῖν (where for λέξαντος *a* has ἐλέγξαντος and *B* ἐλέγξοντος). Hermann thought that the schol. wrote καλῶς ἐλέγξαντος, '*eoque certe vestigium verae scripturae servavit*'; but it is more probable that the true reading in the scholium is κακῶς λέξαντος (Schwartz) or κακῶς σε λέξαντος (Dindorf). In the line from our text Dindorf, Nauck and Earle retain λέξαντος: Prinz and Weil follow Hermann, and Wecklein accepts Reiske's emendation.

713 ff. A difficult passage. It is clear from 714 that some kind of an imprecation immediately preceded. In the MSS. 714 immediately follows 713; hence the question at once arises: "Is 713 an imprecation?" Many edd. follow Schaefer in omitting ἄν and reading καὶ μὴν Διός γε μείζονα ζώης χρόνον, rendering "May you live longer than Zeus at least," or the like. To this there is the twofold objection that the MSS. have ἄν and that such an imprecation would surely have seemed impious to an Athenian audience. Such language is not at all consistent with the character of the pious Admetus. Others (so Hermann, Paley) retain ἄν and render, "You had better live longer than Zeus," ἄν ζώης being used like χαίροις ἄν and the like. But this converts the line into an ironical recommendation, not a curse. On the other hand, 719 is an unmistakable wish that misfortune of some kind may befall Pheres. Hence Nauck is probably right in placing 714 immediately after it. 713 will then be a mere "potential optative-clause," "And yet you fain would live longer than Zeus himself." The schol. oddly observes: καὶ ζήσειας μείζονα παρὰ ⟨τὸν⟩ τοῦ Διὸς χρόνον. ὁ γὰρ μὴν καὶ ἂν παρέλκει, which looks as though he wanted to take the line as a wish, but found μήν and ἄν in his way. Another schol. is: ἔζησας τοσοῦτον χρόνον ὅσον ἔχει ὁ Ζεύς, which (if ἔζησας be not corrupt) looks as though some read an indicative in place of ἂν ζώης. On the form ζώης (so L P rightly; ζώοις the other MSS.) see Nauck *Eur. Stud.* II. p. 70. That critic would put 714 and 715 after 719 and not transpose any of the other lines; but the arrangement in the text, which is that of Wecklein, seems better, though it involves more changes.

717. Van Herwerden wished to insert γ' after σῆς. The particle seems to be needed, "Yes, a proof of your cowardice"; this use of γε in answers is too familiar to need illustration. L and P have the variant σημεῖα γ' ὦ κάκιστε ταῦτ' ἀψυχίας, which is weaker, as the emphatic τῆς σῆς is lost. Wecklein brackets 717-18 as an interpolation, on the ground that 717 and 721 are too much alike; but this seems hardly necessary. Admetus reiterates his charge in spite of the old man's denial.

719. φεῦ is followed by a wish in the same way *I. A.* 666.

722 ff. Note the triple rhyme φίλον, τὸ σόν, νεκρόν. Was this intentional, to give a mocking, sneering effect to the lines? ἐν ἀνδράσιν: so 732, *I. A.* 945 ἐγὼ τὸ μηδέν, Μενέλεως δ' ἐν ἀνδράσιν. *Orest.* 1528 οὔτε γὰρ γυνὴ πέφυκας οὔτ' ἐν ἀνδράσιν σύ γ' εἶ is, of course, different. *Androm.* 591 σοῦ ποῦ μέτεστιν ὡς ἐν ἀνδράσιν λόγου; illustrates the origin of the idiom.

725. θάνῃ: here all the best MSS. show the form in ῃ. Cf. 247.

726. κακῶς ἀκούειν: so *male audire* in Latin. μέλει: so L P, rightly, the other MSS. having μέλλει. These two verbs are often confused in MSS. — The line is one of those immoral sentiments which drew down on Euripides the censure of Aristophanes and other men of the old school. Of course Euripides himself should not be taxed with upholding the opinion here expressed.

731. τε: L P have δέ, doubtless a copyist's error. σοῖσι: so L P a. B has τοῖσι σοῖσι (with σοῖσι cancelled by the first hand). The variant is interesting as showing how easily the article may creep into the text where it does not belong; see note on 318.

732. Ἄκαστος: *B* has ἄκλαυστος, a curious instance of text-corruption.

733. For the construction, cf. *Cycl.* 691 εἰ μή σ' ἑταίρων φόνον ἐτιμωρησάμην and fr. 559.

734. ἔρρων: *B a* have ἔρροις, *L* ἔρρου, *P* ἔρρο (with an erasure of one letter after the o). The schol. observes: ἔρροις νῦν αὐτός: φθείρου. εἶτα ἐξ ἑτέρας ἀρχῆς· καὶ αὐτὸς καὶ ἡ ξυνοικοῦσά σοι γηράσκετε ἄπαιδες, ὡς ἐστὲ ἄξιοι, καὶ ταῦτα ἐμοῦ ζῶντος. τινὲς δὲ ἔρρων γράφουσι σὺν τῷ ν̄, ἵνα ᾖ μετοχὴ ἀντὶ ῥήματος τοῦ ἔρρε. Ἔρρου we may dismiss at once, as ἔρρομαι is never used by classic writers. There remain ἔρροις and ἔρρων. Of these ἔρρων is clearly the more idiomatic and elegant; ἔρροις is too weak, as an imperative is needed rather than the milder optative, and the asyndeton ἔρροις — γηράσκετε is also an objection. See Nauck *Eur. Stud.* II. p. 71. νυν: so Lascaris; the MSS. have νῦν. It is, of course, the intensive νυν which is required. χἠ ξυνοικήσασά σοι: Admetus uses this formal phrase to avoid calling her μήτηρ.

735. ἄπαιδε παιδὸς ὄντος: a fine oxymoron.

736. τῷδ' ἔτ': so Elmsley; τῶδε γ' *B a*, τῶδ' ἔτ' *L P*. Cf. 719, where Kirchhoff would read τοῦδ'ἔτ' for τοῦδέ γ'.

737. νεῖσθ': the pres. of νέομαι, like that of εἶμι, is generally used with a future sense. The word is poetic.

739. τοὺν ποσίν κ.τ.λ.: a common proverbial expression. Cf. *Andr.* 397, *I. T.* 1312, 938, and esp. Soph. *Antig.* 1327 βράχιστα γὰρ κράτιστα τὰν ποσὶν κακά. Jebb *ad loc.* compares Pindar *Pyth.* 8, 32 τὸ δ' ἐν ποσί μοι τράχον. *a* has τοὔμποσίν, *B* τούμποσί, which may well be relics of the original spelling. See Meisterhans p. 85.

740. ὡς ἄν: on final clauses with ὡς ἄν in Euripides, see Schanz *Beiträge* II. pp. 100, 104, where Weber has collected the statistics. See also *M. and T.* 325 ff. and Gildersleeve in *Am. Jour. Phil.* IV. p. 422. — Pheres passes out at, or soon after, 730, and at the command of Admetus (739) the procession starts again and moves off from the scene to the left. The chorus joins the procession, and takes a solemn farewell of Alcestis, as Admetus had directed (609–10). At 746 it probably vanishes through the left-hand parodos. The anapaestic system 741–6 is, of course, sung during the march.

741. σχετλία τόλμης: καρτερικὴ τῆς τόλμης χάριν the schol., who therefore felt the gen. to be causal. The original meaning of σχέτλιος (from ἔχω) seems to have been "clinging to a thing," hence "persistent," "steadfast," "stubborn." The genitive may be really, as Earle suggests, a "gen. of part taken hold of," like the gen. with ἔχεσθαι.

743–4. χθόνιός θ' ἄδης ἑρμῆς τε δέχηθ' *B*. But Hermes χθόνιος (= ψυχαγωγός or ψυχοπομπός) is properly mentioned first, as Alcestis would meet him first and be guided by him down into the realm of Hades. Hence the other reading is preferable. παρεδρεύοις: the appropriate word, "be the chosen attendant"; προσεδρεύοις, the reading of L P, is obviously less apposite, though προσεδρεύω is an Euripidean word (Orest. 403).

747. The servant comes out of the door of the ξενών (i.e. probably the side-door to the right of the main entrance to the palace). The semi-comic nature of the following scene has often been remarked upon. Heracles is here the gluttonous hero of comedy; cf. Aristoph. Pax 741. ἀπὸ παντοίας χθονός: a very unusual expression, to which I have found no parallel elsewhere in the tragedians, "from every possible country." Aeschylus does not use παντοῖος: Sophocles has three cases, Euripides at least four.

749. ξένον: so Dobree for ξένου. The genitive would be a not impossible construction; but the prevailing usage favors the emendation, and the change is really very slight.

752. ἀμείψασθαι πύλας: "The proper meaning of the middle probably is, 'to have the position of the door changed with respect to oneself,' i.e. to have it behind, whereas it was just now in front" (Paley). ἀμείβεσθαί τι may mean "to pass beyond a thing" either *inwards* or *outwards*, and so either to *enter* or to *leave* it, according to the connection. Cf. the Homeric ἀμείψεται ἕρκος ὀδόντων, and Hesiod *Theog.* 749 f.

753. οὔτι: one is tempted to read οὐδέ, "he did not *even* receive the proffered cheer with proper moderation"; but the change is not absolutely necessary.

755. B has φέροιεν which is clearly a blunder. The speaker is himself one of the slaves in question.

756. ἐν χείρεσσι: so a (χείρεσι the other MSS.). Cobet and others long ago asserted that this epic form is out of place here in a trimeter and in a comic portion of the play. See Sel. Conj. for some of the emendations that have been suggested. But the epic form, as Jebb points out in his note on *Antig.* 1297, was probably used intentionally, to give a mock-heroic tone to the passage. Cf. ἐμοῖσιν in 793, γούνασι 947 (also in trimeters). κίσσινον: ivy wood was a favorite material for drinking-cups. Monk compares fr. 135, *Cycl.* 390, Hom. *Od.* IX. 346. Add Theoc. I. 26 ff., where there is an elaborate description of such a cup (κισσύβιον). See also Athenaeus XI. p. 476 f., 477 a, b.

757. μελαίνης μητρός: i.e. τῆς Γῆς. μέλαινα is a common epithet of the Earth, perhaps not so much from her color as from her position among the dark, mysterious chthonian divinities. εὔζωρον: "pure," "unmixed," Lat. *meracus*. Hesychius wrongly defines the word by εὐκέραστον; but Photius has rightly εὐζωρότερον, ἀκρατότερον. Suidas has both definitions. The derivation from (εὖ, ζωρός) and use of the word are both in favor of the signification "unmixed." It is a rare term. μέθυ: originally *honey*-wine, as the cognate words show, but used of wine in general from Homer down. See Brugmann, *Vergl. Gram.* II. p. 205. (Has the word any connection with Hebrew *meseq*? The resemblance of οἶνος and *yayin* has often been noted.)

759. μυρσίνης: so Canter for μυρσίνοις. See note on 172. On the use of the myrtle at symposia, see Guhl and Koner *Leben d. Griech. u. Röm.*⁶ p. 310. Myrtle chaplets were so much in demand at Athens that the flower-market was called αἱ μυρρίναι (see Aristoph. *Thesm.* 448).

760. ἄμουσ': "cognate" accus., like σεμνόν in 772. — The words δισσὰ... ἥδε are not in *L P* (in *L* a later hand has added them in the margin). They are not essential to the sense, and may well be an interpolation. I have bracketed them as suspicious.

761. ἐν Ἀδμήτου: sc. δόμῳ, as often.

764. τέγγοντες: best taken with ἐδείκνυμεν, "we did not let the guest see that we were shedding tears." Others take ὄμμα as direct object of ἐδείκνυμεν and also to be understood with τέγγοντες, "we did not show our faces (eyes) to the guest while we were weeping."

768. οὐδ' ἐξέτεινα χεῖρ': on gestures of mourning see Sittl *Gebärden d. Griech. u. Röm.* pp. 65 ff., where this passage should have been cited. The schol. compares Aesch. *Choeph.* 8 οὐδ' ἐξέτεινα χεῖρ' ἐπ' ἐκφορᾷ νεκροῦ. Monk cites Eur. *Suppl.* 772 ἀλλ' εἶμ' ἐπαρῶ χεῖρ' ἀπαντήσας νεκροῖς.

769 ff. A pleasing and characteristic touch. Such a state of things must have existed in many Greek households.

771. ὀργάς. Euripides is fond of the plural of ὀργή, using it nearly twenty times. Compare in English "whenever he falls into one of his rages."

773. οὗτος: used here in unceremonious address, as often. So *Hec.* 1127, 1280, *Hel.* 1627, *Or.* 1567, etc. **πεφροντικός**: this use of the perf. participle with verbs of looking is very rare in Attic, though not uncommon in late writers. See Jacobs' ed. of Philostratus p. 590 and Lobeck's *Phrynichus* p. 119 for examples. There seems to be no other case of the construction in Euripides.

775. εὐπροσηγόρῳ: a favorite Euripidean word; cf. *Hippol.* 95, *Herc. F.* 1284, *Suppl.* 869, fr. 1132, 45. It means properly "easy of address"; cf. Latin *adfabilis*, our "affable."

776. ἄνδρ' ἑταῖρον: so ἑταῖρος ἀνήρ in *Il.* XVII. 466, *Od.* VIII. 584. The presence of an apparently pleonastic ἀνήρ in such cases is probably due to the fact that the other substantive was once an adjective. So ἑταῖρος (for ἐτάριος) probably originally meant "following"; see *Bezzenberger's Beiträge* IV. p. 327. Traces of the adj. use of ἑταῖρος may still be seen in classic Greek, e.g. Plat. *Gorg.* 487 D τοῖς σαυτοῦ ἑταιροτάτοις.

777. συνωφρυωμένῳ: Nauck would read συνωφρυωμένος, which would be more idiomatic; but the change is unnecessary. If authors always used the most idiomatic constructions, their works would be "like plum-puddings made only of plums," as some one has well put it.

778. θυραίου... ἔχων: these words recur in 1012, which is probably an interpolation from this line, or is due to a mistake of the same kind as gave us 312 (1012 − 778 = 234 = 6 pages of 39 lines each — a singular coincidence if accidental. See note on 312).

779. καὶ σοφώτερος: a sly hit. Heracles, though somewhat exhilarated, is not by any means drunk; and his speech is consistent enough from one point of view.

780. οἶδας: Nauck (*Eur. Stud.* II. p. 71) argues at great length that we should read οἶσθας: but in this passage, Athenaeus IV. 175 d. (a fragment of Philemon, 44 Kock), and Xen. *Mem.* IV. 6, 6 the MSS. *all* have οἶδας. See also Rutherford *New Phryn.* pp. 227–8, who cites the testimony of the grammarians. He observes: "Nauck is rash in the extreme to alter οἶδας to οἶσθας in *Alc.* 780. . . . There is, in fine, not one assured instance of the form οἶσθας in Attic of any period."

781. οἶμαι μὲν οὔ: note the colloquial tone. Plutarch (*Consol. ad Apoll.* 107 B and C) has δοκῶ for οἶμαι, doubtless quoting from memory. — This scene where Heracles expounds his easy philosophy is delicious. Wecklein calls attention to the rhymes 782–5, which heighten the humorous effect.

782. Proverbial; cf. Soph. *El.* 1173 (cited by Jerram), Menand. *Monostich.* 69.

783. A favorite Euripidean cadence; cf. 848. Plutarch has ἔστιν αὐτῶν, probably through confusion with some other line which was also in his mind.

784. τὴν (ἡμέραν) αὔριον μέλλουσαν εἶναι: cf. Soph. *Trach.* 945 οὐ γὰρ ἔσθ' ἥ γ' αὔριον, Alexis fr. 241 K. Through this ellipsis of ἡμέρα, αὔριον was fairly on the way to become a true feminine substantive. In the line in our text it would be easy (though, I think, needless) to read τὴν ἡμέραν μέλλουσαν and take αὔριον as a gloss which has displaced the true reading.

785. τὸ τῆς τύχης: an intentionally vague expression. Elmsley proposed τά for τό: the plural is more common, but that is not a decisive reason for the change. προβήσεται: cf. *Med.* 907 καὶ μὴ προβαίη μεῖζον ἢ τὸ νῦν κακόν, *Orest.* 511 πέρας δὴ ποῖ κακῶν προβήσεται; and esp. *Med.* 1117 καραδοκῶ τἀκεῖθεν οἷ προβήσεται. *Hippol.* 342 ποῖ προβήσεται λόγος; ib. 936 φεῦ τῆς βροτείας· ποῖ προβήσεται; φρενός may also be compared. The sense must be: "for it is uncertain how far fortune will proceed," i.e. what will be its outcome. Wecklein would read 'ποβήσεται: but the emendation, though undeniably elegant, is not, I think, necessary.

786. ἁλίσκεται τέχνῃ: cf. fr. 811 τἀφανῆ | τεκμηρίοισιν εἰκότως ἁλίσκεται. Pflugk cites Soph. *O. T.* 110 τὸ δὲ ζητούμενον | ἁλωτόν, *Phil.* 863 τὸ δ' ἁλώσιμον ἐμᾷ φροντίδι, παῖ, πόνος ὁ μὴ φοβῶν κράτιστος.

790. τὴν πλεῖστον ἡδίστην: cf. Soph. *Phil.* 631 τῆς πλεῖστον ἐχθίστης ἐμοὶ . . . ἐχίδνης, *O. C.* 743 εἰ μὴ πλεῖστον ἀνθρώπων ἔφυν | κάκιστος, and from Eur. himself *Med.* 1323 ὦ μέγιστον ἐχθίστη γύναι, *Hippol.* 1421 μάλιστα φίλτατος.

792. ταῦτα: as Hermann pointed out, Markland's conjecture πάντα is quite needless; ταῦτα = "these of yours."

795. πίῃ: πία MSS. πύλας: the MSS. have τύχας, except that in α the first hand has written in the margin γρ. πύλας. The schol. says: γράφεται πύλας ἵν' ᾖ· ὑπερβὰς τὰς πύλας· εἰ δὲ τύχας, καταφρονήσας. I should be inclined to read τύχας were it not for the fact that the words τάσδ'... πυκασθείς are almost certainly an interpolation from 829 and 832. The interpolator wrote πύλας, as in 829. Then some one, wishing to avoid a repetition and obtain a more appropriate meaning, emended πύλας to τύχας. The change then reacted in turn on 829, where a has τύχας πύλας by the first hand. The expression ὑπερβαλὼν τύχας can hardly be paralleled, and I believe that Wecklein is right in bracketing τάσδ'... πυκασθείς.

796. ὁθούνεκα: = ὡς or ὅτι, as not infrequently in the tragedians.

797. φρενῶν: so *L P*; the other MSS. have κακοῦ. Of the two readings φρενῶν is clearly the better; but neither is satisfactory, though Jerram compares *Hippol.* 983 ξύστασις φρενῶν. The view of Kirchhoff, that there was a lacuna in the archetype at the end of 795, which was filled out in different ways by grammarians or copyists, is extremely probable. The true reading cannot be restored with certainty; Nauck's τρόπον is very plausible, though I have not ventured to receive it into the text.

798. A bold nautical metaphor; μεθορμίζειν, "to shift (a vessel) from one anchorage to another," is repeatedly used by Eur. in this figurative way (*Bacch.* 931 ἐξ ἕδρας μεθώρμισα [τὸν πλόκαμον], cf. *Med.* 258, 443). πίτυλος: the plash of wine poured into the cup; but when used in connection with μεθορμιεῖ the nautical meaning of the term would instantly occur to an Athenian hearer. Hence I must agree with Earle in regarding σκύφον as an ἀπροσδόκητον added at the last moment by way of joke, though Mr. England (*Class. Rev.* IX. p. 52) seems to hold a different opinion. Euripides uses πίτυλος of the plashing of oars (*I. T.* 1050, 1346, cf. *Troad.* 1123), of the sound of falling tears (*Hippol.* 1464), of the noise of beating with the hands (*Tro.* 1236), of the crash of spears striking in the onset (*Heracl.* 834), of the sudden and violent impulses of madness (*I. T.* 307, *Her. F.* 1189) or panic (*Her. F.* 816). Difficult is *Troad.* 817, where δυοῖν πιτύλοιν is generally taken as meaning "two encounters" or the like; cf. *Heracl.* 834.

799. Some English poet has the line "For mortal thoughts beseem a mortal mind"; but I have been unable to find the source of the quotation.

800. Earle calls attention to the sigmatism of this line. Note also the repetition of συνωφρυωμένοις (cf. 777). The effect is to give the words a highly contemptuous tone.

801. ὡς... κριτῇ: quoted by the schol. on Soph. *Aj.* 395 to explain the use of ὡς ἐμοί in that passage.

802. This line has *two* substituted dactyls, showing how far Euripides deviated from the metrical usage of Sophocles and Aeschylus. "Quid quod Alcestis, quae inter fabulas est summa metri severitate compositas, versum continet, qualis 802 ... quo loco ne id quidem excusationi est quod vocabula, quae initium efficiant versus, arcte inter se cohaereant? Sed ne cui suspicio incidat, opus esse corrigi illum versum, tenendum est, Herculem illa pronuntiare verba paullo liberiore utentem metro" (Mueller *De ped. sol.* p. 98). That the line is not corrupt is sufficiently shown by the other cases of resolution cited by Mueller *l. s. c.* See also Rümpel *Die Auflösungen im Trimeter d. Euripides Philol.* XXIV. pp. 407-21.

803. ἐπιστάμεσθα: so L a, rightly, as the metre shows. The other MSS. have ἐπιστάμεθα.

807 ff. The στιχομυθία which follows has given a great deal of trouble. As far as 809 everything seems to be clear; but with 810 the difficulty begins. Prinz regards 810-11 as spurious, without assigning any adequate ground for doing so. They are probably genuine; but it cannot be denied that when they follow 809 (as in the MSS.) they occasion difficulty. As Nauck points out (*Eur. Stud.* II. p. 75), Euripides would never have been so careless as to let 811 immediately precede 812, leaving it to the reader to divine that οἰκεῖος ἦν refers to the dead person and οὐκ ἔφραζε to Admetus. By removing 810 and 811 a perfect connection is restored at 809-12. But what is to be done with 810-11? Nauck would insert them immediately after 813. But 813 and 814 give an excellent connection as they stand. It is the ominous phrase δεσποτῶν κακά that makes Heracles observe ὅδ' οὐ θυραίων πημάτων ἄρχει λόγος. (Cf. *Her. F.* 537-8.) On the other hand, where can the indignant question 810 come in so fittingly as after the broad hint in 817 that the guest's presence is undesirable? I am therefore strongly in favor of the arrangement in the text, which is due to Wecklein — all the more because I had come to the same conclusion quite independently after long and careful study of the passage.

812. ἔφραζε: for the use of the imperf. (almost = οὐκ ἐβούλετο φράζειν), see Goodwin *M. and T.* 38.

813. χαίρων ἴθ': a polite intimation that the conversation is to be dropped.

815. τί ... σ' ὁρῶν: σε ... ὁρῶν L P, a much inferior reading, as it loses the force of the expressive τί. — The implication is, " (Yes), for had they been θυραῖα, I should not have been displeased," etc.

816. ἀλλ' ἦ πέπονθα δεῖν': a stereotyped phrase expressing surprise and vexation at an unpleasant discovery. So *I. A.* 847 (cited by Earle); cf. *Bacch.* 642, *Or.* 1616. δεινὰ πάσχειν seems to have been almost a slang expression; cf. Aristoph. *Ran.* 252, *Eccl.* 650, etc. Euripides is excessively fond of the adj. δεινός.

817. ἐν δέοντι: cf. *Hippol.* 923, *Med.* 1277, *Or.* 212.

810. οὔνεκ': οὔνεκα is the *only* form found in Sophocles, and is the preponderating form in Aesch. and Eur. (see Kühner-Blass II. p. 251, 10). Moreover it (I am speaking of the *preposition*) is attested by at least *one* Attic inscription (C. I. A. IV. b, 491, 8) of the fifth century. (C. I. A. IV. b, 422 No. 4 is doubtful, as there Kirchhoff believes the word to be a conjunction and the lacuna makes it impossible to decide the question. See Meisterhans p. 177, 25 and note.) Hence those who would change it to εἵνεκα (as Prinz does in this instance) are probably in the wrong. εὖ πάσχειν: "be hospitably treated." Nauck would read εὖ πράσσειν: but his objection, that πάσχειν cannot refer to "das innere Behagen," amounts to nothing; for it is not "das *innere* Behagen" that Euripides means.

811. This line is a most conspicuous example of the power of the Greek particles, a power which so often may be felt but cannot be expressed in translation. οἰκεῖος : θυραῖος (so *a*) is in my opinion a mere guess, though Lascaris, Matthiae, Hermann, Woolsey,* Verrall and others prefer it. The sarcasm would undeniably be more forcible with that reading; but the authority of *a* cannot stand for an instant against *B L P*. The schol. says οὐκ ἦν ξένη, ἀλλὰ πάνυ οἰκεῖα, which may look either way. — The place which in the text is occupied by 810-11 is filled in the MSS. by the two bracketed lines which follow (818-19). These are open to two objections: they break the στιχομυθία, and the schol. has on 820 the note: ταῦτα δὲ τὰ τρία⟨ιαμβεῖα⟩ ἔν τισιν οὐκ ἔγκειται. Hence Kirchhoff rejects 818-20 as an interpolation; while Nauck would reject 816-19, reading τέσσαρα instead of τρία in the scholium. The whole trouble is, I think, due to 818-19. Wilamowitz and Klotz defend them; but surely it is not accident that almost at the very place where the στιχομυθία is interrupted the schol. remarks that three lines are not found in some copies. Either the lines are an interpolation, or they were arbitrarily rejected by some ancient scholars. I firmly believe them to be spurious. 820, on the other hand, makes a good connection with 811, and should probably be retained. I conceive the history of the passage to have been about as follows: 810-11 originally stood after 817. By a copyist's blunder they were torn from their proper context and inserted after 809. Then, observing the lacuna thus left, some one composed 818-19 and inserted them in the gap; and, being either careless or ignorant, he interrupted the στιχομυθία. In composing the two lines he probably had in mind 215-17, 427 or 923, or all of them. The τρία of the schol. is then a mistake for δύο. Hannemueller's proposal to reject 817-20 and read πέπονθε δεινά τις in 816 is ingenious but futile, as the corrective μὲν οὖν in 821 is fatal to it.

820. The text is that of *L P*; *a* has τι φροῦδον ἤ, *B* τι φροῦδον γένος ἤ (γένος deleted by the first hand). The reading of *L P*, with its *constructio ad sensum*, is bolder and more characteristic; and τι φροῦδον is probably due to some grammarian who wished to bring the gender of τις in accord with that of τέκνων. The γένος of *B* (whence Earle conjectures μῶν ἢ γένους τι φροῦδον) is, if I mistake not, the remnant of a grammatical gloss on the gender (γένος) of φροῦδος (or φροῦδον). The schol. says: ἆρα, φησίν, ἀφανὴς ἐγένετό τις τῶν παιδῶν ἢ ὁ γέρων πατὴρ ἀπέθανεν. (Note that he says γέρων πατήρ, not πατὴρ γέρων with Wecklein; though he may have transposed.)

826. ᾐσθόμην . . . ἰδών: "I noticed that I saw." So England; this is, I think, better than to take ᾐσθόμην and ἰδών separately, with Earle.

---

* Woolsey's objection to οἰκεῖος, that "it supersedes all further inquiry," is obviated by Wecklein's arrangement of the lines, as Heracles *at once infers* (820) from the servant's words that Admetus has lost a near relative.

827. πρόσωπον: probably corrupt (Prinz). Those who retain it explain it as referring to the expression of the face, like Latin *vultus* (so Earle, who compares *Ion* 925, and others). But surely the order—eyes, hair, expression—is very odd; though cf. *Med.* 1071 f. (χείρ, κάρα, σχῆμα, πρόσωπον). In place of πρόσωπον we should expect either (1) an adjective qualifying κουράν, e.g. Herwerden's δυσπρόσωπον, which Wecklein accepts, or (2) a noun denoting dress or general appearance, e.g. Stadtmüller and Mekler's πεπλώματ'. None of the conjectures that have been made seems really satisfactory (see Sel. Conj.), πρόσοψιν (cf. *Or.* 388) among the rest.

828. κῆδος: euphemistic for νεκρόν.

829. βίᾳ δὲ θυμοῦ: "against my inclination," like βίᾳ φρενῶν. τάσδ'... πύλας: here these words appear in their proper connection. See note on 795.

831. κᾆτα κωμάζω: so *a* (except for the ι subscript); *B* has κατακωμάζω, *L* κᾆτ' ἐκώμαζον, *P* κἀπεκώμαζον. "The preceding imperfects seem to have caused the alteration of κωμάζω—which is properly used as denoting an action not fully ended—into ἐκώμαζον, and the other reading(s) then easily arose" (Woolsey). The source of *L P* probably had κᾆτ' ἐκώμαζον: the reading of *P* is due to the common mistake of π for τ.

832. πυκασθείς: note the contemptuous force, "*loaded* with garlands." See note on 796. σοῦ τὸ φράσαι: there is much doubt about the construction of these words. At least three possibilities arise: (1) ἀλλά may be corrupt for some verb of blaming or wondering; (2) σοῦ may be "exclamatory genitive" and τὸ μὴ φράσαι the articular inf. used in exclamations (*M. and T.* 805), as is held by Monk, Paley, Weil, Wecklein, Earle and others, probably with reason (cf. *Med.* 1051 f.); (3) ἦν may be understood, "it was your fault not to tell," as the schol. and Woolsey explain it. F. W. Schmidt's τόδ' ἦν for τὸ μή and Matthiae's μοι for μή are ingenious but not convincing.

833. προσκειμένου: Scaliger's certain emendation for προκειμένου. See 551 and note.

834. ποῦ νιν: ποῖ νιν Monk; but εὑρήσω, not μολών, predominates in the writer's mind.* In *Hippol.* 1153 ποῖ (ποῦ *A*, πῇ *Christus patiens* 1863) γῆς ἄνακτα τῆσδε Θησέα μολών | εὕροιμ' ἄν and Soph. *Aj.* 403 ποῖ μολὼν μενῶ the participle, on the other hand, stands nearer to the adverb than the verb does, and so predominates. The order is significant.

835. Λάρισαν: λάρισσαν the MSS.; but the grammarians and inscriptions show conclusively that the form with one σ is the correct one. See Nauck *Eur. Stud.* II. pp. 77 ff.; Meisterhans p. 75, 12. ξεστόν: i.e. made of polished stone. Cf. *Hel.* 986 τῷδ' ἐπὶ ξεστῷ τάφῳ. Such monuments must have been familiar to every spectator, common as they were in Athens. Nauck's χωστόν for ξεστόν is quite unnecessary. As Earle well observes, "the objection that any proper monument could hardly be set up at such short notice is of little moment; for the poet intended his audience to think of the lovely sculptures

---

* See on the other side Wecklein *Beiträge zur Kritik des Euripides* p. 540.

of the Ceramicus, situate ἐπὶ τοῦ καλλίστου προαστείου τῆς πόλεως (Thuc. II. 34, 5)." Besides, when a monarch commands, work is done quickly. ἐκ προαστίου: the metre requires the form without ε in this place, Pindar fr. 129, 2, Soph. *El.* 1431 (cf. Soph. fr. 647 γῆς προαστίας) and Polemo *Anth. Pal.* XI. 38 (see Nauck *Eur. Stud.* II. p. 77). Nauck regards προάστιον as the correct form of the word, and προάστειον as an erroneous form which was perhaps introduced under the influence of ἀστεῖος. There seems to be no passage where the metre requires the form with ε; but Suidas (*s. v.*) and Choeroboscus (Cramer's *Anecd.* II. p. 250) speak of προάστειον as the regular form, and Suidas mentions the Sophoclean usage as exceptional. This may mean merely that the grammarians in introducing the form προάστειον found that the passages from Sophocles would not fall into line, and so one of them wrote the note in question. The change from ι to ει is much less natural than that from ει to ι, but the analogy of ἀστεῖος may be sufficient to account for it. The question must for the present remain *sub judice.* See Lobeck *Paralip.* p. 253, where the grammarians are cited. The metrical inscriptions give no help in this case. The force of the phrase ἐκ προαστίου is also in doubt. What relation does ἐκ here express? (A) Some connect ἐκ προαστίου with κατόψει, "You will see the tomb *from the suburb.*" (B) Others still take ἐκ = ἔξω or ἐκτός (so the schol. and Jerram). Others (C) take it in the sense of "next to," "adjoining" (so Bauer-Wecklein). Others again (D) suppose an ellipsis of ἰὼν εἰς τὸν ἀγρόν or the like (so Paley). The true explanation is, if I mistake not, that of England (E), who says: "Is it not better to take it as = ἐν προαστίῳ, as it were 'looking at you from the suburb'"? As so often, the Greek prefers the point of view of motion to that of rest. The speaker thinks of the image as coming (as it were) from the suburb to meet the eye of Heracles. See for an excellent statement of this and allied uses of ἐκ Matthiae *Greek Gr.* (Eng. trans.[5]) § 596. Euripides even uses the ἐκ construction with verbs of standing and sitting; see Jebb's elaborate note on *Antig.* 411, and cf. Donkin in the *Classical Rev.* IX. p. 350. The tomb would naturally be *in* the suburb, like those in the Ceramicus, which the poet doubtless had in mind. As far as sense and metre go, Euripides *might* have written here ἐν προαστίῳ, though it is not probable that he did so.

837. Exit Servant. καὶ χεῖρ': *a* has ψυχή τ'; an inferior reading probably due to the influence of *Or.* 466 ὦ τάλαινα καρδία ψυχή τ' ἐμή.

839. Ἠλεκτρυόνος ἐγείνατ': ἠλεκτρύονος *C* (which, however, is of slight authority), ἐγείνατ' Blomfield. *a* has ἠλεκτρύωνος, the other MSS. ἠλεκτρυῶνος: all have γείνατ'. The epic form γείνατ' can scarcely be right, as in trimeters the omission of the augment occurs very rarely, and then only in the beginning of the verse. Hence it seems necessary to read ἐγείνατ', and this in turn necessitates reading Ἠλεκτρύονος. The usual form of the gen. is that in ω (cf. *Herc. F.* 17 Ἠλεκτρύωνα); but in Apollod. *Bibl.* 2, 4, 5, 6 the MSS. have the form with *o*. See also Nauck *Eur. Stud.* II. p. 78, Kühner-Blass I. p. 476 (with the "Nachträge" *ad loc.*). Wilamowitz has proposed the very ingenious and elegant conjecture Ἠλεκτρυώνη 'γεῖνατ', which *may* be the true reading; but the probabilities seem to me to favor Ἠλεκτρυόνος.

841. κάς τόνδ' ἱδρῦσαι δόμον: εἰς because of the motion implied in ἱδρῦσαι, "(bring and) set down." Cf. *Ion* 1573, *Hel.* 46.

842. ὑπουργῆσαι χάριν: Monk compares Aesch. *Prom.* 635 σὸν ἔργον, Ἰοῖ, ταῖσδ' ὑπουργῆσαι χάριν, Soph. fr. 315 ἢ φῂς ὑπομνῶς ἀνθυπουργῆσαι χάριν.

843. μελάμπτερον: the MSS. have μελάμπεπλον, but, as Musgrave long ago pointed out, the schol. seems to have μελάμπτερον, for he says: εἰδωλοποιεῖται μελαίνας πτέρυγας ἔχων ὁ Θάνατος. Μελάμπεπλον is appropriate enough; but μελάμπτερον is the finer and more poetic term. Cf. *Hec.* 71, 705, Hor. *Sat.* II. 1, 58. Besides, as μελάμπεπλος occurs in this play (according to one reading) in 427 and in the interpolated line 819, it might easily have displaced the other word.

845. About this line much critical controversy has raged. The older edd. retained the MSS. reading πίνοντα, and took προσφαγμάτων as "partitive genitive" with it. Then arose the question why Heracles expects to find Thanatos *drinking* of the blood-offerings. To this various answers have been given. Koechly (*Litt.-hist. Taschenb. von Prutz* 1847 p. 381) suggested that the poet merely intended to produce a comic effect, adding that the guess of Heracles is "eine köstliche Vermuthung für einen Trinker von Profession"! Much more plausible is the view of J. Lessing (*De Mortis apud veteres figura* p. 25 note 5) that the poet had in mind the passage of the Homeric Νέκυια (*Od.* XI. 23 ff.) where the shades taste the blood of the victim. The habit thus attributed to the shades might well be extended to the ἄναξ νεκρῶν, Thanatos (cf. Rohde *Psyche* p. 540 note 1). F. W. Schmidt (*Sat. Crit.* p. 29; cf. his *Krit. Stud.* II. p. 24) objects that πίνοντα would assume that the burning of the body was already in progress. But Heracles has just learned that Alcestis is dead; he has not seen Admetus for some time, and knows that the funeral-rites are going on (θάπτει 834). Why then should he *not* suppose that "der Akt der Leichenverbrennung schon im Gange war"? Besides, even if the objection were just, a poet does not always speak by the card. Schmidt conjectures πεινῶντα, "hungry for" the offerings, which is accepted by Prinz and Bauer-Wecklein. Nauck, Weil and Earle retain πίνοντα: Dindorf conjectured ἴζοντα, Hartung πίτνοντα (!). The schol. read πίνοντα, which I believe to be sound. προσφαγμάτων: for the part. gen. after πίνω Weil compares *Od.* XXII. 11 ὄφρα πίοι οἴνοιο. So also *Od.* XV. 373, XI. 96 (in the very passage which, according to Lessing, Euripides had in mind). The force of προ in πρόσφαγμα is much disputed. Some think it refers to the offering of the blood-sacrifice *in front of* the tomb, others that a πρόσφαγμα was so called because offered *in behalf of* some one, others still that the sacrifice was given this name because it *preceded* the offerings of milk, honey and wine which were made to the dead. I have little doubt that the term originally denoted a *preliminary* sacrifice of some kind and then was gradually made to include other kinds of blood-offerings.

846. λοχαίας: this reading was recovered from the schol. (γράφεται λο-χ⟨α⟩ίας) and the cod. Flor. of the *Etymol. Mag.*, where the line is cited thus (with wrong division of words): κἄνπερ λοχαία σαυτὸν ἐξέδρας. The MSS. have λοχήσας. Cf. fr. 727 b, where σῖτον λοχαῖον is used of grain in which one can lie in wait (ἐν ᾧ ἔστι λοχῆσαι, *Etym. Mag. l. s. c.*).

847. περιβάλω: so Monk; περιβαλῶ of *L P* is due to some one who took both this verb and μάρψω to be fut. indic. The other MSS. have περιβαλών, which is clearly wrong, as the preceding δέ shows. Nauck would read τε for δέ: but in such cases δέ has a slight *climactic* rather than adversative force, almost = "and what is more," though weaker. ἐμαῖν: Nauck suspects this word to be corrupt. *a* has ἐμά by the first hand, which the second has corrected to ἐμάν and the third to ἐμαῖν. There is probably not sufficient ground for emendation.

849. πρὶν ... μεθῇ: *M.* and *T.* 648.

851. αἱματηρὸν πέλανον: here not of a sacrificial cake, but of the clotted blood of the offering. Cf. *I. T.* 300, *Rhes.* 430, *Or.* 220, etc. τῶν κάτω: explained by Κόρης and ἄνακτος, which are in "partitive apposition" with it; τὴν κάτω (sc. ὁδόν), the reading of the Aldine, is a neat but needless emendation.

852. *B* has ἀνηλίου: but ἀνηλίους, the reading of the other MSS., is shown by the position and sense to be right. Cf. *Herc. F.* 607.

854. Wecklein compares *Il.* I. 441 πατρὶ φίλῳ ἐν χερσὶ τίθει.

856. πεπληγμένος: πεπλεγμένος has been conjectured, but lacks MS. authority. Cf. 405 and *Herc. F.* 1393.

857. F. W. Schmidt thinks this line is spurious, and calls attention to the repetition of γενναῖος three lines below. But Greek writers were less sensitive to blemishes of this sort than we are.

859. ἐλάδ' *B*, obviously a mere "copyist's blunder." The Attic inscriptions show that during the classical period the gemination of consonants was pretty carefully observed.

860 f. Exit Heracles, to the left. Admetus and the chorus return by the same way by which they left the scene at 740 ff. Admetus sings a short anapaestic lament, followed by a responsive song between him and the chorus. The whole scene from 861–934 is a κομμός: see Aristotle *Poet.* 12, 3.

862. χήρων μελάθρων: cf. in English "her widowed couch." αἰαῖ: as to the number and form of the interjections there is much difference in the MSS. Thus in 860 *l* has added a second ἰώ, and so Hermann and Earle read. In 862 *B* has μοι only once; at the end of the line, too, there is disagreement (see Critical Apparatus). The reading in the text is that of Prinz and Nauck; Wecklein omits αἰαῖ altogether, Hermann and Earle double it. The arrangement of the anapaests, too, differs in different editions; the text follows Prinz.

863. πᾷ: restored by Porson (see his note on *Hec.* 1062). *l* has πῇ, the other MSS. ποῖ. The adverb of rest, not that of motion, is required; and πῇ would be quite out of place in a lyrical passage and surrounded by Doric forms (cf. ὀλοίμαν just below).

864. The same question occurs in *Med.* 97, *Suppl.* 796, *Rhes.* 751. On the construction (originally a deliberative question, implying a wish, "how can I" = "would that I could") see *M. and T.* 728.

865. ἔτεκεν: this, the reading of L P, is confirmed by the metre.

866. κείνων ἔραμαι: to restore the symmetry of the clauses F. W. Schmidt would read νεκύων ἄγαμαι. There seems, however, not to be sufficient reason for any change. The repetition κείνων ... κεῖν' expresses very forcibly the speaker's yearning, and κείνων (euphemistic) is no more vague or weak than κἀκεῖ in 744. Cf. Aristoph. *Vesp.* 751 κείνων ἔραμαι, κεῖθι γενοίμαν, which looks like a parody, or at least a reminiscence, of this passage.

868. αὐγάς: see note on 667.

869. πόδα πεζεύων: a striking example of the "cognate" accusative. I have not been able to find another instance of πόδα πεζεύειν.

870-71. A difficult passage. The schol. gives two explanations: τοιοῦτον ἐνέχυρον ὑπὲρ ἐμοῦ, ἵνα κἀγὼ ἀποθάνω. λυπούμενος γὰρ δι' αὐτὴν ἀπόλλυμαι, and ὅμηρον: ἐνέχυρον. τοῦ δὲ ζῆν φησιν ὅμηρον αὐτῷ γεγονέναι τὴν Ἄλκηστιν· ἀντὶ γὰρ αὐτοῦ δέδοται τῷ Ἅιδῃ. The former is, I think, the correct one, as ἀποσυλήσας shows. Admetus regards Alcestis as his pledge or security for living. But Thanatos has robbed him of this security and has delivered it to Hades; so that Admetus has now no guarantee that his life will continue to be spared. This is, of course, illogical, as it is the *death* of Alcestis which is the real security. Admetus, like most weak characters, would fain "have his cake and eat it too." If the other explanation were correct, ἀποσυλήσας would be out of place, for Thanatos would only be *doing his duty* in taking away Alcestis and handing her over to Hades. ἀποσυλήσας implies violence or fraud, and hence could not be used of a mere legal transfer. The figure is that of stealing hostages from an enemy.

872. κεῦθος: except in fr. 781, 63 this word seems not to occur elsewhere in Euripides. Sophocles has it once (*Antig.* 818), Aeschylus twice (*Eum.* 1013, *Suppl.* 714).

873. Hermann read here πεπονθώς, in agreement with the subject of βᾶθι, while Musgrave read πέπονθάς γ'. These changes they found necessary because they read in 890 πέρας δ' οὐδὲν with L P. But if we accept there πέρας δέ γ' (so *a*, and *B* except for the division of δέ γ'), there is no need of changing πέπονθας. (ἀλγέων in 890 is to be scanned with synizesis.)

874. δι' ὀδύνας ἔβας: cf. *El.* 1210, *Phoen.* 1561, cited by Monk. So in English "to pass through suffering," with a similar underlying *material* conception.

877. This line is certainly corrupt, as we have only -πον to correspond to -ζει φαν- of 894. The difficulty lies, in all probability, in ἄντα (so the MSS.). Hartung conjectured σ' ἔναντα, which is probably right. See Sel. Conj. for other emendations. Cf. *Or.* 1478 ἔναντα δ᾽ ἦλθεν, Soph. *Antig.* 1299 τὸν δ᾽ ἔναντα προσβλέπω νεκρόν.

878. ἤλκωσεν: a very strong word. Cf. *Suppl.* 223 (which, however, is not quite a parallel case). *B* has here ὁμοῦ φρέν᾽ ἤλκωσε, with wrong division of words and loss of a syllable and a ν. The value of that MS. is greatly diminished by the *extreme* carelessness with which it was written.

879-80. The construction of ἁμαρτεῖν and ἀλόχου has been much disputed. At least *seven* views have been advanced: (1) we may punctuate ἔμνησας ὅ μου φρένας ἤλκωσεν (τί γὰρ ἀνδρὶ κακὸν μεῖζον;), ἁμαρτεῖν πιστῆς ἀλόχου (so Schaefer); (2) we may suppose an ellipsis of ἤ; (3) we may take ἁμαρτεῖν as = τοῦ ἁμαρτεῖν (so Wuestemann and Earle); (4) we may suppose an ellipsis of τούτου, with which ἁμαρτεῖν is in "explanatory apposition" (so Wecklein); (5) we may assume an inversion of the clause for ἁμαρτεῖν πιστῆς ἀλόχου — τί μεῖζον κακόν; (so Hermann and Paley); (6) we may render "*quid enim tristius est ad amittendum quam fida uxor*"? taking ἀλόχου as gen. after μεῖζον (so Hermann formerly); (7) we may take τί directly with ἁμαρτεῖν, "What loss is greater than (the loss of) a faithful wife"? (so Bauer). Explanation (1) is flat in the extreme; (2) and (3) are, I believe, impossible. I have not been able to find any instance of a simple infinitive after a comparative without ἤ or τοῦ. Verse 11 ὃν θανεῖν ἐρρυσάμην, is different, as there is no comparative and θανεῖν is *not* for τοῦ θανεῖν (see *M. and T.* 807). (4) and (5) are harsh, and the same may be said of (7). I believe that (6), which Hermann proposed and then retracted, is substantially correct. Render: "What is worse (lit. 'a greater evil') for a man to lose (ἁμαρτεῖν epexegetical inf., 'as to losing it') than a trusty wife?" Cf. in English "A good wife is *a bad thing to lose.*" The only alternative that I can see is to boldly emend τί γὰρ to τίνος and render "What is there the loss of which (lit. 'losing what') is a greater evil than (to lose) a faithful wife?" πιστῆς ἀλόχου being for τοῦ πιστῆς ἀλόχου ἁμαρτεῖν (*comparatio compendiaria*). But probably the change is needless. πιστῆς: so *L P a*, and Stobaeus *Flor.* 69, 12. This is clearly better than φιλίας of *B*, which comes from 876 φιλίας ἀλόχου. μή ποτε ... ὤφελον: the view that in this construction "μή originally belonged to the inf. and afterward came to negative the whole expression" (*M. and T.* 736) seems improbable. The position of μή is against it, and besides does a case like ὤφελε μὴ τοῦτο ποιεῖν, "he ought not to be doing this," ever occur in classic Greek? Cf. *Il.* XVIII. 367. Of course, cases like εἴθ᾽ ὤφελε μὴ γενέσθαι (where μή and γενέσθαι form *one idea*) do occur (e.g. *Med.* 1). The other alternative, that μή was prefixed after the original meaning of ὤφελον was obscured and it came to be looked upon as a real wish-construction, has the analogy of εἴθε and εἰ γάρ with ὤφελον in its favor, and is probably the correct view.

883. μία γὰρ ψυχή: this order of the words (so *B a L*) is certainly right; ψυχῇ γὰρ μιᾷ (*sic*), the reading of *P*, does not suit the metre, and ψυχῇ δὲ μιᾷ (*sic*), that of *l*, is wrong, as the explanatory γάρ is needed, and besides has too slight MSS. authority. τῆς ὕπερ ἀλγεῖν: "The use of the verb ὑπεραλγέω with a genitive, 'to grieve for or because of a thing,' is attested by the Greek lexicons from Stephanus down. Only four passages, however, are cited as examples of this usage until we come down to late writers. These are: *Alcestis* 883, Hippol. 260 τῆσδ' ὑπεραλγῶ, *Antig.* 630 ἀπάτης λεχέων ὑπεραλγῶν, Aristoph. *Aves* 466 οὕτως ὑμῶν ὑπεραλγῶ. It is clear at a glance that in all these cases the verb follows the genitive, so that it is perfectly possible to read ὕπερ with anastrophe. Hence they by no means prove that the compound verb ὑπεραλγεῖν was used by classical writers with a genitive in this sense. While I will not venture to assert that it was never so used by them, I have not been able to find a certain instance" (Ed. in *Harvard Studies* VII. p. 221). There is certainly none in Homer, Hesiod, Pindar or the tragedians and comedians.

885-6. Blomfield compared *Il.* X. 63 καὶ θαλάμους κεραϊζομένους. θανάτοις: Seidler long ago pointed out that Euripides often uses the plural of θάνατος when speaking of a violent or premature death.

887-8. ἀτέκνοις ἀγάμοις τ': it is hard to decide between the dative, which is the reading of *L P*, and the accus., which is that of the other family. The accus. is grammatically the *difficilior lectio*, and as it is supported by the schol., I should be inclined to accept it were it not for the fact that we have ἀγάμους ἀτέκνους τε in 882, which might so easily have affected the reading in 887-8. Most edd. accept the accusative.

889. δυσπάλαιστος: so *Suppl.* 1108 ὦ δυσπάλαιστον γῆρας, Aesch. *Choeph.* 673, *Suppl.* 451.

890. *L P* have δ' οὐδέν: see note on 873. δέ γ' οὐδέν is probably right; "setzest du doch deinen Thränen keine Grenze" (Wecklein). δ' ἔτ' οὐδέν has occurred to me as a possible reading. τιθεῖς: see note on τιθεῖς in 57. With the whole line cf. *Andr.* 1217 οὐκ ἔχων πέρας κακῶν.

892-3. Cf. 416 f., where the chorus use the same hackneyed means of consolation.

894. πιέζει: cf. *Suppl.* 249 πιέζειν τὴν τύχην ἡμᾶς λίαν. θνατῶν: so *L*; the other MSS. have θνητῶν. Cf. τύχα in 889.

896. τῶν ὑπὸ γαῖαν: sc. οἰχομένων. Monk wished to read γαίας against the MSS., but the accus. is more idiomatic. The idea of motion was present in the poet's mind. Cf. *Hec.* 147 τοὺς θ' ὑπὸ γαῖαν (so the MSS., γαίας Porson).

897. ῥῖψαι: for this intransitive use, cf. *Cycl.* 166 ῥίψει τ' ἐς ἄλμην λευκάδος πέτρας ἄπο (cited by Monk); also *Hel.* 1325, Theognis 176, Xen. *Cyneg.* 9, 20 *ad fin.* Jerram compares Milton's "out of doors he flung."

898. τύμβου ... τάφρον ἐς κοίλην: see note on 607 ἐς τάφον τε καὶ πυράν. The poet evidently has a *deep* grave in mind.

901. σὺν ἂν ἔσχεν: written as one word in *B L P*. *l* has γε συνέσχεν, a συνέχεν, with σ written above by the first hand. Lenting first divided the words as they stand in the text. The difficulty came, of course, from the "tmesis."

903. Jacobs has suggested, not without some degree of plausibility, that Anaxagoras is here referred to. This conjecture is based on Cicero's *Tusc. Disp.* III. 14, 29–30, where he translates a passage from Euripides (ἐγὼ δὲ ⟨ταῦτα⟩ παρὰ σοφοῦ τινος μαθών, etc. fr. 964 N.) and observes: "*quod Theseus a doctis se audisse dicit, id de se ipso loquitur Euripides; fuerat enim auditor Anaxagorae, quem ferunt nuntiata morte filii dixisse 'sciebam me genuisse mortalem.'*" The view of Jacobs is, however, opposed by Hermann (see his note) and by Decharme (*Revue des Études grecques* 1889 p. 236, cited by Earle). If it is correct, the words ἐν γένει are probably a "blind," as there is no evidence that Anaxagoras was akin to Euripides. We know, too, that the philosopher had more than one son (Diog. Laert. II. 3, 9). On the relations between Euripides and Anaxagoras, see for the ancient sources Schaubach *Anaxagorae Fragmenta* pp. 20–21, and for the modern Zeller *Gesch. d. Griech. Phil.* I.[4] p. 975 n. 2. The dissertation of Köhler *Die Philosophie des Eur.*, Th. I. *Anaxagoras u. Euripides*, I have been unable to consult.[*]

904. ἐν γένει: so Soph. *O. T.* 1016 ὀθούνεκ' ἦν σοι Πόλυβος οὐδὲν ἐν γένει, [Dem.] XLVII. 70 οὐ γάρ ἐστιν ἐν γένει σοι (cited by Jebb *ad loc.*). κόρος: so *l*; κοῦρος the other MSS., but a dactyl is required by the responsion (ᾧ κόρος = ἦλθεν ἁ- of 927). Liddell and Scott are incorrect in stating that the form κοῦρος is always used in the lyric passages of the tragedians.

905. ὤλετ': ᾤχετ', the reading of *L Γ*, would give the same sense, but is less appropriate with ἐν δόμοισιν.

906. μονόπαις: most edd., following the schol., have taken this word as here = μόνος or μονογενής, so that κόρος μονόπαις will = κόρος μόνος παῖς ὤν. So *Or.* 964 Περσέφασσα καλλίπαις θεά, where καλλίπαις probably means not καλοὺς παῖδας ἔχουσα but καλὴ παῖς οὖσα. See as to this usage Lobeck *Paralip.* pp. 371-2, Kühner-Blass II. p. 314 *ad fin*. This *may* be the correct view; but I suspect that we should punctuate after δόμοισιν and take μονόπαις as a possessive compound in agreement with τις, the adj. being used *resumptively*, as so often in Pindar — "I had a kinsman whose son, a youth worthy to be lamented, died in his home — and yet but one son had he." ἔμπας: cf. *Cycl.* 535 ἔμπας δ' οὔτις ἂν ψαύσειέ μου, Aesch. *Prom.* 190 ἀλλ' ἔμπας μαλακογνώμων ἔσται. On the forms of the word, cf. the schol. on Soph. *Aj.* 122 Ἴωνες ἔμπης φασίν, Ἀττικοὶ δὲ ἔμπας καὶ ἔμπα. This statement is confirmed by the facts. Homer knows only ἔμπης: while Aeschylus has only ἔμπας (four cases); Sophocles has ἔμπας (three times) and ἔμπα (once, *Aj.* 563; cf. Pind. *Nc.* IV. 36); Euripides has only ἔμπας (two cases). The word here = ὅμως. Its derivation has never been satisfactorily explained. If from ἐν πᾶσι, how account for ἔμπης and ἐμπᾶ (to say nothing of the Pindaric ἔμπαν)?

907. ἅλις: ἰδίως τὸ ἅλις τέταχεν ἐπὶ τοῦ μετρίως · μετρίως ἔφερε τὸ κακόν, καίπερ ἄτεκνος ὤν schol. Hesychius says *s. v.* ἅλις: ἱκανῶς, πληρεστάτως, αὐτάρκες. ἔστι

---

[*] See also Parmentier *Euripide et Anaxagore*, in *Mémoires couronnés de l'académie de Belgique*, vol. XLVII. (1892).

δὲ καὶ μετρίως, ὡς Εὐριπίδης 'Αλκήστιδι. The edd. compare *Med.* 629 εἰ δ' ἅλις ἔλθοι Κύπρις κ.τ.λ.

909. προπετής: cf. *Hec.* 152 ἢ δεῖ σ' ἐπιδεῖν τύμβου προπετῆ... πάρθενον, and better Plato *Legg.* VII. p. 792 D αὐτὸν προπετῆ πρὸς τὰς ἡδονὰς γιγνόμενον, though neither is an exact parallel. The sense here is clearly "*verging upon old age*," just *slipping down into* it, as it were.

910. πόρσω: so Gaisford for πρόσω. The responsion (cf. 934) requires a long penult. The Doric form πόρσω occurs in Pindar and the tragedians, but not in Homer. Πόρσω is probably not "old Attic"; at least the inscriptions do not favor ρσ (see Meisterhans p. 76). For πόρσω with the gen. of part. cf. Plato *Apol.* 38 c ὁρᾶτε γὰρ δὴ τὴν ἡλικίαν ὅτι πόρρω ἤδη ἐστὶ τοῦ βίου, and the like.

911. σχῆμα δόμων: "not a mere periphrasis for δόμοι, but giving a picture of the old, familiar *form* of the house, as it strikes his eye" (so Jerram, who compares *Andr.* 1 'Ασιάτιδος γῆς σχῆμα, *Hec.* 619 ὦ σχῆματ' οἴκων). Add Soph. *Phil.* 952 ὦ σχῆμα πέτρας δίπυλον (cited by Monk).

912. μεταπίπτοντος: as in English "when the luck is changing"; but the underlying figure is that of the fall of dice.

914. τὸ μέσον: τὸ διάφορον τῆς νῦν τύχης καὶ τῆς πάλαι schol.; τὸ μέσον in this sense is Herodotean (I. 126 οἱ δὲ ἔφασαν πολλὸν εἶναι τὸ μέσον, IX. 82 τῆς θοίνης ποιηθείσης ἦν πολλὸν τὸ μέσον), but rare in other writers.

915 f. Cf. the description of the nuptials of Peleus *I. A.* 1036 ff. σύν: " Im Ganzen steht σύν bei Euripides etwa 65 mal bei *sachlichen* Begriffen, eine geringe Frequenz, wenn man bedenkt, dass Aeschylos und Sophokles bei weit kleinerem Umfange je 44 und 56 Beispiele dieser Art darbieten" (Mommsen *Beitr. z. d. Lehre d. Griech. Präp.* p. 135).

917. φιλίας: so the MSS. The schol. says γράφεται πιστῆς, a variant which is due to 880, where see note. A comparison of 876, 880 and 917, with their variants, is most instructive, as showing the way in which the readings of our text have been influenced.

918. πολυάχητος: a very rare word, probably ἅπαξ λεγόμενον in classic writers.

920-21: an echo of a legal phrase like οἱ ἐξ ἀμφοτέρων γεγονότες ἀστῶν, Aristotle *Const. Ath.* 42, 1 or μὴ μετέχειν τῆς πόλεως ὃς ἂν μὴ ἐξ ἀμφοῖν ἀστοῖν ᾖ γεγονώς, ib. 26, 4; cf. *Politics* 1278 a 34. One is almost tempted to propose ἀστῶν ὄντες σύζυγες εἶμεν. ἀριστέων: Dobree for ἀρίστων. The emendation is supported by Soph. *Aj.* 1304 ἆρ' ὧδ' ἀριστεὺς ἐξ ἀριστέοιν δυοῖν | βλαστὼν ἂν αἰσχύνοιμι τοὺς πρὸς αἵματος, as well as by the analogy of ἐξ ἀμφοτέρων ἀστῶν. A noun, not an adj., is required. καὶ ἀπ': κἀπ' *L*, but the metre allows καὶ ἀπ', which is supported by the other MSS. εἶμεν: so Heath (εἶμεν *P a*). The other MSS. have ἦμεν, which is defended by Nauck (*Eur. Stud.* II. p. 79). The form εἶμεν is rare in tragedy, but seems well assured in *Hippol.* 349 (ἂν εἶμεν *A L P a d*, ἂν ἦμεν *B C E c*, ἂρ' ἦμεν Nauck), a trimeter. There the potential optative ("*probably* I have experienced," etc.) well suits the connection, as Phaedra has just admitted that she is a *novice* in such matters. Homer has εἶτ' *Od.* XXI. 105, and Soph. *O. T.* 1046 the analogous form εἰδεῖτ' for εἰδείητε (Jebb on *Antig.* 215). See for other examples Kühner-Blass II. p. 221, 3. Nauck's objection to εἶμεν, then, will not hold. The question is simply which is the *better* reading; neither is *impossible*. The MSS. are pretty evenly divided P a against B L), though ἦμεν has, on the whole, slightly better authority. If ὡς is *causal*, either ἦμεν or εἶμεν may be used (cf. *M. and T.* 713-14); if, on the other hand, it merely introduces indirect discourse (ὀλβίζοντες implying a verb of saying), εἶμεν is certainly right, as in such cases the Greek retains the original *tense*, though after secondary tenses the *mood* may change. The scholiast's paraphrase καὶ ἐμακάριζον ἡμᾶς ὡς ἐσμὲν εὐγενεῖς favors εἶμεν, which I have adopted with most edd. Cf. *Troad.* 1253 μέγα δ' ὀλβισθεὶς ὡς ἐκ πατέρων | ἀγαθῶν ἐγένου. ἦμεν of B L may be due to iotacism; but the passage is one where it is almost impossible to feel *sure* of the true reading.

923. **μέλανες στολμοί**: sc. ἀντίπαλοι, a somewhat bold ellipsis.

925. **λέκτρων κοίτας**: so *Med.* 435 f. τὰς ἀνάνδρου κοίτας ὀλέσασα λέκτρον (if the text be sound).

926. **παρ'**: here the preposition has the force of "during" or "in the midst of"; see L. and S. *s. v.* παρά II. Some (so Earle) render it more literally, "alongside of," implying contrast. *Heracl.* 611, cited by Paley, is different, as there παρά denotes alternation rather than succession. The use in our passage, whether local, or, as I am inclined to think, temporal, is a rare one, and I know of no exact parallel in Euripides.

927. **ἀπειροκάκῳ**: cf. Thuc. V. 105 μακαρίσαντες ὑμῶν τὸ ἀπειρόκακον οὐ ζηλοῦμεν τὸ ἄφρον. The word comes to the surface again in late writers. Cf. ἀπειρόκαλος.

929. **βίοτον καὶ ψυχάν**: not a mere pleonasm. βίοτος denotes the physical side of life, ψυχή the emotional and intellectual. See Schmidt *Synonymik* § 75, 2.

930. **φιλίαν**: so the MSS. A writer in the *Quarterly Rev.* XV. p. 123 proposed the reading ἔλιπε, φιλία, "she has left you, the dear one," φιλία being a semi-substantive in apposition with δάμαρ (so Earle). But cf. 282 σὴν γὰρ φιλίαν σεβόμεσθα, where φιλία refers to conjugal love, as here.

931 ff. A troublesome passage. The MSS. have πολλοῖς, and all but B (δάμαρτας) read δάμαρτος. The schol. paraphrases by τί ξένον; πολλοὶ τὰς γυναῖκας ἀπώλεσαν, which looks (though of this we cannot be *certain*) as though he read δάμαρτας. (A) Hermann retains both πολλοῖς and δάμαρτος, and understands φιλίαν, to be supplied from 930 as the object of παρέλυσεν: "*multis iam solvit mutuum amorem mors uxoris.*" This is hard indeed, and can scarcely be right. (B) Others retain πολλοῖς and read δάμαρτα (so Prinz) or δάμαρτας (with B and Reiske). But παρέλυσεν will then be ambiguous = *abstulit* or *vires resolvit*. If it = *abstulit*, πολλοῖς will be 'dative of disadvantage' where we

should expect a 'genitive of separation.' Another possibility (C) would be to read πολλῶν and δάμαρτα or δάμαρτας: the sense would then be good, "from many men already has death taken away (unyoked) their spouse" or "wives." On the whole, however, I incline to the view of Canter and most recent editors (D), that we should read πολλοὺς and δάμαρτος. The change from πολλοῖς to πολλοὺς is very slight, and δάμαρτος has the authority of all the MSS. but B. The rendering will then be, "many a man already has death separated from his spouse." Παραλύσει, with the accus. only, occurs in 117 in the sense of "set free," "release"; but δάμαρτος in our passage is best taken as gen. of separation with παρέλυσεν, not as depending on θάνατος. It must be admitted, however, that the reading in the text is ambiguous, and might perfectly well be translated, "many a man already has the death of a wife *unnerved*." But both (B) and (C) are liable to a similar ambiguity, owing to the double meaning of παραλύειν. παρέλυσεν: Matthiae for παρέλυσε, as the strophe (909) has a long syllable and *syllaba anceps* is not permissible here.

936. ὅμως: cf. in English "though it doesn't look so, I think so *all the same*," which at the same time shows how ὅμως came to mean "nevertheless."

939. χρῆν: Elmsley for χρή. The harshness of the combination is palliated in some measure by the metrical ictus. See note on 379.

943. This line was rejected by Nauck (*Eur. Stud.* II. p. 80), who observes: "Im dritten Verse erscheint τερπνῆς als unpassend; wenn Admet vorher gesagt hat, sein verödetes Haus sei ihm unerträglich, so kann er nicht füglich fortfahren dass keine Anrede die er an jemand richte oder die an ihn gerichtet werde, sein Eingehen in das Haus zu einem ergötzlichem machen werde." He conjectures that the line was interpolated in order to supply a finite verb to go with the participles προσειπών and προσρηθείς. Not conclusive: Admetus is thinking of the cheerful welcome which he used to receive from Alcestis, which might well be said to make his home-coming delightful. Nauck, great scholar though he was, was sometimes led by his love of verbal accuracy to sacrifice literary effect.

947. γούνασι: the epic form of the plural occurs in trimeters also in *Hec.* 752, 839, *Andr.* 893, being required by the metre in all four places.

948. πίπτοντα: so the MSS. Wecklein (*Jahrb. f. kl. Phil.* Suppl. IX. p. 171) would read πίτνοντα. He lays it down as a principle that the "forma πίτνειν aut metri causa poetae tragici eadem qua πίπτειν usi sunt aut temperata cadendi significatione ut vel tarditatem vel decorem vel mollitiem depingat." This rule is in general borne out by the usage; but he does not make it entirely clear that πίπτειν is not sometimes employed "temperata cadendi significatione." To enforce the rule strictly he has to emend some *ten* passages. Hence I have not ventured to read πίτνοντα here against *all* the MSS. δεσπότιν: this rare word (= δέσποινα) occurs also in *Med.* 17, 694, 970; fr. 1132, 53. Sophocles has it twice, Aeschylus and Pindar not at all.

951. γάμοι: "nuptials," "wedding-feasts." The rendering of some editors, "*uxores*," is absurd, as Woolsey points out. **ξύλλογοι γυναικοπληθεῖς**: the edd. from Monk down remark that this is a reminiscence of Aesch. *Pers.* 122 γυναικοπληθής ὅμιλος. γυναικοπληθής seems to be δὶς εἰρημένον.

952. ἐξανέξομαι: cf. *Med.* 74 ταῦτα παῖδας ἐξανέξομαι πάσχοντας; *Heracl.* 967, *Andr.* 201. The word is a very strong one.

954. κυρεῖ: Monk would read κυρῇ, which would require ὅστις ἄν (*M. and T.* 529). *Hippol.* 427 ὅτῳ παρῇ, which Monk compares, is different, being a "general relative condition with omitted ἄν" (*M. and T.* 540); and the same is true of ὅτι νεύσῃ in 978 of our play. In the passage in the text Admetus has particular enemies in mind, and so uses the indicative. — It is with profound knowledge of human nature that the poet represents Admetus as lamenting, not his own selfishness and cowardice, but the *consequences* to which it has led and will lead.

960. κύδιον: so the MSS. If the comparative is right, τοῦ τεθνάναι must be understood. Cf. *Andr.* 639 f. κύδιον (so L P and Stobaeus; κύδιστον A, κέρδιον Wecklein *) βροτοῖς | πένητα χρηστὸν ἢ κακὸν καὶ πλούσιον | γαμβρὸν πεπᾶσθαι, and Hesych. κύδιον· κρεῖττον, αἱρετώτερον. Purgold conjectured κέρδιον, which Wecklein approves; but there seems to be no *certain* example of κερδίων, κέρδιον in the tragedians. Perhaps we should read κέρδος, ὦ φίλοι, or κέρδος ἦν with Blomfield (cf. *Med.* 798, Aesch. *Prom.* 745); but, on the whole, I am inclined to believe that the MSS. are in the right.

962 ff. From the time of the schol. down these words have been taken as a personal statement of the poet's own experience. The schol. observes on μετάρσιος ᾖξα: καὶ περὶ μετεώρων ἐφρόντισα, οἷον ἀστρολόγησα καὶ ὁρμὴν ἐπὶ τοῦτο ἔσχον. As was noted by the ancient grammarians, these addresses of the poet to the audience correspond in a manner to the parabasis of the comedy. Cf. Pollux IV. 111 τραγικὸν δὲ οὐκ ἔστιν (sc. ἡ παράβασις)· ἀλλ' Εὐριπίδης αὐτὸ πεποίηκεν ἐν πολλοῖς δράμασιν κ.τ.λ.

965–6. κρεῖσσον and ηὗρον (— ⏑) do not correspond exactly with μή μοι and ἔλθοις (— —) of the antistrophic lines 976, 977. But no emendation is necessary, as Glyconics and Pherecrateans allow this imperfect responsion in the first foot (see Christ *Metrik*[2] p. 521 f.). It is noteworthy that 962, a Pherecratean, introduces a Glyconic system; which is unusual.

967. σανίσιν: here, like Lat. *tabulae*, of the wooden tablets which were covered with wax for writing. σανίς occurs in other senses in *Or.* 1221 and *Hel.* 1572. The ancient belief that the inhabitants of Thrace and Thessaly were skilled in magic incantations shows itself over and over again in the literature.

968. κατέγραψεν: Monk added the ν because the ultima must be long to correspond with that of τελευτᾷ in 979. The schol. quotes Heraclitus, who says: τὸ δὲ Διονύσου (sc. ἱερὸν) κατεσκεύασται [ἐπὶ] τῆς Θρᾴκης ἐπὶ τοῦ καλουμένου Αἵμου, ὅπου δή τινας ἐν σανίσιν ἀναγραφὰς εἶναί φασιν ('Ορφέως). Among the

---

* See his *Beiträge zur Kritik des Euripides* p. 541 f.

pseudo-Orphic works current in later times was a treatise περὶ φαρμάκων; see Lobeck *Aglaophamus* p. 748 f. Note that the chorus here mention the Thracian Orpheus, and the Asclepiads, who probably had their origin in Thessaly (see Walton *Cult of Asklepios* pp. 18 ff.) and would naturally be familiar to the Thessalians of Pherae. The poet is true to the local coloring.

971. ἀντιτεμών: "Der Ausdruck ist hergenommen von den ῥιζοτόμοι, welche durch Einschneiden besonderer Wurzel und Pflanzen Arzneimittel bereiteten (Bauer-Wecklein). Cf. *Andr.* 120 εἴ τί σοι δυναίμαν | ἄκος τῶν δυσλύτων πόνων τεμεῖν, Aesch. *Ag.* 17 ἀντίμολπον ἐντέμνων ἄκος, and the word ἀντίτομος.

972 ff. For the sentiment, cf. the famous lines of Aeschylus quoted in the note on 424. In the MSS. ἐλθεῖν of 975 and ἔστιν of 974 have exchanged places, thus disturbing the responsion. The true reading was restored by G. A. Wagner.

975. κλύει: Wecklein reads μέλει, on the ground that κλύειν cannot be used of sacrifices. But the sacrifices were accompanied by prayers, and κλύειν, like the English "hearken to," may be loosely used. Cf. Aesch. *Ag.* 1064 κακῶν κλύει φρενῶν, which is nearly as bold an usage.

976. μείζων: Wuestemann compares *Med.* 630 εἰ δ' ἅλις ἔλθοι Κύπρις, 627 ἔρωτες ὑπὲρ μὲν ἄγαν ἐλθόντες.

978. ὅ τι νεύσῃ: τοῦτο ἀναγκαστικώτατα πράττει. οἷον καὶ ὁ Ὁμηρικὸς Ζεὺς ὑπόκειται τῷ τῆς Ἀνάγκης ζυγῷ, ἀφ' οὗ ⟨ἂν⟩ ἐπινεύσῃ τινί· 'οὐ γὰρ ἐμὸν παλινάγρετον οὐδ' ἀπατηλὸν οὐδ' ἀτελεύτητον ὅ τι κεν κεφαλῇ κατανεύσω' schol. For the omission of ἄν, see note on κυρεῖ, v. 954.

980. Χαλύβοις: *L P* have Χαλύβοισι, but the responsion requires the shorter form. Cf. fr. 472, 5 τμηθεῖσα δοκὸς ... Χαλύβῳ πελέκει, Aesch. *Prom.* 712 λαιᾶς δὲ χειρὸς οἱ σιδηροτέκτονες | οἰκοῦσι Χάλυβες, *Sept.* 711 f., etc. Hence the names χάλυβος and χάλυψ for iron. See Xen. *Anab.* V. 5, 1 and Strabo XII. 19 (549 M.). σὺ βίᾳ: *P* has οὐ βίᾳ (O for C). σίδαρον: so *L a*; the other MSS. have σίδηρον.

981. ἀποτόμου: this word seems to be ἅπαξ εἰρημένον in this sense in classic Greek, but is not uncommon in late writers, esp. Diodorus. Earle compares Aesch. *Prom.* 18 τῆς ὀρθοβούλου Θέμιδος αἰπυμῆτα παῖ, and Jerram Tacitus *Ann.* XVI. 17 *animo praeruptus*. μόρος ἀπότομος in l. 118 is slightly different, being more like the Homeric αἰπὺς ὄλεθρος.

983. καὶ σ' ἐν: Nauck proposed καὶ σέ γ': but the preposition is often used with verbs of binding and loosing where it might be omitted. So *Bacch.* 444 κάθησας ἐν δεσμοῖσι πανδήμου στέγης (cf. *Heracl.* 861), *Hippol.* 1244 ἐκ δεσμῶν λυθείς (cf. fr. 128, 2). There may also be here the notion of *catching one in a noose or net*; cf. *Herc. F.* 153 ὃν ἐν βρόχοις ἑλὼν κ.τ.λ. Hence there is not sufficient ground for altering the text. The schol. probably read ἐν, for he says: καὶ σοῦ οὖν περιγέγονεν ἡ Ἀνάγκη, ὦ Ἄδμητε, ἐν ἀφύκτοις δεσμοῖς.

986. ἄνω: this word seems pleonastic with ἀνάξεις, and its position, too, is strange, as one would naturally take it with φθιμένους. Earle proposes to read βροτῶν, taking ἄνω as part of a gloss on ἀνάξεις. But why make a gloss on such a simple word? Possibly we should read in 985 οὐ γὰρ σύ γ' ἄξεις and retain ἄνω: cf. 853. The sense will then be: "for you, at least will not bring up the dead," whatever Orpheus may have done. ἀνάξεις may then be a note on ἄξεις ... ἄνω which has crept into the text. But, on the whole, I am inclined to believe ἄνω corrupt. Perhaps we should read ἄγαν (with κλαίων), or ἄναξ, with a comma after φθιμένους (cf. Soph. Phil. 150 μέλον πάλαι μέλημά μοι λέγεις, ἄναξ, and the like).

989. σκότιοι: proleptic = εἰς σκότον. The schol. absurdly takes it = νόθοι: cf. Hesych. s. v. σκότιος and Il. VI. 24. Earle is probably right in holding that the figure is taken from the setting (or waning) of a heavenly body. The use of αὔξειν and φθίνειν in this figurative sense is very common. φθίνουσι: so L P; φθινύθουσι, the reading of the other MSS., is forbidden by the responsion (κέλευθον 1000).

982. The MSS. have θανοῦσ' ἔσται, which in all but a is preceded by a καί. The old conjecture of Portus, φίλα δ' ἔτι καὶ θανοῦσα seems to me preferable to the more modern emendations; ἔσται would be so apt to be supplied to show the construction, and the τι of δ' ἔτι could so easily fall out. Next, I think, in order of merit is Prinz's φίλα δὲ θανοῦσ' ἔτ' ἔσται, which palaeographically is very easy; though it sacrifices the καί, which word improves the sense and has excellent MSS. authority. Nauck proposed θανοῦσ' ἐς ἀεί, Wecklein θανοῦσα κεῖται (cf. Soph. El. 1134 θανὼν ἔκεισο). See also Sel. Conj.

994. The extraordinary frequency of the metaphor of *yoking* with reference to the marriage relation is extremely noticeable in the Greek writers, and the same is true of the Latin, though to a less extent. I have noted over one hundred instances of the metaphor, and the number might easily be increased. A good parallel to the cases in the text is *Ion* 901 ἵνα με λέχεσι ... ἐζεύξω: cf. *Troad.* 671. κλισίαις: here in its original sense (from κλί-νω) = λέχεσι. "A rare usage, perhaps without nearer parallel than *I. T.* 857 seqq. Ἀχιλλέως | ἐς κλισίαν λέκτρων | δόλι' ὅτ' ἀγόμαν" (Earle). In Pindar *Pyth.* IV. 133 ἀπὸ κλισιᾶν perhaps means "from their banqueting-couches," though some take κλισιᾶν = "seats" and others (with the schol. *ad loc.*) think it means "tents." But I know of no exact parallel to the passage in our text.

997. θεοῖσι δ' ὁμοίως: a fine example of "brachylogy."

1000. δοχμίαν κέλευθον: the tomb of Alcestis was in a conspicuous place in the suburb (see note on 836), so that the traveller, as he climbed up the ascent, would see it from a distance and turn aside from the road into the path that led to it. On the situation of the ancient Pherae, see Bursian *Geog. v. Griechenland* I. p. 69; Wordsworth's *Greece* ed. Tozer p. 302.

1001. ἐμβαίνων: L P (with the schol.) have ἐκβαίνων, which Usener (*Jahrb. f. Phil.* 139, p. 369) defends, on the ground that the words 1002-4 would be said *after* the person has seen the monument and as he is *going back from* the side-path into the main road, not when he *first enters* the path. This is not at all conclusive; τις may refer to the towns-people and kin of Alcestis as well as to strangers; and those *acquainted* with the tomb would naturally pay their greeting *as they came in sight of the monument*. Cf. *Hel.* 1165 f. ὦ χαῖρε, πατρὸς μνῆμ᾽· ἐπ᾽ ἐξόδοισι γὰρ | ἔθαψα, Πρωτεῦ, σ᾽ ἕνεκ᾽ ἐμῆς προσρήσεως· ἀεὶ δέ σ᾽ ἐξιών τε κεἰσιὼν δόμους | Θεοκλύμενος παῖς ὅδε προσεννέπω, πάτερ. Moreover, the passages which Usener cites to support the construction κέλευθον ἐκβαίνειν (Eur. *Bacch.* 554, *Il.* VI. 128, *Od.* XVIII. 206) are not one of them parallel, the preposition in all of them being not ἐκ but κατά. I have not been able to find *one* example of ὁδὸν or κέλευθον ἐκβαίνειν in the sense which Usener would assign to it (the nearest approach being ταύρῳ νάπος ἐκβαίνοντι in a late epigram, Adaeus in *Anth. Pal.* IX. 300). I suspect that κέλευθον ἐκβαίνειν would have meant to Euripides "to overstep," "stray beyond the path"; cf. *Her. F.* 82 ὡς οὔτε γαίας ὅρι᾽ ἂν ἐκβαῖμεν λάθρᾳ, *Bacch.* 1044 ἐξέβημεν Ἀσωποῦ ῥοάς.

1002. προύθαν᾽: προύθανεν or προὔθανεν the MSS., but the responsion with 991 requires the shorter form.

1005. φᾶμαι: so Monk; the MSS. have φῆμαι. (Cf. αὗτα above.) The word not merely = "speeches," but has a distinct religious sense, "solemn addresses." Aeschylus uses the word of solemn song, *Suppl.* 663 ἁγνῶν τ᾽ ἐκ στομάτων φερέσθω φήμα φιλοφόρμιγξ.

1006 ff. Exodos. Heracles returns from the left, leading the veiled Alcestis.

1009. μομφάς: μορφάς all the MSS. but *L a*, a blunder due to the frequent confusion between a long-tailed μ and a ρ. ὑπὸ σπλάγχνοις ἔχειν: cf. Theocr. VII. 99 παιδὸς ὑπὸ σπλάγχνοισιν ἔχει πόθον. Euripides uses σπλάγχνον no less than eleven times. Cf. esp. *Med.* 220, *Hippol.* 118.

1011. ἐγγὺς παρεστώς: so *I. A.* 465 παρὼν ἐγγύς, and in English "near at hand." φίλος: possibly we should read φίλον, "my friend" = σέ. If φίλος is retained ἐξετάζεσθαι will be passive, "to be proved to be": see L. and S. s. v. IV. I know no other instance of this use of the verb in Euripides. If we read φίλον, ἐξετάζεσθαι will, of course, be middle, "to question my friend."

1012. προκείμενον: referring to the πρόθεσις of the body.

1014. A line which does not belong here. See note on 778.

1017. μέν: so *B* and *a*; *L P* have the one δή, the other δέ. "Id (μέν) cum excidisset propter sequentis syllabae similitudinem, correctores addiderunt δή, quod hic multo deterius est" (Hermann).

1021. Θρῃκίας: θρηϊκας *L P*, on which [θρηικ]ίους of *l* is a gloss. The metre, of course, demands Θρῃκίας (— ∪ —), not Θρῄκας or Θρῆκας. The variant arose from the correct spelling ΘΡΗΙΚΙΑΣ: see Meisterhans p. 50. For the genitive, see Goodwin *Gr. Gram.* 1119.

1023. Note the euphemism, and the prayer added to avert evil consequences from the mention of possible misfortune. Cf. *Heracl.* 511, 714 and the like.

1022 f. In *B* this passage was copied with excessive carelessness. See App. Crit.

1024. προσπολεῖν: πρόσπολον L P, which gives equally good sense; but the infin. is more idiomatic. (Hermann observes, "in prima dipodiae arsi finalis syllaba longioris vocabuli, quae nullum accentum habet, non perite collocatur"; but to this rule there are *very* numerous exceptions. Cf. just below in 1027 ἄξιον πόνον, etc.)

1027. πόνον: so B. a has πόνων (ω for ο), L P πόνου. As B L P have ο in the ultima, and B a both have the final ν, πόνον seems, on the whole, well accredited; but πόνου gives equally good sense. Certainty in such a case is scarcely possible, as the MSS. are so evenly balanced. Πόνον is, of course, in apposition with ἀγῶνα, and if we read πόνου, ἄξιον would agree with ἀγῶνα. I have preferred πόνον, as being the *difficilior lectio;* but it *may* be a mere "copyist's error." To be dogmatic in such cases is the sheerest folly.

1029. τὰ ... κοῦφα τοῖς νικῶσιν: a very unusual order, doubtless adopted for metrical convenience, as well as to make κοῦφα emphatic. Cf. Soph. *Antig.* 710 ἄνδρα ... τὸ μανθάνειν, Trach. 65 σὲ ... τὸ μὴ πύθεσθαι.

1031. βουφόρβια: ἀγέλη βοῶν schol. The word occurs also in *I. T.* 301, fr. 485. It is here used of cattle taken separately, not of whole *herds;* as Monk pointed out, Euripides obviously had *Il.* XXIII. 259 ff. in mind in arranging the scale of prizes.

1032. ἐντυχόντι: some take this as meaning 'to me that chanced upon (the games).' So the schol., who paraphrases by ἐπειδὴ ἔτυχον ἐκεῖσε, τὸ μὲν κερδαίνειν αὐτὴν εὐκλεὲς ἡγησάμην, τὸ δὲ ἐᾶσαι αἰσχρόν. Others take ἐντυχόντι = 'that happened upon (the *prize*)'; the sense being 'since I had won her, I thought it disgraceful not to keep her.' I incline to the former view, though some high authorities (among them England) prefer the other.

1035. κλοπαίαν ... λαβών: periphrasis for κλέψας.

1036. μ': L P have γ', the two letters being frequently confused in the MSS. A γ and a μ with one arm shorter than usual often look extremely alike in cursive writing.

1037. ἀτίζων: all the best MSS. have ἀτιμάζων, which the metre will not admit of. Fortunately, however, Cod. Harl. 5743 has the true reading. The MS. in question is of little value except in this passage, and I suspect that ἀτίζων is a lucky guess rather than an independent variant. Scaliger proposed ἀτίζων *ex conj.*, not knowing that it stood in the Harleian. ἀτιμάζων is merely a gloss which has displaced the word which it was meant to explain. Cf. *Suppl.* 19 νόμιμ' ἀτίζοντες θεῶν, ib. 865 τἀρκοῦντ' ἀτίζων, *Rhes.* 251, 327, etc. ἐχθροῖσιν: αἰσχροῖσιν L P; but ἐν αἰσχροῖσιν τιθεὶς is weak and tautological after ἀτίζων. Probably in an ancestor of L P only ροῖσιν was legible, and the gap was filled at a venture by some one. "Matthiae ἐν αἰσχροῖσιν referendum censet ad τύχας, non quo uxoris sortem mihi turpem esse putem, ob ignaviam, quam pater Admeto exprobraverat. At de hac re ille, quum Herculi se expurgare vult, non cogitat" (Hermann).

1038. ἀθλίου: so all the MSS. but a, which has ἀθλίους. A decision between the two readings is very difficult. The order favors ἀθλίους, but may be due to the exigencies of the metre. The weight of MSS. authority, on the other hand, favors ἀθλίου, which is clearly the *difficilior lectio*. It has been suggested that ἀθλίου is due to some one who was offended by what seemed to him to be the *masculine* ending of ἀθλίους, not knowing that Euripides has a predilection for the two-ending declension of adjectives. But if so, why did he not at once read ἀθλίας? The slight rhyme ἀθλίας τύχας would hardly have deterred him. Hence, though not with great confidence, I have followed *B L P*. The tragedians use ἄθλιος freely both of persons and things.

1039. προκείμενον *B P*. Cf. 551 and 833, in both of which the MSS. have προ- for προσ- in this compound. The sense, of course, requires προσκείμενον.

1040. εἴ του: *L P* have εἴπερ, but the restrictive περ is not needed here. Perhaps εἰπ^G = εἴπερ was read by mistake for εἴ τ̄ = εἴ του.

1045. μ' ἀναμνήσῃς: so (except for the ι subscript) *L P*. *a* has με μιμνήσῃς (with erasures above ι and between μ and ν), *B* με μιμνήσκεις. To read μή με μιμνήσκεις is, of course, impossible. Kirchhoff, Nauck, Weil, Bauer-Wecklein and Earle read μὴ 'μέ· μιμνήσκεις κακῶν. This is ingenious but not convincing; as Leutsch has pointed out (*Philologus* XXIII. (1866) p. 27), the tragedians never elsewhere use the present μιμνήσκω, and μιμνήσκεις κακῶν sounds abrupt and almost discourteous. Probably in an ancestor of *B* the word ἀναμνήσῃς was so mutilated that only μνη or μνησ was legible, and the gap was wrongly filled out. The reading of *a* looks like a conflation of μιμνήσκεις and ἀναμνήσῃς. Cf. μή ... προσθῇς below. A long study of the question has convinced the writer that the testimony of *L P* is not only not to be despised, but is in many cases to be preferred to that of the other family.

1048. συμφορᾷ: συμφοραῖς *a*, but in speaking of a single misfortune the singular is more natural.

1050. The edd. pass very lightly over this passage, which, simple as it seems, is in reality one of the most difficult in the play. To show how complicated the question of its syntax and interpretation is, I append a list of some of the possibilities that have been, or may be, suggested. The question centres about the meaning and use of ὡς and of πρέπει.

A. The schol. paraphrases: καὶ γὰρ νέα φαίνεται ὡς ἐκ τῆς ἐσθῆτος, which looks as though he read νέα γάρ, ὡς ἐσθῆτι καὶ κόσμῳ, πρέπει, taking πρέπει = "appears," and so Woolsey. But νέα πρέπει, "she appears young," is hardly classic Greek, and there is certainly nothing like it in the tragedians. The nearest approach to it that I can find is Aesch. *Pers.* 247 τοῦδε γὰρ δράμημα φωτὸς Περσικὸν πρέπει μαθεῖν, and even here the meaning "is conspicuous" or "clear" has not quite passed into that of "seems," as the addition of the inf. shows. Even in this construction ὡς is usually added; cf. Eur. *Suppl.* 1056, Soph. *El.* 664 πρέπει γὰρ ὡς τύραννος εἰσορᾶν.

B. Another possibility is to assume the ellipsis of οὖσα with πρέπει, "for she clearly is (πρέπει οὖσα) young, to judge by her dress and ornaments." Cf. Aesch.

Ag. 30 ὡς ὁ φρυκτὸς ἀγγέλλων πρέπει ("clearly announces") and the like. But I know of no example of this usage in Euripides.

C. Again, we may take ὡς as post-positive with νέα, "for as a young woman (naturally would be), she is conspicuous by (or "in respect to") her clothing and ornaments." For the dative, cf. 512, *Hel.* 1204 Ἄπολλον, ὡς ἐσθῆτι δυσμόρφῳ πρέπει, etc. Young women, especially the unmarried (Aristoph. *Aves* 670), wore much jewelry, and Admetus, seeing the queen's rich attire, would naturally suppose her to be young.

D. Or, still taking ὡς as post-positive, we may construct πρέπει ὡς νέα, ἐσθῆτι καὶ κόσμῳ, "she is clearly young (is conspicuous as young) by her dress and ornaments." The case would then be like Soph. *El.* 664 πρέπει ὡς τύραννος εἰσορᾶν if the εἰσορᾶν were omitted. But for this it will be hard to find a parallel, and I doubt whether it is possible.

E. Or ὡς may be *causal*, "for she is young, inasmuch as she is conspicuous by her dress and ornaments."

F. Or ὡς may be *demonstrative*, "for she is young; so conspicuous is she by her clothing and ornaments." Cf. *Hippol.* 1054 ὡς σὸν ἐχθαίρω κάρα, *El.* 155, Aesch. *Ag.* 894, Soph. *O. C.* 1242, etc.

G. Or we may take πρέπει as impersonal in its ordinary sense, "for she is young, as is in keeping with (beseems) her dress and ornaments."

H. Some would take πρέπει as impersonal in the sense of "is clear," "for she is young, as is evident from her dress and ornaments." This is not, I think, possible, as there seems to be no parallel for this use of πρέπει.

I. We might read νέᾳ and render "for she seems like (resembles) a young woman, to judge by her dress and ornaments"; but this would, I fear, imply *doubt* as to the *reality* of her youth!

Explanations A, B, D, H and I we may, I think, dismiss, the first four as not borne out by Euripidean usage, and the last as inappropriate in sense and involving a change of the text. G, too, seems very dubious, as in classical Greek πρέπει is rarely, if ever, used *impersonally* with the dative of the *thing* (cases like Aesch. *Ag.* 462 γυναικὸς αἰχμᾷ πρέπει . . . χάριν ξυναινέσαι are, of course, not real exceptions, as there the *inf.* is really the *subject* of πρέπει); though instances like fr. 292, 3 ἐὰν ταῦτα τῇ νόσῳ πρέπει, *Cycl.* 137 φῶς γὰρ ἐμπολήμασιν πρέπει, Plato *Rep.* V. 459 E ὕμνοι . . . πρέποντες τοῖς γιγνομένοις γάμοις, etc. are not uncommon (see Stephanus *s. v.* πρέπω). Nor do I believe that ὡς is *causal*, though I cannot give any very convincing reason for the disbelief. F is, I think, *possible*, though the demonstrative ὡς is very rare in Attic; but, on the whole, I strongly incline to explanation C, supported as it is by the analogy of 512, *Hel.* 1204, Aesch. *Choeph.* 11, *Sept.* 117, etc. The post-positive ὡς is surely unobjectionable, as it is common in the tragedians. There are thirteen cases at least in Aeschylus alone. Cf. *Phoen.* 628 δοῦλος ὥς, Soph. *Tr.* 771 ἐχίδνης ἰὸς ὥς, Aesch. *Choeph.* 493 φελλοὶ δ' ὥς, *Suppl.* 863 ἔχιδνα δ' ὥς, etc. But I must frankly admit that the true syntax and meaning of the passage are far from certain. Dogmatism in such cases is mere folly.

1052. ἀκραιφνής: cf. *Hes.* 537 κόρης ἀκραιφνὲς αἷμα. Cf. also Soph. *O. C.* 1147 (where it means "unscathed," "safe"), Aristoph. fr. 32 Kock, Lysippus fr. 9, Thuc. 1. 19, 34 and 52, 25. The word is not rare in late writers. Bekker's *Anecd.* p. 366 has ἀκραιφνοῦς: ἀβλαβοῦς, οἱονεὶ ἀκηροφανοῦς· κὴρ γὰρ ὁ θάνατος. Suidas says ἀκραιφνές· καθαρόν, ὑψηλόν, τέλειον: Hesychius ἀκραιφνής· καθαρός, ἀκριβής, ἀληθής. Either the meaning of "pure" or that of "safe" will suit our passage. Cf. Latin *integer*.

1055. εἰσβήσας: so εἰσέβησα' *Bacch.* 466, ἐξέβησε *Hel.* 1616, ἐμβῆσαι *Heracl.* 845, ἐμβῆσας *Cycl.* 467. The first aorist is therefore well attested for Euripides. All the MSS. but *a* have εἰς θάλαμον βήσας, which is clearly erroneous, as the anapaest in the fifth foot is not admissible.

1056. ἐπεσφρῶ: the most plausible explanation of this curious form is that of Brugmann (*Fleckeisen's Jahrb.* 1880 pp. 217 ff., *Vergl. Gram.* II. p. 962), that from the stem φρ-η- "to bring" (I. E. *bher-*) were made forms after the analogy of ἵημι (φρῶ, φρές, φρῆναι, φρείς). See Veitch s. v. φρέω for the Euripidean instances. The old derivation from προίημι is surely untenable. The simple verb probably never occurs (in *fr. com. adesp.* 489 Kock εἰσφρες is to be read) except in grammarians.

1058. ἐλέγξῃ: so all the MSS. but *B* (ἐλέγχῃ). The reading of *B* is probably a mere blunder. The scribes constantly confuse and exchange the forms of the present, future and aorist tenses*; and here there is no reason for emphasizing the *continuance* of the action.

1059. ἄλλης: so *L Γ*, rightly. ἄλλοις (so the other MSS.) is due to the influence of the following dative. For the phrase ἐν δεμνίοις πίτνειν, cf. *Hel.* 1099 ὦ πότνι' ἣ δίοισιν ἐν λέκτροις πίτνεις, and (in a different sense, of the sick Orestes) *Or.* 35 πεσὼν ἐν δεμνίοις κεῖται, ib. 88 πόσον χρόνον δὲ δεμνίοις πέπτωχ' ὅδε; (where perhaps we should read δ' ἐν δεμνίοις).

1063. πρὸς ἧξαι: England; προσήοιξαι *L*, προσήξε *Γ*, προσήξαι the other MSS. Hesychius has προσήικται· προσέοικε, which gloss Nauck refers to this passage (*Eur. Stud.* II. p. 85), though he does not venture to decide whether we should read the third person here or the second in Hesychius. He doubts, however, the genuineness of the lection, for the reasons that neither προσήγμαι nor any other form of προσείσκω occurs elsewhere (though, as he points out, ἤικτο and εἴκτο are attested for Homer, and ἤικται for Nicander *Theriaca* 658), and that the juxtaposition of constructions so different as ἴσθ' ἔχουσ' and προσήιξαι is harsh. The true solution of the difficulty is, I believe, that the words are wrongly divided in the MSS.; πρός is an adverb, as in *Hel.* 962 καὶ πρὸς σῶσον, ib. 110, *Or.* 622, *Phoen.* 611, *Heracl.* 641, Aesch. *Choeph.* 293, etc. As to the change of construction, it is not harder than many in Euripides, and besides is softened by the καὶ πρός.

1065. μή μ' ἕλῃς ᾑρημένον: see Otto *Sprichwörter* s. v. *vincere*.

---

* See Wecklein *Beiträge zur Kritik des Euripides* p. 522 f. for a list of mistakes of this class.

1067. θολοῖ: a very expressive figure. Cf. Pherecrates fr. 115 K. and the parallels cited by Kock *ad loc.* Soph. *Aj.* 206 has θολερῷ κεῖται χειμῶνι νοσήσας of the mad Ajax. See also Aesch. *Prom.* 883 θολεροὶ λόγοι (with Wecklein's note) and Hesychius *s. v.* θολῶσαι.

1068. πηγαί: cf. *Herc. F.* 99, 450, 1355; Aesch. *Prom.* 404, *Ag.* 852, Soph. *Antig.* 803, and esp. *Trach.* 852 ἔρρωγεν παγὰ δακρύων. The figure is that of a spring suddenly bursting forth and sweeping down in a torrent. **τλήμων**: B and P have τλῆμον, but the metre requires the form with ω. So *Andr.* 348 ὦ τλήμων ἐγώ (at the end of a trimeter); cf. Soph. *O. C.* 185.

1071. ἥτις εἴη: ὅστις εἶ σύ the MSS. The edd. from Hermann down have seen that an address in the second person, "whoever you are," is out of place here. Hermann proposed ὅστις εἶσι, "whatever one shall come," whether a hostile or a friendly deity. See Sel. Conj. for other suggestions. I suspect that Euripides wrote ἥτις εἴη (see *M. and T.* 555). The emendation is palaeographically easy, as a carelessly written H often looks extremely like CY in the MSS.; and ἥτις ποτ' εἶ σύ in 1062 would help to facilitate the change. Then some "intelligent reader," noticing that ἥτις εἶ σύ would include only *women*, changed ἥτις to ὅστις.

1072. ὥστε σήν: lacking in *L P*. In *P* some one has added ἐκ θεοῦ *ex conj.*

1073. πορεῦσαι: cf. πορεύσας in 444.

1074. The words καὶ ... χάριν seem tame, but probably no change should be made. καί σοι τήνδ' ἐπόρσυν' ἂν χάριν has been conjectured, but εἰ γὰρ ... εἶχον is a wish, not a condition.

1077. ὑπέρβαλλ': so Monk, ὑπέρβαλ' *a*. The aorist imv. with μή in prohibitions does sometimes occur in poetry (*M. and T.* 260), but as it is rare and one λ of ὑπέρβαλλ' might so easily be lost, Monk's conjecture is probably right. ὑπέρβαιν', the reading of the other MSS., would mean "transgress," "err," which is much less appropriate here than "go to excess." IN might easily come from a carelessly written ΛΛ; or, as Earle observes, ὑπέρβαιν' may be due to the influence of παραινεῖν just below it.

1078. Cf. Terence *Andr.* 307 *facile omnes, quom valemus, recta consilia aegrotis damus.*

1079. προκόπτοις: "a metaphor taken from clearing ground" (Earle). — The text of 1080, 1081 and 1085 I have given according to Galen, *De plac. Hipp. et Plat.* pp. 388, 394 Mueller; for the MSS. variants, see App. Crit. The most noticeable difference is in 1085, where Galen reads ἡβάσκει (our MSS. of Euripides having ἡβᾷ σοι): cf. Photius ἡβάσκει· ἀκμάζει, Macedonius in *Anth. Pal.* VI. 30 κακοῦ δ' ἐπὶ γήραος ἡμῖν | ἄλυτος ἡβάσκει ... πενίη. A harder question is whether in 1080 we should read ἐξάγει with Galen or μ' ἐξάγει with the Euripidean MSS. In *Suppl.* 79 and *Ion* 361 we have the pronoun; but that fact does not prove that Euripides used it here, where it can so easily be supplied from the context. Moreover, "Porson's rule" (see note on 671) if strictly interpreted favors ἐξάγει: and as Galen's MS. of the *Alcestis* seems to have been better than ours (witness ἡβάσκει just below), I have adopted that reading.

1086. The χρόνον just below χρόνος of 1085 looks suspicious, and Nauck conjectured ὀρθῶς λέγοις ἄν. But the threefold repetition (χρόνος — χρόνον — χρόνος) may be intentional, to increase the emphasis; and probably no change should be made.

1087. νέου γάμου πόθοι the MSS., but Schmidt's emendation νέοι γάμοι πόθου is almost certainly right. Some early scribe simply exchanged the endings of νέοι, γάμοι and πόθου, one of the commonest kinds of error in copying. Euripides often uses the plural γάμοι of a single marriage.

1088. οὐκ ἂν ᾠόμην: cf. the English "I wouldn't have thought that of you."

1089. A difficult place. The text follows *a*; B has χηρεύσῃ λέχος, while L P show the curious variant χηρεύεις μόνος. Monk read χηρεύσεις μόνος, which gives good sense (cf. Soph. O. T. 479), though μόνος is somewhat pleonastic. But, if I mistake not, μόνος is part of a gloss on χηρεύσει or χηρεύσῃ. A much stronger case may be made out for the reading χηρεύσεις λέχος: χηρεύεις and χηρεύσει will then be different mistakes for χηρεύσεις, and λέχος "accus. of specification" with the verb, "remain widowed as to your couch." But in that case λέχος is otiose, and could well be spared. Kirchhoff and Earle read χηρεύσῃ: but the *middle* does not occur elsewhere in Aeschylus, Sophocles or Euripides, and I doubt if it is to be found in any good writer. On the whole, it seems best to read χηρεύσει λέχος, making λέχος the subject, "will your couch remain empty"? Cf. Od. IX. 123 f. ἀλλ' ἦ γ' (sc. νῆσος) ... ἀνδρῶν χηρεύει, and the English "widowed couch." So 862 χήρων μελάθρων. The reading χηρεύσῃ may be due to iotacism, or be the work of some one who took χηρεύσει to be second person and preferred the form in -ῃ. (It is just *possible* that χηρεύσει, λέχος and μόνος are *all* glosses, and that the true reading was ἀλλ' ἄνευ κοίτης (or λέκτρων) μενεῖς, or something of the sort.)

1094. This line has been much tortured by the critics. The MSS. have the reading in the text (except that B has καλὸν and *l* καλεῖν), which I believe to be correct without any change at all. There is, of course, an ellipsis of ἴσθι: μήποτε needs no alteration (see *M. and T.* 688 for other cases of μή with a participle after οἶδα in *Oratio Obliqua*). The construction is *exactly* like that in Soph. *Antig.* 1063 ὡς μὴ 'μπολήσων ἴσθι τὴν ἐμὴν φρένα, except that ἴσθι is not expressed. In L the first hand has written ἴσθι above ὡς to show the ellipsis, and the schol. says ἴσθι μηδέποτε καλέσων με νυμφίον. For emendations that have been suggested, see Sel. Conj. The passage is a good example of the way in which a perfectly sound text has sometimes been tampered with.

1095. ἐπῄνεσ': for this use of the aorist, see *M. and T.* 60. So *Med.* 707, *I. A.* 440, *Herc. F.* 1235, *Or.* 1672, *Phoen.* 771, Soph. *Aj.* 536, *El.* 1322, etc. The usage in the case of this verb may fairly be called a settled idiom of the language.

1097. γενναίων: so *B a*, γενναίαν *L P*, γενναίως Lenting. I have retained γενναίων with Hermann; cf. *Hippol.* 409 ἐκ γενναίων δόμων. The phrase τήνδε γενναίαν could only mean "this high-born lady," an epithet which could not fail to arouse curiosity when applied to a slave; but Admetus shows no surprise.

1098. ἄντομαι: so *L P*, rightly. The other family have αἰτοῦμαι, obviously a gloss on the rarer and more distinctively poetic word. The substitution was aided by the resemblance in form between the two words. Cf. *Suppl.* 279 πρός σε γενειάδος ... ἄντομαι, *Heracl.* 226.

1100. Cf. *Rhes.* 596 λύπῃ καρδίαν δεδηγμένοι.

1101. ἐς δέον π. χ.: a curious phrase. The meaning seems to be, "perhaps the kindness (or "favor") may result advantageously" (or "opportunely"). Bauer-Wecklein render ἐς δέον "wie es soll, zum guten." Earle and others take it = ἐς καιρόν, which is supported by cases like Soph. *Antig.* 386, *O. T.* 1416, and by the analogy of ἐν δέοντι. Herod. 1. 119 ἐς δέον ἐγεγόνεε and 186 ἐς δέον ἐδόκεε γεγονέναι are disputed, some rendering ἐς δέον 'as it should be,' others 'opportunely.' The difference, however, is not great. Cf. also Demos. IV. 14 εἰς δέον λέγουσιν, ib. XX. 41 εἰς δέον δὲ νῦν γέγονεν αὐτῷ τὸ ... λαβεῖν ... τὴν ἀτέλειαν.

1102. μὴ ᾽λαβές: on this aphaeresis see Christ *Metrik*[2] pp. 34 ff. The MS. variants here are due in part to a misunderstanding of it. Tyrwhitt restored the true reading.

1105. ἄθρει: so the first class. ὅρα of *L P* is probably a gloss. Euripides uses ἀθρεῖν some fifteen times.

1107-8. Nauck rejects 1108 (which is not in the text of *B*, but has been added in the margin by the first hand), and 1107 as well. He deems the whole of 1107 corrupt except προθυμίαν, which word he holds to be a variant of πίθου μόνον (*Eur. Stud.* II. p. 83 f.). This seems quite needless. The omission of 1108 in *B* does not prove very much, as that MS. is written "unsäglich flüchtig" (Wilamowitz) and abounds in slips. 1107 is intentionally vague, "I, too, have some secret knowledge that leads me to show this eagerness (for you to receive her)." Heracles in this scene is paying back Admetus for the *double-entendres* of 513 ff. Though the vengeance is comic and harmless, the king does not escape unpunished for his deceit. κἀγώ implies that it is now Heracles' turn. There is no ground for any change. **ποεῖς**: see Christ *Metrik*[2] p. 26 (§ 36) and Wecklein *Cur. Epigr.* pp. 53 ff.

1112. δοκεῖ: so *L P*; βούλει the other MSS. The use of the impersonal verb without a dative, seeming unusual, led to the emendation βούλει. So often in the MSS. δοκεῖ has been changed to δοκεῖς or δόκει. See Jebb on *Antig.* 1102. **δόμους**: so the Venetian copy of *L*; δόμοις of the other MSS. is clearly due to δόμοις in 1110.

1115. μόνῃ: μόνου Nauck, which is undeniably 'neat'; but probably change is unnecessary.

1117. προτεῖναι: προτείνειν L P, πρότεινε a. θιγεῖν: θίγειν the MSS. as usual (θίγε a). προτεῖναι was proposed by Elmsley *ex conj.*, and is confirmed by B. "*Nam et aoristus accommodatior est praesente* (i.e. the act is momentary), *et ex ea scriptura intelligitur unde πρότεινε et θίγε venerint*" (Hermann). προτείνειν is due to the wish to have the other verb in the same tense as the (supposed) present θίγειν.

1118. καρατομῶν: so Lobeck; καρατόμῳ the MSS. Mr. Brennan (*Class. Rev.* VII. pp. 17 ff.) has defended the reading of the MSS. on the ground that καρατομῶν "is in reality ridiculous, for Perseus was a model of courage." But surely the most courageous man would be justified in using caution under such circumstances. As another has well said (*Class. Rev.* VII. p. 204), "the attitude of Admetus is the real point of the comparison. He is unwilling to look at the stranger for fear he should be attracted by her beauty and so even for a moment false to his wife's memory; and in thus standing with hand outstretched but averted face (ταῦτα λέγει ἀπεστραμμένος schol.), he is like Perseus, who dares not with all his courage look at the features which turned beholders into stone." The elision of the dative ι in tragedy has been almost universally given up by scholars, and all cases where it seems to occur are capable of easy emendation. See Jebb's critical note on Soph. *O. C.* 1436. — Cf. *Rhes.* 586 χρὴ καρατομεῖν ξίφει, and *Troad.* 564, *Phoen.* 606, where καρατόμος is used. For the Gorgon simile, cf. *Orest.* 1520, *Herc. F.* 990, *Phoen.* 455.

1121. πρὸς αὐτήν: B has πρὸς, the other MSS. δ' ἐς. Euripides uses both πρός and εἰς (ἐς) with βλέπειν: but as when the imperative βλέψον is used in this way the conjunction is *almost always* omitted (cf. 390, *Hel.* 1442, *Heracl.* 225, *Herc. F.* 1227, *I. A.* 1238; *I. A.* 320, etc.), I have followed B.*

1123. τί λέξω: so L P. The other class has λεύσσω (λεύσω B), which Earle reads, changing λεύσσω in the next line to λέξω. But cf. *Hec.* 488, *Cycl.* 375 ὦ Ζεῦ, τί λέξω, *Hel.* 483, and the like; and for λέξω in 1124 there is no MS. authority. It seems more likely that the reading λεύσσω in 1123 is due to the influence of the λεύσσω just under it in 1124. Nauck would read φάσμα for θαῦμα, on the ground that "statt des unverhofften Wunders muss man eine unverhoffte Erscheinung erwarten." He compares *Ion* 1395 τί δῆτα φάσμα τῶν ἀνελπίστων ὁρῶ; *Or.* 879 ὁρῶ δ' ἄελπτον φάσμ', ὃ μήποτ' ὤφελον. Add *I. A.* 1585 ἄελπτον εἰσιδόντες ἐκ θεῶν τινος | φάσμ'. But, as Nauck himself points out, the phrase θαῦμ' ἀέλπιστον occurs in Soph. *Trach.* 673, a play which shows a strong Euripidean influence. Moreover, a general term like θαῦμα may include an "unverhoffte Erscheinung" as well as any other form of prodigy. In *Or.* 879, the very passage quoted by Nauck, B has θαῦμα, and in *I. A.* 1581 we have θαῦμα δ' ἦν αἴφνης ὁρᾶν just before the φάσμα is mentioned. Hence, though the emendations are plausible, I am inclined to believe that no change is necessary. φάσμα would hardly have been used here unnecessarily when it occurs just

---

* See on the other side Wecklein *Beiträge zur Kritik des Euripides* p. 538.

below in 1127. — Dobree punctuates ὦ θεοί, τί λέξω θαῦμ᾽ ἀνέλπιστον τόδε; γυναῖκα λεύσσω κ.τ.λ., which may be right.

1125. "All the MSS. except *a* (which has ἤ) read ἤ, and all except *P* (which has ἐμπλήσσει) have ἐκπλήσσει. Nauck and Prinz suspect the words ἐκπλήσσει χαρά, the former on the ground that the ideas expressed by ἐκπλήσσειν and χαρά are not congruous. But surely if one can say ἐκπλαγῆναι χαρᾷ cf. Aesch. *Choeph.* 231) or ἡδονῇ (cf. Soph. *Trach.* 626), the expression χαρά ἐκπλήσσει τινά ought to be both possible and natural. So in English we can say 'joy crazes a man' as well as 'a man is crazed with joy.' On the other hand, the simple genitive θεοῦ is certainly hard. If it is possessive, 'some delusive joy of the divinity,' it is ambiguous, and if it is a genitive of source we miss some verb indicating motion or origin. Should we not insert one letter and read μ᾽ ἐκ θεοῦ? This seems better than to escape the difficulty by altering χαρά to χάρις with Kviçala (*Studien zu Euripides* II. p. 36)" (Ed. in *Harvard Studies* VII. p. 220). Since the above was written, I find that Buecheler proposed μ᾽ ἐκ θεοῦ many years ago (on quite different grounds); and the conjecture therefore belongs to him. His reason for making it was that θεοῦ, θεῶν, etc., when synizesis occurs, are almost always, if not always, preceded by a long syllable. The conjecture is thus confirmed by evidence of another kind.

1126. Radermacher's ἄλλη for ἀλλά improves both sense and metre so much that I have ventured to receive it into the text. The caesura between the conjunction ἀλλά and the clause with which it belongs seems very clumsy.

1127. τόδε: so Herwerden; ᾗ is, of course, understood. For the ellipsis, cf. *Iph. T.* 67 ὅρα, φυλάσσου μή τις ἐν στίβῳ βροτῶν. τόδ᾽ εἰσορῶ of *B* and τόδ᾽ of most MSS. will then be different attempts to supply the verb. For μή with the subjunctive after ὁρῶ and οἶδα, see *M. and T.* 366. Kirchhoff thinks ὅρα γε a gloss, and that μή τι has come by a "copyist's error" from ἀλλ᾽ ἤ τι (i.e. MHTI from AΛΛHTI). Hence he would read ἀλλ᾽ ἤ τι φάσμα νερτέρων τόδ᾽ εἰσορῶ; One might also think of μὴ νερτέρων τι φάσμα γ᾽ εἰσορῶ τόδε (*M. and T.* 264; cf. v. 315) or μὴ νερτέρων τι φάσμα νῦν τόδ᾽ εἰσορῶ, which would account better for the addition of ὅρα γε: but, on the whole, I prefer the reading in the text.

1128. "Mediums" seem to have been in ill repute in ancient times as well as in modern.

1130. τύχην: so the MSS. The sense will then be "that you disbelieve your good fortune," which seems apposite enough, as Admetus has just asked doubtingly, "do I really behold my wife, whose funeral I was holding just now?" I cannot see why Reiske's emendation τύχῃ is at all necessary. "Aliud est non fidere sorti, quod est instabilem futuram putantis: de qua re hic non est sermo; aliud non credere verum esse, quod accidit. De eo hic solo agitur" (Hermann).

1135. As to envy felt by the gods, Wecklein aptly compares Herod. III. 40, VII. 46, V. 21. Do the words of Heracles also convey a gentle hint that it is time to thank him and his divine parent? At all events, the promptness with which Admetus turns to him is noticeable.

1137. φιτύσας: this, the reading of *B*, is certainly right, as the metre requires the antepenult to be long. The phrase ὁ φυτεύσας (φιτύσας) πατήρ is a favorite one with the tragedians; cf. *I. A.* 1177, Soph. *O. T.* 793, 1514, etc.

1138. τἄμ' ἀνώρθωσας: τἄμ' ὤρθωσας *L P* (αν lost after αμ). In *L* the second hand has tried to fill out the line by reading τἀμά γ'. Cf. *Suppl.* 1227 σὺ γὰρ μ'ἀνορθοῖς.

1140. δαιμόνων τῷ κυρίῳ: so the schol., *a* and *d*. *B L P* have δαιμόνων τῷ κοιράνῳ. Those who retain κοιράνῳ take δαίμονες in the sense of "departed spirits," *manes*, comparing 1003 and Hesiod *Op.* 121 τοὶ μὲν δαίμονές εἰσι . . . ἐσθλοί. That δαίμων sometimes has this sense cannot be denied; but, as Weil points out, "tous les morts ne s'élevaient pas au rang de δαίμονες, qui était reservé à une minorité privilégiée." To this privileged minority Alcestis would belong; but surely no unprejudiced person on hearing the phrase δαιμόνων κοίρανος would ever *think* of Thanatos. He would naturally suppose that Zeus was meant, or if the connection showed that δαιμόνων meant "departed spirits," that Pluto was in the speaker's mind. Those who believe that in this play Hades and Thanatos are identified, find support for their theory in this passage; but see note on l. 261. Moreover, as Jerram points out, an attributive genitive, like δαιμόνων, usually has the article when the other noun has it, so that we should expect τῶν δαιμόνων if we accept τῷ κοιράνῳ. On the other hand, if we read δαιμόνων τῷ κυρίῳ, "with that one of the divinities who had her in his power," all is clear and simple. There is no need of interpreting with Matthiae δαίμονι ἐκείνῳ ὅς κύριός ἐστι τούτου, τοῦ ἀνάγειν τοὺς τεθνηκότας, or with Hermann δαιμόνων τῷ τοῦ ζῆν ἢ μὴ ζῆν κυρίῳ: with κυρίῳ, αὐτῆς or τῆς γυναικός is to be understood. The use of the article and the order of the words are just what we should look for if the *adj.* κυρίῳ is used; δαιμόνων, too, has its ordinary sense, and, in short, all is plain and regular. I cannot doubt for an instant that κυρίῳ is the true reading. See on this whole passage Lessing *De Mortis apud veteres figura* p. 19; Robert *Thanatos* p. 35.

1132 ff. A clumsy device for explaining the silence of Alcestis. The poet obviously did not wish to have more than two *speaking* actors on the "stage" at once; a fact which would mark the play as early even if we did not know its date.

1145-6. πρὶν ἂν ἀφαγνίσηται: i.e. "before the consecration to the powers of the lower world, which has been laid upon her, has been taken off." Cf. vv. 75-6. ἀφαγνίζειν is very rare in classic writers, if not indeed ἅπαξ εἰρ. Suidas defines ἀφοσιῶ by ἀφαγνίζω.

1150. τυράννῳ: so *B P L*; τυράννου *a l*. Euripides often uses τύραννος as an adj., e.g. *Hippol.* 843, *Med.* 957, *Andr.* 3, etc.

1153. δρόμον: Wilamowitz's brilliant emendation for δόμον of *L P* (which reading is also mentioned by the schol.). ὁδόν of *B* is probably a gloss on δρόμον: while πόδα of a is doubtless an emendation made by some one who had in mind *Hec.* 939 f. ἐπεὶ νόστιμον | ναῦς ἐκίνησεν πόδα and the construction πόδα βαίνειν (*El.* 94, 1173). The figure in ἔλθοις δρόμον is that of a ship making her "run" (cf. *Hel.* 1080 νέως δρόμος, etc.), so that the meaning is, "may your return home be safe and speedy."

1154. πάσῃ τ': so a (except that the ι is omitted, as usual). The other MSS. have πᾶσι τ', but πάσῃ must be right, as the τ' shows; for the adj. must belong with the following word.. **τετραρχίᾳ**: Δημοσθένης Φιλιππικοῖς. τεττάρων μερῶν ὄντων τῆς Θετταλίας ἕκαστον μέρος τετρὰς ἐκαλεῖτο, καθά φησιν Ἑλλάνικος ἐν τοῖς Θετταλικοῖς· ὄνομα δέ φησιν εἶναι ταῖς τετράσι Θετταλιώτιν, Φθιώτιν, Πελασγιώτιν, Ἑστιαιώτιν. καὶ Ἀριστοτέλης δὲ ἐν τῇ κοινῇ Θετταλῶν πολιτείᾳ ἐπὶ Ἀλεύα τοῦ Πύρρου διῃρῆσθαί φησιν εἰς δ' μοίρας τὴν Θετταλίαν. ... ὅτι δὲ Φίλιππος καθ' ἑκάστην τούτων τῶν μοιρῶν ἄρχοντα κατέστησε δεδηλώκασιν ἄλλοι τε καὶ Θεόπομπος ἐν τῇ μδ' (Harpocration; cf. Photius and Suidas s. v. τετραρχίᾳ). Nauck would read τετραπτόλει, as the tragedians do not elsewhere use τετραρχία and the mention of a τετραρχία in Thessaly in the heroic age is an anachronism. But I suspect Euripides did not think of this point. Does not Shakespeare make Hector quote Aristotle? It looks as if the use of the word "tetrarchy" for a political division of a country originated in Thessaly; and if so, Euripides is probably using the technical Thessalian word.

1157. **μεθηρμόσμεσθα**: cf. Aesch. *Prom.* 313 καὶ μεθάρμοσαι τρόπους | νέους. Wakefield and Earle conjecture μεθωρμίσμεσθα, which is very elegant; but there seems to be no convincing reason for the change.

1158. **εὐτυχῶν ἀρνήσομαι**: the typical instance of this construction; see *M. and T.* 910, and cf. *Or.* 1581.

1159 ff. These lines occur also at the close of the *Andromache, Bacchae, Helena* and (with a change in the first line) *Medea*.

METRICAL APPENDIX.

As might be expected from its early date, the *Alcestis* shows a relatively strict metrical treatment. This is true both of the iambic trimeters, which have comparatively few (about fifty) cases of resolution, and of the logaoedic verses, which show very close responsion and very few irregular resolutions (see Rumpel *Die Auflösungen im Trimeter des Euripides* in *Philologus* XXIV. pp. 407 ff.; K. F. Mueller *De pedibus solutis in dialogorum senariis Aesch. Soph. Eur.*; the appendix to Earle's *Alcestis*, and Groeppel *De Euripidis versibus logaoedicis* p. 91 f.).

In the schematization of the lyric metres I have not followed any one authority to the exclusion of others. In his metrical schemes of the play (in vol. III. of the *Kunstformen*) J. H. H. Schmidt pays, as usual, too much attention to mere outward symmetry, and cannot be implicitly trusted. More satisfactory, so far as it goes, is the treatment of Rossbach-Westphal in the third edition of their *Griechische Metrik*. I have also found Christ's *Metrik* and Gleditsch's *Metrik* (in the 2d vol. of I. Mueller's *Handbuch d. klass. Alt.-Wiss.*) of great service. Of course, many different arrangements and schemes are possible, and no single one will meet the approval of all scholars. I have adopted in part the notation employed by Schmidt, as his system, thanks to the admirable way in which it has been presented, is now in vogue in this country.

Metres of the Play.

1–27 iambic trimeters.
28–37 anapaestic system.
38–76 iambic trimeters.
77–85 anapaestic system.
86–92 = 98–104 logaoedic:—

86 = 98 $\cup$ | $\underline{\angle}$ $\cup$ | $\underline{\angle}$ $\cup$ | $\underline{\angle}$ $\cup$ | $\underline{\angle}$ (troch. dim. cat. with anacrusis).
87 = 99 — | $\underline{\angle}$ $\cup$ | $\underline{\angle}$ $\cup$ | $\underline{\angle}$ $\cup$ | $\underline{\angle}$ "   "   "   "   "
88 = 100 $\underline{\angle}$ $\cup\cup$ | $\underline{\angle}$ $\cup$ | $\underline{\angle}$ $\cup$ | $\underline{\angle}$ (First Glyconic).
89 = 101 $\underline{\angle}$ > | $\underline{\angle}$ $\cup\cup$ | $\underline{\angle}$ $\cup\cup$ | $\underline{\angle}$ (log. tetrap. cat.).
90 = 102 $\cup$ | $\underline{\angle}$ $\cup\cup$ | $\underline{\angle}$ $\cup\cup$ | $\underline{\angle}$ (log. trip. cat. with anacrusis).
91 = 103 — | $\underline{\angle}$ $\cup\cup$ | $\underline{\angle}$ $\cup\cup$ | $\underline{\angle}$ | $\underline{\angle}$ (sync. log. tetrap. cat. with anacrusis).
92 = 104 $\underline{\angle}$ > | $\underline{\angle}$ $\cup$ | $\underline{\angle}$ | $\underline{\angle}$ (sync. troch. dim. cat.).

93–97 = 105–111 (anapaestic systems).
112–121 = 122–131 (logaoedic) : —
112 = 122 ⌣ | ⏓ ⏑ | ⌞ | ⏓ ⏑ | ⏓ (sync. troch. dim. cat. with anacr.).
113 = 123 ⏓ ⏑ | ⏓ ⏑ | ⌞ | ⏓ (sync. troch. dim. cat.).*
114 = 124 ⏓ > | ⏓ ⏑ ⏑ | ⏓ (log. trip. cat.).
115 = 125 ⏓ ⏑ ⏑ | ⏓ ⏑ ⏑ | ⏓ (log. trip. cat.).
116 = 126 — | ⏓ ⏑ ⏑ | ⏓ (log. dip. cat. with anacrusis).
117 = 127 ⏓ > | ⏓ ⏑ ⏑ | ⌞ | ⏓ (Second Pherecratean).
118 = 128 ◡ | ⏓ ⏑ | ⏓ ⏑ | ◡ ⏑ ⏑ | ⏓ (troch. tetrap. cat. with anacr.).
119 = 129 — | ⏓ ⏑ | ⏓ ⏑ | ⏓ ⏑ | ⏓   "   "   "   "   "
120–21 = 130–31 ⏓ ⏑ ⏑ | ⏓ ⏑ ⏑ | ⏓ ⏑ ⏑ | ⏓ ⏑ | ⌞ | ⏓ (sync. log. hexap. cat.).
132–5 anapaestic system.

(See also Rossbach-Westphal *Griechische Metrik* pp. 494–5, 165 ; J. H. H. Schmidt *Kunstformen d. Gr. Poesie* vol. III. pp. II–III.)
136–212 iambic trimeters.
213–225 = 226–237 logaoedo-trochaic : —
213 = 226 ⏑ | ⌞ | ⏓ ⏑ | ⏓, — | ⏓ ⏑ | ⏓ ⏑ | ⏓ (two troch. tripodies cat., the first syncopated, both with anacrusis).
214 = 227 ⌣ | ⏓ ⏑ | ⏓ ⏑ | ⏓ ⏑ | ⏓, — ⏑ | — ⌣ | ⏓ ⏑ | ⏓ (two troch. dims. cat., the first syncopated with anacr.).
215 = 228 — | ⏓ ⏑ ⏑ | ⏓ ⏑ | ⏓ ⏑ | ⌣ (First Glyconic with anacr.).
216 = 229 ⏓ ⏑ ⏑ | — ⏒ | ⏓ ⏑ | ⏓ (First Glyconic).†
217 = 230 ⏓ ⏑ ⏑ | ⏓ ⏑ | ⌞ | ⏓ (First Pherecratean).
218 = 231 ⏓ ⏑ | ⏓ ⏑ | ⏓, ⏓ ⏑ | ⏓ ⏑ | ⏓ (two troch. trip. cat.).
219 = 232 ⏑ | ⏓ ⏑ | ⏓ ⏒ | ⏓ ⏑ | ⏓, ⏓ ⏑ ⏑ | ⏓ ⏑ | ⌞ | ⏓ (troch. tetrap. cat. with anacr. + First Pherecratean).
220 = 233 ⌣ | ⏓ ⏑ | ⏓ (troch. monom. cat. with anacr.).
221 = 233 b — | ⏓ ⏑ | ⏓ ⌣ | ⏓ ⏑ | ⏓ ⏒ | ⏓ ⏑ | ⏓ (troch. trim. cat. with anacr.).
222 = 234 ⏑ | ⏓ ⏑ | ⏓ ⏑ | ⏓ ⏑ | ⏓ ⏑ | ⌞ | ⏓ (sync. troch. trim. with anacr.).
223 = 235 ⏓ ⏑ | ⌞ | ⏓ (sync. troch. trip. cat.).
224 = 236 ⏑ | — ⏑ ⏑ | — ⏑ ⏑ | — ⏑ | ⏓ (log. tetrap. cat. with anacr.).
225 = 237 ⏑ ⏑ | ⏓ ⏑ ⏑ | ⏓ ⏑ | ⌞ | ⏓ (First Pherecratean with anacr.).

(See also Rossbach-Westphal pp. 286–7 ; Schmidt pp. IV–V ; Christ *Metrik*[2] p. 629.)
238–43 anapaestic system.
244–47 = 248–51 : —
244 = 248 ⏓ ⏑ ⏑ | ⏓ ⏑ ⏑ | ⏓ ⏑ | ⏓ (log. tetrap. cat.).

---

* Often called *Ithyphallicus*.
† The irrational long in the second foot (να στυλ | μον) of 216 is highly suspicious, as the antistrophe has ⏓ ⏑. Schmidt and Rossbach-Westphal read στόλον, which, however, does not seem to be used in this sense. Groeppel reads δειρὴν βρόχῳ in 229.

METRICAL APPENDIX.   171

245 = 249 ⏗ ⏑ ⏑ | ⏗ ⏑ | ⏘, | ⏗ ⏑ ⏑ | ⏗ ⏑ | ⏘ | ⏗ (sync. log. trip. + First Pherecratean).

{ 246 = 250
{ 247 = 251 iambic trimeters.

252–8 = 259–65 iambo-logaoedic:—

252 = 259 ⏑ | ⏗ ⏑ | ⏗ ⏑ ⏑ | ⏗ ⏑ | ⏗ (Second Glyconic with anacr.).

253 = 260 ⏑ ⏑ | ⏗ ⏑ | ⏘ | ⏗ (troch. trip. cat., syncopated, with anacr.).

254 = 261 ⏑ ⏗ | ⏑ ⏖ ⏑ | ⏗ ⏗ | ⏑ ⏗, ⏗ ⏗ | ⏑ ⏗ | ⏑ ⏘ | ⏗ (two iambic dims., the second syncopated).*

255 = 262 ⏖ — | ⏗ ⏑ ⏑ | ⏘, | — ⏑ ⏑ | — ⏙ (sync. log. trip. + Adonic).

256 = 263 ⏗ ⏑ ⏑ | ⏗ ⏑ | ⏘ | ⏗ (First Pherecratean).

257–8 = 264–5 iambic trimeters.

266–72 logaoedic:—

266 ⏖ ⏑ ⏑ | ⏖ ⏑ ⏑ | ⏘ | ⏗ (sync. troch. dim. cat.).

267 ⏗ ⏑ | ⏗ ⏑ | ⏗ ⏑ | ⏗ (troch. dim. cat.).

268 — ⏑ ⏑ | ⏘ | ⏗ (sync. troch. trip. cat.).†

269 ⏑ ⏑ | ⏗ ⏑ | ⏗ > | ⏗ ⏑ | ⏗ > (troch. dim. with anacr.).

270 ⏗ ⏑ ⏑ | ⏗ ⏑ ⏑ | ⏗ (log. trip. cat.).

271 — ⏖ ⏑ | — ⏗ | — ⏗ | — (anapaest. tetrap. cat.).

272 — | ⏗ ⏑ | ⏗ ⏑ | ⏖ ⏑ ⏑ | ⏖ ⏑ ⏑ | ⏘ | ⏗ (sync. troch. trim. cat. with anacr.).

(See also Rossbach-Westphal pp. 494–5; Schmidt pp. VI–VII.)

273–9 anapaestic system.

280–302 iambic trimeters.

303–403 = 406–415 dochmiac-trochaic:—

303 = 406 ⏑ ⏟ ⏗ ⏑ — | ⏗ ⏑ | ⏗ ⏑ | ⏗ (dochmius + troch. trip. cat.).

304 = 407 ⏑ | ⏗ ⏑ | ⏗ ⏑ | ⏗ ⏑ | ⏗ (troch. dim. cat. with anacr.).

305 = 408 ⏑ ⏑ ⏑ ⏗ ⏑ — (dochmius).

306 = 409 ⏑ ⏑ | ⏗ ⏑ | ⏘ | ⏗ ⏑ | ⏙ (sync. troch. dim. cat. with anacr.).

307 = 410 > ⏑ ⏑ ⏗ > — (dochmius).

308 = 411 ⏑ | ⏖ ⏑ ⏑ | ⏗ ⏑ ⏑ | ⏗ (log. trip. cat. with anacr.).

309 = 411 b — | ⏖ ⏑ ⏑ | ⏗ ⏑ | ⏙ (troch. trip. cat. with anacr.).

400 = 412 ⏑ ⏑ | ⏗ ⏑ ⏑ | ⏗ ⏑ | ⏘, | ⏗ ⏑ | ⏗ ⏑ | ⏘ ⏗ (sync. log. trip. with anacr. + sync. troch. tetrap.).

401 = 413 ⏑ | ⏗ ⏑ | ⏘ | ⏗ ⏑ (sync. troch. trip. with anacr.).

402 = 414 ⏗ ⏑ ⏑ | ⏗ ⏑ | ⏗ (log. trip. cat.).

403 = 415 ⏗ ⏑ ⏑ | ⏗ ⏑ | ⏘, ⏗ ⏑ ⏑ | ⏗ ⏑ | ⏗ ⏑ (two log. trips., the first sync.).

416–34 iambic trimeters.

435–444 = 445–454 logaoedic:—

435 = 445 ⏗ ⏑ ⏑ | ⏗ ⏑ ⏑ | ⏗ (log. trip. cat.).

* This line may also be regarded as an iambic tetrameter catalectic.
† May also be taken as an Adonic.

436 = 416 — | ‿ ⏑⏑ | ‿ ⏑⏑ | ‿ ⏑ | ‿ ⏑ (log. tetrap. with anacr.).
437 = 447 ⏑ ⏑ | ‿ ⏑⏑ | ‿ ⏑ | ‿ ⏑ | ⌐ ‿ (sync. log. pentap. with anacr.).
438-9 = 448-9 — | ‿ ⏑⏑ | ‿ ⏑⏑ | ⌐ | ⌐, | ‿ ⏑⏑ | ‿ ⏑⏑ | ⌐ | ‿ (two sync. log. tetrapodies, the first with anacr., the second catalectic).
440 = 450 ‿ ⏑⏑ | — ⏑⏑ | ‿ (log. trip. cat.).
441 = 451 ‿ ⏑ | ‿ ⏑ | ⌐ | ‿ (sync. troch. dim. cat.).
442 = 452 ⏑ ⏑ | ‿ ⏑⏑ | ‿ ⏑ | — ⏑ | ⌐ ‿ (sync. log. pentap. with anacr.).
443-4 = 453-4 — | ‿ ⏑⏑ | ‿ ⏑ | ‿ ⏑ | ⌐, | ‿ ⏑⏑ | ‿ ⏑⏑ | ⌐ | ‿ (First Glyconic with anacr. + First Pherecratean).

455-65 = 466-75 logaoedic : —
455 = 466 ‿ ⏑⏑ | ‿ ⏑ | ⌐ | ‿ (First Pherecratean).
456 = 467 ⏑ — | ‿ ⏑⏑ | ⌐ | ‿ (Second Pherecratean).
457 = 468 ⏑ ⏑ | ‿ ⏑⏑ | ⌐ | ‿ (First Pherecratean with anacr.).
458 = *** ‿ > | — ⏑⏑ | ⌐ | ‿ (Second Pherecratean).
459 = 469 ⏑ ⏑ ⏑ | ⌐ | ‿ ⏑ | ‿ ⏑ | ⌐ | ‿ (sync. troch. hexap. cat.).
460 = 470 ⏑ ⏑ | ‿ ⏑⏑ | ‿ ⏑ | ‿ ⏑ | ⌐ ‿ (sync. log. pentap. with anacr.).
461 = 471 ⏑ ⏑ ⌐ | ‿ (anapaestic monometer, syncopated).
461 b = 471 b ⏑ | ‿ ⏑⏑ | ‿ ⏑ | ‿ ⏑ | ⌐ ‿ (sync. log. pentap. with anacr.).
462 = 472 ‿ _ | ‿ _ | ‿ _ | ‿ _ (dactylic tetram.).
463 = 473 ‿ ⏑⏑ | ‿ ⏑⏑ | ‿ ⏑⏑ | ‿ ⏑⏑ (dactylic tetram.).
464 = 474 ‿ ⏑⏑ | ‿ ⏑⏑ | ‿ ⏑⏑ | ‿ ⏑⏑ |, ⏑ | ‿ ⏑ | ⌐ | ‿ (dact. tetram. + sync. troch. trip. cat. with anacr.).
465 = 475 ⏑ | ⌐ | ‿ ⏑ | ‿ ⏑ | ⌐ | ‿ (sync. troch. pentap. cat. with anacr.).
476-567 iambic trimeters.
568-77 = 578-587 logaoedic : —
568-9 = 578-9 ‿ ⏑ | ‿ > | ‿ ⏑⏑ | ⌐, | ⏑ ⏑ | ‿ ⏑⏑ | ‿ ⏑ | ‿ ⏑ (sync. Third Glyconic + log. trip. with anacr.).
570-71 = 580-81 ⏑ | ‿ ⏑⏑ | ‿ ⏑⏑ | ‿ ⏑ | ‿ ⏑ | ⌐ | ‿ (sync. log. hexap. cat. with anacr.).
572 = 582 ‿ ⏑ | ‿ ⏑ | ⌐ | ‿ (sync. troch. dim. cat.).
573 = 583 ⏑ | ‿ ⏑ | ‿ ⏑ | ‿ ⏑⏑ | — (Third Glyconic with anacr.).
574 = 584 ‿ ⏑ | ‿ ⏑ | ⌐ | ‿ (sync. troch. trip. cat.).
575 = 585 ‿ ⏑ | ‿ ⏑⏑ | ‿ ⏑ | ‿ (Second Glyconic).
576 = 586 — | ‿ ⏑⏑ | ‿ ⏑ | ‿ > | ‿ (First Glyconic with anacr.).
577 = 587 ‿ > | ‿ ⏑⏑ | ⌐ | ‿ (Second Pherecratean).
588-96 = 597-605 dactylo-epitritic, logaoedic.
588 = 597 — | ‿ ⏑⏑ | ‿ ⏑⏑ | ‿ (dact. trip. cat. with anacr.).
589 = 598 ⌐ ⏑ — — | ‿ ⏑⏑ | ‿ ⏑⏑ | ‿ (2d Epitrite + dact. trip. cat.).
590 = 599 ⌐ ⏑ — — | ‿ ⏑⏑ | ‿ ⏑⏑ | ‿ " " " " "
591 = 600 ‿ ⏑⏑ | ‿ ⏑⏑ | ‿ (dact. trip. cat.).
592 = 601 ⏑ ⏑ | ‿ ⏑⏑ | ‿ ⏑⏑ | ‿ ⏑ | ⌐ | ‿ (sync. log. pentap. cat., with anacr.).

METRICAL APPENDIX. 173

593–4 = 602–3 – | –́ ⏑ ⏑ | –́ ⏑ ⏑ | –́ ⏑ | –́, | –́ ⏑ ⏑ | –́ ⏑ ⏑ | –́ (sync. log. tetrap. with anacr. + log. trip. cat.).

595 = 604 –́ ⏑ | –́ > | –́ | –́ ⏑ | –́ | –́ (sync. troch. hexap. cat.).

596 = 605 ⏑́ ⏑ ⏑ | –́ | –́ ⏑ | –́ ⏑ | –́ | –́   "   "   "   "

606–740 iambic trimeters.

741–6 anapaestic system.

747–860 iambic trimeters.

861–871 anapaestic system.

872–7 = 880–94 (μέλος ἀμοιβαῖον) logoedic *:—

872 = 889 ⏑ | –́ ⏑ | –́ | –́ ⏑ | –́ ⏑ | –́ | –́ (sync. troch. hexap. cat. with anacr.).

873 = 890 ⏑ | –́ ⏑ | –́ ⏑ | –́ | –́ ⏑ | –́ (sync. troch. pentap. cat. with anacr.).

874 = 891 ⏑ ⏑ ⏑ –́ ⏑ – (dochmius).

875 = 892 ⏑ | –́ ⏑ | –́ | –́ ⏑ | –́ ⏑ | –́ ⏑ | – (sync. troch. hexap. cat. with anacr.).

876 = 893 ⏑ | –́ ⏑ | –́ ⏑ | –́ ⏑ ⏑ | –́ ⏑ ⏑ | –́ (log. pentap. cat. with anacr.).

877 = 894 ⏑́ – | –́ ⏑ | –́ ⏑ | –́ | –́ (sync. troch. pentap. cat. with anacr.).

895–902 anapaestic system.

903–10 = 926–34 logaoedo-trochaic:—

903 = 926 ⏑ | –́ ⏑ | – (troch. monom. cat. with anacr.).

904 = 927 –́ ⏑ ⏑ | –́ ⏑ ⏑ | –́ ⏑ ⏑ | –́ ⏑ (log. tetrapody).

905 = 928 – ⏑ | – ⏑́ | –́ | – (sync. troch. dim. cat.).

906 = 929 ⏑ ⏑ | –́ | –́ | –́ | –́ (sync. troch. dim. cat. with anacr.).

907 = 930–31 ⏑ | ⏑́ ⏑ ⏑ | ⏑́ ⏑ ⏑ | ⏑́ ⏑ ⏑ | –́ (troch. dim. cat. with anacr.).

908 = 932 ⏑ ⏑ | – ⏑ ⏑ | –́ | –́ (sync. log. trip. cat. with anacr.).

909 = 933 – | –́ ⏑ ⏑ | –́ | –́   "   "   "   "   "   "

910 = 934 ⏑ ⏑ | – ⏑ | –́ | –́ (sync. troch. trip. cat. with anacr.).

911–925 anapaestic system.

935–961 iambic trimeters.

962–971 = 973–81 logoedic:—

962 = 973 ⏑́ – | –́ ⏑ ⏑ | –́ | –́ (Second Pherecratean).

963 = 974 –́ ⏑ | –́ ⏑ ⏑ | –́ ⏑ | –́ (Second Glyconic).

964 = 975 –́ > | –́ ⏑ ⏑ | –́ ⏑ | –́   "   "

965 = 976 –́ ⏑̆ | –́ ⏑ ⏑ | –́ | –́ (Second Pherecratean).

966 = 977 –́ ⏑̆ | –́ ⏑ ⏑ | –́ ⏑ | –́ (Second Glyconic).

967 = 978 –́ > | –́ ⏑ ⏑ | –́ | –́ (Second Pherecratean).

968 = 979 –́ > | –́ ⏑ ⏑ | –́ | –́   "   "

969–70 = 980 –́ ⏑ | –́ ⏑ ⏑ | –́ ⏑ | –́, | –́ ⏑ ⏑ | –́ ⏑ | –́ ⏑ (Second Glyconic + log. trip.).

971 = 981 –́ ⏑ ⏑ | ⏑́ ⏑ ⏑ | –́ (log. trip. cat.).

972 = 982 – ⏑ ⏑ | – ⏑ | –́ | –́ (First Pherecratean).

* The ejaculations made by Admetus stand *extra metrum*.

983-994 = 995-1005 logaoedic.
983-4 = 995-6 $\angle \cup \cup \mid \angle \mid \angle \cup \cup \mid \angle, \mid \angle \cup \cup \mid \angle > \mid \angle$ (choriambic dimeter + log. trip. cat.).
985 = 977-8 $\angle > \mid \angle \cup \cup \mid \angle, \mid - \cup \cup \mid \angle \mid \angle$ (sync. log. trip. + sync. log. trip. cat.).
986 = 999 $\angle > \mid \angle \cup \cup \mid \angle \cup \mid \angle$ (Second Glyconic).
987-9 = 1000 $- \mid \angle \cup \cup \mid \angle - \mid \angle \cup$ (log. trip. with anacr.).
990 = 1001 $\angle \cup \mid \angle \cup \cup \mid -$ (log. trip. cat.).
991 = 1002 $\cup \mid \angle \cup \cup \mid \angle \cup \mid \angle \mid \angle$ (First Pherecratean with anacr.).
992 = 1003 $\cup \mid \angle \cup \cup \mid \angle \cup \mid \angle \mid \angle$ " " " "
993 = 1004 $- \mid \angle \cup \cup \mid \angle \cup \mid \angle \mid \angle$ " " " "
994 = 1005 $\angle > \mid \angle \cup \cup \mid \angle \cup \mid \angle \cup$ (log. tetrap.).
1159-63 anapaestic system.

GREEK INDEX.

[*The Roman numerals refer to the page of the Introduction; the Arabic numbers to the line of the play under which the word is discussed in the Critical Notes.*]

A.

Ἄγαλμα, meaning of, 613.
ἀγών, meanings of, 489.
ᾅδης, as common noun, 13.
ἀεί and αἰεί, 40.
ἄζομαι, 326.
ἀθρέω, 1105.
-αι, elision of, in 1st and 3d person, 90.
Αἰγαίων, 595.
αἰδόφρων, 658.
αἵματα, meaning of plur., 496.
αἱμόρραντος, 134.
αἰνέω, meaning of, 12.
ἄκλαυστος, sigmatic and non-sigmatic forms of, 173.
ἄκοιτις, 201.
ἀκραιφνής, 1052.
ἅλις = μετρίως, 907.
ἁλίσκεσθαι, use of, 786.
ἄλλως, meaning of, 333.
ἀμβαλεῖν, use of form, 526.
ἀμείψασθαί τι, 752.
ἄν, ellipsis of partic. with, 181.
ἄν, omitted after ἔστιν ὅπως, 52.
ἄνα = ἀνάστηθι, 276.
ἀντιτέμνειν, 971.
ἄντομαι and αἰτοῦμαι, 1098.
ἀπαντλέω, metaphorical use of, 354.
ἀπειρόκακος, 927.
ἀπλακών and ἀμπλακών, 242.
ἀπ' ἀρχῆς, 111.
ἀπὸ παντοίας χθονός, 747.

ἀπότομος, 118, 981.
ἄρδην, 608.
ἀρταμέω, 494.
ἀτίζων, 1027.
αὖθις... πάλιν, 188.
αὐλός, 351.
αὐχέω, meaning of, 95.
ἀφαγνίζειν, 1145.
ἀφορίζειν, 81.

B.

Βαίνω, first aorist of, Euripidean, 1055.
βάρβιτος, nature of, 345.
βίοτος, how different from ψυχή, 929.
βλέπειν, with εἰς and πρός, 1121.
βουφόρβια, 1031.

Γ.

Γ for Π, 96.
γαμεῖν, not γαμήσειν, Attic form, 372.
γούνασι, form, 947.

Δ.

Δαίμων, meaning of, 1140.
δαφοινός, 581.
δέ, climactic force of, 847.
δεινὰ πάσχειν, 816.
δέσποινα, title of deities, 163.
διάδοχος, as substantive, 655.
διαπρέπειν, with gen., 642.
δόμοι = οἶσία, 160.
δυσπάλαιστος, 889.
δύσφορα and δυσμενῆ, 617.

GREEK INDEX.

E.

Ἔγχος = ξίφος, 76.
ἔζων and ἔζην, 295.
ἐθέλειν and θέλειν, 644.
εἶμεν, form, 920.
εἴν, form, 232.
ἐκ προαστίου, force of prep., 835.
ἐκπρεπής and εὐπρεπής, 353.
ἐκφέρεσθαι, 601.
ἐκφορά, 422.
ἐμβαίνειν and ἐκβαίνειν κέλευθον, 1001.
ἔμπας, 906.
ἐν γένει, 904.
ἐν δεμνίοις πίτνειν, 1059.
ἐν σοὶ ἐσμεν καὶ ζῆν καὶ μή, 279.
ἐν τῇδ' ἡμέρᾳ, use of prep., 513.
ἐντυχόντι, meaning of, 1032.
ἐξ, denoting agency, 629.
ἐξέρχεσθαι, use of, 640.
ἐξώπιος, 546.
ἐπ' αὐτῇ and ἐπ' αὐτοῖς, 148.
ἐπεστράφη, meaning of, 187.
ἐπῄνεσα, idiomatic use of aor., 1095.
ἐπιγαμεῖν, meaning of, 305.
ἐπιπάροδος, xlix.
ἐπίστασθαι = δύνασθαι, 566.
ἐς δέον, 1101.
ἐς τρίτην μηνός, 320.
ἔστιν ὅποι, opt. without ἄν after, 117.
ἔστιν ὅπως, opt. without ἄν after, 52.
ἑταῖρος, as adj., 776.
ἔτεμον and ἔταμον, 215.
εὔζωρος, 757.
εὐμαρής, 492.
εὐπροσήγορος, 775.
ἐχθροξένους and κακοξένους, 558.
ἔχιδνα, emblem of cruelty, 310.
ἔχειν = "comprehend," 51.

Z.

Ζῆν χρῆν, 184.

Θ.

Θαρσεῖν, form in ρσ, 38.
θολοῦν, 1067.
Θρῃκίας, orthography of, 1021.

I.

I of dative not elided in tragedy, 1118.
ι, mistaken for ρ, 228.
ἱερέα and ἱερῇ, 25.
ἱερός with gen., 75.
Ἴπνοι, 596.
ἱππόστασις, 590.

K.

Καί . . . τε, 647.
καλλίναος, of a lake, 589.
καλῶς αὐτοῖς κατθανεῖν ἧκον βίου, 291.
καρατομῶν, 1118.
κατά, with gen. and accus., 237.
κατάρχεσθαι, 74.
καταστήσασα = ποιήσασα, 283.
κατηύξατο, form of augment, 162.
κάτω χθονός and κατὰ χθονός, 45.
κεδνὰ πράξειν, 605.
κείνων ἔραμαι, 866.
κεῦθος, 872.
κλαίω = "catch it," 64.
κλέω and κλείω, 447.
κλισία = λέχος, 994.
κοινοῦσθαι, with accus., 426.
κορηθεύσει, meaning, 313.
κόρος, form, 964.
κυαναυγής, use as epithet, 254.
κύδιον, 960.
κυρίῳ and κοιράνῳ, 1140.
κῦρσαι and κυρῆσαι, 473.
κωμῆται, of Thessalians, 476.

Λ.

Λακεῖν = "sing," 351.
Λάρισα, orthography of, 835.
λέγειν = "talk about," 697.

GREEK INDEX. 177

λιπαραί, epithet applied to Athens, 452.
λοχαῖος, 846.
λύειν = λυσιτελεῖν, 627.
Λυκίαν, constr. of, 114.

M.

Μαραίνεσθαι, "pregnant constr." with, 236.
μεθαρμόζειν, 1157.
μεθορμίζειν, 798, 1157.
μέθυ, 757.
μελαμπέπλῳ στολῇ and μελαγχίμοις πέπλοις, 427.
μέν = "I suppose," 146.
μέσον, τό, = "the difference," 914.
μετακύμιος ἄτας, 91.
μετάστασις, of the chorus, xlix.
μή, with subj. to express apprehension and desire to avert, 318.
μή ... ὤφελον, 879.
μηλοθύτης, 119.
μιμνήσκω, pres. not used by tragedians, 1045.
μονάμπυξ, 428.
μονόπαις, 906.
μονόστολος, 406.
μοῦνος, μούνως, not Euripidean, 122.
μυρρινός, rare word, 173.

N.

Ναυκληρία, meaning, 112.
νεανίας, as adj., 679.
νεβρός, 585.
νεολαία, 103.
νέομαι, used in fut. sense, 737.
νεοσσός = "child," 403.
νόμοις and δόμοις, 574.
νοσφίζειν, 43.

Ξ.

Ξενῶνες, 547.

O.

Οθνεῖος, 532.
οἶδα μή, with partic., 1094.
οἶδας and οἶσθας, 780.
οἰκετεύειν, 437.
οἰκτίρειν, orthography of, 193.
ὀρφανεύω, 165.
ὁρῶ and οἶδα, with μή and subj., 1127.
ὅς εἰ, meaning, 640.
ὅσιος, meaning, 10.
ὅστις γε, causal use of, 620.
ὄστρακον or ἰρδόνιον, 98.
οὐκ οἶδ' εἰ and nescio an, 48.
οὕνεκα, the form, 810.
οὐράνιος, in Euripides, 230.
οὕτω, post-positive, 333.
οὐχ' οὕτως = haud impune, 680.
ὀφθαλμότεγκτος, 184.
ὄχημα, 66.

Π.

Παιάν, use of the word, 424.
παρά = "during," 926.
παραλῦσαι, form, 117.
παρθένεια = "virginity," 177.
πάροδος, 77 f.
πάρος, with gen. of time, 223.
πάτριος and πατρῷος, 249.
πέλτης = πελταστῶν, 408.
πέμψαντος ... μέτα, 66.
πέραν = πέρα, 585.
πεφροντικὸς βλέπειν, 773.
πίτνειν = "to be cut off," 103.
πίτνειν and πίπτειν, 948.
πίτνειν and πιτνεῖν, 183.
πίτυλος, Euripidean uses of, 798.
πλάθειν, 119.
πλέον, orthography of, 229.
πλήρης, meaning, 132.
πόδα πεζεύειν, 869.
ποεῖν, form, 1107.
ποιμνίτης, use of word, 576.
πολεῖν, 29.
πολυάχητος, 918.
πορεύειν, with two accus., 444.
πόρσω, 910.
πράσσω, not "old Attic," 148.

GREEK INDEX.

πρέπει, meaning and constr., 1050.
πρεσβεύειν, 282.
πρίν, with indic., 128.
προβήσεται or 'ποβήσεται, 785.
προθυμίαν ἔχειν, 51.
προκόπτειν, metaphorical use of, 1079.
προπετής, 909.
πρός, adverbial use of, 1063.
πρός, "for the interest of," 57.
προσζευγνύναι or συζευγνύναι, 482.
προσκήνιον, doors in, xlix, 547.
προσπέτεσθαι, 421.
πρόσφαγμα, 845.
πυρά, meaning, 608.
πύργος, metaphorical use of, 311.

Ρ.

Ρεῖθρον, used in plur. by Soph. and Eurip., 458.
ῥῖψαι, intransitive use of, 897.

Σ.

Σ, doubled in first aor., 230.
σανίς, meanings, 968.
σεσίγηται, force of tense, 78.
σκληρός, metaphorical use, 500.
σοῦ τὸ φράσαι, constr., 832.
σσ, for ττ, 148.
στατίζεσθαι, 90.
στείχειν ἐπί τινα, 74.
στερείς, form, 227.
σύγκασις, 410.
σύμμετρος, 26.
σύν, in Euripides, 915.
συνδυάς, 474.
σφε, as sing., 553.
σχέτλιος, 741.
σχῆμα δόμων, 911.
σώζω, orthography of, 292.

Τ.

Τέραμνα and τέρεμνα, 457.
τιθεῖς and τίθης, 57.

τοξήρης, 35.
-τον and -την, in dual of hist. tenses and opt., 272.
τόνδ' ἄνδρα = ἐμέ, 331.
τετραρχία, 1154.
τί γένωμαι, meaning, 153.
τί κακὸν μεῖζον ἁμαρτεῖν ἀλόχου, constr. of, 879.
τύραννος, as adj., 1150.

Υ.

Ὑμέναιοι, meaning, 576.
ὑπεραλγεῖν, with gen., 883.
ὑπερβάλλειν and ὑπερβαίνειν, 1077.
ὑπὸ σπλάγχνοις ἔχειν, 1009.
ὑποβάλλειν, meaning, 639.
ὑπορράπτειν, metaphorical use of, 537.
ὑπουργῆσαι χάριν, 842.

Φ.

Φᾶμαι = "solemn addresses," 1005.
φεῦ, followed by a wish, 719.
φθάνω, with partic., 662.
φθιτός, 100.
φίλτατα, τά, 340.
φιτεύω and φυτεύω, 294, 1137.
φλόξ, without adj., 4.
φρονεῖν δοκῶ vs. δόξω φρονεῖν, 565.
φροῦδος, fem., 94.

Χ.

Χάλυβοι, 980.
χεῖρ' ἐκτείνειν, 768.
χείρεσσι, form, 756.
χρῆν, without ἄν, 384.

Ψ.

Ψυχορραγεῖν, 20.

Ω.

Ω and ο, confused in MSS., 88.
ὡραῖος, 516.
ὡς ἄν, in final clauses, 740.

ADVERTISEMENTS

GREEK TEXT-BOOKS

Allen's Medea of Euripides	$1.00
Baird's Greek-English Word-List	.30
Collar and Daniell's Beginner's Greek Composition	.90
College Series of Greek Authors: See circulars for details.	
Flagg's Hellenic Orations of Demosthenes	1.00
Flagg's Seven Against Thebes	1.00
Flagg's Anacreontics	.35
Goodwin's Greek Grammar	1.50
Goodwin's Greek Moods and Tenses	2.00
Goodwin's Greek Reader	1.50
Goodwin and White's New Anabasis, with Illustrated Vocabulary	1.50
Goodwin and White's Selections from Xenophon and Herodotus	1.50
Greek (and Latin) School Classic Series: See circulars for details.	
Bain's Odyssey, Book VI.	.35
Bain's Odyssey, Book VII.	
Gleason's Gate to the Anabasis	.40
Rolfe's Anabasis, Book V.	.40
Sewall's Timon of Lucian	.50
Harding's Strong and Weak Inflection in Greek	.50
Hayley's Alcestis of Euripides	
Higley's Exercises in Greek Composition	1.00
Hogue's Irregular Verbs of Attic Prose	1.50
Jebb's Introduction to the Study of Homer	1.12
Leighton's New Greek Lessons	1.20
Liddell and Scott's Greek-English Lexicon	9.40
Liddell and Scott's Greek-English Lexicon, abridged	1.25
Parsons' Cebes' Tablet	.75
Perrin and Seymour's School Odyssey:	
Books I.-IV., with vocabulary	1.25
Books I.-IV., IX.-XII., with vocabulary	1.50
Rangabé's Practical Method in Modern Greek	2.00
Seymour's School Iliad:	
Books I.-III., with vocabulary	1.25
Books I.-VI., with vocabulary	1.60
Seymour's Homeric Vocabulary	.75
Seymour's Selected Odes of Pindar	1.40
Sidgwick's Greek Prose Composition	1.50
Tarbell's Philippics of Demosthenes	1.00
Tyler's Selections from Greek Lyric Poets	1.00
White's Beginner's Greek Book	1.50
White's First Greek Book	1.25
White's First Lessons	1.20
White's Oedipus Tyrannus of Sophocles	1.12
White's Passages for Translation at Sight, Part IV.	.80
White and Morgan's Anabasis Dictionary	1.25
Whiton's Orations of Lysias	1.00

GINN & COMPANY, Publishers,

Boston.   New York.   Chicago.   Atlanta.   Dallas.

COLLEGE SERIES OF GREEK AUTHORS

Edited under the supervision of

JOHN WILLIAMS WHITE,
Professor of Greek in Harvard University,

AND

THOMAS D. SEYMOUR,
Professor of the Greek Language and Literature in Yale University,

With the coöperation of eminent scholars, each of whom is responsible for the details of the work in the volume which he edits.

AESCHINES AGAINST CTESIPHON "On the Crown." Edited by Professor RUFUS B. RICHARDSON. 279 pages. $1.40.

AESCHYLUS, Prometheus Bound, and the Fragments of Prometheus Loosed. Edited by N. WECKLEIN, Rector of Maximilian Gymnasium in Munich. Translated by the late Professor F. D. ALLEN, of Harvard University. 178 pages. $1.40.

ARISTOPHANES, Clouds. Edited by Professor HUMPHREYS, of the University of Virginia. 252 pages. $1.40.

EURIPIDES, Bacchantes. Edited by Professor BECKWITH, of Trinity College. 146 pages. $1.25.

EURIPIDES, Iphigenia among the Taurians. Edited by Professor FLAGG, of the University of California. 197 pages. $1.40.

HIPPOLYTUS. Edited by Professor HARRY, of Georgetown College, Ky.

HOMER. Introduction to the Language and Verse of Homer. By Professor SEYMOUR, of Yale University. 104 pages. 75 cents.

HOMER, Iliad, Books I.-III. and Books IV.-VI. Edited by Professor SEYMOUR, of Yale University. $1.40 each.

HOMER, Iliad, Books XIX.-XXIV. Edited by Professor CLAPP, of the University of California.

HOMER, Odyssey, Books I.-IV. and Books V.-VIII. Edited by Professor PERRIN, of Yale University. $1.40 each.

LYSIAS, Eight Orations. Edited by Assistant Professor MORGAN, of Harvard University. 223 pages. $1.40.

PLATO, Apology and Crito. Edited by Professor DYER, formerly of Cornell University. 204 pages. $1.40.

PLATO, Gorgias. Edited by Professor LODGE, of Bryn Mawr College. 308 pages. $1.65.

PLATO, Protagoras. By Professor TOWLE, formerly of Iowa College. 179 pages. $1.25.

SOPHOCLES, Antigone. Edited by Professor D'OOGE, of the University of Michigan. 196 pages. $1.40.

THUCYDIDES, Book I. Edited by the late Professor MORRIS. 349 pages. $1.65.

THUCYDIDES, Book III. Edited by Professor SMITH, of the University of Wisconsin. 320 pages. $1.65.

THUCYDIDES, Book V. Edited by Professor FOWLER, of Western Reserve University. 213 pages. $1.40.

THUCYDIDES, Book VII. Edited by Professor SMITH, of the University of Wisconsin. 202 pages. $1.40.

XENOPHON, Hellenica I.-IV. Edited by Professor MANATT, of Brown University. 286 pages. $1.65.

XENOPHON, Hellenica V.-VII. Edited by Professor BENNETT, of Cornell University. 240 pages. $1.40.

GINN & COMPANY, Publishers,

Boston.   New York.   Chicago.   Atlanta.   Dallas.

www.ingramcontent.com/pod-product-compliance
Lightning Source LLC
Chambersburg PA
CBHW032000230426
43672CB00010B/2214